THE IRISH IN US

The Irish in Us

DIANE NEGRA, EDITOR

Irishness, Performativity, and Popular Culture

Duke University Press   Durham & London   2006

© 2006 Duke University Press All rights reserved
Printed in the United States of America on acid-free paper ∞
Designed by Rebecca Giménez
Typeset in Minion by Tseng Information Systems, Inc.
Library of Congress Cataloging-in-Publication Data appear
on the last printed page of this book.

Contents

ACKNOWLEDGMENTS

The contributors to this book produced their essays while juggling many personal and professional responsibilities, and I would like to thank them for their strong commitment to this project and their good humor along the way.

Dudley Andrew, Margot Backus, Ruth Barton, Sarah Churchwell, Elizabeth Butler Cullingford, Luke Gibbons, Neil Ewen, Eric Homberger, Shelley McGinnis, Lorcan McGrane, Glenn Medler, Martha Nochimson, Carol O'Sullivan, Yvonne Tasker, and Spurgeon Thompson have supported this project in myriad ways. Shelley Cobb has been both resourceful and tenacious in working on digital illustrations. My colleagues in Film and Television at the University of East Anglia helped to relieve me of some of my teaching and administrative responsibilities at a crucial phase in the completion of the book. Grainne Humphreys at the Irish Film Institute generously assisted with obtaining media materials. At Duke University Press I have enjoyed ideal editorial guidance and wonderful support from Ken Wissoker, while Anitra Grisales has tracked the progress of the manuscript with extraordinary care and attention to detail. The press's readers provided a set of first- and second-stage reports that were rigorous, challenging, and inspiring.

The chapter "Irishness, Innocence, and American Identity Politics before and after September 11" constitutes a slightly updated version of an essay that first appeared in 2004 in *Keeping It Real: Irish Film and Television* from Wallflower Press.

DIANE NEGRA

The Irish in Us: Irishness,
Performativity, and Popular Culture

In *Charlie's Angels: Full Throttle* (2003), the African American comedian Bernie Mac attempts to infiltrate a Dublin-based tanker by
presenting a driver's license identifying himself as Paddy O'Malley.
When a criminal on the tanker doubts him, Mac launches into a comic
tirade of outrage. "You never heard of no black Irish?" he asks. "Who do
you think invented the McRib, Lucky Charms, the Shamrock Shake? . . .
My family suffered for lack of potatoes." This catalogue of associative
links to Irishness delivered by a black comedian is but one example of a
popular culture increasingly likely to produce comedy tied to the "everything and nothing" status of Irishness. The joke here turns on an assumption the film presumes its audience to share; namely, that whatever else
it may be, Irishness is reliably, invariably, a form of whiteness.

Over the last ten years, a particular set of cultural and economic pressures has rapidly transnationalized Irishness. Recruited for global capitalism, Irishness has become a form of discursive currency, motivating
and authenticating a variety of heritage narratives and commercial transactions, often through its status as a form of "enriched whiteness." The
scene from *Charlie's Angels* underscores one of the most central concerns of this book — namely, the status of Irishness as a category of racial
fantasy. While Irishness surged into a globally marketed identity under
the aegis of the Celtic Tiger, its terms in American culture have been
particularly functional in accommodating new diversity imperatives. As
Catherine M. Eagan observes in her essay for this volume, "in celebrating
their Irishness, Irish Americans are also finding a way to celebrate their
whiteness." Or, as Vincent J. Cheng contends, "in the United States today,

Irishness may be both popular and comfortable precisely because it remains an identifiable (and presumably authentic) ethnicity that is nonetheless unthreatening and familiar."[1] With a greater level of permission now given to claim heritage amidst the cultural romance of identities, Irishness has emerged as an "a la carte ethnicity," the ideal all-purpose identity credential.[2] In this sense, concepts of Irish whiteness play a particular part in what Ghassan Hage has termed "the psychopathology of white decline," the terror that whiteness in America is losing its social purchase.[3]

The Irish in Us seeks to explore some of the coordinates on the expanding map of Irishness in contemporary popular culture, and to investigate the ideological implications of the ways that Irishness has become particularly performative and mobile at the millennium. This book originates in concerns about the imbrication of Irishness with a number of ideological agendas, including the depoliticization of difference, the reclassification of forms of whiteness as "ethnicity," and niche-market saturation leading to a process in which commodities that have lost their luster are reendowed with (ethnic) meaning.[4] Drawing from the tenets of Cultural Studies, the book dispenses with an absolute "truthful" version of Irishness, looking instead to the many fictions that proliferate around Irish identity in our current environment. In this vein, essays on such topics as the explosion of Irish-themed merchandising over the last ten years, themes of Irishness on series television, the genealogical practices of heritage seekers, and performances of Irishness in celebrity culture are brought together in this collection to examine how Irishness is claimed, enacted, and performed in the current transnational environment. Richard Dyer has noted that "whiteness can determine who is to be included and excluded from the category and also determine among those deemed to be within it. Some people—the Irish, Latins, Jews— are white sometimes, and some white people are whiter than others."[5] A strong connecting thread among the essays is their shared concern with the flexible racial status of Irishness (its "complex oscillation between otherness and whiteness," in the words of one contributor) in an era of highly charged racial-identity politics.

Catherine M. Eagan's essay poses questions about the romance of the Irish-black connection that will be addressed by the majority of essays here. These analyses are carried out in line with Hazel Carby's observation that "the last decade of the 20th century was a particularly interesting conjunctual moment between the global production of blackness and Irishness."[6] One of the key phenomena with which this book is concerned is the way that Irishness seems to move between a quasi blackness and a politically insulated ethnic whiteness. It is crucial to candidly assess the implications of the ways that Irishness now functions as a form of identity currency and the way that it stands at the heart of so many mass-marketed white homeland fantasies. In examining the role of Irishness among American fictions and fantasies of race and ethnicity at the end of the twentieth century and the beginning of the twenty-first, we must acknowledge that assertions of Irish whiteness may well act to displace and/or neutralize the identity claims of blacks and Latinos. Conjunctions of Irishness and blackness are not inevitably conservative formulations, as Lauren Onkey's essay — a nuanced reading of the racialized persona of Van Morrison — demonstrates. Similarly, as Michael Malouf shows, in the Irish context, performances of cross-racial and cross-cultural solidarity may be far more complex and multifaceted than they first appear. Nevertheless, we must also take note of Natasha Casey's account, which documents the increased commingling of the rhetoric of supremacist hyper-whiteness with "suburban whiteness" at Irish-themed culture and music festivals. In the United States in particular, new processes of transcultural mixing and matching seem to be catalyzing desire for monoethnic stability.

The commercial scene of Irishness has vastly expanded since Dinitia Smith observed in 1996 that "in almost every realm of culture there is a resurgence of things Irish."[7] In the realm of commodified Irishness there is now a price point for every taste and budget. While associations of Irishness with antimaterialism and whimsy have existed at least since the publication of Yeats's *The Celtic Twilight: Faerie and Folklore*, these associations are now ironically hyper-commercialized. Virtually every form of popular culture has in one way or another, at one time or another, presented Irishness as a moral antidote to contemporary ills ranging from globalization to postmodern alienation, from crises over the meaning and practice of family values to environmental destruction. While fantasies of Ireland posit a culture unsullied by consumerism and modernity,

Irishness is nevertheless a buy-in category and it comes in a staggering variety of consumable forms available across a broad spectrum of outlets. From the massive international success of the music/dance revue *Riverdance*, to the juggernaut of Celtic-themed merchandising, and the spate of Irish-themed material on Broadway, Irishness, it seems, circulates ever more widely in contemporary culture. Natasha Casey's essay in this collection offers one of the first sustained analyses of the myriad ways in which U.S. consumers buy their Irishness across a spectrum of social valuation, ranging from upper-middle-class Irish theme weddings to shamrock tattoos as emblems of whiteness.

In the 1990s, Irish-oriented writing proved a staple category on the best-seller lists, with Frank McCourt's Pulitzer Prize–winning *Angela's Ashes* (1996) generating a powerful origin myth for corporate Irish America. McCourt's memoir, translated into nineteen languages and selling over four million copies worldwide, spent over ninety weeks at or near the top of the *New York Times Book Review* best-seller list and was subsequently adapted into a feature film that saw release in late 1999.[8] Irish-interest magazines such as *Irish America* are now stocked regularly at newsstands and bookstores, while Celticvision is among the offerings for U.S. cable subscribers. The 1998–2001 U.S. network television seasons offered further evidence of the currency of Irishness, ushering in seven new dramas and sitcoms that centralized the Irish-American experience, and increasingly using Irishness as an ethnic code for reinstating social values perceived to be lost in millennial American culture.[9] In these narratives Irishness serves as a point of access into a purified vision of family and community life that specifically compensates for the exigencies of contemporary U.S. culture. Of course, such uses of Irishness are by no means confined to television. Stephanie Rains shows in her essay here how the genealogy industry has worked to define a specific "Irish Americanness" that negotiates social memory to produce a coherent and consoling sense of heritage.[10]

In the 1990s, Irishness emerged as an increasingly valuable ethnic credential for talk-show hosts such as Conan O'Brien and Rosie O'Donnell, while *Ballykissangel*, a British soap opera set in Ireland, flourished on PBS.[11] The past decade has also seen the emergence of the New Irish

It's like being in a nineteenth century romantic novel. With better food and a happier ending.

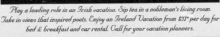

Play a leading role in an Irish vacation. Sip tea in a nobleman's living room. Take in views that inspired poets. Enjoy an Ireland Vacation from $37 per day for bed & breakfast and car rental. Call for your vacation planners.*

IRELAND
The ANCIENT BIRTHPLACE of GOOD TIMES.

*Price per person based on double occupancy and Group A car rental.

For a free vacation kit, send in the coupon to Ireland Vacations 1994, P.O. Box 7728, Woodside, New York 11377 or call 1-800-SHAMROCK, extension 37.

Name _____

Address _____

City _____ State _____ Zip _____

1. Tourist ads promised visitors a respite from contemporary culture; their vision of Ireland highlighted an encounter with the past that would not require sacrificing present-day comforts.

Cinema and the success of a growing number of Irish American–themed films.[12] Meanwhile, there is an increasing tendency for print and broadcast advertisements to deploy Irishness, notably in relation to goods and services that have no inherent connection to this ethnic category.[13] Long linked in the American imagination with the experience of poverty and the rigor of sexual repression, Irishness now factors in campaigns for Porsche automobiles and Candies stiletto-heeled shoes as a marker of luxury and eroticism.[14] In television franchises such as *Buffy the Vampire Slayer* and its spin-off *Angel*, as Gerardine Meaney shows in her essay for this volume, Irish masculinity can be eroticized and updated while remaining enmeshed in themes of tragic familialism all too familiar from the work of Yeats and Synge. For Meaney, recent representations such as these "veer dramatically between liberal and conservative impulses in their racial thought process."

As American and global audiences became more attuned to the consumption of Irishness in print, film, and television fiction, Irishness was also increasingly amplified or borrowed by a variety of popular cultural performers. The year 1998 saw the emergence of a fascinating case of ethnic impersonation as the (now deceased) novelist Patrick O'Brian was forced to acknowledge that he had invented an Irish name and biography. Then in his eighties, the British author had for decades passed as Irish, frequently referencing his upbringing in the west of Ireland, and his fluency in the Irish language. The O'Brian case underscored the importance of myths of origin in the heritage-publishing climate that has seen the rise to prominence not only of Frank McCourt, but of authors such as Malachy McCourt, Alice McDermott, and Thomas Cahill.[15] O'Brian's fictional biography established the author as the right kind of narrator for an immensely successful series of novels about seafaring while at a broader level indicating the desirability of Irishness as a platform for discursive legitimacy.

Irishness has increasingly operated as a soundtrack as well as a narrative prototype. The *Riverdance* touring show has played to eighteen million people and grossed more than a billion dollars worldwide, and the associated CD long remained the top-selling album on *Billboard*'s world music chart.[16] Irish music has been effectively synthesized with pop in a wide range of popular cultural contexts. Irishness has been deployed

2. An explosion of Irish-themed advertising campaigns (such as this one for General Foods International Coffees) sought to de-genericize a variety of products and services in 1990s U.S. culture.

3. As Irishness became hip it sloughed off associations with Catholic sexual repression and was increasingly eroticized, as in this Candie's advertisement.

as a soundtrack in such films as *Titanic* (1996), while performers such as Phil Collins, Rod Stewart, and Shania Twain released Celtic-flavored pop songs. National Public Radio features a regular "Thistle and Shamrock" program of Irish music, while strains of "Danny Boy" were mixed into the pop group Chumbawamba's 1998 single "Tubthumping," and Canadian Celtic recording artist Loreena McKennitt's "The Mummers' Dance" was remixed as a highly successful dance track. Indeed a 1998 article referred to "watching Celtic music become the millennium's Muzak."[17] Even when the song structures of Irish traditional music are not overtly used, the instrumentation associated with it has been deployed in aural flourishes to connote moments of authenticity and intimacy in both television and film. Uilleann pipes have been used in ads for General Electric and Mobil, and one of NBC's dramatic hit series, *Providence* (1999–2003), used similar instrumental cues to signal viewers at key transitional moments in its dramatic narrative of familial reintegration and regional romanticization.

The closing decades of the twentieth century also saw the emergence of a category of globally saleable popular/rock music associated with distinctively Irish performers. Acts such as the Cranberries and the Corrs are not perceived as incidentally Irish; rather their national heritage is positioned as a mark of quality. A 1994 *Time* article, for instance, praised Sinéad O'Connor and Cranberries lead singer Dolores O'Riordan for an awareness of a particular past that "helps distinguish their songs from the typical rootless algae of pop music."[18] In her revealing case study, Lauren Onkey notes that Northern Irish music star Van Morrison launched his career playing R&B, then increasingly drew on a rhetoric of Irishness to "source" his music. Rejecting overly binaristic explanations which would cast Morrison as a blackface performer, Onkey finds that instead, in a complex balance of "blackness" and Celticism, he creates for himself an Irishness significantly mediated by his affinity for black musical forms. Mary McGlynn's essay, meanwhile, examines and critically questions the phenomenal late-1990s popularity of country star Garth Brooks in Ireland, asking what it was about Brooks's nostalgic vision that resonated with a fast-changing Irish society. Lest we misunderstand this process as simply one-sided, McGlynn goes on to show that Brooks's own affiliations with Irishness broadened and extended the persona of a country music star whose southern white masculinity was in danger of appearing parochial.

In an August 2001 editorial, Thomas L. Friedman noted that "people all over the world are looking to Ireland for its reservoir of spirituality, hoping to siphon off what they can to feed their souls, which have become hungry for something other than consumerism and computers."[19] American recourse to a consoling Irishness was most recently and evidently demonstrated in the aftermath of 9/11, which saw widespread celebration of Irish American heroes.[20] In my essay here, I discuss some of the ways that Irishness factored at a time when Orientalist tropes of those who look Middle Eastern were matched by a set of tropes about what white masculinity looks like and is.

The tendency of Irishness to travel into a wide range of international popular cultural contexts has prompted controversies in critical and intellectual circles over "invented Irishness." Some of the most well-recognized figures in the cultural Celtic Tiger (Jim Sheridan, Frank McCourt, Michael Flatley, Martin McDonough) have produced Irish-themed films, books, plays, and dance shows as expatriates. These developments occurred in tandem with what some critics termed the "theme-parking of Ireland," as pressures intensified for the nation to remake itself for tourist consumption.[21] The expectations of diaspora tourists that Ireland's present is always their past are less and less likely to be sustainable in contemporary Dublin or Galway, yet homeland fantasies may now no longer require an actual homeland visit. Although Bord Failte exhorts prospective tourists with its most recent slogan, "Ireland—Live a Different Life," it is perhaps more likely for Irishness to be tapped to enrich one's existing life. More than any other national identity, Irishness now both travels and inspires travel, increasingly manifesting symptoms of complete virtuality. In Los Angeles, entertainment figures congregate at Dublin's, a theme-park Irish bar on the Sunset Strip. Travelers to New York can stay at the Fitzpatrick Grand Central, an Irish theme hotel, which maintains Irish staff, and offers such amenities as a pub, an Irish-themed restaurant, and an "in-room Irish Film Festival" of Irish-oriented videotapes that can be viewed by guests. Several of the essays in *The Irish in Us* counter virtual Irishness with identification of media forms and tropes they find to be less essentializing. Maeve Connolly argues that "the cinematic figure of the traveler can offer a point of resistance to essentialized images of Irishness," while Maria Pramaggiore finds in two contemporary Irish films a critical deconstruction of essentialized national identity achieved in part through an emphasis on pregnancy . . . as a state of performance.

While popular cultural representations seemed to generate an Irishness for every taste and purpose, offering a means of being both white and ethnically differentiated, an extraordinarily successful campaign to "brand" Ireland as a site for tourism and a new frontier for American and global business was taking place. At the end of the 1990s Irish government figures indicated that Ireland was the fastest growing tourist destination in Europe, with a 129 percent increase in the number of overseas visitors in the preceding ten years.[22] Meanwhile, articles in American newsmagazines assessing the state of Europe at the close of the twentieth century hyped Ireland as the economic and social ideal, ranking it first overall in the "musts for a better society" and noting that the nation seems "ready for anything."[23] Much of the growth of the Irish economy has been tied to new technology and service sectors and the arrival in Ireland of U.S. and multinational firms. In February 2000, at ceremonies marking the opening of a new Dell computer plant in Ireland, Prime Minister Bertie Ahern observed that Dell had become the largest foreign employer in Ireland and asserted that Ireland receives 25 percent of American investment monies in Europe. With recent economic developments slackening the pace of growth in Ireland, and sparking speculation of a new, post–Celtic Tiger phase, this seems an appropriate moment to measure ideological (as well as financial) investments in Ireland and consider the way that media fictions take hold of such investments.[24]

While the relations between American popular-culture industries, Irishness, and whiteness may have intensified in the contemporary period, such relations have key historical features as well. Two of the essays in this collection produce historically minded case studies that in many ways prefigure and/or lead up to the contemporary performativity of Irishness. Sean Griffin reads several Twentieth Century Fox wartime musicals such as *Sweet Rosie O'Grady* and *Coney Island* as representative of a particular phase of the Irish assimilation into whiteness. Amanda Third's essay produces a historical/psychoanalytic account of the colonialist ideological residue that influences the semiotics of red hair in popular culture. Her analysis offers a trenchant explanation of the ways that female redheadedness has come to signify a largely benign Irish-inflected whiteness.

In the 1990s, Ireland and the United States, which have long maintained a unique cultural relationship, seemed to draw even closer as their economic interests merged, shoring up a cultural contract characterized chiefly by what Dudley Andrew has referred to as a state of "demi-immigration" in twentieth-century Ireland.[25] In America, Irishness now seems increasingly to serve as the ideal guilt-free white ethnicity of choice, subject to a predominantly (and peculiarly) ecumenical vision. Little wonder then that when Americans are asked to report their ethnic backgrounds, Irishness (once a socially stigmatized ethnic category) is now overreported. When Bill Clinton went to Ireland in 1996, he epitomized the personalization of this national trend—in speeches during his trip abroad, the U.S. president spoke of "my people" and meant the Irish. Developments such as these over the past decade have sustained Richard Alba's point made at the start of the 1990s that "ethnic identities have become ways of claiming to be American, and this is a profound change from the past. Ethnic identity can be a means of locating oneself and one's family against the panorama of American history, against the backdrop of what it means to be American. No longer, then, need there be any contradiction between being American and asserting an ethnic identity. Increasingly, they are accepted as the same thing."[26]

As Irishness has achieved greater and more complex representability there has been a growing discourse on the ways that operative definitions of Irishness within Ireland are being Americanized.[27] Some of the complexities of this process are hinted at in a 2001 print advertisement for Allied Irish Bank that tellingly conjoins American capital interests with Irish middle-class experience. The image features several Dublin row homes perpendicular to a street sign that reads "Sraid an Bhalla/Wall Street." Such an image can also be seen to highlight the ways that Irishness was made saleable for American consumers in the 1990s, whether in the form of an Irish-themed commodity, a tourist package, or a stock investment.[28]

Not all of the essays here situate themselves in relation to the "Irish

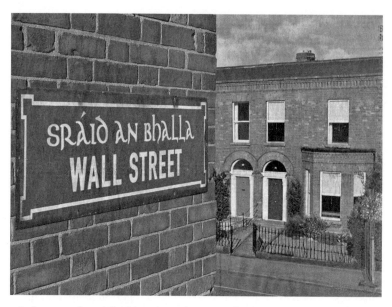

4. In the 1990s, a financialized American culture merged with Irish middle-class experience, as seen in this AIB advertisement.

Atlantic," although, as Colin Graham has observed and Lauren Onkey echoes in her essay here, the United States played a key role in producing and consuming the authenticity of Irishness. In the U.S. context particularly but more broadly as well, Ireland in many ways has come to ground a set of consoling fictions about forms of social health that could be recovered amidst dawning perceptions of the losses global capitalism inflicts. Many of the essays are, in effect, a set of case studies about how and why Ireland came to take up that position. A number of them detail textures and trends of the late 1990s, a period in which (to use Hazel Carby's phrase) Irishness seemed to have "gone global."[29] It appears now that during that time representations of Irishness reached a high-water mark.

The drawing to a close of the most intense period of Irish thematization may have found its signal moment in the controversial visit of George W. Bush to Ireland in June 2004; at the very least the visit marked an emergent change in the supposed reliability of Irishness for an American hegemonic regime. Transfixing the country and becoming the subject of national debate that went on for weeks, Bush's stopover starkly demonstrated a calculated effort to invoke Irish "innocence" and "neutrality" to mediate the deep resentment in Europe toward the Bush government. Although he stayed for less than twenty-four hours in Ireland, Bush prompted the largest security operation in Irish history. His visit sparked extensive protests by a broad coalition of students, clerics, trade unions, and politicians (including the mayor of Dublin) opposed to the war in Iraq and Ireland's decision to allow U.S. military jets to refuel at Shannon Airport.[30] Adding to the controversy was an interview Bush gave to Carole Coleman, the Washington correspondent for state broadcaster RTE, in which Coleman repeatedly challenged Bush's evasive and disingenuous responses to questions about the Middle East and domestic policy post-9/11. When she did so Coleman placed herself in the almost unique journalistic position of openly contesting the president under an administration that has continually offered low press availability, acted to suppress dissent, and scorned the functions of a "watchdog" press. Coleman's interview prompted the White House to admonish her by telephone, to withdraw from a commitment by Laura Bush to be interviewed by RTE, and to launch a complaint with the Irish Embassy in Washington.[31]

When considered alongside other presidential visits of the past, this trip may have marked the end of certain features of Celtic Tigerism (notably the assumption of a Hiberno-American "special relationship" expressed through heritage rhetoric), as a clash between indigenous Irishness and American political and ideological isolationism dramatically emerged on the world stage. As this book goes to press and in a period slightly preceding and following the visit, Irishness has gone decidedly down-market, seemingly becoming de-exoticized as national air carrier Aer Lingus transforms itself into a budget airline offering bargain-basement transatlantic fares. An apparent status change has themes of Irishness relocating from middlebrow dramas to reality television and the only openly Irish-themed offering in primetime, the ABC sitcom *It's All Relative*, equating Irishness with intolerance and homophobia. Meanwhile, the traditional directional flow of Irish-U.S. migration is being strikingly reversed as the "New Irish" immigrants of the 1980s and 1990s return to Ireland in an exodus that is "hard to quantify, but unmistakable."[32]

The title of this book invokes a 1935 James Cagney film in part to indicate the historical reach and scope of proprietary claims to Irishness, before turning largely to contemporary subject matter in an era in which the stakes for affiliating with Irishness have been significantly raised. The contributors to *The Irish in Us* analyze the social and representational consequences of Ireland's transformation into an economic magnet, producing essays that simultaneously reflect the extent to which Irishness has become a magnetic topic for Cultural Studies. The heightened interest in Irish history, culture, literature, sociology, and media has been reflected in the growth of Irish Studies programs in the United States, Britain, and Ireland, the increased number of academic conferences devoted to Irish Studies, and the dedication of a number of special theme issues in scholarly journals to topics in this field.[33] In 1995, Noel Ignatiev's reverberant *How the Irish Became White* opened up a pathway for beginning to analyze the racial dynamics of Irishness in the United States, while Maureen Dezell's 2000 *Irish America Coming Into Clover: The Evolution of a People and a Culture* has tracked "the recent surge of enthusiasm for all things green."[34] In 1999 and 2000, after a more than ten-year lag since Luke Gibbons, Kevin Rockett, and John Hill first published *Cinema and Ireland* (1988), three new books on Irish media appeared: James Mac-Killop's *Contemporary Irish Cinema: From* The Quiet Man *to* Dancing at Lughnasa, Lance Pettitt's *Screening Ireland*, and Martin McLoone's *Irish Film: The Emergence of a Contemporary Cinema*. An important precursor to this study, Elizabeth Butler Cullingford's *Ireland's Others: Gender and Ethnicity in Irish Literature and Popular Culture*, was published in 2001. Another major work, Ruth Barton's *Irish National Cinema*, appeared in 2004.

Drawing from but also expanding on this scholarship, *The Irish in Us* addresses the range of sites around which the meanings of Irishness currently circulate and seeks to provide a theoretical account of the Hibernophilia that drives the consumption of Irish-themed plays, dance performances, film, and television and the economies of tourism, genealogy, and kitsch. Irish Studies still clings in many ways to a monolithic sense of Irishness, while critical race and ethnicity studies have too often (until very recently as I detail below) conceptualized whiteness as monolithic. The fraught racial status of Irishness has only recently emerged as a topic of intense discussion in Irish Studies. *The Irish in Us* seeks to expand such existing conversations by making direct connections between Irish Studies and critical race and ethnicity studies; it proceeds from the assumption that claiming Irishness often authorizes a location and celebration of whiteness in ways that would otherwise be problematic. With studies of whiteness becoming more influential in humanities and social-science scholarship, there is recent evidence of a turn toward more particularized analyses that focus on the relation to whiteness of a single ethnic or national group; this turn is one in which this book seeks to participate.[35]

Bringing a range of methodological approaches to bear on historical and contemporary manifestations of Irishness, the essays gathered here seek to intervene on the process of essentializing Irishness that has proven so commercially attractive to individuals, to culture industries, and to governments. They call for forms of Irishness that are conscious and critically self-reflective of their relation to whiteness while being flexible, inclusive, and multicultural in the best sense. For instance, while most of the laudatory accounts of Celtic Tiger Ireland tended to overlook or radically oversimplify the social consequences of the nation's transformation into an economic magnet, new critical and creative work is emerging to historicize and analyze the emergence of an increasingly multiracial Ireland. Such work underscores the importance and the complexity of Ireland's (frequently uneasy) transformation from a nation renowned for its emigrant outflow to one that has now (for the first time) become the destination of immigrants. The award-winning short film *Yu Ming Is Ainm Dom* (2003), for example, interrupts dominant equations of Irishness with politically conservative formulations of whiteness. In telling the story of a disenfranchised Chinese shop clerk who spins a globe at random, puts his finger on Ireland and then prepares to emigrate by studying the Irish language, the film demonstrates a warm sympathy for the sort of immigrants who cause political consternation to some observers of the increasingly multiracial Irish national landscape. When Yu Ming arrives in Dublin and discovers that he cannot make himself understood, he despondently concludes that his Irish must be "terrible." His fortune is reversed, however, when in applying for work at a Dublin bar (the barman's misunderstanding offer of a pint of Guinness is accompanied by a short parodic dance imitating the "Oirishness" he presumes any tourist will expect), he is finally understood by an older male customer who informs him that Irish is more of an official language than a practically spoken one. Looking in on the conversation, the barman stands back in wonder, finally asking a colleague, "Did you know that old Paddy could speak Chinese?" The film then concludes with Yu Ming relocating to the Gaeltacht where he is last seen happily welcoming customers in a consummate display of "Irish hospitality."

Yu Ming is not an entirely unproblematic fiction (in part because it installs a fantasy of the ideal immigrant and having done so then safely confines this immigrant to Connemara). Yet a powerful idea in the film is that destabilizations of "cultural authenticity" provide new opportunities for it to be made transferable. *Yu Ming is Ainm Dom* offers a glimpse of a set of new social and economic possibilities that Michael Malouf characterizes in terms of "the possibility of taking on and adopting multiple identities in a way that opens up the potential for developing communities that might also describe multiple ways of being citizens." In an era in which Irishness is regularly claimed by a variety of white, first-world interests it can also be appropriated by others for whom it may reenergize concepts of egalitarianism, self-actualization, and the promise of a better future. In the sense that representations such as this "speak back" to evermore consolidating and repressive political and economic systems, they may signify an important way forward. In other words, by turning current concepts of Irishness inside out, it is just possible that they might generate the kind of Irish clichés we can live with.

Notes

1. Vincent J. Cheng, *Inauthentic: The Anxiety Over Culture and Identity* (New Brunswick, N.J.: Rutgers University Press, 2004), 32.

2. For an account of the commodification of ethnic identities in America see Marilyn Halter, *Shopping for Identity: The Marketing of Ethnicity* (New York: Schocken Books, 2000). The phrase *a la carte ethnicity* is used by Ruth Barton in *Irish National Cinema* (London: Routledge, 2004), 3.

3. Ghassan Hage, *White Nation: Fantasies of White Supremacy in a Multicultural Society* (New York: Routledge, 2000), 9.

4. I thank Spurgeon Thompson for his illumination of these issues via e-mail.

5. Richard Dyer, *White* (London: Routledge, 1997), 51.

6. Hazel Carby, "What Is This 'Black' in Irish Popular Culture?" *European Journal of Cultural Studies* 4, no. 3 (2001): 327.

7. Dinitia Smith, "The Irish Are Hot in the U.S. Again," *New York Times*, 3 October 1996, B1, B4.

8. Indeed, McCourt's memoir spawned a family industry. In addition to his own follow-up, *'Tis*, there were *A Monk Swimming*, a best-selling memoir by the writer's brother, part-time actor Malachy McCourt, and *The McCourts of Limerick*, a documentary on the family made by the brothers' nephew, a New York City policeman.

9. These include *Turks* (CBS), *Trinity* (NBC), *To Have and To Hold* (CBS), *Costello* (Fox), *Love and Money* (CBS), *Madigan Men* (ABC), and *The Fighting Fitzgeralds* (NBC). In 1998, television critic Mike Flaherty observed that "the silence about these series has been deafening. Probably because the Irish occupy an unfortunate middle ground in America: Numbering roughly 40 million, they're too large to be thought a minority, yet not large enough to be seen as the Establishment" ("Remote Patrol," *Entertainment Weekly*, 16 October 1998, 69).

10. *The Irish Face in America* (New York: Bulfinch Press, 2004), a coffee-table book edited by Julia McNamara, distinctly fetishizes heritage physiognomy. The book emphatically insists on a "democratic" Irishness, mixing its profiles of celebrities with profiles of "regular" people throughout.

11. Although such analysis lies outside the bounds of this book, the success of *Ballykissangel* should certainly be placed within the context of PBS's growing stake in marketing heritage ethnicities to affluent audiences.

12. Notable in this regard is Edward Burns, the actor/filmmaker from New York, whose debut film, *The Brothers McMullen* (1995), pioneered a new self-consciousness about Irish American working-class identity. Understood to closely reflect the director's own regional and ethnic identity, the film exemplified the way that Irishness has become increasingly marketable in a multicultural environment.

13. Examples include television and print campaigns for General Foods International Coffees, AT&T long-distance service, the cholesterol medication Zocor, Folgers coffee, Dr. Pepper soda, Platinum MasterCard, and Mobil Oil—all of which use Irishness to sanitize the commodified nature of the product being offered.

14. Colin Coulter aptly describes the Candies ad as depicting "an impossibly gymnastic pre-coital clinch" but is unaware that the male partner in the ad's couple is not, as he puts it, "one particular male model selected by a single advertising agency" (Colin Coulter and Steve Coleman, eds., *The End of Irish History?: Critical Reflections on the Celtic Tiger* [Manchester: Manchester University Press, 2003], 1–2) but Mark McGrath, the lead singer of pop group Sugar Ray, and a rather well-known personality among the demographic groups to whom the ad makes its address. The stunt casting here surely heightens the ad's effect.

15. The authors respectively of *Angela's Ashes* (New York: Scribner, 1999); *A Monk Swimming* (New York: Hyperion, 1998); *Charming Billy* (New York: Delta, 1998); and *How the Irish Saved Civilization* (New York: Anchor, 1995).

16. See Brian Lavery, "Riverdance Aims to Tap into the Future," *International Herald Tribune*, 16–17 October 2004, 11.

17. "The Celtification of Pop," *Entertainment Weekly*, 20 March 1998.

18. "Singing to a Silent Harp," *Time*, 7 November 1994, 19.

19. Thomas L. Friedman, "The Lexus and the Shamrock," *New York Times*, 3 August 2001.

20. Such celebration is documented and furthered by Niall O'Dowd's *Fire in the Morning: The Story of the Irish and the Twin Towers on September 11* (Dingle: Brandon, 2002).

21. See Spurgeon Thompson, "The Romance of Simulation: W. B. Yeats and the Theme-Parking of Ireland," *Eire-Ireland* 30, no. 1 (1995): 17–34. For a discussion of the links between heritage tourism and Irish-heritage cinema, see Ruth Barton, "The Ballykissangelization of Ireland," *Historical Journal of Film, Radio, and Television* 20, no. 3 (2000): 413–26.

22. From a total of 2.4 million visitors in 1988, the number of tourists in 1998 swelled to 5.5 million, a number roughly equal to the population of Ireland. Warren Hoge, "Ireland: Popularity Grows," *New York Times*, 11 September 1999, A4.

23. Fields Wicker-Miurin, "A Measure of Success," *Newsweek*, December 1999/February 2000, 32–33.

24. The recent emergence of a series of postcards that excessively assemble castles, Colleens, hurling matches, and scenic vistas in a collage format that completely abandons any sense of pictorial realism offers one example of an attempt to redress the growing gap between tourist expectations and Irish realities.

25. Dudley Andrew, opening remarks at the Theatre of Irish Cinema Conference (Yale University, New Haven, Conn., 1 February 2001). These remarks were developed into an article, "The Theatre of Irish Cinema," which appeared in the *Yale Journal of Criticism* 15, no. 1 (2002): 23–58. It is perhaps more likely that middle-class American Hibernophiles would now feel themselves demi-immigrated to Ireland. Significantly, American applications for Irish citizenship doubled through the 1990s.

26. Richard D. Alba, *Ethnic Identity: The Transformation of White America* (New Haven, Conn.: Yale University Press, 1990), 318–19.

27. See for instance Hugo Hamilton's "Thanks for Nothing, Michael Flatley," *Irish Observer*, 19 June 1998. On the issue of Europeanization in Ireland, see Thomas L. Friedman, "The Lexus and the Shamrock." Friedman describes Ireland as "the European country that has been the biggest beneficiary of globalization and the one that is most ambivalent about those benefits."

28. The commodification of heritage Irishness fit well into a cultural framework that increasingly stressed that both product purchases and financial investments were

a reflection of self, a staging of identity. A hypercompetitive 1990s U.S. economy urged consumers to "financialize" themselves, and thus confuse any distinction between capital and self. In such a climate, as Randy Martin has argued, "the management of money's ebbs and flows is not simply in service of accessible wealth, but presents itself as a merger of business and life cycles, as a means for the acquisition of self." *Financialization of Daily Life* (Philadelphia: Temple University Press, 2002), 3.

29. Carby, "What Is This 'Black'?" 336.

30. Angelique Chrisafis, "Irish Batten Down Hatches for Bush," *Guardian*, 25 June 2004. For an account of the visit see "Protestors 'Drive' Bush From Ireland," CNN .com, 26 June 2004, <http://www.edition.cnn.com/2004/WORLD/europe/06/26/us .eu.protests.reut/>.

31. Miriam Lord, "Angry White House Pulls RTE Interview," *Irish Independent*, 26 June 2004.

32. The characterization appears in Nina Bernstein, "Immigrants Reverse Their Trek as American Dreams Fade," *New York Times*, 10 November 2004, B1.

33. New academic programs in Irish Studies have been created while existing programs have dramatically expanded in recent years, in part due to the high profile of Irish literary figures such as Seamus Heaney and Seamus Deane and the growing scope of Irish American philanthropy directed at such endeavors. Some of the most prominent programs are at Notre Dame (Keough Institute for Irish Studies), New York University (Glucksman House), Southern Illinois University, the University of St. Thomas, Boston College, and the University of Massachusetts, Boston. In addition to the American Conference for Irish Studies (the major disciplinary organization for Irish Studies in this country), which holds an annual academic meeting, institutions sponsoring conferences dedicated to Irish Studies have in recent years included Yale University, Drew University, and Virginia Tech. A number of high-profile journals have recently dedicated special issues to Irish Studies including *Cultural Studies*, *South Atlantic Quarterly*, *Historical Journal of Film, Radio and Television*, the *Yale Journal of Criticism*, and *boundary 2: an international journal of literature and culture*.

34. Maureen Dezell, *Irish America Coming Into Clover: The Evolution of a People and a Culture* (New York: Doubleday, 2000), 5. This mass-market book lightly historicizes but does not theorize the current vogue for Irishness. See also Noel Ignatiev, *How The Irish Became White* (New York: Routledge, 1995).

35. Into this category we might place Matthew Frye Jacobson and David Roediger, eds., *Special Sorrows: The Diasporic Imagination of Irish, Polish and Jewish Immigrants in the United States* (Berkeley: University of California Press, 2002); and Jennifer Guglielmo and Salvatore Salerno, eds., *Are Italians White? How Race Is Made in America* (London: Routledge, 2003), as well as Thomas J. Ferraro's *Feeling Italian: The Art of Ethnicity in America* (New York: New York University Press, 2005).

CATHERINE M. EAGAN

"Still 'Black' and 'Proud' ":
Irish America and the Racial
Politics of Hibernophilia

As the twentieth century came to a close, Americans were in the midst of a mania for all things Irish.[1] *Riverdance* had lost its star, the Irish American Irish step dancer Michael Flatley, but it was becoming a franchise and was spawning a series of popular spin-offs. Thanks to the Internet and relaxed immigration laws, a more authentic variety of Irish culture could now travel unfettered across the ocean; Americans no longer had to look to St. Patrick's Day and John Ford's *The Quiet Man* (1952) to stoke their inner ethnic fires. In a more sober vein, Irish on both sides of the Atlantic were commemorating the Irish famine 150 years after its most destructive year, 1847, with lecturers, public art installations, and memorials, while Irish American legislators across the country were proposing Irish famine curricula to educate American youth about a tragedy few of them, even those of Irish descent, knew anything about. At the time of this writing, the closing of 2004, I would no longer describe American Hibernophilia as a mania. By this point, American interest in Irish and even Irish American culture has simply become pervasive.

Yet if talk of the popularity of Irish and Irish American culture is no longer new, the racial politics of its popularity is still only partially admitted or understood. Alan Parker's 1991 film *The Commitments*, inspired by Roddy Doyle's 1989 novel of the same name, has frequently been cited to demonstrate Irish people's consciousness of their connection to African Americans. But the film's popularity in the United States also exposes the ways in which the issue of race impacts and influences Irish American ethnic pride. In an early scene, Jimmy Rabbitte tries to inspire his mates to form an Irish rhythm-and-blues band by showing them a video of James Brown in concert. As they watch the video with a mix of curiosity and confusion (they actually think Brown is hurt when he limps off the stage), Jimmy instructs, "The Irish are the blacks of Europe, lads . . . An' Dubliners are the blacks of Ireland . . . An' the northside Dubliners are the blacks o' Dublin. Say it once, say it loud, I'm black an' I'm proud." The prospective band members respond to Jimmy's pronouncement with blank stares, but when I first saw the film in San Francisco, shortly after its release, the film's audience responded to Jimmy's pronouncement with roars of approval.[2] This dialogue and its enthusiastic reception are so important because they demonstrate the Irish and Irish American tendency to link "Irishness" to a heritage of oppression that is in many ways very distant from their present-day lives.[3]

Irish American Catholics, some raised with a nationalist perspective on Irish history, figure importantly in these dynamics, having heard stories or songs of the penal laws, revolutionaries who died for the Irish cause, poor Irish sold into slavery in the West Indies, or the "coffin ships" that brought immigrants to the New World after the devastation of the famine. Historically, Irish Americans have been at odds with African Americans, but the slavery legend and stories of the Atlantic passage in particular invite comparisons with blacks, who endured the infamous Middle Passage to the Americas once they were sold into slavery.[4] For the bulk of Irish Americans who had never made the connection, the Irish involved in the civil rights struggle in Northern Ireland may have introduced it.[5] In the 1960s, Northern Irish Catholic activists often described their struggle as analogous to that of African Americans in the Deep South, and some cited the nonviolent tactics popularized by Dr. Martin Luther King Jr. as an inspiration.[6] Bernadette Devlin McAliskey broadcast the connection between Irish and black struggles when she visited America in 1969 and handed over her recently awarded keys to New York City to the Black Panther Party. Her cool reception by the Irish American establishment[7] shows, however, that whatever connections Irish Americans may have made between the Irish cause and those of other colonized or oppressed peoples, they were generally hostile to the suggestion that Irish Americans and African Americans had anything in common — the Boston busing riots come to mind as evidence of that perspective. In fact, scholars have seen the resurgence of Irish American ethnic enthusiasm in this era as a reaction against the inroads made by African Americans and others into American culture; John McCarthy has suggested that Irish American support of Noraid, an organization founded to send financial support to Northern Irish political prisoners and their families, was fueled by feelings of marginalization in the neighborhoods Irish Americans had once controlled, and Howard Stein and Robert Hill have theorized that Irish Americans' involvement in the new ethnic movement, which promoted European American ethnic identities and rights in response to the civil rights movement, was underpinned by two interdependent binary oppositions: the Irish "against the WASP-Jewish establishment on the one hand, and the minorities on the other."[8] But Irish American Democrats of the era were supporters of the civil rights movement and embraced their immigrant ancestors' antidiscrimination rhetoric. Though few young Irish Americans were so prominent, the experience California politician and activist Tom Hayden had of awakening to connections between the Irish and African Americans may not have been atypical; in his recent memoir *Irish on the Inside*, he writes: "After a decade in the civil rights movement, I associated being 'white' with either supremacy or emptiness. Then, in 1968, accused of being less than a red-blooded American by the authorities, having been beaten up and indicted in Chicago, having been targeted for 'neutralization' by J. Edgar Hoover, I saw marchers in Northern Ireland singing 'We Shall Overcome' and, in an epiphany, discovered that I was Irish on the inside."[9]

Perhaps it is these Irish American liberals and their children — now accustomed to a more integrated society and increasingly exposed to Irish perspectives on race due to the growing popularity of Irish and Northern Irish culture and the greater number of Irish immigrants — who don't shy away from making the connection between the Irish and African Americans and who cheered at Jimmy's line in *The Commitments*. Irish Americans accustomed to thinking of the Irish and African Americans as brothers in struggle may also have been among those who reacted with anger when they heard that the Boston Housing Authority had included the shamrock in a list of potentially divisive symbols in the materials for their sensitivity training workshops.[10] The anger that met this revelation indicates some Irish Americans' failure to admit their shift from a past history of oppression to a present history of assimilation and power. Distanced from their past suffering and culturally adrift in a multicultural world in which they are identified as "whites" alongside Anglo-Saxon Protestants, these Irish Americans, most often as consumers of culture but also as participants in politics and academia, are revealing their desire to re-become the "other" and deny their past and present participation in the white power structure.

In this essay, I will revisit some of the observations I made in the late 1990s about the racial politics of Hibernophilia—in the main, that Hibernophiles celebrate intersections of the "Celtic" and the "black," or "African," even as they deemphasize how the "whiteness" of "Irishness" might compromise those intersections.[11] Aside from updating and extending these observations into an analysis of the racial politics of Irishness in a new millennium and a post–September 11 world, I will organize my investigation by focusing on three different, if sometimes intersecting, spheres: the sphere of popular culture, inhabited by the likes of Broadway and the movies; the sphere of literary historical imagination, represented here by two of the recent novels that explore the Irish-black connection; and the sphere of education, as occupied by the public school, the university, the museum, and the public-television documentary. Within these spheres, many Irish Americans search for a reconnection to their roots and a way to intertwine those roots with the roots of other oppressed peoples, whether within or outside the United States. I will evaluate the possible rewards and pitfalls of such a project and suggest how the whiteness of the Irish and of Irish Americans informs it.

Irish Americans: CWASPS or White Negroes?

The rejuvenation of Irish Americans' interest in their past struggles has coincided with historians' and cultural theorists' interest in looking at the Irish and Irish Americans as victims of colonial oppression and racism.[12] Whereas in previous decades, interest in these issues may have sprung from family lore, the nationalist politics of the day, or somewhat superficial rejuvenations of ethnic pride, present-day Irish Americans' knowl-

HARPER'S WEEKLY.
JOURNAL OF CIVILIZATION

Vol. XX.—No. 1041.]   NEW YORK, SATURDAY, DECEMBER 9, 1876.   ["PRICE TEN CENTS."]

1. Thomas Nast, "The Ignorant Vote: Honors Are Easy," *Harper's Weekly*, 9 December, 1876.

edge of their past is often wide-ranging and sophisticated. As distinct from Irish Americans in earlier decades, Irish Americans in the present historical moment are becoming much more interested in not just their Irish but their American stories of discrimination and hardship and in how those stories connect to the experiences of racial others in America. For example, an increasing number of Irish Americans know that the popular Anglo-American press once depicted their ancestors with simian and Africanoid features. A cartoon originally published in the late nine-teenth century, Thomas Nast's "The Ignorant Vote: Honors Are Easy," is often cited, whether in informal conversation, lectures, or publications (see figure 1). While not as well known, H. Strickland Constable's "Ireland from One or Two Neglected Points of View" represents the kind of racial pseudoscience that legitimized Ireland's colonization and anti-Irish dis-crimination in America by linking the Irish to the African race, of which a smaller, but still significant, number of Irish Americans are aware (see

2. H. Strickland Constable, "Ireland From One or Two Neglected Points of View," 1899.

figure 2).[13] Finally, some Irish Americans are also familiar with the recent academic interest in whiteness; one of the focal points of whiteness studies is the supposed transformation of Irish immigrants from nonwhites to whites in the crucible of American race relations.[14] Whether familiar with these aspects of anti-Irish racism and eventual Irish assimilation or not, most Irish Americans would admit that they live as whites today, or, as Maureen Dezell defines it, as "CWASPs (Catholic — or Celtic — White Anglo-Saxon Protestants)."[15]

For those Irish Americans in touch with the Irish history of oppression and uncomfortable with the whiteness of their Irish identity in contemporary, multicultural America, Irishness sometimes serves as a kind of nonwhite or pre-white identity that facilitates their disassociation of themselves from mainstream WASP culture. At academic symposia on Irish and Irish American history and culture that are open to the public, audiences often mention Noel Ignatiev's book *How the Irish Became White*, voicing their interest in his idea that the once "black" Irish became white only in America.[16] Irish-themed publications like *Irish America* and the *Irish Voice*, as well as the mainstream media, often run articles linking the histories of the Irish and Irish Americans to those of other oppressed groups in America. A survey of issues of *Irish America* magazine in the mid-1990s reveals articles on Daniel O'Connell's support of the abolitionist cause (January–February 1996); on the deep connections between the Caribbean island of Montserrat and Ireland (September–October 1993); on New York's Seneca Village, where blacks and newly immigrated Irish once coexisted (March–April 1997); on an African American and a Native American who made the magazine's list of distinguished Irish Americans (March–April 1997); on the donation the Choctaw Indians made to Irish famine victims (September–October 1995); and on Irish involvement in Ethiopian famine relief (September—October 1993). The connections between Irish, Irish Americans, and African Americans are also disseminated on the Internet: three examples are the website for Tangled Roots, a project out of Yale University dedicated to "exploring the histories of Americans of Irish Heritage and Americans of African Heritage"; the page Irish Slavery in America, which stems from the website of the Gerry Tobin Irish Language School; and the webpage for Boston's Irish Immigration Center devoted to its "Cross Cultural Program," which includes a program called "Black and Green in Boston," a day of seminars and events in its tenth year.[17]

As Irish Americans reconnect to their roots and recall the supposedly pre-white Irish and Irish American identities in their history, ahistorical conflations sometimes occur. For example, an informant for sociologist Mary Waters's study of ethnicity's role in the lives of suburb dwellers cobbled together a bizarre narrative of Irish immigrant hardships that may reveal many Irish Americans' subconscious motivations for recalling their ethnic identities:

> Q: Did your ancestors face discrimination when they first came here?
> A: Yes, from what I was told they were [sic]. I know that Irish people were treated almost like blacks for a while. They weren't allowed in certain buildings. They were discriminated against. From what my mother says there were even signs in Philadelphia for Irish people not to come into the restaurants. I think they were even forced to ride in the back of the bus for a while there.[18]

Significantly, the speaker unconsciously equates "discrimination" with the experience of African Americans, conflating her knowledge of segregation in the Jim Crow south with the experiences of Irish immigrants to America. Memories of the Irish experience of prejudice in America, both real and imagined, have no parallel in the modern-day Irish American experience. This may contribute not only to the conflation of Irish and African American experiences of oppression by Waters's informant, but also to current Irish American interest in Northern Ireland, which has continued unabated since the 1960s. Irish Americans' distance from past suffering can contribute to their interest in hearing about both contemporary and historical examples of Irish solidarity with the oppressed of color, particularly those of the African diaspora, around the world.[19]

The realization of past hardship and injustice and the related desire to rectify the sense of loss of relevance and identity in postmodern, multicultural America may especially affect those who are only recently "getting in touch" with their heritage. In a study of America's "culture wars," Todd Gitlin comments on whites' lack of a meaningful ethnic or racial identity as he reports the findings of the 1991 Berkeley Diversity Project. In an effort to characterize the feelings of some white students at the University of California, Berkeley, Gitlin writes, "If not an oppressor, the white male is a blank, made to feel he lacks roots, culture, substance. 'Being white,' as one student put it, 'means having no box to check on admission forms.' "[20] Time and again, articles about the new rage for things Celtic in the late 1990s reported the feelings of loss that people hoped to fill with a consciousness of their heritage. A now-defunct website from the 1990s, Every Celtic Thing on the Web, once reassured assimilated Irish Americans: "So if you thought we'd been cleared, diluted, educated, famined, marched, migrated, transported, transplanted, or otherwise fandaggled [*sic*] out of existence—you're *dead wrong.*"[21] Eddie Stack, cofounder of San Francisco's Irish Cultural Center, opined at the time that what people find in "that bit of Celtic, Scottish or Irish blood they have, is a sense of belonging and a sense of something that is kind of genuine, which is hard to get in America."[22] For those hoping to access the genuine, websites like Irish Culture Guide and Celtic.com are available to help.[23]

Irish Americans' rediscovery of their ethnicity, for so long obscured by the muck of green beer and shamrocks, certainly has the potential to be a healthy antidote to the "identity panic" Gitlin has described.[24] One might go so far as to praise those Irish Americans who seek to "cast off the shroud of whiteness" that has kept them from creating a living, vibrant ethnic identity for themselves.[25] But for many Irish Americans, casting off that shroud is merely a way to reassert a lost innocence and still benefit from the privileges of whiteness. Scholars who have contributed to the field of whiteness studies have written extensively about how this so often happens. As Gitlin puts it, the rediscovery of ethnicity in our own times offers whites "pride and victimization, assertion without the need for defensiveness."[26] Historian David Roediger cautions that the "ethnic cultures that are bolstered as a response to [the] panic of alienation are always in danger of being swallowed by the 'lie of whiteness' "; in his view, whiteness always threatens to distract European Americans from true cross-cultural and class collaboration.[27] If the break with whiteness is not complete, whiteness merely becomes "recoded" as ethnicity or culture, Ruth Frankenberg observes.[28] Howard Winant goes further and charges that those who allow whiteness to masquerade as ethnicity are engaged in a "white racial project," even though the people involved may not overtly insist on white superiority and hierarchy.[29]

Waters clarifies how many Irish Americans may use ethnicity to identify with blackness even as they unconsciously, or unintentionally, hold onto whiteness. She writes, "But that [ethnic] 'community' is of a type that will not interfere with a person's individuality . . . They work and reside within the mainstream of American middle-class life, yet they retain the interesting benefits — the 'specialness' of ethnic allegiance."[30] In other words, ethnicity is not something that influences Irish Americans' lives unless they want it to. They can embrace their ethnicity through purchases, leisure activities, and even political involvement but still enjoy the advantages of being white in America's racially hierarchical society. Irish Americans who claim a commonality of oppression with blacks in a lecture hall, a movie theater, or a heated conversation in a pub still go home as whites once they have left that context.

Irish Americans are not the only Americans invested in these assumptions. Cultural products centered on Irish themes, perspectives, or histories are increasingly marketed to American culture at large. I hope to expose not just the white racial projects of Irish Americans, but mainstream Americans, and suggest ways in which gestures toward an authentic cross-racial solidarity might be made. As Elizabeth Butler Cullingford says of emerging cultures, "imaginative connections . . . can be used to demonstrate that the post-colonial condition is widely shared, to destabilize essentialist conceptions of national identity, and to energize political action . . . They operate . . . through the power of empathy, which can be a potent mobilizing force."[31] Though Irish Americans have long been associated with the white dominant culture, their difficult history in this country and suppressed memories of tragic events like the famine indicate that they may still have enough in common with postcolonial, "emerging" cultures to empathize with nonwhite communities of color.

"Scattered" and "in Chains": Irish and Black Connections in the Popular Imagination

No analysis of the collective Irish American romance with the idea of Irish-black solidarity would be complete without a discussion of *Riverdance*, which took the United States public by storm in 1996. While *Riverdance* is typically thought of as centered on Irish dance and Irish themes, it is in fact self-consciously multicultural, focusing on the intersections between different cultures, and particularly Irish and African American cultures. In 1997, the official website for the show defined *Riverdance* as "nothing less than the story of humankind. And it tells a story—of a people who came to the small island from many other places and who one day had to leave, many of them against their will, to find survival elsewhere. They found a new world and, in it, new people with new ways— but, above all, a common humanity in which they join, like tributaries to a great river."[32] The frequently imperial and white supremacist terms of some of these cultural exchanges, however, are erased from the narrative. The show's sequence featuring an African American gospel choir is a prime example of the romanticized narrative of shared oppression that fills this erasure. An Irish singer has just painted a scene of hardship that forces the Irish to leave their homeland. The dancers, who walk upstage toward a backdrop of a bridge that represents their crossing over the Atlantic to America, pantomime this departure. The gospel choir then comes forward and sings a hymn about the suffering of "our children," "scattered . . . torn . . . [and] in chains" and waiting for their freedom. In this fusion of oppressed peoples, African Americans vocalize Irish suffering even as the history of Irish-black conflict and the differences in subject position of the two groups are elided.[33]

Natasha Casey agrees that Irish American audiences love the solidarity overtures of the revue because they are reminded of what they imagine to be their past egalitarianism.[34] Irish Americans may admit their whiteness in the main, but at least the more liberal variety pride themselves on being sympathetic to minority struggles, as I outlined earlier.[35] Despite these sympathies, *Riverdance*'s audiences, as they identify with the dancers and watch them commune with people of other cultures, are invited to ignore current distances between white Irish Americans and people of those other cultures.

Frank McCourt's memoir *Angela's Ashes*, which competed for Americans' attention in the mid-1990s, also makes connections between oppressed peoples and avoids any discussion of strife or inequality between them. Like *Riverdance*, *Angela's Ashes* has been incredibly popular, among Irish Americans and other Americans alike, transforming the memoir and its author into institutions. The book printed and sold internationally in the millions, got an early boost as an Oprah Winfrey Book Club pick, and inspired a film adaptation. McCourt's story, which turns on the poverty he experienced in Ireland before he immigrated to America, is certainly refreshing in that it doesn't resort to a tired "damn the English" formula. Instead, McCourt astutely blames the family's poor fortune on alcoholism and the failed promise of a neocolonial state. But the success of his memoir's opener relies on the reader's identification of the Irish with oppression. McCourt writes, "People everywhere brag and whimper about the woes of their early years, but nothing can compare with the Irish version: the poverty; the shiftless loquacious alcoholic father; the pious defeated mother moaning by the fire; pompous priests; bullying schoolmasters; the English and the terrible things they did to us for eight hundred long years."[36] Though this passage parodies the Irish obsession with their suffering to some extent, it is also deadly serious — the suffering of Limerick's poor is painful to read about. In addition, the identification of the Irish with suffering is later bolstered by analogies between the Irish and oppressed peoples of color. While Irish racism is acknowledged, as it is not in *Riverdance*, it is never reconciled with the humorous and sentimental moments in the memoir in which the solidarity between the Irish and blacks is assumed and celebrated.

References to blacks are sprinkled throughout the book; Frankie fantasizes about going to America, where Joe Louis, who's also from a poor family, will show him how to fight and Billie Holiday will sing only to him.[37] He has a dream of being a coalman, turned black from his work, and decides that if he could, he'd "be black every day of the year even

Christmas when you're supposed to give yourself a good wash for the coming of the Infant Jesus."[38] More tellingly, McCourt explains that in the movie house, the lower classes are "the kind of people if you don't mind who are liable to cheer on the Africans when they throw spears at Tarzan or the Indians when they're scalping the United States Cavalry."[39] For McCourt and his readers, the suffering of the Irish makes them the natural friends of the oppressed everywhere.

But this background narrative of solidarity is undercut by Frankie's uncritical reportage of Irish condescension toward other oppressed peoples. Outside of the movie house and in the light of day, the Limerick lower classes are very conscious of their distinct difference from Africans in particular. When Frankie and his brother Malachy are lugging coal home for Christmas, they get black all over them and a woman in a shop tells them "get away from that door, 'tis Christmas Day and she doesn't want to be looking at Africa."[40] Priests speak of little pagan black babies condemned to Limbo.[41] Frankie's Irish dance teacher makes the children put sixpence in a kind of Sambo bank and challenges Frankie to remove his hand before the mouth with the "huge red lips" bites him.[42] Though Frankie as a rule seems to embrace and identify with blackness, as seen above, his child narrator voice reports these slurs on blacks without commentary. The collected references to blackness and black culture speak to a white identity that McCourt seems unconscious of, or might explicitly deny (using Frankie's perspective as evidence), but that threatens to undercut his framework of the commonality of oppression. McCourt's Irish American readers may have similar blind spots.[43]

Riverdance and *Angela's Ashes* stood at the pinnacle of Americans' mania for Irish culture in the late 1990s. Films like *Gangs of New York* (2002) and *In America* (2003) may not have earned the same frenzy of attention, but they draw on the same themes and assumptions. Martin Scorsese's *Gangs of New York*, set in the nineteenth-century New York neighborhood called Five Points, focuses primarily on the Yankee-Irish cultural and neighborhood war of the period, with Bill Cutting (Daniel Day Lewis) representing nativist Anglo-American racism and Amsterdam Vallon (Leonardo DiCaprio) representing Irish pride. The Irish-black relationship is not the focus of the film, but the offhand ways in which the film ahistorically represents the Irish-black relationship are important to notice. Jim Sheridan's *In America* more overtly encourages audiences to emotionally invest themselves in an Irish immigrant family's friendship with an African immigrant in Hell's Kitchen, another historically rough New York neighborhood. In many ways, this is a typical American story: one need only read *The Adventures of Huckleberry Finn* (1884) or screen any number of movies, from *The Defiant Ones* (1958) to *The Green Mile* (1999), to witness black characters rescuing white characters from alienation and desperation. But in *In America*, the Nigerian immigrant Mateo (Djimon Houusou) also helps the family reconnect with their Irishness in a foreign land.

Pitting the racist natives against the Irish immigrants positions the Irish as the heroes of *Gangs of New York*. But since Scorsese also wants to tell the story of the violence that traumatized the city during the 1863 draft riots, he has to use some sleights of hand to sustain the Irish heroic image. This is because Irish Americans are infamous for taking out their anger at the Civil War draft, which put them in front of the cannons and allowed more prosperous Americans to buy their way out of service, on New York's African Americans. Predominantly Irish mobs terrorized and lynched African Americans over several days. To uphold the audience's sense of the Irish as protagonists, the film deflects Irish racism onto one character, McGloin, a racially insecure Irishman who defects to Bill Cutting's camp after the death of Amsterdam's father, "Priest" Vallon (Liam Neeson) and the dissolution of his Irish gang, the Dead Rabbits. More importantly, the film de-emphasizes the Irish role in the draft riots. On the day the riots begin, the Irish are too involved in their battle with the nativists to even participate. In his voice-over narration, Amsterdam Vallon briefly mentions that some of the participants in the riots were Irish, but the Irish are merely one group in a list of immigrants and poor that he describes as rushing to participate.

The film also makes it appear that both Vallons and their gang are racially tolerant. This suggestion of racial egalitarianism is established early; when viewers follow "Priest" Vallon and his son through their underground lair, a network of catacombs beneath an abandoned church, viewers see shadows of blacks dancing in one of the caves. And during a night of drinking and whoring, Cutting comments to Amsterdam (who is living undercover as Cutting's right-hand man) that the blacks' tap dancing is an unholy combination of black and Irish dancing — a "jig jig." Juxtapositions like these imply that nineteenth-century poor Irish immigrants and free blacks coexisted peacefully, perhaps even in some sort of fellowship.[44] Later in Amsterdam's life, he and his gang run with an African American character named Jimmy Spoils. In one scene, Spoils actually helps the gang round up votes for Tammany Hall, which was firmly proslavery. Later in the film, Jimmy is killed in the draft riots, and Amsterdam mourns his death.

In all these ways, audiences can cheer for the struggles of the lowly Irish against the racist Know-Nothings and not face the fact that the lion's share of those participating in the draft riots and in the lynching of African Americans were Irish. Viewers are not challenged to reconcile their sympathy for the Irish American cause with their repulsion at Irish racism. As a result, audiences' cheers for the Irish will not make them feel uncomfortable. Scorsese might have been able to use such discomfort productively — after all, the film encourages viewers to admire Cutting even as they despise him for his anti-Irish and anti-immigrant views. The one instance in which viewers see Amsterdam participating in America's racist society is when he accompanies Cutting to a production of *Uncle Tom's Cabin*. He and Cutting join others in the audience in throwing tomatoes at the man who plays Lincoln, and some in the audience taunt the "niggers" Uncle Tom and Topsy. But it's clear in this scene that Amsterdam is merely playing along in his undercover role and isn't really invested in what's happening.

In America, a film often praised for the emotional tug it exerted on its audiences, is set much more closely to the present and is based loosely on the immigrant experiences of Sheridan and his family in the early 1980s.[45] The family did indeed move to Hell's Kitchen and so presumably interacted with people of color, if they did not experience such a close relationship with an African immigrant. In an interview on National Public Radio's "All Things Considered," Sheridan suggested that the film might affect American viewers so deeply because "everybody in America has an immigrant soul" and because the movie connects to each viewer's immigrant history.[46] Aside from the fact that this statement ignores those Americans who were brought here by force or who found their land taken over by an occupying power, it reveals the way in which Sheridan pulls on the heartstrings of Americans who like to imagine themselves as coming up from nothing.

Irish American filmgoers, of course, might be particularly attached to this narrative of struggle and victory. The young Irish immigrant family at the center of the film is starting at the bottom, living in a crack house. The young girls of the family, Christy and Ariel, initially befriend the African immigrant and artist Mateo on their first Halloween in America, when they boldly knock on his door and yell for tricks or treats. We later witness Mateo playing with the girls in a carefree manner that Johnny has lost since the death of his youngest child and only son, Frankie. In one critical sequence of scenes, a fight between Johnny and Sarah over whether to continue her high-risk pregnancy is followed by an argument between Johnny and Mateo, whom Johnny sees staring at him disapprovingly as he angrily leaves the apartment. As one might expect, the end result of the argument between the two men is that Johnny confesses his suffering and Mateo inspires Johnny to be thankful for the wonderful family he has. By the end of the scene, Johnny has realized that Mateo is dying, and he leaves Mateo's apartment, mollified. Throughout the rest of the film, Mateo serves as the conduit to bring the family together again, even as he is dying of AIDS.[47]

Even as Mateo helps reconnect the members of the Sullivan family to each other, he rekindles the Sullivan parents' attachment to aspects of their Irishness they have lost. Mateo's somewhat pagan sense of spirituality resembles a Celtic, or at least peasant, worldview; he talks of ancestors coming to visit on Halloween night, and refers to his impending death as a journey to "the other side," a concept that Johnny, surprisingly, has to ask him to explain. In another scene, Sarah notices that one of Mateo's paintings features a black man bleeding blue blood; she comments that the Irish word for black man is *fear gorm* (blue man) and that the literal words *black man, fear dubh,* mean "the devil." It is almost as if Mateo has originally come to them from the "other side," like E.T., the extraterrestrial (the family sees this movie together midway through the film), so that he can help the family and then depart. Unlike Mateo and E.T., the Sullivans will remain on earth, but with a new sense of connectedness to each other and their Irishness.

"Banished Children of Eve": Irish and African Americans in the Contemporary Novel

One of the most difficult things for a historian to uncover is people's racial beliefs about themselves.[48] Fiction is a genre that can sometimes come closest to the truth, since it can surpass the factual and let imagination reach its own logical conclusions. But one artist's imaginings are sometimes just that and can be at least idiosyncratic and at most controversial. I've already shown, for example, how *Riverdance*, *Angela's Ashes*, *Gangs of New York*, and to a lesser extent *In America* support a subtext of Irish-black solidarity by glossing over Irish-black conflict. Novelists, who explore the issue of Irish-black connection in a more extended fashion, are to be congratulated for endeavoring to imagine the personal connections and conflicts between Irish and black people that undoubtedly have occurred yet always seem to fly under the radar of mass movements and political blocs. But, as Cullingford warns, "one man's sympathetic identification is another woman's 'cannibalistic' appropriation, and the construction of aesthetic parallels that elide historical differences or asymmetries of power may appear racist or falsely totalizing."[49] Thus, even as one is grateful for creative work that explores cross-cultural relationships, one must assess it for whether it avoids such pitfalls.

The novels that plumb the depths of Irish-black connections frequently have a common thread—they are set in the past, centered on events that crystallize the complications of the Irish–African American relationship, and interested in interracial love relationships. The past decade has seen the publication of Peter Quinn's *Banished Children of Eve* (1995), focusing on Irish immigrant and free black relationships in Civil War–era New York and featuring a love relationship between a mulatto woman and an Irish American blackface minstrel; Colum McCann's *This Side of Brightness* (1998), concerning itself with the interracial friendships of the white and black diggers of the New York subway tunnels and with the legacy of the marriage of an African American digger and an Irish-American woman; Kate McCafferty's *Testimony of an Irish Slave Girl* (2002), treating white Irish slavery in seventeenth-century Barbados and dramatizing a marriage between Irish and African slaves; Kevin Baker's *Paradise Alley* (2002), covering the three days of the Civil War draft riots and featuring a marriage between an Irish immigrant woman and an ex-slave; and Pete Hamill's *Forever* (2003), beginning in its American section with New York's Irish-African revolt of 1741 and ending with the long-awaited consummation of a relationship between its Irish American hero and a Dominican American woman at the turn of the twentieth century. For the purposes of this essay, I will examine two of the above-mentioned novels — *Forever* and *Banished Children of Eve* — as case studies in the relative degrees to which fiction can move Americans closer to an understanding of how cross-racial relationships are affected by the very different racial histories and status of white American "ethnics" and African Americans.

Like many of the above-mentioned authors, Pete Hamill's interest in centering his novel *Forever* on New York's 1741 Irish-African revolt seems to come from his desire to remind Americans of the oppression Irish immigrants were subject to in the early Republic (Mary Burton, an Irish servant girl and friend of Cormac O'Connor, the Irish-born protagonist, calls herself a " 'feckin' slave' "[50]) and reveals an example of the cross-racial solidarity that tends to get lost in Americans' understanding of Irish-black relations.[51] While these reminders are important, particularly for Irish Americans unsympathetic to the present-day suffering of their former collaborators, Hamill's portrayal of Irish oppression in Ireland and in America bears the exaggerated style of legend and ultimately derails what could have been an emotional yet honest look at Irish-black relations over the centuries.

Near the tale's beginning in early eighteenth-century Ireland, Cormac's father, anticipating his murder by the local English earl, reminds his son in a parting letter to never oppress the weak.[52] Cormac obeys this injunction, living among slaves and indentured servants and participating in the Irish-African revolt soon after he arrives in New York, hot on the trail of the earl (who is, fittingly, a slaveholder). An additional motivation for Cormac to retain a connection with New Yorkers of the African diaspora comes from an African shaman named Kongo at the unsuccessful conclusion of the revolt; as a gesture of gratitude, Kongo grants Cormac the gift of eternal life and tells him he can be released from immortality only by making love to a dark-skinned woman.[53] With this literally fantastic and at times heavy-handed plotline, Hamill seems to be suggesting that the Irish-black connection forged in "slavery" is one that must be honored and preserved and one that is literally redeeming.

But Hamill manages to sustain this conceit of Cormac's connection with African Americans and refusal to oppress the weak only because Cormac doesn't follow the typical racial trajectory of the Irish in America. This is because he never really becomes part of the Irish American community again; lest someone realize he is not aging, he keeps a low profile and remains at a distance from people in general. Other than a deep friendship with Tammany Hall's Boss Tweed in the nineteenth century and with Healy, an eccentric Irish American novelist and screenwriter, in the twentieth, Cormac is completely outside of the mainstream of society, let alone the Irish American mainstream. Cormac remains a Celtic pagan, worshipping the gods of Ireland and Africa, responding to and playing the music of the African diaspora, eroticizing the African female body, and remembering his Irish and black friends throughout the novel.[54] Even when Hamill touches on the Civil War draft riots, he sidesteps an opportunity for Cormac to muse on the conflict between his outlook and that of the Irish rioters from whom he saves an African American man.[55] The Irish American assimilation into whiteness in the mid-nineteenth and twentieth centuries, at the cost of cross-racial solidarity, is almost completely ignored.

Certainly, Hamill acknowledges that Americans, if not the English, see Cormac as white. But his and all Irish Americans' connections to whiteness are seemingly erased by the destruction of the Twin Towers on 11 September 2001. When Kongo visits Cormac soon after the destruction, heralding the impending end to his immortality, Cormac tells him he has "lived to see all memory, African, Irish, Italian, Jewish, German, Polish, English, all memory of injury and insult, all nostalgia for lost places and smashed families, all yearning for the past . . . merge[d] into New York."[56] Near the novel's end, Cormac touches the belly of his Dominican American girlfriend Delfina, thinking of their mixed-race child growing in her womb, and recognizes that New York has always been a crucible: "Here in [New York's] streets the alloy of Irish and Africans invented the new world. Here is where Master Juba's spirit floated in the wings, dancing beside his Irish friend John Diamond, the two of them inventing tap-dancing. Harlem was the true northern border of the Five

Points, after all the Know-Nothing race bullshit broke the Irish away from the children of Africans. Except for those who loved one another. Except for the Africans who took Irish wives and the Irishmen who took African wives and loved them until death did them part."[57]

With these two passages, Hamill innocently suggests that 9/11 has brought people together and erased the racial polarization of the nineteenth and twentieth centuries. Hamill implicitly invites Irish American readers to enter vicariously into Cormac's egalitarian relationships with various blacks as if they, too, haven't been implicated in or shaped by the history of Irish America in the intervening years. Indeed, in a conversation and book reading with novelist Peter Quinn in San Francisco, Hamill talked about how race relations in New York improved markedly after 9/11 and naively disassociated himself from his own "whiteness." His unself-conscious comment that whiteness isn't a central part of his identity, which he jokingly emphasized by explaining that he doesn't think of his whiteness when he gets up and looks at himself in the mirror every morning, was a disappointment.[58] Anyone claiming to write a novel about interracial solidarity who isn't cognizant of the unconscious centrality of whiteness to their identity and status cannot do so successfully.[59]

Peter Quinn's historical novel *Banished Children of Eve*, published nine years earlier, is more successful in its detailed and nuanced analysis of how race and the racial formation of identity informs the main characters' lives and love relationships, their involvement in blackface minstrelsy, and their perspective on the Civil War draft.[60] Like Hamill, Quinn begins with a series of allusions to connections between Irish and African Americans. He retells the story of T. D. Rice's move from doing "Paddy" imitations to "jumping Jim Crow" as a blackface minstrel on the American popular stage; speaks of the Five Points as a home for both "darkies and Paddies"; compares the conditions of early Irish indentured servants to those of black slaves; describes the revolts Irish Americans planned with black slaves; notes how the English regarded Irish music as "savage"; and even features one character flipping through scientific estimates of the inferior skull sizes of Irish and Africans.[61] Quinn makes it clear that Irish and African American characters, at the bottom of the proverbial American barrel, very often contend with one another in antebellum America—both Irish and black characters are given ample opportunity to blame each other for their poverty and unemployment. In one desperate scene, Irish and blacks are at each other's throats over coal and even freshly killed horsemeat after they hijack a horse-drawn coal cart.

At times, it seems as if references like these risk equating Irish and black suffering and failing to take into account the critical difference that whiteness made in Irish American lives, rather like some popular cultural products and Hamill's *Forever*. In addition, Irish American characters are so often allowed to voice their belief that African Americans are taking their jobs that Quinn risks excusing their racism as a survival tactic. But the complex characters of McSweeney and Mulcahey demonstrate that Quinn recognizes more factors at work than his characters are able or willing to. McSweeney is a perpetually drunk factory worker who is put off by the draft riots, believing that it is one thing to rave against "Negroes," and quite another to kill them. Walking along on the fringe of the riots, he recalls the words of Joe Starkey, a representative of the Industrial Congress, who tried to show the Irish that Negroes weren't their enemy. " 'It's "Down with Niggerdom," not "Down with the niggers." Down with the system that makes one man a serf and the other a slave, then sets them at each other's throat. Down with them who put us here to kill one another over who'll sweep the floor.' "[62] Tellingly, McSweeney is killed by a stray bullet from the rioting as he formulates this critique of the riots and their Irish American rioters. Mulcahey, a blackface minstrel, survives the riots, but he never makes the kind of sophisticated and self-aware critique of Irish American racism that McSweeney does. He and his minstrel friends conceive of themselves as beyond racial boundaries, reflecting some historians' theories that blackface minstrels thought of themselves as subversive critics of mainstream white society.[63] However, Mulcahey's actions contradict his sense of racial egalitarianism. Mulcahey claims to be crazy about his mulatta lover Eliza, but he refuses to marry her. Quinn also reveals that Eliza knows the minstrels tolerate her in their group only because she is the only person of color, she's light-skinned, and she maintains a cheery disposition.[64] Mulcahey also has an ambivalent relationship with his young African American sidekick, Squirt (the illegitimate son of a mixed marriage of an Irish mother and an African American father). At one point, for example, Mulcahey thinks to himself that Eliza's attempt to teach Squirt to read is fruitless because he has "too much of the squirming, fidgeting darkie" in him.[65] The ultimate result of Mulcahey's ambivalence is horrific; he hesitates to save Squirt from an Irish mob during the draft riots, and the mob drags Squirt away, presumably to be lynched.

With characters like these, Quinn's novel takes steps toward admitting the tragic consequences of nineteenth-century Irish American racism, and his story may cause some Irish American readers to reflect upon the costs of their pursuit of assimilation and failure to join in mass solidarity with their fellow oppressed. While at times Quinn conflates Irish American and African American "blackness," as Hamill does, he ultimately peels back many more layers of Irish American identity.

Commemorations and Curricula

Perhaps the greatest promise for understanding the connections between Irish, blacks, and other oppressed peoples in a productive and transformative way is held by education. But the curricular innovations that might try to address these connections are affected by multicultural politics and the American mainstream's desire for celebrations of ethnicity and common oppression. These and other factors can determine whether new curricula become a force for productive complication or oversimplification. In the years leading up to and following 1997, the year in which the 150th anniversary of the worst year of the Great Irish Famine was commemorated in Ireland and the United States, education about the famine, the Irish, and the Irish experience in America could be witnessed in many different kinds of educational arenas: documentaries, museum exhibits, commemoration lectures, legislation to include the famine in the public school curriculum, and the public school curriculum itself. At times, this commemoration and education converged with Irish Americans' romanticized notions of Irish-black solidarity in unhealthy ways. But at their best, these convergences encouraged Irish Americans and other white Americans to make present-day connections with people of color who have also experienced hardship at the hands of racism, capitalism, and government bureaucracies. The commemoration of the Irish famine in the years surrounding 1997 led to important changes in the curricula of public schools in New Jersey and New York, underscoring the importance of educational arenas in promoting a more sophisticated understanding of racial identity politics and the promise and the failures of cross-racial relationships.[66]

These two famine curricula, one adopted by the New Jersey public school system in 1996 and the other by the New York public school system in 2001, emerged from the series of activities and memorials commemorating the famine in the mid-1990s. While a correspondent for *Irish America* magazine commented in 1995 on the difficulty of conveying "the horrors of the Great Hunger of 1846–50 to a group of middle-class Irish Americans, most of them well-heeled, well fed and enjoying most of the benefits of the American dream,"[67] the willingness of "well-heeled" Irish Americans to identify with a history of oppression had intensified by 1997, the key year for reviewing the legacy of "Black '47." To their credit, many of the scholars involved in these commemorations did their best to educate their Irish American audiences about the "human catastrophe" of this mass starvation in a serious, politically objective manner. They used folklore, songs, literature, and more traditional historical and sociological sources to revive the cultural memory of this catastrophe, the perceived repression of which, many theorize, has led to national, community, and personal dysfunction. Despite the scholars' best efforts, the attendees of these events were at times overeager in their excoriation of the English and their willingness to engage in competitive suffering matches with Jews, Native Americans, African Americans, and other oppressed peoples. As Lawrence Osborne points out in his controversial *Village Voice* article "The Uses of Eire: How the Irish Made up a Civilization," Irish and Irish Americans can very easily slip into capitalizing on their oppression in order to achieve "a certain politically correct credibility." Elsewhere in his article, Osborne more baldly states his objections to Irish American interest in parallels between their hardships and the hardships of nonwhite peoples: "The Irish, when all is said and done," he writes, "are not *black*."[68]

Some academic speakers at commemoration events anticipated this conflation, and endeavored to demystify the devastating famine experience of the nineteenth-century Irish or remind Irish Americans of their racial privilege and complicity in racial oppression despite their past suffering. But Irish American reception of such efforts was often negative, and agitated audience comments and questions sometimes created a tense atmosphere. Famine historian Jim Donnelly describes the tendency of audiences to assume the famine was a case of genocide: "And so strong are popular feelings on these matters in Ireland and especially in Irish America that a scholar who seeks to rebut or heavily qualify the nationalist charge of genocide is often capable of stirring furious controversy and runs the risk of being labeled an apologist for the British government's horribly misguided policies during the famine."[69]

The Irish cultural and postcolonial critic Luke Gibbons, who spoke to Irish American audiences as a part of the Irish government's traveling series of commemoration lectures, demonstrated how slippery this slope can be. One of the more conscientious critics concerning issues of race, he argues in his essay "Race Against Time" that the Irish were simultaneously "white" and "native," even as he cautions against making "simplistic equation[s] of the plight of the native Irish with that of the black population in the southern states of the USA."[70] Similarly, his commemoration lecture argued that the famine was a case of "passive injustice," not an instance of genocide like what Jews and some colonized people of color experienced.[71] Such nuanced arguments would initially appear to have nothing in common with the supposedly "politically correct" Irish Osborne excoriates. However, Gibbons's passionate rejection of Osborne's argument in the commemoration lecture threatened to eclipse his careful differentiation of the Irish experience from that of colonized people of color. Gibbons explained Osborne's position as follows: "The Irish, he says, are white, full stop, and should stick to their own caste. Whatever propagandists might say, the Irish and the British, for 'all intents and purposes,' are 'the same race, indistinguishable from each other.' If this is so, one wonders why . . . the British authorities were so slow to spot the obvious similarities and did not respond to the Irish famine the way they would have if a similar catastrophe threatened Yorkshire and Cornwall."[72] Gibbons's contradictory admission and denial of Irish whiteness inadvertently rendered him complicit in what Howard Winant might call Irish Americans' white racial project: recalling their oppression while continuing to enjoy the benefits of white privilege, thus appropriating the suffering of people of color for their own psychic ease.

The danger of appropriating others' suffering played out on a governmental level when, across the country, legislators and constituents began to lobby for teaching the Irish famine in the public schools.[73] Racial politics engulfed the legislative initiatives; British diplomats and the British press reacted with strong opposition to any suggestion that the famine was genocide, as did Jews, who emphasized the uniqueness of the Holocaust.[74] Further, the implication that the global perception of Irish racial inferiority was equivalent to the global perception of the racial inferiority of Africans, Native Americans, and other groups threatened to offend American minorities. New York politicians caused the most controversy. Democratic Assemblyman Joseph Crowley of Queens, New York, one of the primary architects of the New York state bill, argued that the famine was the "Irish holocaust," and that the "British government used the blight as a tool of subjugation."[75] In a speech heralding the passage of the bill, which described the famine as "akin to genocide, slavery and the Holocaust," New York Governor Pataki (an Irish American, unbeknownst to some) irresponsibly called the famine "a deliberate campaign" to starve the Irish people.[76]

The challenge of doing justice to the history of the famine without allowing it to become a chess piece in a game of competitive suffering was faced most directly by the scholars, politicians, and community members who worked to develop famine curricula for the public schools in New York and New Jersey.[77] Both were designed to fit into broader curricula dealing with human rights crimes around the world. The idea of an Irish famine curriculum, Thomas J. Archdeacon explains, was accepted in New Jersey due to a 1994 decision to teach the Holocaust along with other "genocides." The authors of the New Jersey statute, Senators Ewing, McGreevey, and Sinagra, hoped that students might come to " 'understand that genocide is a consequence of prejudice and discrimination' " and that they might accept the " 'personal responsibility that each citizen bears to fight racism and hatred whenever and wherever it happens.' "[78] New York folded the teaching of the famine into its preexisting Human Rights Curriculum, which included teaching of the Holocaust and American slavery.[79] Both state planning teams tried to address the problem of assuming a universalism of suffering that denied the very different histories of the Irish and African experiences. But the New Jersey Famine Curriculum, designed by James Mullin, so stacks the deck in favor of concluding that the Irish were victims of racism and genocide that it ultimately fails to encourage the freedom of thinking and complex levels of questioning necessary for such a curriculum to be relevant in a multicultural, multinational world.[80]

The New Jersey curriculum succeeds in impressing the horror of the famine on students. There is no denying that the history of the famine is horrific, and the case for it being a kind of genocide is compelling. British Treasury Secretary Charles Edward Trevelyan's 1846 evaluation of the famine's causes and effects, reprinted for the opening "Teacher and Student Summary" of the curriculum, is particularly chilling: "The cure [for the overpopulation of Ireland] has been applied by the direct stroke of an all-wise Providence in a manner as unexpected and as unthought-of as it is likely to be effectual."[81] Mullin helpfully contextualizes the famine by directing teachers to introduce concepts like laissez-faire economics and the population theories of Malthus.[82] Yet there is very little comparative perspective to other genocides, particularly the Jewish Holocaust in Europe, which goes unmentioned.[83] Students are merely asked to assess the behavior of the British toward groups as varied as American Revolution soldiers, East Indian famine victims, the Chinese who resisted opium importation, African slaves, and South African Boer "concentration camp" victims to counter Cecil Woodham-Smith's assertion that the cruelty the British showed the Irish was not typical of their behavior. Finally, students are presented with the "case for genocide" and are asked a series of questions to guide them in determining whether the Irish were victims of it.

In the chapters leading up to this determination, students have been introduced to the concept of racism and have read numerous comparisons of the Irish to black slaves. This portion of the curriculum would doubtless prove to be the most influential in students' decision making. Mullin includes philosopher George Berkeley's relation of a "Negro saying" after his visit to an American plantation in 1739, that " 'If Negro was not a Negro, Irishman would be Negro [sic].' " He also reprints the often cited judgment of Charles Kingsley that the Irish were "white chimpanzees."[84] Though the "Racism" unit of the curriculum promises to "examine this [anti-Irish] racism in the context of racism against other peoples,"[85] these quotes, and the political cartoons comparing Irishmen to apes and Negroes, are reprinted to build a simplistic case for equating the racisms. Under a reprint of the *Harper's Weekly* cartoon "The Ignorant Vote: Honors Are Easy" (see figure 1), the editor's text reads, " 'Equal Burdens': Here the stereotype of the belligerent Irishman meets the stereotype of the happy slave. Irish were called 'white Negroes.' "[86] There is a certain defensiveness here: after the cartoons, in the beginning of a section titled "Out of Africa, Out of Ireland," Mullin writes, "Before all white Europeans are lumped together with the British as colonists and slave keepers, let us consider Britain's treatment of the Irish and the Africans, and the many parallels of subjugation and enslavement to be drawn."[87] Though this is an important and worthwhile project, Mullin then splices together the histories of cruel treatment of blacks and Irish somewhat indiscriminately. Mullin details the cruel behavior exhibited toward the Irish under Cromwell, including the forced migration of the Irish to the west, the kidnapping of Irish to serve as laborers in Barbados, and the supposed orchestration of marriages between black slaves and white Irish servants to increase planters' slaveholdings.[88] Mullin then asks, "How many half Irish children became slaves through this custom? How many Black Americans have Irish ancestors because of it? If a servant is forced to mate with a slave in order to produce slave children for her slave master, is she not a slave?"[89] While it is important to show students that racism is driven by economics, the near equation of the British attitudes toward these very different peoples in very different historical eras is disturbing, in particular because a generation of New Jersey schoolchildren will be exposed to this oversimplification.

This oversimplification is all too common in academia as well. It has become commonplace to reference the aforementioned cartoons and racial pseudoscience that sometimes ranked the Irish at or below the developmental level of Negroes, but this "evidence" must be evaluated alongside contemporaneous historical realities and scientific beliefs that contradicted it. For one, much about the English attitude toward the Irish, and the English conception of racial categories generally, had changed between the time of Cromwell's rule and of the Irish famine and the publication of racist cartoons. Increased contact with Africans, expanding missionary activity and trade, and the beginnings of the second phase of imperialism had increased the likelihood that the Irish would have been viewed as racially superior to blacks. If, as Luke Gibbons claims, a "historical backdrop" of Saxon hatred of the Celtic race lent "force to accusations of genocidal intent with regard to the nineteenth-century Great Famine" and other instances of anti-Irish racism, it is nevertheless the case that overestimating the intensity of anti-Irish racism and drawing parallels between it and antiblack racism as late as the nineteenth century is risky.[90]

An important scientific factor ignored by such parallels is the theory of the Great Chain of Being, an Enlightenment racial ranking system still influential in the nineteenth century that ordered plants, animals, and humans in gradations of sophistication, and clearly placed white Europeans on a level superior to black Africans. As Stephen Jay Gould explains, the chain's hierarchical ordering of organisms was seen as a "static ordering of unchanging, created entities—a set of creatures placed by God in fixed positions of an ascending hierarchy representing neither time nor history, but the eternal order of things."[91] The racial rhetoric directed at the Irish in nineteenth-century English and American political speeches and cartoons, then, was potent; comparing Irish to apes and Negroes threatened to turn everything European peoples understood as "natural" about race on its head.

Whether this rhetoric did succeed in changing the European understanding of race and came to mirror actual beliefs about the severity of Irish inferiority is highly debatable. As postcolonial critic David Lloyd contends, Charles Kingsley's labeling of Irish he saw in Sligo as "white chimpanzees" (cited by the curriculum) is an attempt to resolve the haunting "disturbance in the visual field" that the white-skinned Irish present.[92] Because of their white skin and heritage, the Irish participated in the British Empire, voted as members of the British Parliament, and held their own antiblack racist attitudes.[93] Kingsley was likely so disturbed by what he saw in Sligo because he had not previously questioned the whiteness of the Irish.[94] But Mullin ignores these subtleties and marshals the Kingsley quote and many others to equate anti-Irish and antiblack racism and by extension the "Irish genocide" of the famine with slavery and other crimes against humanity. Given this backdrop, Mullin cannot expect that students will make any determination other than his: the Irish famine was clearly a case of genocide.[95]

By contrast, the scholars who developed the New York State Irish Famine Curriculum traveled quite a distance on the road to reaching the goal of investigating the famine, and the matter of Irish oppression, in a balanced way. Developed by an impressive group of Irish and American scholars, the famine curriculum makes connections between the genocides of other peoples without being prescriptive about whether the Irish famine was genocide. Maureen Murphy, one of the authors of the curriculum, writes, "Our lessons are about responsibility: what we do and what we fail to do. Although we were concerned about the matter of those in charge who failed to take appropriate action, we were more concerned with providing models of compassion and responsible behavior to students." Students are provided with creative lessons that ask them to decide how to distribute famine assistance in the most effective way; to distinguish between moral and civil law; and to plan an event recognizing the problem of world hunger at their schools. The curriculum also makes the connection between the Irish famine and American history and avoids romanticizing Irish America. Students not only consider anti-Irish discrimination, but also examine the draft riots and use the lessons they learn as the basis for their analyses of present-day discrimination against immigrants.[96]

The curriculum authors do compare the sufferings of Irish, Irish Americans, Africans, and African Americans at various points, but they avoid the kind of racially explosive quotations and cartoon caricatures that Mullin uses so extensively. The unit on former slave and abolitionist Frederick Douglass's visit to Ireland, designed to link the famine to American slavery, is a good example of their more balanced approach. Douglass visited Ireland as part of an abolitionist tour in 1845, students learn, and was greatly saddened by the condition of the poor there. In keeping with its focus on racial interrelationships, one of the "Student Learning Objectives" is that students "Discuss and evaluate Frederick Douglass' comparison of life as an enslaved African with conditions of the poor in Ireland."[97] To help students address this question, the curriculum provides them with a summary of Douglass's life and with the passage from Douglass's autobiography in which he comments on the similarities between the songs of the poor Irish and enslaved African Americans. The curriculum then encourages teachers to remind students that Irish men and women were free before students begin formulating their answers. The curriculum does romanticize the Irish reception of Douglass somewhat—Douglass did have some run-ins with racism in Ireland, and contemporary observers noted that the Irish fervor for the abolition of black slavery was short-lived. Students may thus feel confused by the contrast between his reception in Ireland and his treatment by the Irish in America, if their teachers choose to acquaint them with that in a following unit; the continuity between Irish ideas of whiteness and racial equality and Irish American concepts of the same are not discussed.[98] Still, the curriculum forces students to thoughtfully engage in a comparison of levels of human suffering, which is valuable.

If the teaching apparatus supporting the comparison of Irish and black oppression is a little thin in the Douglass example, it is extensive in the unit on the draft riots. The draft riots are an important subject of study in a famine curriculum not only as an example of the legacy of the famine for Irish American history, but also as a tragic outpouring of anger at anti-Irish discrimination and of racism against the blacks that had sometimes been seen as brothers in struggle in racially homogeneous Ireland. The students begin by reading a summary of the draft riots that describes instances of animosity but also cooperation between Irish immigrants and African Americans in the years between 1830 and 1850; relates the Democrats' charge that the Irish were risking their lives on the battlefield to free a people that would eventually move north and take their jobs; portrays the loyalty of Irish immigrant soldiers who fought for the Union Army; and describes the controversial conscription law and the murderous riots that followed. The students then analyze the *New York Times*'s reports of the riots for anti-Irish (or generally, anti-mob) bias, even as they confront the murderous violence of the rioters.[99] The curriculum authors caution teachers: "Teaching this activity reminds students that history is a messy business. Experience with the activity has demanded [*sic*] that it can be very difficult for students to balance empathy for both Irish and African-Americans with the events that took place during the Civil War. It is especially difficult to understand that explaining an event does not mean that you are justifying that event. During this activity, teachers should be sensitive to racial and ethnic tensions and stereotyping in their classes . . . It is also important to discuss the value of dialogue, mediation, and peaceable resolution to conflict."[100]

The section's only failure is that it never looks at how racism and prejudice, not only angry reactions to bad treatment, can lead to violence. Nast's "The Ignorant Vote" (see figure 1), reprinted in Mullin's curriculum, and Constable's "Ireland from One or Two Neglected Points of View" (see figure 2) demonstrate how anti-Irish racism and comparisons of Irish immigrants to blacks may have fueled Irish American racial insecurity and anger.[101] Given the racial conflict in late-nineteenth-century New York and the curriculum's goal of connecting the experiences of the Irish to modern-day experiences, this oversight is surprising.

The strongest section is the one dealing with the issue of genocide. The authors give teachers detailed advice about how students will need to weigh conflicting opinions: "This . . . is a subject that is challenging, and should be explored by students who are building investigative skills and developing the ability to weigh varying points of view and draw rational conclusions . . . The activity is also meant to encourage responsible class discussions about genocide in the form of a *democratic dialogue* . . . It is critical that [students] gather thorough information before drawing conclusions about the cause of massive starvation and death. Students will have to do extensive research in order to determine whether genocide had occurred in Ireland, and they may not agree with each other."[102]

Students aren't limited to the sphere of the eighteenth- and nineteenth-century British Empire to judge whether genocide was inflicted on the Irish, as in the New Jersey curriculum; examples of the Jewish Holocaust, the murder of Armenians by Turks, the Middle Passage, the plummeting population of Native Americans in Mexico between 1520 and 1620, and the murder of the Tutsi by Hutu in Rwanda are presented for comparison.[103] Students are cautioned that they must beware of "applying present concepts and values to past events" when they make these comparisons.[104] Earlier, there is a discussion of how some British blamed the famine on the "character" of the Irish, but there is little heavy-handed discussion of anti-Irish racism.[105]

The New York State Great Irish Famine curriculum, with its strong American and Irish American history components, does a better job than the New Jersey curriculum of avoiding equations of Irish and black oppression, even as it relates some liberating tales of solidarity among the working-class, or "colonized." Still, as I've suggested above, neither curriculum adequately considers how race and racial identity informed Irish and Irish American actions, and this is regrettable.[106] The children who will most likely be exposed to this curriculum live in a world where the influence of race on human interaction is strong. Understanding more about the racial politics of the nineteenth century might help students navigate the racial politics of their own time. Otherwise, the general Irish American public may never complicate its image of the Irish as freedom fighters with an understanding of how Irish Americans ultimately colluded with the white hegemony that so exploited their ancestors on their arrival in America. Thoughtful human rights curricula like the one approved for New York, especially if the inhumane treatment of the Irish during the famine is included in them, can serve as important counters to the oversimplification and romanticizing of Irish-black relationships so often presented by popular culture. They can do so, however, only if they interrogate how theories of race, racial difference, and racial superiority have fueled crimes against humanity in very different ways over time and space. If they do, the children who follow their parents into an enthusiasm for Irish and Irish American culture will do so with a strong sense of the rewards and dangers of ethnic pride and make the cross-racial connections necessary to a thriving multicultural society with a sense of optimism as well as caution.

Conclusion

As I suggested in my introduction, the desire for racial innocence and multicultural belonging has led an increasing number of European Americans to distance themselves from their whiteness. Witness the experiences of Paul Kivel in one of his antiracist workshops: "Recently I was doing a workshop on racism . . . A white, Christian woman stood up and said, 'I'm not really white because I'm not part of the white male power structure that perpetuates racism.' Next a white gay man stood up and said, 'You have to be straight to have the privileges of being white' . . . Finally, a straight, white middle class man said, 'I'm not white, I'm Italian.' My African-American co-worker turned to me and asked, 'Where are all the white people who were just here a minute ago?' Of course I replied, 'Don't ask me, I'm not white, I'm Jewish!' "[107]

Kivel's anecdote is a humorous but all-too-real depiction of how all kinds of white Americans are seeking to distance themselves from white privilege. This may be why the mania for Irish American culture seen in the late 1990s has shifted into a pervasive feature of American life in the twenty-first century—Irish and Irish American popular culture does a great deal to achieve that reconnection for people, whether they're of Irish ancestry or not. As the *National Review* suggested in a 1998 article, the mania for things Irish could not have been sustained only by the fourteen percent of Americans who claim Irish ancestry. The article suggests that what may draw Americans to performances of Irishness is both their desire to vicariously play the underdog in struggle with the English or with Anglo-Americans and to get close to the passion for life seemingly evinced by the Irish and sometimes elusive to WASP culture.[108]

The success of Irish- and Irish American–themed popular culture, novels, and educational initiatives in mainstream America may have been additionally reinforced by the post–September 11 American obsession with New York. So much of this essay centers on New York and New York Irish Americans because that is what culture producers and educators are interested in. This may have been driven by the complex history of Irish-black interaction there, by the focus on this region by the majority of academics, popular writers and performers, and novelists who write on Irish America and the Irish-black connection, and by Americans' increased interest in New York. The 2002 dedication of the Irish Hunger Memorial in Battery Park was delayed because of the World Trade Center catastrophe, and Irish President Mary McAleese, on hand for the eventual dedication, connected the tragedies. She said: "Doesn't it seem almost prophetic though, that the site for the Irish Famine Memorial should be in the memory-shadow of that tragic absence that is the Twin Towers of the World Trade Center. The spirit of the people of this city now fills that space with their courage, generosity, kindness, resilience and decency. That spirit took the tragedy visited upon this country by the poison of human hatred and turned it spontaneously into the triumph of love. There can be no better next-door neighbour for the new memorial, for this is now an area where a bustling noisy city, silently but powerfully holds its most sacred memories."[109]

McAleese's speech, paralleling Hamill's novel, encourages Americans to believe in their innocence, as seen in the post–9/11 rhetoric about how terrorists "hate us for our freedom." In the concluding essay of this volume, Diane Negra demonstrates that this romance with American innocence was indulged in part through the figure of an Irish American fireman whose defiant rhetoric at a 9/11 benefit concert made him a national sensation. In the post–September 11 moment, Negra argues, fire and police departments struggling to adapt to a multicultural world that faulted them for everything from lack of diversity to racial profiling were able to momentarily put aside their white privilege, such a liability in popular American discourse, and become innocent heroes.[110] The placement of the famine memorial in such close proximity to the World Trade Center site, though planned long before September 11, connects the innocence of famine victims to the innocence of World Trade Center victims and by extension to a dubious sense of white Americans' racial innocence and the American nation's political innocence in fueling the mentality that led to the bombing.

Many white Americans these days like to think they are untouched by racism or racist sensibilities. The diverse kinds of Irish Americans that attend *Riverdance*, read *Angela's Ashes*, design famine curricula, and enthusiastically consume comparisons of their oppression to that of blacks most likely see themselves as above the fray, telling themselves that prejudiced Irish Americans live only in South Boston. Irish Americans' failure to confront their white privilege and white racial frame of reference, both in the present day and in earlier times, must end if they truly seek to "throw off the shroud of whiteness." The Irish have simultaneously inhabited the identities of white oppressor and colonized victim, and understanding that duality is vital so that meaningful and transformative collaborations, instead of idle and ultimately superficial expressions of fellow feeling, can occur between Irish and black communities, wherever they reside. It is also a necessary first step to ensure that Irish Americans seeking to reestablish a connection to their ethnic roots do not slip into some kind of defensive white supremacist mentality. Historical and present-day instances of Irish Americans crossing the constructed boundaries of race to make real connections with African Americans should be documented and celebrated, but always with a consciousness of how whiteness has historically undermined those connections and may still have the power to do so. If Irish and Irish American culture is indeed attracting many varieties of assimilated whites and even self-consciously "ethnic" whites, Irish Americans may have the opportunity to be the vanguard for increasing numbers of Americans willing to distance themselves from the emptiness and destructiveness of whiteness. If historians, artists, and other culture producers insist on recognizing the duality inherent in the Irish position, Irish American audiences cannot turn commonalities of oppression into a convenience, a temporary inhabiting of otherness that does nothing to alter their understanding or consciousness. But if we cannot rely on the popular to point out the risk of opportunism that lies on the road to significant expressions of solidarity, let us hope for the continued influence of creative work and educational initiatives that provide a complex picture. Hopefully, the next wave of creative work and pedagogy will aid Irish and other Americans in an ongoing investigation of what present-day Irish American struggles with racial identity and cross-racial relationships can tell us about the ongoing racial formations of American identity.

Notes

I thank Diane Hotten-Somers, Joseph Lennon, and Anthony Hale for so generously offering their insight on the original version of this article, and I thank David Roediger and Lafayette Bluford Adams for their insight on the present version. I am also grateful to Maureen Murphy for providing me with a hard copy of the New York State Irish Famine Curriculum. Thanks also to Diane Negra, who liked the original version of this article enough to include it in her book proposal and who has been such a helpful editor. Finally, I would like to dedicate this article to Adele Dalsimer, who read and commented on an earlier version before its 1999 publication. Her encouragement, at that moment and at so many other moments in my graduate school career, has led to the article's publication here.

1. For a more detailed discussion of this period, see Catherine M. Eagan, " 'Say It Loud, I'm Black and I'm Proud': Irish Americans, Irish Studies, and the Racial Politics of Hibernophilia in 1990s America," *Working Papers in Irish Studies* 99, no. 1 (1999): 1–28.

2. *The Commitments*, dir. Alan Parker, Beacon Communications, 1991. Dialogue

transcription based on Roddy Doyle, *The Commitments* (New York: Vintage Contemporaries, 1989), 9. The delivery of this scene is quite different in the novel. In the novel, Outspan and Derek gasp with recognition when Jimmy suggests they are the "niggers" of Europe. As in the case of their decision to change *niggers* to *blacks*, Parker and Doyle may have changed the scene to respect American and Irish American sensibilities. They may have feared that Irish American filmgoers' status as white in multicultural America, at some distance from the anti-Irish racism historically directed at their ancestors, would cause them to be confused by Outspan and Derek's identification with being niggers. Thus the blank stares substituted by the film for the gasps of recognition in the novel. In addition, the film has Dean respond, "Maybe we're a little white for that kinda thing." The soulful success of the band proves Dean wrong, to the delight of American audiences and compact disc buyers. The soundtrack was so successful that a recording company came out with a CD that defensively promoted the original black singers of the songs made newly popular by the film. See Wilson Pickett, Aretha Franklin, Otis Redding, Isaac Hayes et al., *Before the Commitments* (Atlantic, 1991). Another line in the novel but not the screenplay is the lament of Joey the Lips, the older inspirational saxophone player who once played with American R&B greats, that he "wasn't born black" (Doyle, 125).

3. In this essay, I will talk about this Irish and Irish American "tendency" with the full awareness that the Irish and Irish Americans have very different historical and social relationships to African Americans. So, too, do different sectors of the Irish American population. An Irish-identified longtime labor organizer, a suburban family new to Irish culture, or a conservative Republican may regard the Irish-black relationship with varying levels of awareness and sophistication. Still, mainstream American and Irish American cultural products, whether niche or mass market, assume Irish-black synergy and solidarity in very similar ways. Thus, when explaining Irish American tendencies, I will usually speak of Irish Americans as a group, but will highlight the important differences in various Irish American perspectives on the Irish-black relationship when appropriate.

4. Whenever I wish to speak generally about the descendants of Irish people and the descendants of African people, or whenever I am speaking about a group that comprised both Irish immigrants and Irish Americans, or both Africans and African Americans, I will use the terms *Irish* and *black*.

5. As Dennis Clark points out, post–World War II Irish Americans had little connection to their ethnic identity, due to assimilation, the changes wrought by Vatican II, and the "youth culture" that drew young people away from their families and from the traditions associated with them. Dennis J. Clark, *Irish Blood: Northern Ireland and the American Conscience* (Port Washington, N.Y.: National University Publications, 1977), 12–13.

6. See Andrew J. Wilson, *Irish America and the Ulster Conflict, 1968–1995* (Washington, D.C.: Catholic University of America Press, 1995), 18–22.

7. "Biography of Bernadette Devlin," Bookrags.com, <http://www.bookrags.com/biography/bernadette-devlin/>, accessed 4 October 2004.

8. John P. McCarthy, *Dissent from Irish-America* (New York: University of America Press, 1993), 89; Howard F. Stein and Robert F. Hill, *The Ethnic Imperative: Examining the New White Ethnic Movement* (University Park: Pennsylvania State University Press, 1977), 140.

9. Tom Hayden, *Irish on the Inside* (London: Verso, 2001), 4.

10. See Tatsha Robertson, "Old Symbols, New Debates; Shamrock Flap Emblematic of Differing Views," *Boston Globe*, 7 August 1999. Byron Rushing, an African American state representative from the Boston area, explained to the *Globe* that the shamrock may be an innocuous symbol for the "luck of the Irish" to some, but "can become as intimidating as the clenched fists raised as black-power salutes by some African Americans in the 1960s and 70s" when "used as a rallying point by those intent on showing their power over other groups." Coincidentally, the *Boston Globe* had run a story in February of that same year about Boston blacks' resentment of the ubiquitous shamrock. As the subtitle of the article puts it, "To many minority groups, the shamrock adorning several fire engines and ladder trucks is a reminder that the Boston Fire Department remains an old-boy network controlled by white and mostly Irish-American men." David Armstrong, "Traditional Ways Trample on Women and Minority Groups," *Boston Globe*, 8 February 1999.

11. Here I follow Matthew Frye Jacobson's lead in *Whiteness of a Different Color: European Immigrants and the Alchemy of Race* (Cambridge: Harvard University Press, 1998). In writing his book, he found that "scarcely a sentence [of his manuscript] went by in which one phrase or another did not seem to require quotation marks," and he decided to dispense with them (ix). I will do the same, simply for the sake of readability, though I recognize what Jacobson calls the "social fabrication" of these terms.

12. A few of these critics, most notably David Lloyd, have carefully emphasized that the colonization of Ireland, while in some senses a model for England's colonization of Africa and Asia, did not produce an experience equivalent to that of Third World countries. See for example the introduction to Lloyd's *Anomalous States: Irish Writing and the Post-Colonial Moment* (Durham, N.C.: Duke University Press, 1993). But many critics have left important questions of racial difference unaddressed as they compare the Irish "blacks of Europe" to their counterparts in colonial and postcolonial Africa, Asia, and the Americas.

13. Thomas Nast, "The Ignorant Vote: Honors Are Easy," *Harper's Weekly*, 9 December 1876; H. Strickland Constable, "Ireland from One or Two Neglected Points of View," 1899. I thank George Bornstein for responding to an e-mail query about the latter illustration's author and title. Bornstein discusses both cartoons in greater detail in his *Material Modernism: The Politics of the Page* (Cambridge: Cambridge University Press, 2001), 145–46.

14. The seminal texts of whiteness studies as they apply to Irish racial formation

are Theodore Allen, *The Invention of the White Race*, vol. 1, *Racial Oppression and Social Control* (London: Verso, 1994); Noel Ignatiev, *How the Irish Became White* (New York: Routledge, 1995); Jacobson, *Whiteness of a Different Color*; and David Roediger, *The Wages of Whiteness: Race and the Making of the American Working Class* (New York: Verso, 1999). Ignatiev's book is perhaps the most well known among the general public. For a somewhat different perspective on the issue of whether the Irish actually "became" white in America or already identified with some form of white racial identity, see Eagan, " 'I Did Imagine . . . We Had Ceased to Be Whitewashed Negroes': The Racial Formation of Irish Identity in Nineteenth-Century Ireland and America" (Ph.D. diss., Boston College, 2000).

15. Maureen Dezell, *Irish America: Coming into Clover; The Evolution of a People and a Culture* (New York: Doubleday, 2000), 67.

16. The first time I noticed this was at a symposium on Irish America at Boston College in April of 1996, when a woman in the audience contributed Ignatiev's idea that the Irish had only belatedly "become" white to the discussion; seven years later, at a New College of California seminar I presented on the Irish relationship to whiteness, most of the people in the audience were familiar with his book and its argument.

17. See "Welcome to Tangled Roots," Tangled Roots, <http://www.iicenter.org/crossculture.html>, accessed 4 October 2004.

18. Mary C. Waters, *Ethnic Options: Choosing Ethnic Identities in America* (Berkeley: University of California Press, 1990), 161. It should be noted that the popular memory of "No Irish Need Apply" signs, which is most likely the source of the informant's confused story, is currently being contested. See Richard Jensen, " 'No Irish Need Apply': A Myth of Victimization," *Journal of Social History* 36, no. 2 (2002): 405–29.

19. Instances of Irish-black solidarity typically under discussion include the 1741 Irish-African revolt in New York City; Frederick Douglass's visit to Ireland and Daniel O'Connell's support for the abolition of slavery; and the San Patricio battalion, an army unit of Irish U.S. Army deserters that fought with the Mexican side in the Mexican-American war.

20. Todd Gitlin, *The Twilight of Common Dreams: Why America Is Wracked by Culture Wars* (New York: Henry Holt, 1995), 125.

21. Every Celtic Thing on the Web, <http://celt.net/og/>, accessed 1 April 1997. The 20 July 1998 version of Every Celtic Thing did not conclude the introductory section with "you're *dead wrong*," but with "well—perhaps we had." Sometime after 1998, however, Every Celtic Thing on the web disappeared. Typing in the old URL, <http://celt.net/og/>, now leads to the website of the person who must have been Every Celtic Thing's original creator, Cath Filmer-Davies.

22. Pat Craig, "Celtic Revival: Why the Scots and Irish Are Searching For Roots," *In Sync, Contra Costa* (Walnut Creek, Cal.) *Times*, December 1996, 8.

23. See <http://www.irishcultureguide.com> and <http://www.celticonline

.com>. The biggest difference in Celtic or Irish-themed websites since the late 1990s is that they have become highly corporate. Many more websites are devoted to selling Celtic products, whereas when I first began my research, initial search engine hits yielded websites designed by individual enthusiasts celebrating Irish and Celtic culture and getting "lapsed Celts" excited about it. The shift in site purpose indicates that Irishness has "arrived" to full commercialization, as Natasha Casey discusses in her contribution to this volume. Paddynet, another website from the late 1990s, no longer seems connected to Irishness at all—the devotion of its main page to genealogy is the only "Irish" remnant. Yet the genealogy links are meant to be used by all kinds of people—the page features pictures of families of multiple racial backgrounds in a banner above the text. Paddynet, <http://www.paddynet.com>, accessed 4 December 2003.

24. Gitlin, *Twilight of Common Dreams*, 122.

25. Daniel Cassidy, introductory address (presented at Gates of Gold Irish American Literary and Cultural Festival, New College of California, San Francisco, California, March 2002). Cassidy directs the Irish Studies program at the New College of California.

26. Gitlin, *Twilight of Common Dreams*, 139.

27. Roediger, *Towards the Abolition of Whiteness*, 13.

28. Ruth Frankenberg, "Locating Research on Whiteness" (paper presented at the Making and Unmaking of Whiteness Conference, University of California at Berkeley, 12 April 1997).

29. Howard Winant, "White Racial Projects: A Comparative Perspective" (paper presented at the Making and Unmaking of Whiteness Conference, University of California at Berkeley, 12 April 1997). Versions of Frankenberg's and Winant's papers can be found in Birgit Brander Rasmussen, Eric Klinenberg, Irene J. Nexica, and Matt Wray, eds., *The Making and Unmaking of Whiteness* (Durham, N.C.: Duke University Press, 2001).

30. Waters, *Ethnic Options*, 151–52.

31. Elizabeth Butler Cullingford, *Ireland's Others: Gender and Ethnicity in Irish Literature and Popular Culture*, Critical Conditions: Field Day Essays and Monographs (Cork: Cork University Press, 2001), 133.

32. "The Story," Riverdance: The Website, <http://www.riverdance.com/theshow/thestory/12/index.htm>, accessed 4 December 2003.

33. *Riverdance: The Show*, dir. John McColgan, Tyrone RTE Video, 1996, videocassette.

34. Natasha Casey, "*Riverdance*: The Importance of Being Irish American," *New Hibernia Review* 6, no. 4 (2002), 15.

35. Indeed, according to the Survey Research Center at the University of California at Berkeley, "surveys from 1972 onwards show that among white ethnic groups, the Jews are the least prejudiced and the Irish come in second." Quoted in Kathleen Sulli-

van, "Blending Green and Black in a Cultural Melting Pot: African American and Irish to Explore Roots, Sufferings, and Similarities," *San Francisco Examiner*, 13 March 1998.

36. Frank McCourt, *Angela's Ashes* (New York: Scribner, 1996), 11.

37. McCourt, *Angela's Ashes*, 295, 275.

38. Ibid., 263.

39. Ibid., 216–17.

40. Ibid., 100.

41. Ibid., 119.

42. Ibid., 142.

43. McCourt sees more clearly when Irish American racism is the subject, as it is in the second installment of his memoir, *'Tis*, and thus Irish American readers are forced to face their contradictory attitudes toward racial difference in a way they are not in *Angela's Ashes*. Fellow hotel worker Eddie Gilligan refers to the hotel's Puerto Rican workers as "spics" when he explains to Frank that he'd be down in the kitchen with them if he weren't Irish. In the next moment, however, Eddie speaks of the spics with admiration when he tells Frank about how they urinated in the coffee urn meant for a Daughters of the American Revolution luncheon in the hotel: "Then Eddie smiles and laughs and chokes on his cigarette because he's Irish-American and he thinks the PRS are great for what they did to the Daughters of the British Empire. He calls them PRS now instead of spics because they did something patriotic the Irish should have thought of in the first place. Next year he'll piss in the coffee urns himself and laugh himself to death watching the Daughters drink coffee that's Puerto Rican and Irish piss . . . Now Eddie says maybe the PRS aren't that bad at all. He wouldn't want them marrying his daughter or moving into his neighborhood but you have to admit they're musical and they send up some pretty good baseball players, you have to admit that." Frank McCourt, *'Tis: A Memoir* (New York: Scribner, 1999), 39.

44. There were certainly cases of Irish-black cohabitation in nineteenth-century New York. For example, Seneca Village, the shantytown displaced by Central Park, was inhabited by blacks and Irish, and New York's sixth ward, which had some Irish-black couples, remained peaceful during the draft riots. But the film's systematic elision of Irish-black strife and Irish racism inaccurately suggests that these instances of Irish-black solidarity were the norm. For two different views of the Irish-black relationship in early America, see Graham Hodges, " 'Desirable Companions and Lovers': Irish and African Americans in the Sixth Ward, 1830–1870," in *The New York Irish*, edited by Ronald Baylor and Timothy J. Meagher (Baltimore: Johns Hopkins University Press, 1996); and Ignatiev, *How the Irish Became White*.

45. *In America*, dir. Jim Sheridan, Fox Searchlight Pictures, 2003.

46. Jim Sheridan, interview by Melissa Block, *All Things Considered*, NPR, 25 November 2003.

47. As Cullingford points out, Sheridan uses Irish-black relationships in his other films. *In the Name of the Father* features a strong relationship between the falsely im-

prisoned Gerry Conlon and an Afro-Caribbean prisoner; and *The Boxer*'s protagonist demonstrates his solidarity with a black Nigerian boxer. Cullingford, *Ireland's Others*, 149–50.

48. See Eagan, "'I Did Imagine . . .'" for an attempt.

49. Cullingford, *Ireland's Others*, 133.

50. Mary goes on, "They call us indentured servants, but that's the fancy way to say it. The true feckin' word is slave. Just like all these black fellas from Africa. There's no bloody difference." Pete Hamill, *Forever* (Boston: Little, Brown, 2003), 165.

51. My description of Hamill's motivations is based on my memory of his comments during a reading of *Forever* and a conversation with Peter Quinn at the University of San Francisco, 29 May 2003. The evening was part of San Francisco's Irish Arts Foundation's Thomas Flanagan Memorial Lecture Series.

52. Hamill, *Forever*, 132.

53. Cormac will recognize her because her body will be "adorned with spirals," as Kongo tells him. Hamill, *Forever*, 261. The spirals resemble the spiral earrings once worn by his mother, an Irish Jew.

54. Ibid., 395, 411, 334, 554, 596.

55. Ibid., 384.

56. Ibid., 534.

57. Ibid., 598.

58. Hamill, reading and conversation with Peter Quinn.

59. White filmgoers are not likely to question the novel's final erasure of Irish Americans' whiteness—there is talk of making *Forever* into a movie. Colin Farrell and Jennifer Lopez are reportedly being considered for the roles of Cormac and his Dominican American "dark-skinned woman," Delfina. "Daily Dish," *Daily News*, 6 February 2003.

60. Peter Quinn, *Banished Children of Eve* (New York: Penguin, 1994).

61. Ibid., 57–58; 42; 82–83; 67; 154.

62. Quinn, *Banished Children of Eve*, 549–50.

63. See for example Eric Lott, *Love and Theft: Blackface Minstrelsy and the American Working Class* (New York: Oxford University Press, 1995).

64. Quinn, *Banished Children of Eve*, 328.

65. Ibid., 272.

66. As of 1998, bills had been passed in New York, New Jersey, Illinois, Connecticut, and California. Glen Elsasser, "Irish-Americans Demand Famine Be Taught in Schools," *Chicago Tribune*, 16 March 1998. Only New Jersey and New York have created and begun to implement curricula.

67. Mark Day, "Remembering the Famine," *Irish America* (November–December 1993), 16.

68. Lawrence Osborne, "The Uses of Eire: How the Irish Made Up a Civilization," *VLS*, *The Village Voice*, June 1996, 20.

69. James S. Donnelly Jr., "The Construction of the Memory of the Famine in Ireland and the Irish Diaspora, 1850–1900," *Éire-Ireland* 31, no. 1–2 (1996): 26–27.

70. Luke Gibbons, "Race Against Time: Racial Discourse and Irish History," in *Neocolonialism*, edited by Robert Young, special issue of *Oxford Literary Review* 13, no. 1–2 (1991): 150.

71. Gibbons, "Doing Justice to the Past: The Great Famine and Cultural Memory." Lecture delivered at the Great Famine Commemoration: An Gorta Mór, 1845–1850. United Irish Cultural Center, San Francisco, 4 December 1996.

72. Gibbons, "Doing Justice to the Past."

73. Bill Blakemore and Carol Simpson, "Irish Famine Part of Curriculum in New Jersey and New York," ABC *World News Sunday*, 16 March 1997.

74. Thomas J. Archdeacon, "The Irish Famine in American School Curricula," *Éire-Ireland* (spring–summer 2002).

75. Sarah Metzgar, "Senate Approves Irish Famine Studies," *Times Union* (Albany, N.Y.), 16 July 1996.

76. Robert Scally, "Teaching the Irish Famine in America" (lecture delivered at the Great Famine Commemoration: An Gorta Mór, 1845–1850, New York University, 8 December 1996). As Archdeacon reports, Governor George Pataki tried to quell some of the negative reaction to his speech by clarifying that the bill's intention was not to equate the famine with the Holocaust but to include the famine "with genocide, slavery and the Holocaust . . . in the human rights issues to be taught in New York's schools." Quoted in Archdeacon, "The Irish Famine in American School Curricula." As a Democratic assemblyman for California, Tom Hayden also proposed a bill to mandate the teaching of the famine in the public schools, but he was more careful from the outset to stress that the legislation would not assert equivalencies of oppression. Bee Capitol Bureau, "Potato Famine a Curriculum Must?" *Sacramento Bee*, 18 March 1997.

77. In the New York edition of the famine commemoration lectures in which Gibbons participated, New York University historian Robert Scally dealt with the danger of equating very different varieties of oppression. Restating Governor Pataki's claim that the famine is equivalent to " 'genocide, slavery, and the Holocaust' " as a question, Scally told his audience that while there may be similarities between these events, it is important to determine the historical processes behind them, not to imply through claiming "kinship" that "the human experience that resulted was the same on the part of the victims either in numbers or duration." Scally, "Teaching the Irish Famine in America." Scally was one of the advisors to the New York State Famine Curriculum development. Maureen Murphy, "New York State's 'Great Irish Famine Curriculum': A Report," *Éire-Ireland* (spring–summer 2002).

78. Quoted in Archdeacon, "The Irish Famine in American School Curricula."

79. Murphy, "New York State's 'Great Irish Famine Curriculum.' "

80. Developed by James Mullin and the Irish Famine Curriculum Committee that

he chaired, the curriculum begins with a dedication that credits "the work of New Jersey Senator James E. McGreevey, Rutgers Economics Professor Jack Worrall, historian Dr. Christine Kinealy, teacher Jim Master, and author Liz Curtis." James V. Mullin, *The Great Irish Famine*, New Jersey Secondary Schools Curriculum, approved for inclusion in the Holocaust and Genocide Curriculum in 1996, revised as of November 1998, <http://www.nde.state.ne.us/SS/irish/irish_pf.html>, accessed 11 November 2003.

81. Ibid., 14.

82. Ibid., 27–30.

83. Certainly, the varying definitions of genocide provided by Mullin provide some justification for considering the famine as an instance of genocide. From the American Heritage Dictionary: genocide is the "systematic, planned annihilation of a racial, political or cultural group." From the 1948 United Nations Convention on Genocide: "deliberately inflicting on the group conditions of life calculated to bring about its destruction in whole or part" is considered genocide. And from Richard L. Rubenstein, author of *The Age of Triage: Fear and Hope in an Overcrowded World*: "A government is as responsible for a genocidal policy when its officials accept mass death as a necessary cost of implementing their policies as when they pursue genocide as an end in itself." Quoted in Mullin, *Great Irish Famine*, 98. But students are asked to read these definitions, read various "British, Irish and American Voices" on the treatment of the Irish, read about cruel British colonial policies, and then decide whether the Irish experienced genocide without ever being asked to compare the Irish "genocide" to the Nazis' systematic plan to round up and exterminate Jews.

84. Mullin, *Great Irish Famine*, 56.

85. Ibid., 35.

86. Ibid., 43.

87. Ibid., 47.

88. Ibid., 48.

89. Ibid., 49.

90. Luke Gibbons, *Transformations in Irish Culture* (Cork: Cork University Press, 1996), 208 n. 12.

91. Stephen Jay Gould, *The Flamingo's Smile: Reflections in Natural History* (New York: Norton, 1985), 282–83.

92. David Lloyd, "Race under Representation," in *Neocolonialism*, edited by Robert Young, special issue of *Oxford Literary Review* 13, no. 1–2 (1991): 76. On a trip to Sligo in 1860, Kingsley wrote his wife, " 'But I am haunted by the human chimpanzees I saw along that hundred miles of horrible country . . . to see white chimpanzees is dreadful; if they were black, one would not feel it so much, but their skins, except where tanned by exposure, are as white as ours.' " Quoted in Lloyd, "Race under Representation," 76.

93. Much of my argument in this section is drawn from my dissertation's critique of the use of nineteenth-century scientific racial theory and political cartoons to equate

anti-Irish and antiblack racism. See Eagan, " 'White,' If 'Not Quite,' " in " 'I Did Imagine . . .' " It is also disturbing that students are not encouraged to make connections between the famine emigrants and nineteenth-century (or present-day, for that matter) Irish Americans. Emigration is only discussed in the contexts of horrific images from Liverpool and Grosse Ile. (See Mullin, *Great Irish Famine*, chapter 5, 79–96.) Yet some of the racist cartoons Mullin uses to demonstrate anti-Irish racism are from American magazines. Nast drew "The Ignorant Vote" as late as 1876, by which time Irish immigrants had demonstrated their mettle in the Civil War and were solidly on the path to assimilation. Nast's cartoon jokes that the potentially fearsome voting power of newly naturalized Irish immigrant voters and Reconstruction-enfranchised black voters would be cancelled out, but it masks how most white, native-born Americans perceived the racial status of lace-curtain and more prominent Irish Americans at this time and bears very little relation to British anti-Irish attitudes during the famine.

94. At one point, Mullin quotes eighteenth-century British philosopher David Hume's judgment that Africans are naturally inferior to whites without ever commenting on the fact that the Irish were acknowledged by many to be white Europeans, despite British hatred for them. Mullin writes, "In his essay, 'Of National Characters' he wrote: 'I am apt to suspect that Negroes, and in general all other species of men (for there are four or five different kinds) to be naturally inferior to the whites. There never was a civilized nation of any other complexion than white.' " *Great Irish Famine*, 55.

95. Only twice does Mullin make a distinction between anti-Irish and antiblack racism. Once he comments that the terms used to denigrate blacks were "even more defamatory" than those used to insult the Irish and soon after he admits that "the Irish occupied a position way below [the English], but just above the Africans." Right after these disclaimers, Mullin launches into a litany of anti-Irish comments. The first is a satirical poem from *Punch*, dating from 1848:

Six-foot Paddy, are you no bigger —
You whom cozening friars dish —
Mentally, than the poorest nigger
Grovelling before fetish?
You to Sambo I compare
Prostrate like an abject fool.

He also quotes the *Punch* article "The Missing Link," which suggested that the missing link between "the Gorilla and the Negro" was the "lowest species of Irish Yahoo." *Great Irish Famine*, 54–56. In the face of uncritically used quotes like these, it is hard to believe Mullin's assurances that the English viewed the Irish as more sophisticated than Africans.

96. Maureen Murphy, Alan Singer, and Maureen McCann Miletta, *The Great Irish Famine Curriculum: A Curriculum for All Subjects, Based on the New York State Learning Standards, Using Primary Sources, Literature, Dance and Music, Mathematics, His-*

tory, Science, Art and Theatre, Geography, Economics, Government, Career Develop-ment, and Technology (Albany: University of the State of New York, State Education Department, 2001).

97. Ibid., 151.

98. For a more in-depth discussion of Frederick Douglass's time in Ireland, see Eagan, " 'I Did Imagine . . . ,' " 121–32.

99. Murphy, Singer, and Miletta, *Great Irish Famine Curriculum*, 848–54.

100. Ibid., 843.

101. Though Constable's drawing dates from quite late in the century, Irish im-migrants and Irish Americans were compared to Africans and apes throughout the nineteenth century, and they were doubtless aware of it. For more examples of car-toons that made this comparison, see L. P. Curtis, *Apes and Angels: The Irishman in Victorian Caricature*, rev. ed. (Washington, D.C.: Smithsonian Institution Press, 1997). One cartoon drawn in the aftermath of the draft riots, "The Meeting of the Friends," depicted simian Irishmen with the heads of lynched African Americans in their hands. Henry L. Stephens, "The Meeting of the Friends: City Hall Park" (New York, 1863).

102. Murphy, Singer, and Miletta, *Great Irish Famine Curriculum*, 455.

103. Ibid., 461–63.

104. Ibid., 455.

105. Ibid., 387, 421.

106. As I've discussed above, there is a similar absence in Quinn's *Banished Chil-dren of Eve*. Interestingly, Quinn was an advisor to the development of the curriculum. Murphy et al., *Great Irish Famine Curriculum*, iv.

107. Paul Kivel, *Uprooting Racism: How White People Can Work for Racial Justice* (Philadelphia: New Society Publishers, 1996), 10.

108. "Fighting Irish," *National Review*, 26 October 1998.

109. "Speech of Irish President, Mary McAleese, at the opening of the Irish Hun-ger Memorial, 16 July, 2002," <http://www.emsc.nysed.gov/nysssa/gif/mcaleese%20 speech%20at%20hunger%20memorial.htm>, accessed 3 December 2003.

110. See Diane Negra's essay "Irishness, Innocence, and American Identity Politics Before and After September 11," in this volume.

SEAN GRIFFIN

The Wearing of the Green:
Performing Irishness in the
Fox Wartime Musical

Themes of Irishness are not what film historians tend to mention when describing Twentieth Century Fox's wartime musicals. More commonly remembered are the studio's series of "Good Neighbor" musicals set in Latin American vacation spots (such as *Down Argentine Way* [1940], *That Night in Rio* [1941], and *Weekend in Havana* [1941]), with Brazilian star Carmen Miranda "chica-chica-boom-chic"-ing her way across the screen. Yet, in *Springtime in the Rockies* (1942), Carmen Miranda's character is introduced to the rest of the cast (and hence, the viewing audience) as "Rosita Murphy." The suggestion that Miranda could be of Irish descent is played for humor, but the tie between the Latin and the Irish points to how ethnicity (and its slippery nature) were emphasized in Fox's musical output during this period.

The Good Neighbor films were not the only musicals the studio made at the time. When they were not reveling in south-of-the-border getaways, Fox musicals were joyously remembering America at the turn of the century. Starting in the later thirties with films like *In Old Chicago* (1937) and *Alexander's Ragtime Band* (1938), the early forties saw a veritable onslaught of period musicals, so much so that some industry wags referred to the studio as "Nineteenth Century Fox." The two musical formulas may seem initially different—one exotically other, the other nostalgically American—but the period musicals tended to emphasize race and ethnicity as much as the Good Neighbor musicals. Instead of overtly comparing "white" America to Latin American culture, a number of the turn-of-the-century musicals focused on Irish Americans. As many have shown, Fox's Good Neighbor musicals plainly attempted to do their part in helping U.S. foreign policy during wartime.[1] What has not been noted is how Fox's turn-of-the-century musicals also attempted to negotiate wartime attitudes about race and national identity in the United States, often through representations of Irish Americans. An analysis of three of these period Fox musicals also reveals how Irishness was used to deal with social shifts in gender roles during the war, tying them to concepts of race and ethnicity. The metaphoric use of Irishness in these films was made possible by the increasingly elective nature of Irish ethnicity in mainstream American thought. By World War II, Irish Americans increasingly could choose to announce their ethnic heritage or to blend in as part of the rest of white America.

Contemporary Irish Studies has increasingly focused on the construction of Irishness as simultaneously ethnic and white. Particularly in the wake of the Celtic Tiger economy of the 1990s, a number of historians and critics have researched how the dual nature of Irishness functions in contemporary U.S. culture.[2] Irishness presently seems to allow a number of ostensibly white Americans the ability to ethnically label themselves in an age that increasingly values and celebrates multicultural diversity. At the same time, though, asserting this ethnic heritage helps keep the white power structure dominant without seeming racist. Hence, contemporary Irishness in the United States works to help resolve conflicts between national identity and racial/ethnic issues. These Fox musicals reveal parallels between how Irishness often functions in the United States today and how it was employed in the national culture during World War II. The films employ Irishness in an almost metaphoric fashion, using it to safely cover larger concerns about race/ethnicity and gender.

In trying to resolve these issues, though, using Irishness as a metaphor also potentially *undermines* assumptions that racial/ethnic and gender identities are natural and inevitable. The films do this by creating spaces for viewers to consider race/ethnicity and gender as ideological performances rather than biological essentialisms. Such spaces are enhanced by the carnivalesque nature of the musical genre, which often works to open up rather than close down various possibilities in conceptions of race, gender, and their intersection. Although made over half a century ago, these musicals often end up exemplifying Colin Graham's contemporary contention that Irish identity has become "an impossible category."[3]

Beneath the Blarney: Irishness as Metaphor

Coney Island and *Sweet Rosie O'Grady* were released in 1943, and *Irish Eyes Are Smiling* hit screens in the following year. Betty Grable became the top box-office attraction in the country in 1943 by starring in the first two films, while *Irish Eyes Are Smiling* was the first starring vehicle for June Haver. Intriguingly for this discussion, while these films are fundamental to these women's star status, Grable and Haver did not carry aspects of Irishness into their star personae (although Haver's off-screen image did heavily invest in her Catholicism).[4] Probable reasons for this lack of association with Irishness will be examined shortly but, at present, some basic outlining of the films themselves seems advisable (particularly because, while major box-office successes during their initial release, these pictures are not familiar to most people today).

Coney Island follows the intense yet friendly rivalry between two shady entrepreneurs. Eddie Johnson and Joe Rocco (played by George Montgomery and Cesar Romero) continually try to better each other, in business (at the titular amusement park) as well as in romance. Central to both areas of competition is singer Kate Farley (Grable), who performs at Rocco's beer hall. The sweetheart of her predominantly Irish working-class clientele, Kate exhibits a singing style and personality that are loud, feisty, and brash.[5] Eddie wheedles his way into managing the beer hall and immediately sets to revamping Kate's performing style — specifically trying to tone her down. In trying to make her more upscale, for example, he handcuffs her hands and feet before one performance to limit her histrionics. Kate, of course, is furious, but the favorable reaction and sense of respect she gets for going "high class" soften her response (and her attitude toward Eddie). Such a shift is also indicated by the change in her repertoire: from "Irish Eyes Are Smiling" and "Put Your Arms Around Me Honey" to slow romantic ballads newly written for the film. Kate eventually gets the attention of Broadway, completing her rise to fame. A few romantic complications arise as Kate realizes how she is functioning as a pawn in the two men's rivalry, but all is resolved between her and Eddie in time for her successful opening night.

Sweet Rosie O'Grady presents a similarly combative romantic relationship against a show-business background. Irish American singer Rosie has left the New York beer halls for Britain, where she has changed her name to Madeline Marlowe and become a star on the legitimate stage. As the film opens, a duke is on the verge of proposing to her. As she sails back to America as Madeline Marlowe, though, her secret is exposed by an intrepid Irish American reporter from the *Police Gazette* (Robert Young). Incensed, Rosie/Madeline initiates revenge by telling other reporters that she is actually secretly engaged to the reporter, and that he plans to live off her income. Such moves and countermoves continue throughout the film, but the two eventually come together as Rosie realizes American audiences love her even more under her real name than as Madeline.

Irish Eyes Are Smiling may seem initially different from the first two, since it claims to be a biography of songwriter Ernest Ball (Dick Haymes), writer of such tunes as the title song and "Mother Machree." Still, the (highly fictionalized) rise of an Irish American male in show business is combined with a young female performer's quest for stardom. Nicknamed "Irish," and played by Haver, the performer's romance with Ernie is constantly complicated by their attempts to succeed onstage. (For clarity's sake, when referring to this character, "Irish" will be placed in quotes.) As in the Grable films, the relationship between the two leads is highly contentious, with each repeatedly storming off after taking umbrage at the misunderstood actions of the other. Of course, after all the reversals of fortune, the film ends with the two embracing on the stage of a big Broadway show featuring his first score—and her as the Great White Way's newest star.

The formulaic sensibility of these films extends beyond the narratives and into stylistic choices. Each is filmed in three-strip Technicolor, using the period atmosphere for a maximum of splashy, colorful, and brightly lit sets and costumes. Such elaborateness is accentuated in the musical numbers, which are granted even greater amounts of stylized artifice since all the numbers are stage performances. Furthermore, the standardized plots often seem like the merest excuses for a variety of loosely justified musical numbers, the extravagances that customers probably really paid to see. The three films together create a mini-cycle of musicals that programmatically retell narratives of Irish American characters climbing the ladder of success. The rags-to-riches plots of these musicals plainly and consistently invoke the typical Horatio Alger narrative, showing Irish Americans climbing the ladder of success and affirming the possibilities of acceptance and assimilation.[6]

Most scholars, though, consider that Irish Americans had largely been assimilated long before World War II.[7] The first large waves of Irish Catholic immigrants began in the mid-1800s, so almost a century of assimilation had been underway by the time these films were produced. By the early 1900s, immigration from southern and eastern Europe had increased dramatically, and Irish Americans began to be positioned as exemplars of immigrant assimilation on whom other groups should attempt to model themselves. One can see this growing acceptance of Irish Americans into the inner circle of whiteness by the 1920s, as Diane Negra's work on the career of actress Colleen Moore and the image of the Irish American girl has ably shown.[8] In a number of Moore's films, gradual acceptance of the Irish as white was demonstrated in happy endings in which Moore's Irish lasses wed upstanding white American men. By the time Fox was producing its period musicals, the whiteness of Irishness seemed generally accepted. Irishness would still be invoked in films during the war—in the GIS played by James Cagney or Gene Kelly, or Bing Crosby's Oscar-winning turn as Father O'Malley in *Going My Way* (1944).[9] But these stars also often played characters whose national heritage was effaced under a general assumption of whiteness. For instance, Mickey Rooney's reign as the top box-office star just before the U.S. entrance into the war came from playing all-American (i.e., ethnically unmarked) boys such as Andy Hardy. During the war, the Production Code Administration reviewed every film to note down all portrayals of crime, alcohol or drug use, and portrayals of "Races or Nationals." The reports for the trio of Fox musicals under analysis do not list any characters as Irish under "Races or Nationals," seemingly indicating that the Irish American characters were considered white.

Reinvoking the Irish American assimilation narrative in these period Fox musicals might seem somewhat pointless, then, if that specific ideological struggle had indeed been settled. The struggles of Irish émigrés, though, seem to be used in these films as a sort of safe zone for mediating other contemporary concerns. First, one needs to acknowledge how these films mediate racial discourse in wartime America. Although the full horror of the Nazi "Final Solution" was not well known in the United States at the time, the country was aware of the racial aspects of the war, and thus grew more conscious of how American culture dealt with racial and ethnic diversity. The Hollywood studios joined in the effort to show America as a land of acceptance and opportunity for all races and ethnicities.[10] For example, in order to encourage African American participation in the war effort, studio executives met with Walter White, head of the NAACP, to try to improve depictions of African Americans in Hollywood films.[11] The number of Good Neighbor films produced by Fox and other studios worked similarly to show U.S. acceptance of other cultures. In their own way, the ethnic discourse in these Irish turn-of-the-century films also attempts to reassure the spectator of American tolerance. In the clearest example, Rosie O'Grady ends up finding even greater stardom and acclaim when she embraces her ethnic identity and stars on Broadway under her real name. The film thus indicates that Rosie's worries about widespread racial and ethnic intolerance in the United States are misplaced. Similarly, music publishers initially refuse Ernest Ball's sentimental ballads about the Emerald Isle, but the American public ends up clamoring for them. In all these films, the Irish easily find success, happiness, and acceptance in America, providing evidence that the country has successfully resolved whatever racial and ethnic inequity may have once existed. Judging by box-office returns, such general celebrations of Americana and nationalist ideals were warmly welcomed by wartime audiences.

The invocation of Irishness in Fox's musicals may also be tied to another aspect of racial discourse during the war. Part of the country's general awareness of the racist politics of Nazi Germany was an acknowledgment of the "Aryan ideal": northern European "white" skin tone, blonde hair, and blue eyes. Such a description perfectly encapsulates the female performers on whom Fox centered its musicals: Alice Faye, Sonja Henie, Betty Grable, and June Haver.[12] Grable *was* of German descent, and spent her childhood in the German American section of south St. Louis; June Haver was born Beverly Jean Stovenour, a name of Prussian heritage.[13]

Fan magazines and interviews did not stress these backgrounds, tending to present the women less complicatedly as just "all-American" girls.[14] The films work to specifically repudiate any claims of Aryan racial superiority in these blonde, blue-eyed, "peaches-and-cream" pinup girls by connecting these physical characteristics to being *Irish*. It would not be until after the war that the blonde female Fox stars would play characters from a Germanic background. For example, Grable and Haver would not star as the Hungarian American vaudeville stars *The Dolly Sisters* until 1946. Haver would also later play the daughter of German American songwriter Otto von Tilzer (S. Z. "Cuddles" Sakall) in *Oh, You Beautiful Doll* (1949).

The centrality of the female star in Fox musicals links Irishness to shifting conceptions of gender roles and how women were expected to behave. In fact, as Negra's work points out, this was not the first time representations of Irishness had been used to deal with gender issues. She writes that, in the 1920s, "when traditional American femininity was 'under siege' to some extent due to the ascendancy of the New Woman as a dominant female stereotype, the figure of the Irish Colleen . . . served as a comforting return to natural and unproblematic femininity."[15] Granted, these Colleens often engaged in mischievous pranks, but such actions were usually excused as the childish exuberance of a basically sweet young thing. Further, that energy was positioned as something that could be cherished *yet harnessed* by an adult American male. In 1920s films, Colleen characters assimilate by becoming the happy and dutiful brides of American males. Thus, images of Irish American females were often used to counter the rise of the independent New Woman.

World War II saw a new upsurge in self-sufficient women, with women finding work in welding, mechanics, and other traditionally masculine jobs. As men marched off to war by the thousands, women also became the de facto heads of the household. A major difference between this period and the 1920s was that the government (and major industries) encouraged women to take on such roles. Icons like Rosie the Riveter grounded a campaign urging women to do their part to keep the nation's economy thriving and help win the war. Hence, Fox's wartime musicals differed slightly from 1920s Hollywood films in how they used Irishness to discuss gender. Like the 1920s Colleen figures, Grable's and Haver's characters *do* end as part of a happy heterosexual couple, but they are anything but sweet and childlike—and *mischievous* is too mild a term for their actions. Rather, they are highly combative and temperamental adult women. Most of the humor in both *Coney Island* and *Sweet Rosie O'Grady* comes from the verbal and physical sparring between the romantic couples. As pointed out earlier, Grable's character in *Coney Island* is so physical that the male lead tries to rein her in by shackling her hands and feet. A running joke in *Sweet Rosie O'Grady* has Rosie angrily braining men with flowerpots. "Irish" in *Irish Eyes Are Smiling* is continually socking guys in the eye with a right hook. (One possible reason why Haver never became as popular as Grable was that film after film had her consistently bristle at men's advances.) Irishness is not used in these films to present sweet old-fashioned girls, but stubborn and often physically violent women.

Archival evidence of the production process behind the films illustrates that such portrayals were carefully conceived. Indeed, the studio very concertedly strengthened the female leads in these films. Notes from story conferences with studio head Darryl Zanuck show how the sweet innocent ciphers in early drafts were transformed into feisty strong-willed characters. Grable's character in *Coney Island*, for example, was initially to be introduced to the story as a singer in a church choir.[16] Zanuck responded to these early drafts: "By making the girl a choir-singer, we have taken all conflict out of the love story. We need two aggressive characters fighting each other."[17] Similarly, initial drafts of *Irish Eyes Are Smiling* presented composer Ernest Ball as a stereotypical hot-tempered Irishman while the girl was so meek and passive that Zanuck himself considered her "nothing but a puppet." Zanuck told the writers to go back and make her "just as tough as anybody else."[18] By the time the film went into production, Ball had been stripped of most of his combativeness (possibly justifying his penchant for writing weepy ballads), and "Irish" ended up the one with the violent disposition. In a press release, Fox even trumpeted the fact that "during the shooting of one . . . fight scene, June [Haver] severely sprained her shoulder muscles and was laid up for two days."[19] In the film's final line of dialogue, "Irish" tells Ernie, "Unless you put your arms around me, kiss me and tell me that you love me . . . one of us is gonna get a black eye!" These films seem to get away with such representations of female assertiveness by ascribing it to a certain ethnic heritage. Hence, just as these musicals use Irishness as a safe zone for addressing American wartime attitudes about race and ethnicity, it is possible that the films also use Irishness as a safe zone for addressing American wartime attitudes about gender.[20]

Getting Their Irish On (and Off): Race/Ethnicity, Gender, and the Carnivalesque

While Irishness was relatively accepted as a form of whiteness by World War II, the emphasis on Irish American women as hot-tempered creatures shows that stereotypical associations about this ethnic group were still common. An early scene from *Coney Island* in which a union of Irish bricklayers rents out the beer hall Kate Farley performs in exemplifies this. Kate and a male quartet entertain the bricklayers by harmonizing to "Irish Eyes Are Smiling." As the scene progresses, though, the performance is interrupted by a full-scale donnybrook among the drunken revelers, who gleefully join in the melee as part of the evening's festivities. In the course of about three minutes, almost every Irish cliché is performed on-screen: maudlin ballads, working-class labor, drunkenness, and a propensity for violence. Such representations are not isolated to this one scene. A lovable souse named Finnegan (played by veteran character actor Charles Winninger) figures prominently, always on the ready to nab a free drink or bluff his way through a fight. Finnegan also gets to perform his own number, a rousing chorus of the old standard "Who Put the Overalls in Mrs. Murphy's Chowder." Used for nostalgic appeal, the song nonetheless recalls stereotypes of dim, drunken, and slovenly Irish immigrants — too poor to own more than one pot for both cooking and cleaning. Such invocations of Irish stereotypes also appear in both *Sweet Rosie O'Grady* and *Irish Eyes Are Smiling* in the form of free-for-all fistfights and boisterous drunken behavior.

Yet, the films do not single out only Irish Americans for such broad brushstrokes. The beer halls in *Coney Island* and *Sweet Rosie O'Grady* are run by non-Irish émigrés. The *Coney Island* hall is owned by Italian American Joe Rocco (played by Cuban American Cesar Romero); before moving to Britain, Rosie O'Grady performed at the beer garden of Ger-

1. Betty Grable on display as Irish American Kate Farley performing in the blackface number "Miss Lulu from Louisville" in *Coney Island* (1943). (Academy of Motion Picture Arts and Sciences)

man American Joe Flugelman (Sig Ruman). Rocco is portrayed as someone with shady dealings and links to underground thugs, hinting at the typical Italian mafioso image; Flugelman is brought out only briefly as an almost poster image of the jolly German tavern keeper. *Coney Island* also contains a harem-girl number in which a group of chorus girls create an exotic Orientalist landscape, complete with a female contortionist specialty act. The number, "In My Harem," is sung by Phil Silvers, who disguises himself as a Turkish maharaja speaking in a tongue more reminiscent of the song "Aba Daba Honeymoon" than any actual Turkish dialect. Use of stereotypes becomes even more apparent when the female leads in two of these films perform in blackface. In *Coney Island*, Grable becomes "Miss Lulu from Louisville," and in *Irish Eyes Are Smiling*, Haver performs "Strut Miss Lizzie." Both numbers have the stars don brunette wigs, light brown makeup, and gaudy clothes to perform "lowdown" rag routines.[21] As numbers in period musicals, such imitations of African Americans directly recall the popularity of blackface minstrelsy in the United States during the nineteenth century.

Potentially demeaning images extend to representations of gender as well in these films. While studio communications indicate the conscious desire to make the female leads more aggressive and independent, Fox musicals had a reputation for being centered on beautiful objectified female bodies. Betty Grable's star image, for example, rests primarily in her status as the most popular pinup girl of the war, and Fox insured her legs at Lloyd's of London. Grable's and Haver's bodies are most definitely on display for the delight of the male gaze in these three films. *Variety* considered *Sweet Rosie O'Grady* merely an excuse "to show Betty Grable in the flesh . . . The Technicolor cameras fairly whistle every time they look at her."[22] An undated press release for the film shows the studio encouraging this objectification: "[when] the gam-and-glamor girl was going through one of her dance numbers . . . she took a tumble and pulled a knee tendon, incapacitating her underpinnings, and thereby the rest of the Grable torso, for a nerve-wracking seven weeks."[23] A male critic in the *Dallas Morning News* reviewing *Coney Island* even indicates how the objectification may have helped male viewers accept aggressive female characters. He evinces a sense of vague annoyance at Grable for "her assertive personality" and for "talk[ing] incessantly," but he concludes that "maybe her generously displayed chassis enhances the values of her histrioni[cs]."[24] Thus, the strong-willed nature of the women in these films is balanced, and possibly even negated, by their presentation as sexual commodities for the heterosexual males in the narrative and in the audience. As with the constant use of racial and ethnic stereotypes, such female objectification seems to work against any argument for Fox's musicals leading the way in their calls for racial and gender equality.

As musicals, though, these films create an ambience that complicates attempts to maintain *any* sort of coherent attitude toward race and gender, whether progressive or reactionary. Specifically, the musical genre often creates a carnivalesque environment in which logic and social propriety can be joyously disregarded. Fox musicals regularly featured narratives filled with rambunctious revelry and combativeness, as star performers such as Carmen Miranda or the Ritz Brothers barged on screen and decimated any sense of logic or plot coherence. The overt physicality of the battle-of-the-sexes romance in this trio of films, as well as the recurrent use of room-clearing brawls, also creates an atmosphere of chaotic energy and anarchic possibilities. As Bakhtin theorized, the carnivalesque can subvert and upend hegemonic norms.[25] For example, within these musicals, such energy seems to create a space for more willful women. The carnivalesque also tends to emphasize artifice, surface, and performativity in its overturning of power dynamics. Thus, while overtly engaging in racial stereotyping and objectification of the female body, these musicals display carnivalesque traits that potentially mitigate against essentialist notions about such stereotyping and objectification.

Further, the *structure* of these films (as well as a number of other musicals), lends itself to a carnivalesque challenge to hegemonic standards. As Gerald Mast succinctly asserts, "while MGM musicals descend from the book tradition of weaving song and story, Fox musicals descend from vaudeville."[26] After World War II, the musical genre (led by MGM) would become dominated by a structure known as "integration." (Integrated numbers help depict the characters and advance the plot by having people singing when they should be talking.) Produced before this point, these Fox musicals were not examples of integration. Instead, all numbers occurred when the characters were onstage performing—whether the films were backstage narratives (as in this trio) or not.[27] All Fox musicals during the war tended to fall into the same pattern: a standardized plot, broken up by various performers (who often played no or little part in the narrative) coming out and doing numbers. Referring to them as "specialty acts" emphasized the regard toward these artists as having a specific talent or act that could be inserted into a film without being directly tied to the storyline. For example, *Coney Island* includes random musical interludes by the female contortionist in the harem number, as well as a harmonica specialty and a whistling quartet. The conclusion of *Irish Eyes Are Smiling* presents a medley of Ernest Ball's greatest hits, sung by a series of performers who have played no part in the narrative—until "Irish" (Haver) and Ball (Haymes) enter to sing the final chorus of the title song and the film fades to the end credits. Such random presentations of performers create a structure strongly influenced by the theatrical tradition of vaudeville.

Unlike the integrated structure that superseded it, the theatrical structure of vaudeville (codified roughly at the turn of the century) did not have any interest in maintaining a coherent, unified vision. Specialty numbers in Fox's vaudeville-influenced films at times can be explained as part of the show being produced in a backstage narrative. Yet, almost as often, the specialties do not have even this tangential relationship to the narrative, and simply appear out of nowhere (as if the producers realized that too much time had gone by without a musical number, and tossed one in haphazardly). Such apparently random decisions create a general sense of chaos that becomes itself a potential source of pleasure. Henry Jenkins's analysis of the "vaudeville aesthetic" in Hollywood cinema describes films that are "marked by a general questioning of social norms . . . [with a tendency] toward heterogeneity, even at the risk of disunity and incoherence."[28] Hence, the vaudeville structure of Fox musicals during the war often enhances the sense of the carnivalesque to open gaps in the films' narrative construction. Through such gaps, various hegemonic norms could be momentarily ridiculed and reversed.[29]

The carnivalesque atmosphere strongly affects the metaphoric nature of Irishness in these musicals. While the films invoke Irish American stereotypes, this identity is also consistently treated as a costume that the protagonists can put on and discard on a whim, encapsulating ideas of masquerade and performativity found in feminist and queer theory.[30] At the bricklayers' party in Coney Island, for example, the characters played by George Montgomery and Phil Silvers bluff their way in by simply nabbing two union badges and then talking with Irish brogues. Often, this notion of Irishness as costume is tied to the objectification of the female stars. Certainly, the outfit Grable wears as she sings "Irish Eyes Are Smiling" in Coney Island presents Irishness as an outfit for display. She is dressed in a Colleen ensemble, but with a very short hemline to show off her famous legs. The costume is also trimmed extensively with green spangles, and is topped with an oversized shamrock-shaped sequined headdress. Haver wore a similar Colleen costume in posters advertising Irish Eyes Are Smiling, albeit without the shamrock headdress.[31]

The shifting presentations of Grable and Haver show them replacing their Irish outfits and trying on other ethnic masks. This is most notable in the blackface numbers in Coney Island and Irish Eyes Are Smiling, which also seem to regard race as a costume. In these numbers, Grable and Haver use café au lait coloring rather than burnt cork, presenting not so much a version of Topsy from Uncle Tom's Cabin as an imitation Lena Horne, the first African American female performer to be treated by Hollywood as a glamour girl—in other words, a body capable of being objectified. *Variety*'s review of *Coney Island* recognized the use of racial transformation for purposes of objectification, describing Grable's "brownskin takeoff of 'Miss Lulu from Louisville'" as "a pictorial review of derriere exercising."[32] A number of reviews for *Coney Island* seemed to endorse the sexual appeal of these transformations. One Southern reviewer somewhat stunningly felt that "a tawny Betty Grable is more attractive than the peaches-and-cream one."[33] The harem number in *Coney Island* also uses Arabic culture merely as an excuse to put the chorus girls in revealing outfits. Consequently, the numbers come off as just another interesting way to showcase the stars' bodies, treating race and ethnicity as a carnival of possibilities. An article on *Coney Island* in *Look* magazine presents the various racial guises that Grable takes on as equally intriguing and spectacular: right next to a photo of her as Lulu is a photo of her in "colleen drag."[34]

The carnivalesque presentation of ethnicity goes beyond the musical numbers and figures in the narratives of the films as well. The plot of *Sweet Rosie O'Grady* is based on the title character discarding her Irish identity to perform as Madeline Marlowe . . . and then somewhat unproblematically switching back. *Irish Eyes Are Smiling* also begins with a case of mistaken identity, as Ernest Ball mistakes chorus girl "Irish" for vaudeville star Belle LaTour. Later on, due to plot contrivances, "Irish" tries to hide from Ernest, and changes her stage name to do so. Such identity shifting is not limited to the women either. Phil Silvers's character in *Coney Island* pretends to be Turkish in one scene, then Irish in the next. Robert Young's character in *Sweet Rosie O'Grady* also adopts different personae as he attempts to pry out information on the title character for his *Police Gazette* columns. The characters often seem to understand these various identities are merely costumes: Grable points out to the crowd how fake Phil Silvers's Turk is; the women's blackface moments are presented quite specifically as stage performances within the narrative. Consequently, the films imply that the viewer should enjoy the surface nature of these identities, and race and ethnicity themselves potentially fall sway to the carnivalesque nature of these musicals.

It is important, though, to recognize and acknowledge that only white characters get to play this game. Linda Mizejewski's research on the use of café au lait coloring in the Ziegfeld Follies argues that the "imitation was permissible precisely because it was identifiable as disguise."[35] That Irish Americans had been accepted into whiteness meant that they could choose to don their Irish identity or take it off as they liked, much as these characters do with both their Irish identity and their café au lait look. In fact, the blackface numbers recall how Irish American performers in the 1800s often specifically used blackface as an assimilation strategy — positioning themselves as *white* people who needed to "blacken up" to play African Americans.[36] Thus, such a carnivalesque view of race/ethnicity can be read as a hegemonic negotiation that attempts to reessentialize the centrality of whiteness. Considering identity as a role you can take up but then discard could also work as a hegemonic negotiation of gender roles in ultimate support of patriarchy: suggesting to all those Rosie the Riveters in the audience that their new "masculine" behavior was just a temporary persona that should be taken off once the war was over.

Yet, the carnivalesque nature of these musicals potentially implies that whiteness is just as much a masquerade as any other racial/ethnic identity. Similarly, all notions of gender also threaten to become a matter of costume and performance in these films. *Irish Eyes Are Smiling* provides the most remarkable example of how the incoherence of the Fox musical potentially subverts its attempts to resolve wartime gender issues in favor of patriarchal norms. As noted, "Irish" is put on display in a variety of ethnic and racial masks. She also wears her gender like a costume. Twice in the film, she dresses in men's clothing, once as a bellhop with upswept hair hidden underneath her cap; then, in Ernie's big Broadway show, she performs a musical number wearing a suit, pants, bow tie, and boater.

The number, "Bessie in a Bustle," describes a girl from County Cork becoming the toast of the Bowery once she buys a bustle. In the first part of the number, June Haver, as "Irish," is presented in a typical fetishized fashion — the bustle emphasizing her bottom, but the skirt cut away in front to show off Haver's legs. Halfway through the number, though, Haver exits as a chorus of others in bustled bottoms crowds the frame. While the members of the chorus are initially hidden behind parasols, the line eventually turns toward the camera to reveal that they are men in drag — all wearing versions of the same outfit that "Irish" first appeared in (with curled ringlets and cutaway skirts). As they do their pirouettes, leaps and *en pointe* steps, "Irish" returns—this time in a man's suit and straw hat (again with upswept hair)—to sing another chorus. While the first chorus seemed to be about her, now the song seems to be about how these female impersonators were ignored until they bought bustles! At the climax of the number, "Irish" takes the lead as she dances with one of the chorus.

"Bessie in a Bustle" was obviously influenced by the notoriety of the "Ladies of the Chorus" drag routine in the popular Irving Berlin Broadway show *This Is the Army* (first produced for the stage in 1942, adapted to film by Warner Bros. in 1943). What is different from the "Ladies of the Chorus" number is the inclusion of Haver's character in *male* drag, giving added emphasis to the parody of the type of objectification typically found in Fox musicals. In treating gender as costume, the number's carnivalesque nature threatens to upend gender normativity. The continuity script of the completed film (which was done by someone sitting in a screening room and taking down the dialogue) indicates the potential ambivalence being created when it refers to the chorus boys in drag as "girls."[37] The purpose of the number within the narrative is minimal. While officially part of the Broadway show showcasing Ernie's songs, "Bessie in a Bustle" was written for the film by studio contractees Mack Gordon and James V. Monaco, *not* by Ernest Ball. Thus, its inclusion is not part of the tribute to Ball's catalogue of tunes. Rather, the number seems to function as the most outrageous example of gender chaos in a film centered on a combative woman and a relatively passive hero. Further, its placement as the penultimate number of the film (followed only by a final medley of Ball's songs), places it as a climactic moment in the film's structure.

Epilogue

"Bessie in a Bustle" stands as a remarkable carnivalesque moment that disrupts whatever these turn-of-the-century Fox musicals may have been attempting to do in mediating attitudes about gender. The metaphoric nature of Irishness also threatens to set essentialist attitudes about race and ethnicity adrift. Another moment from *Irish Eyes Are Smiling* exemplifies how the carnivalesque rambunctiousness of the Fox musical at this time had the potential to spin negotiations of both race and gender out of control. A number of men have made a bet whether one of them can turn the next woman to come out of a restaurant powder room into a musical comedy star. Each of them has secretly sent into the ladies' room a different woman to fix the wager. The one responsible for making the woman a star has sent in a white actress who is already a headliner; Ernie has sent in "Irish"; and a third who has bet that it cannot be done has sent in a black maid. Typical of the chaos of the Fox musical, all three women begin a wrestling match to get through the door first, until "Irish" ends up stumbling out into the restaurant and landing on her ass. While the sequence supports patriarchal dominance (all three men watching to see which woman comes out, with the idea that the man will mold the woman into a star), the physicality that the women display in the ladies' room shows a noticeable lack of concern for either "ladylike" manners or racial deference.

While quite popular on release, this series of films has been generally forgotten by film historians and scholars—and does not feature among the burgeoning studies of Irishness and representation. Yet, the films offer some provocative points in trying to theorize definitions and uses of Irishness. They provide further evidence of "the therapeutic orientation of many of the themes of Irishness" on the one hand.[38] Yet, in using Irishness as a tool to alleviate U.S. concerns about race and gender, the generic structure of the vaudeville-influenced, nonintegrated musical potentially unravels such efforts. While attempting to negotiate issues of race and gender for wartime audiences through the use of Irishness, these Fox musicals often threatened to unleash more than they could contain.

Notes

1. To provide only one contemporary critic's response, Wilella Wildorf of the *New York Post* thought Carmen Miranda "as an advertisement for Roosevelt's good-neighbor policy . . . [was] worth half a hundred diplomatic negotiations." " 'The Streets of Paris' Opens at Broadhurst Theater," 20 June 1939.

2. Such work includes Richard D. Alba, *Ethnic Identity: The Transformation of White America* (New Haven: Yale University Press, 1990); and Colin C. Graham, *Deconstructing Ireland: Identity, Theory, Culture* (Edinburgh: Edinburgh University Press, 2001).

3. Graham, *Deconstructing Ireland: Identity, Theory, Culture*, flyleaf.

4. In 1953, Haver would quit the industry and enter a convent—whether to actually become a nun or for a period of reflection depended on the reports in the gossip columns. By the end of the year, Haver had reemerged, not to renew her screen career but to wed actor Fred MacMurray and become a Hollywood wife.

5. Coney Island historically attracted a number of Irish immigrants and their descendants, creating associations between the park and Irishness in the popular imagination. Shamrock O'Day, the protagonist in Cecil B. DeMille's film *Saturday Night* (1922) is heavily connected to Coney Island, for example, jubilantly riding the park's roller-coaster at the end of the film. Research on Coney Island includes: John F. Kasson, *Amusing the Million: Coney Island at the Turn of the Century* (New York: Hill and Wang, 1978); Michael Immerso, *Coney Island: The People's Playground* (New Brunswick: Rutgers University Press, 2002); and Jon Sterngass, *First Resorts: Pursuing Pleasure at Saratoga Springs, Newport and Coney Island* (Baltimore: Johns Hopkins University Press, 2001).

6. Hollywood musicals had been using variations of this assimilation-through-stardom plot long before these three films, going all the way back to *The Jazz Singer* (1927).

7. See Noel Ignatiev, *How the Irish Became White* (New York: Routledge, 1995); and Theodore W. Allen, *The Invention of the White Race*, vol. 1, *Racial Oppression and Social Control* (London: Verso, 1994).

8. Diane Negra, *Off-White Hollywood: American Culture and Ethnic Female Stardom* (London: Routledge, 2001), 25–54.

9. This would also extend to the rise of Maureen O'Hara to stardom in Hollywood during the 1940s.

10. Of course, such efforts worked to mask the high levels of racism in American society that existed at the time. This racism was manifested in the forced internment of Japanese Americans, the "Zoot Suit" riots between white servicemen and Los Angeles Latinos, and the large number of violent protests against attempts to integrate various industries during the war.

11. This campaign is also detailed in Clayton R. Koppes and Gregory D. Black, "Blacks, Loyalty, and Motion-Picture Propaganda in World War II," *Journal of American History* 73 (September 1986), 383–406; and Thomas Cripps, *Slow Fade to Black: The Negro in American Film (1900–1942)* (New York: Oxford University Press, 1977).

12. Ian C. Jarvie opines "her bleached . . . blonde hair and fair skin make Betty Grable almost a caricature of the peaches-and-cream, allegedly nonethnic ideal" but does not seem to recognize that such features were highly charged signs during World War II. Jarvie, "Stars and Ethnicity: Hollywood and the United States, 1932–51," in *Unspeakable Images: Ethnicity and the American Cinema*, edited by Lester D. Friedman (Chicago: University of Illinois Press, 1991), 97.

13. Spero Pastos, *Pin-Up: The Tragedy of Betty Grable* (New York: G. P. Putnam's

Sons, 1986), 13–16; and James Robert Parrish, *The Fox Girls* (New Rochelle, N.Y.: Arlington House, 1971), 341.

14. A letter in *Photoplay* from Shirley Lange of Toledo, Ohio, expresses how Grable was positioned as all-purpose "American" rather than linked to a specific ethnic heritage. "Seeing candid pictures of Betty, knowing she fears a double chin, and sometimes her hair isn't in perfect ringlets, makes one feel that we have something in common, and that the average pretty American girl . . . has a chance after all" (February 1944, 20).

15. Negra, *Off-White Hollywood*, 25–26.

16. Dorothy Hechtlinger, "Notes on Conference with Darryl F. Zanuck on December 12, 1941, Treatment of 'Coney Island,'" Darryl F. Zanuck Script Collection, University of Southern California, Los Angeles.

17. Dorothy Hechtlinger, "Notes on Conference with Darryl F. Zanuck on April 14, 1942 Temporary Script," Darryl F. Zanuck Script Collection, University of Southern California, Los Angeles.

18. Notes on synopsis by Earl Baldwin, 16 November 1943, Darryl F. Zanuck Script Collection, University of Southern California, Los Angeles, 6–7.

19. Vital Statistics on "Irish Eyes Are Smiling," 26 July 1944, Production Files, Academy of Motion Picture Arts and Sciences, Margaret Herrick Library.

20. Linking the stereotypical propensity of violence in the Irish to female characters may have a generic context as well. Feisty Irish women had potential as subjects of musical comedy, whereas the same clichéd traits in Irish males seemed more potentially threatening and thus more suitable to the gangster films that preceded this era.

21. "Strut Miss Lizzie" was very consciously modeled on "Miss Lulu from Louisville." Conference Notes on "Irish Eyes Are Smiling" Musical Plot[ting], 29 January 1944, Darryl F. Zanuck Script Collection, University of Southern California, Los Angeles, 5.

22. *Variety*, 13 November 1943.

23. Press release for *Sweet Rosie O'Grady*, Production Files, Academy of Motion Picture Arts and Sciences, Margaret Herrick Library.

24. John Rosenfield, "Early 1900s Setting Now Given to Grable," *Dallas Morning News*, 30 July 1943, I-12.

25. For more on theorizing the carnivalesque see Robert Stam, *Subversive Pleasures: Bakhtin, Cultural Criticism and Film* (Baltimore: Johns Hopkins University Press, 1989).

26. Gerald Mast, *Can't Help Singin': The American Musical on Stage and Screen* (New York: Overlook Press, 1987), 228.

27. Examples of nonbackstage, nonintegrated Fox musicals include *Bright Eyes* (1935), *Captain January* (1936), *Stowaway* (1937), *Down Argentine Way* (1940), *Moon Over Miami* (1941), *Weekend in Havana* (1941), and *Song of the Islands* (1942).

28. Henry Jenkins, *What Made Pistachio Nuts?: Early Sound Comedy and the Vaudeville Aesthetic* (New York: Columbia University Press, 1992), 22.

29. For a further elucidation on this issue regarding other racial minority groups and the Fox musical, see Sean Griffin, "The Gang's All Here: Generic Vs. Racial Integration in the 1940s Musical," *Cinema Journal* 42, no. 1 (2002), 21–45.

30. See for example, Mary Ann Doane, "Film and the Masquerade: Theorising the Female Spectator," in *Film Theory and Criticism*, 4th ed., edited by Gerald Mast, Marshall Cohen, and Leo Braudy (Oxford: Oxford University Press, 1992); and Judith Butler, "Imitation and Gender Subordination," in *Inside/Out: Lesbian Theories, Gay Theories*, edited by Diana Fuss (New York: Routledge, 1991), 13–31.

31. Neil Rau, "Irish Film Real Treat," *Los Angeles Examiner*, 20 October 1944.

32. *Variety*, 27 May 1943.

33. Rosenfield, "Early 1900s Setting Now Given to Grable," 12.

34. "*Coney Island*: Ninety Technicolored minutes with Betty Grable," *Look*, 13 July 1943, n.p.

35. Linda Mizejewski, *Ziegfeld Girl: Image and Icon in Culture and Cinema* (Durham, N.C.: Duke University Press, 1999), 131.

36. David R. Roediger, *The Wages of Whiteness: Race and the Making of the American Working Class* (London: Verso, 1991).

37. "LONG SHOT of Irish, Jack and girls on stage holding pose at finish of routine." Continuity and dialogue taken from the Screen, 18 October 1944, Darryl F. Zanuck Script Collection, University of Southern California, Los Angeles. Note the use of *girls* is not in quotes, which would have indicated a more ironic use of the word.

38. Diane Negra, "The New Primitives: Irishness in Recent U.S. Television," *Irish Studies Review* 9, no. 2 (2001), 231.

NATASHA CASEY

"The Best Kept Secret in Retail":
Selling Irishness in Contemporary America

The material conditions of consumer society constitute the
context within which people work out their identities. People's
involvement with material culture is such that mass consumption
infiltrates everyday life not only at the levels of economic processes,
social activities and household structures, but also at the level of
meaningful psychological experience—affecting the construction
of identities, the formation of relationships, the framing of events.
—Peter K. Lunt and Sonia M. Livingstone, *Mass Consumption
and Personal Identity: Everyday Economic Experience* (1992)

That we live in and are deeply affected by our thoroughly con-
sumer-oriented culture is no revelation, as Peter K. Lunt and
Sonia M. Livingstone and numerous others have convincingly
demonstrated.[1] In light of popular historical representations of the Irish,
what is more surprising is that during the past decade themes of Irishness
in the United States have become profitable marketing strategies and distinctive consumption practices shaping new identities and social formations. Beyond ubiquitous shamrocks and shillelaghs, Irishness today in a
myriad of forms is firmly embossed on the U.S. cultural psyche. Amidst
the vagaries of the popular commercial marketplace, Irishness continues
to adapt, accommodate, and appeal to remarkably diverse audiences, indicating that its popularity is unlikely to fade any time soon.

As the roar of the Celtic Tiger has been reduced to a dull growl in
recent years, one of the fastest growing industries in the United States
has been Irish-themed shopping. In stark contrast with previous eras,[2]

today a vast assortment of Irish-themed merchandise is offered in count-less catalogues, on hundreds of Internet sites, in more than five hun-dred Irish "ethnic stores" across the country, on several television shop-ping networks, and even in major department stores such as Macy's and Bloomingdale's.[3] Although other forms of Irish-themed content, such as network television programs (NBC's sitcom *The Fighting Fitzgeralds* and ABC's *Madigan Men* for example) and Hollywood films (a la *Far and Away*), have waned in recent years, Irish-themed shopping continues to grow. Some of the factors at play in this continued growth are obvious, in-cluding increasing access to the Internet, the "logic" of consumer culture itself wherein successful themes are incessantly emulated, and the con-tinued association of Ireland with ideologies of community, authenticity, and tradition. Other reasons are less apparent, such as the vigorous pro-motional efforts of the Irish government on behalf of Irish commerce in the United States (as well as around the world) and complex formulations of Irishness as a form of whiteness (the "racial politics of Hibernophilia" as Catherine Eagan effectively identifies it in this volume).

From $3 shamrock head boppers to lavish upper-middle-class Irish theme weddings at the country club there is an Irish-related product available in every sales category in contemporary America. It seems that irrespective of age, geographical location, gender, class, or political ideol-ogy, as Bord Failte recently advertised "there is something of Ireland in all of us." Just what that something is however is purposefully obscure. One could certainly contend that the manner in which the Irish tourist board peddles its brand of Irishness is merely employment of standard market-ing tropes. Diane Negra's characterization of the Irishness phenomenon as "everything and nothing" ensures that Irishness can and indeed does appeal to a myriad of diverse white U.S. audiences. The resulting main-stream popularity and appeal of Irishness cannot be either disregarded or underestimated.

The motivations behind much contemporary shopping, as Marilyn Halter suggests, can be viewed as attempts to distinguish oneself in an increasingly homogenized and corporatized society. Halter notes that "ethnic marketing highlights the specific nature of the goods and ser-vices being offered as a way to express a distinctive identity, to become more individualized and less lost in the bland mainstream of the generic middle-class customer."[4] There are three distinct though not unrelated sets of customers for Irish-themed products, what I term "sanctioned," "deviant," and "ancillary" consumers. All except the first group have been largely overlooked by Irish cultural studies, however all three groups invest in and deploy diverse and sometimes contradictory notions of Irishness. By outlining the constitutive elements of Irishness in relation to each group I will attempt to explore why Irish-themed products resonate with and continue to appeal to a surprisingly wide variety of Americans at the beginning of the twenty-first century.

Shopping for Shamrocks and Shillelaghs: Sanctioned Consumers of Irishness

Sanctioned consumers of Irish-themed material culture are the most obvious and visible of the three groups under consideration. Labeling these roughly thirty million people "a group" implies a cohesiveness that is somewhat misleading, not to mention improbable, as in reality sanctioned groups invest and utilize Irishness in countless varieties of ways. Nevertheless, for the purposes of this analysis these consumers are grouped together as the people we mean when we typically refer to "Irish America." Sanctioned audiences range from touristic-minded students to second- and third-generation middle-class Irish Americans investing in Waterford crystal to typically "traditional" older Irish Americans (members of the Ancient Order of Hibernians, etc.) and the millions of shoppers in between. Despite obvious distinctions these consumers are allied by virtue of their sanctioned position garnered by way of four primary qualifications.

The first is their status as self-designated Irish Americans or employment of what Elizabeth C. Hirschman has labeled "the emic measure of ethnicity." As Hirschman notes, this measure "is one which permits the individual to ascribe religious and cultural identity to him/herself. It is based on the individuals' subjective self-perceptions."[5] Hirschman, echoing Ronald Cohen, contends that such self-designation "is the only valid measure of ethnicity, since it represents the internal beliefs of the individual and hence reflects the salience and reality of the ethnic affiliation he/she experiences."[6] The second characteristic of sanctioned audiences is their conspicuous consumption and exhibition of mainstream Irish-themed merchandise in both public and private arenas. As Juliet B. Schor notes of this latter dichotomy, "while the literature typically classifies identity and status as alternative sources of consumer motivation, they should not be seen as two independent processes. The self is not public or private, it is always both. Personal identity does not exist prior to the social world, it comes into being with it."[7] Thirdly, sanctioned consumers are allied, as are deviant and ancillary consumers, by virtue of their whiteness. Eagan notes that "the search for heritage, belonging and relevance is intertwined with race in complex and often subterranean ways." It is therefore crucial to recognize whiteness in the context of sanctioned consumers even though these audiences are extremely reluctant to even acknowledge their place in the racial configuration of the United States.

Finally, sanctioned consumers, although largely unaware of it, are allied through their connection with Enterprise Ireland, the Irish government's trade and technology division, which has courted this loosely affiliated group with considerable success, particularly during the last ten years. "The core mission of Enterprise Ireland is accelerating Ireland's national and regional development by working with Irish companies to develop and compete so that they can grow in world markets."[8] The group has more than thirty offices in a diverse range of countries, including China, Saudi Arabia, Malaysia, Australia, and the Czech Republic. Although this indicates that the marketing of Irishness is a global phenomenon, this analysis focuses exclusively on the U.S. case. Most important to note, then, for my purposes are that four of those thirty offices are located in Boston, Los Angeles, Palo Alto, and New York.

Enterprise Ireland, in conjunction with the premier trade association for Celtic-themed retailers in the United States, the North American Celtic Buyers Association (NACBA),[9] organizes several annual trade shows in efforts to network Irish suppliers with American retailers. Sanctioned consumers are overwhelmingly the dominant group at these "trade only" events. They are both the sellers and the conceptualized consumers, and it is their notions of Irishness that provide the ideological framework for such occasions.[10]

Considering the institutional support provided by Enterprise Ireland, it is perhaps no surprise that between 1989 and 1999 Irish ethnic stores in the United States grew by 43 percent. Historically marginalized in established Irish enclaves such as New York and Boston, shops that sell Irish-themed goods can now be found in the most unlikely places including Pelham, Alabama (Callaghan's Celtic Imports); Juneau, Alaska (The Irish Shop of Juneau); Orlando, Florida (Kathleen's House of Ireland); and Sioux Falls, South Dakota (Mrs. Murphy's Irish Gifts). According to a report compiled by Enterprise Ireland and NACBA, the total retail sales of Irish-themed stores in North America was almost $150 million in 1999, prompting the report to characterize such stores as the "best kept secret in US retail."[11] Sales jumped to $181 million by 2001, and even against the generally austere economic landscape of 2002 total retail sales of Irish-themed stores grew a further 6.6 percent to reach $193.3 million.[12] Presently there is at least one Irish-themed store in forty-three of the fifty United States (the majority of these stores are owned by NACBA members). Illinois, for example, has one store for every 45,203 of its inhabitants.[13] No other ethnic heritage can claim a comparable retailing presence.

Clearly, within the United States Enterprise Ireland continues to play a pivotal role in much of this Irish-themed buying and selling. In addition to NACBA, they have worked with QVC (the television shopping network), Busch Gardens theme park in Virginia (where there is an Irish village), and more unlikely collaborators such as Sea World in Florida.[14] However, "best kept secrets" rarely remain that way for long, and over the last few years there has been tremendous growth among Irish-themed catalogue companies and online stores not affiliated with either NACBA or Enterprise Ireland. For example, in 2002 Creative Irish Gifts, one of the most successful Irish-themed catalogue companies, mailed eight million copies of its catalogue, resulting in sales of more than $13 million.[15] In existence before the Celtic Tiger boom of the 1990s, Creative Irish Gifts published its first edition in 1987, introducing U.S. audiences to "Unique Gifts With A Very Special Purpose."[16] The inaugural catalogue announced the company's goal to "create desperately needed jobs by training teens in Belfast and Derry to manufacture the items offered in future catalogs" and offered the "double opportunity . . . to give your family and friends unique mementos from Ireland . . . and to give a Northern Irish child the opportunity of a lifetime."[17] It is likely that this message resonated strongly with the pro-nationalist Irish American audience of the day, galvanized by the 1981 hunger strikes and the symbolic martyrdom of Bobby Sands.[18] This explicit appeal to audiences mindful of "the troubles" at a time of Irish economic stagnation contrasts heavily with contemporary marketing strategies where economically successful Celtic Tiger Ireland provides the backdrop to saleable forms of Irishness. Although Creative Irish Gifts continues to donate a substantial portion of profits to Irish-related causes, less than half of the products in its catalogue are actually made in Ireland. This shift suggests that the origin or at least the verifiable authenticity of such goods is largely irrelevant for the average sanctioned consumer (whom, Creative Irish Gifts, like Enterprise Ireland, explicitly targets).[19]

A 2001 study on Irish-themed pubs noted that "consumers seem to favor establishments that attempt to project and present themselves as 'the real thing.' Ironically, however, they are keenly aware that these environments are not entirely authentic and what they are experiencing is in fact an idealized version of reality."[20] This is an unconvincing argument, though, as it relies heavily on assumptions about the meaning of authenticity, and, as Kent Grayson and Radan Martinec observe, "most scholars who study authenticity agree that authenticity is not an attribute inherent in an object, and is better understood as an assessment made by a particular evaluator in a particular context."[21] The study's authors admit that "authenticity is in the eye of the beholder."[22] But how the consumers in their study define authenticity is unspecified. They insist "while many consumers are able to identify themed environments as knockoffs of the 'real thing,' other consumers have a harder time delineating fact from fiction."[23] This use of artificially stable categories of *fact* and *fiction* suggests that the authors are aware of what these terms mean but that the consumers in question are not.

Creative Irish Gifts did not specify where the 55 percent of their products not made in Ireland came from, but my own purchases from their 2002 Christmas catalogue confirmed the obvious. "Imported" personalized shamrock Santa decorations and pins were unsurprisingly manufactured in China. Clearly economic factors motivated the company to rethink its original goal of providing "desperately needed jobs" for the youth of Ireland. This shift to using (presumably) cheaper manufacturers in China serves only to bestow additional irony on the company name, although Creative Irish Gifts from China doesn't quite roll off the tongue. Perhaps more importantly, this example points to the growing chasm between our relationships with the products we buy and consume and the realities and conditions of their production. As Halter notes, "imported merchandise that gets categorized as ethnic chic, especially garments and home furnishings, often results from escalating levels of worker exploitation. By the time global goods produced by local labor end up in the hands of cosmopolitan American consumers, the process can have been a decidedly inharmonious one."[24] As a way to offset this disconcerting reality and to perhaps compensate for it, many companies stress their altruistic dimension through cause-related marketing. For example, profits from the Creative Irish Gifts catalogue help support the Irish Children's Fund, a program that brings children from the north of Ireland to the United States every summer. Such cause-related marketing both encourages and eases acts of consumption while concomitantly curbing social and ethical questions about the conditions and welfare of the workers producing these goods.

Creative Irish Gifts notes that "clothing and jewelry are definitely our very best selling items."[25] But these two categories alone do not convey the endless types of Irish-themed products available. Beyond the "traditional" St. Patrick's Day accoutrements such as "Light Up Shamrock Stakes," "Shamrock Strewn Placemats," and shamrock mailboxes, you can purchase Irish-themed ornaments, collectibles, cosmetics, sporting goods, posters, housewares, stationery, toys, car accessories, tapestries, food—the list is endless. In addition, many companies and vendors will now "Irish-ize" items.[26] A company executive reported, "For example, they may carry a blouse or dress adorned with roses, but will change the roses to shamrocks for us. When that happens, they will offer us an 'Exclusive,' meaning that only our catalog can carry that item."[27]

It would be easy to write off this entire phenomenon as kitsch, and when one can purchase "proud to be Irish sandals" and "udderly Irish collectible ceramic cows" it is admittedly tempting to characterize it in this manner. But as Sam Binkley suggests, recovering kitsch from its inherently pejorative status may help cast light on the important functions served by otherwise disregarded popular artifacts. "Kitsch tucks us in, making a home in the repetitive fabric of imitative cultural objects, producing a sense of belonging in a rhythmic pattern of routinized experience."[28] Reframing the notion of kitsch in this manner helps advance understanding of these Irish-themed artifacts by crucially tying them to both concepts of community and notions of the everyday.

Applying Binkley's theory of kitsch also erodes convenient high/pop culture distinctions, as now all signifiers of Irishness, whether they are discreet (a shamrock lapel pin, for example) or less so ("luck of the Irish" bowling shirt) can be viewed as part of the same experience or continuum, i.e., "producing a sense of belonging in a rhythmic pattern of routinized experience." Although I am wary of "adding a coat of Bourdieu"[29] to my arguments, the high/low culture hierarchy is indicative of a type of snobbery around popular culture both within Irish Studies and among upper-middle-class Irish and Irish American sanctioned consumers. Discussing Pierre Bourdieu, Nicholas Garnham and Raymond Williams note "the primary distinction operated by the dominant culture and the cultural practices it legitimates (and by doing so those practices it delegitimates) is of culture as all that which is different from, distanced from, the experiences and practices of the dominated class, from all that is 'common,' 'vulgar,' 'popular.' "[30] Binkley's reformulation of kitsch allows us to remove this sort of elitism and taste politicking and replace it with a culture of equivalence in which discreet lapel pins and blatant bowling shirts have more in common than "the dominant culture" would like to admit.[31]

Binkley crucially notes that "kitsch reduces all the complexity, desperation and paradox of human experience to simple sentiment, replacing the novelty of a revealed deeper meaning with a teary eye and a lump in the throat."[32] For sanctioned groups this sentimentality is clearly an important constituent of Irish-themed consumption. Enterprise Ireland noted a similar theme in its analysis of ethnic-store shoppers: "first and second generation Irish Americans and Irish Canadians are the ideal store customers. This group identifies with its Irish heritage and has a strong attachment to Ireland. They are more likely than native-born Irish to be attracted to merchandise that suggests a romantic view of Ireland."[33]

This sense of romance was also evident in my own pilot study, which investigated the consumption of Irishness primarily by sanctioned consumers. I asked participants, "When you hear the word *Ireland* what ideas, images, or words does it conjure up?" A thirty-four-year-old female college math teacher said, "Green, hills, ocean, castles, fairies." A fifty-four-year-old male repair technician said, "Green shamrocks, Book of Kells, Irish traditional music." A forty-nine-year-old environmental specialist said, "Friendly towards Americans, green, and pubs." A twenty-five-year-old female student said, "The country of Ireland, green, Irish dance and music, friendly people, rainbows, Irish language, Celtic symbols." And a fifty-three-year-old female retired teacher said, "Small nation, small population numbers—evidence of nature, earth, sea, stone, green—lives related to and still relating to nature and the environment —a presence of history; big houses which don't belong—small grocery stores where the choices are plenty enough—soil from seaweed; stone walls, holy wells, ruins; tentative friendliness; narrow roads that seem to be going nowhere but beckon."[34] Despite significant cultural transformations in post–Celtic Tiger Ireland, these reported associations suggest that romantic and sentimental conceptions of that country remain dominant.

Taking figures from both Creative Irish Gifts and ethnic stores alone, more than $213 million dollars worth of Irish-themed merchandise was sold in 2002. In view of such consumption patterns, and as Lunt and Livingstone suggest, much more work needs to be done on the relationships between audiences (such as these sanctioned consumers) and material culture to advance our understanding of the connections between and among them.[35]

During the last two decades. as the personal and marketplace capital of Irishness has risen drastically in America, there has been a prolific increase in the use of Irish and/or Celtic imagery among U.S.-based white supremacist groups. These groups constitute the second audience/ consumer set (labeled "deviant") to be considered in this analysis. Deviant consumers are extremely underrepresented in Irish cultural studies partly I suspect because, although they flagrantly exhibit many of the same hackneyed symbols of Irishness as the sanctioned group (Celtic crosses, flags, etc.), they deploy these signs for vastly different political purposes. However, hate groups or white supremacists represent one of the fastest growing consumer audiences of Irishness primarily, though not exclusively, via music and festivals. The early to mid 1990s saw both a revival of hate groups and the rise in popularity of Irishness in mainstream U.S. culture. Both phenomena continue to gain momentum across surprisingly diverse social fields.

Deviant Consumers of Irishness

There are two sets of principles that operate within ethnicity:
the inclusionary-exclusionary principle and the difference-identity
principle. By excluding, one establishes difference. By including,
one establishes identity. Both are, therefore, closely related. The
inclusionary-exclusionary principle states that a group tries to
include only people who display preapproved characteristics and
excludes the others.
—Alladi Venkatesh, "Ethnoconsumerism: A New Paradigm to
Study Cultural and Cross-Cultural Consumer Behavior" (1995)

Just as the Internet significantly facilitated interest in Irishness generally, it also played a pivotal role in the growth of various hate groups in the United States during the last decade.[36] In his analysis of hate groups Brian Levin notes that Stormfront.org was the first major hate site on the World Wide Web.[37] Established in 1995 by Don Black, Stormfront proclaims itself "a resource for those courageous men and women fighting to preserve their White western culture, ideals and freedom of speech and association—a forum for planning strategies and forming political and social groups to ensure victory."[38]

A photo on the site shows Black and David Duke at a Washington, D.C. rally.[39] Behind Black and Duke are six rather incongruous flags. On the far left is an Irish flag (not the official one but a shamrocked "Erin Go Bragh" version) and on the far right is the Red Hand of Ulster (a reworking of the official government of Northern Ireland flag).[40] Sandwiched between these are (from left to right) St. George's Cross (England); a black flag bearing the Stormfront emblem; St. Andrew's Cross (Scotland); and the Red Dragon (Wales). Clem McCartney and Lucy Bryson note that "flags and anthems seem to be more important for those with more right wing political views. This should not be very surprising [as] symbols are only capable of communicating a simple blunt message, which at its most basic distinguishes groups from each other."[41]

The message on display here, however, is both blunt and jumbled. On the one hand, signifiers of English, Irish, Welsh, and Scottish ethnicity operate as Aryan ideological camouflage. In light of the widespread appeal of Irish/Celtic culture, Stormfront's visual assemblage demonstrates astute marketing awareness of the "everything and nothing" nature of these identities. That is, the Irish, English, Scottish, and Welsh flags are semiotically broad enough to encourage mainstream audiences to align themselves with the group, while at the same time the inclusion of the Stormfront flag specifically defines its audience as white supremacist. On the other hand the photograph contains some ideologically confusing signs, most obviously in the symbolic alliance of Irish nationalism with Ulster loyalism! This suggests that understandings of Irishness in the United States are simultaneously multidimensional and contradictory. In an unceasingly racialized society, Irishness has come to connote a distinctive, though rarely publicly announced, ideology of whiteness.

Despite mainstream media tendencies to depict white supremacist groups as simplistic and one-dimensional, whiteness and in this case its associative Irishness are complex ideological practices. Abby L. Ferber points out that "despite commonly held assumptions that white supremacists are uneducated, or especially hard hit victims of economic upheaval, research confirms that, like earlier incarnations of the Klan, contemporary white supremacist group members are similar to the U.S. population in general, in terms of education, income and occupation. Additionally, there are white supremacist periodicals which target highly educated audiences."[42] A variety of events, including festivals where Irish music and dance play a prominent role, are increasingly coded as "European" in efforts to mainstream white supremacist ideologies. One such European festival in St. Louis organized by the National Alliance (a white supremacist group) in 2002 underlines how convincingly the leadership of that group performed respectability, booking various music and dance groups for the event without ever revealing its true nature. The *St. Louis Post-Dispatch* covered the story as follows: "When German and Irish musical groups gathered for a folk festival in south St. Louis earlier this month, they were hoping for a night of food and fun. Instead, the unsuspecting musicians found themselves performing at a recruitment rally sponsored by a white supremacist organization that the FBI says presents 'a continuing terrorist threat.'"[43]

More revealing, however, is the National Alliance's belief that they would attract not only a primarily sympathetic audience at such an event but also potential group members. The following is the National Alliance's own account of the same event: "The second annual Eurofest in St. Louis Missouri was a resounding success with more than 280 people of European descent—i.e. White people—gathering together to celebrate and applaud their vast cultural and racial heritage on Saturday evening 7pm at the fantastically arrayed German Cultural Center . . . The fanfare included beautifully dressed young girls in Irish costumes clogging, tapping, singing and providing orchestral sequences which were the absolute pinnacle of the evening."[44] The National Alliance's membership coordinator, David Pringle, in an interview with Kevin Alfred Storm broadcast on American Dissident Voices radio indicated the rationale behind these types of events:

> STORM: So basically, if you join the Alliance and say you want to join a local unit, if there is one in your area you can expect projects like these are mapped out.
>
> PRINGLE: Right, and that's how we're building community in local areas. For instance, some of these areas put on European Cultural Festivals, or Eurofests; St. Louis put on a very successful Eurofest, as have the Sacramento Unit and other Units, where they'll get several hundred people out for the Eurofest, many of whom may not be racially conscious—they might just like to experience and revel in their heritage—and that could be the perfect place to slip them some Alliance literature and let them see that we're not the bogeymen the media paint us as being.[45]

It would be easy to denounce the St. Louis Eurofest as merely successful false advertising and dismiss the above account as wishful thinking on the part of the National Alliance. Yet their advocacy of this approach for other groups across the country suggests the strategy is an effective one. It also illustrates the alliance's desire and ability to expose their ideas to less marginalized audiences. Condemning these types of groups as ignorant fanatics overlooks their relatively new promotional strategy, which emphasizes a conventional and well-mannered demeanor — "button down terror" as Barbara Perry characterizes it[46] — that is winning them access to wider audiences (both online and face-to-face). This condemnation also ignores the uses of Irishness as a flagrantly white identity marker. Even within my own pilot study on primarily sanctioned (i.e., mainstream) consumers, there were unsolicited comments on race that would not be out of place in white supremacist circles. I asked participants the following, "Irish-themed popular culture has enjoyed unprecedented success in the U.S. in the last decade or so. What do you think accounts for this popularity?" A forty-nine-year-old female offered the following response: "White people are becoming the minority — going back to our roots is important." Interestingly, this same participant listed Irish, German, and American Indian as her ethnic origins. Ultimately the Saint Louis example points to the increasingly narrow divide between celebrations of European ethnic heritages (including Irish) and Aryanism. This precarious divide compels further analysis on the subject.

Another area within white supremacist culture in which the influence of Irishness and/or Celticness is increasingly popular and visible is tattooing. As Margo DeMello notes, "except when worn in private areas, tattoos are meant to be read by others."[47] In the case of supremacist groups, the messages to be read by other subculture members are quite explicit (although sanctioned audiences might be surprised at their use). For example the Anti-Defamation League website contains a "visual database of extremist symbols, logos and tattoos" which includes the three-leaf clover or shamrock.[48] The Florida Department of Corrections maintains that in addition to swastikas and double lightning bolts, identifiers of the Aryan Brotherhood include a shamrock clover/leaf. According to this same source the Aryan Brotherhood is known to "use Gaelic (old Irish) symbols as a method of coding communications."[49] Considering the manner in which tattooing was historically perceived, i.e., "characteristic of the savage others" or "marks of savagery"[50] (read nonwhite), this contemporary tattooing trend with its associated whiteness is quite ironic.

However, as DeMello also observes, Irish and/or Celtic tattoos are popular across a range of mainstream audiences. She notes that "through tattooing, many middle-class tattoo customers are now exploring their "Celtic roots."[51] In a recent *Irish Echo* story, journalist Stephen McKinley profiled an attorney from New York City who said, "[I chose] an Irish band [tattoo] because my dad is from Ireland, and although I am more proud of being American than anything else, I think we should be proud of our heritage as well. I also think it looks cooler than an American flag or an eagle, which are very common."[52] McKinley also comments that "there was a surge in tattooing after the Sept. 11, 2001 terror attacks as people sought to commemorate lost ones or display their patriotism — deep, permanent emotions — permanently on their skin." As a result of the overlap between sanctioned and unsanctioned tattooing practices, many forms of Irish-inspired "ink" are often ideologically ambiguous. These divergent uses nevertheless suggest how proximate the consumption practices of the sanctioned and deviant groups are. As mentioned earlier it is crucial not to suggest that membership in the middle class and white supremacy are incompatible. The seemingly disparate audiences referred to by the *Irish Echo* story and the Florida Department of Corrections are perhaps more closely related than generally assumed.

Amhran na Bhfiann?: The Musical Convergence of "White" and "Irish"

Within white supremacist culture in the United States, the Welsh group Celtic Warrior is one of the most popular contemporary "white power rock" bands.[53] Given the general appeal of all things Celtic/Irish this band's name is unlikely to be decoded in the same manner as others in its category — Angry Aryans (U.S.); White Warriors (Canadian); Aryan Brotherhood Asgard (German); The Klansman (British); Svastika (Swedish).[54] Yet Celtic Warrior, alongside other European white-power bands Celtic Dawn (Irish) and Celtic Moon (German), is clearly just as invested in a militant sense of white racial purity. In fact, countless white supremacist groups in the United States market a wide variety of Irish- and Celtic-themed music. For example, the Heritage Preservation Association, an organization dedicated to protecting and preserving the "symbols, culture and heritage of the American South," sells music such as "Song of the Celtic South" alongside "In Defense of Dixie and Our Flag" and "Confederate Manhood" (only $11 each!).[55] Panzerfaust Records (named for a German World War II antitank weapon) "is a Minnesota-based music label which specializes in the production and distribution of radical pro-White rock music."[56] Its website promises that "the experienced staff at Panzerfaust Records is committed to doing its best in providing the audio ordnance that's needed by our comrades on the front lines of today's racial Struggle."[57] On the Panzerfaust website one can purchase a "Hitler Youth Knife" for $20 alongside a variety of Celtic-themed merchandise including a "Celtic Cross with Odal Runes Pendant" for $12.[58]

Unlike sanctioned audiences, deviant consumers are both candid and adamant in their formulation of Irishness/Celticness as whiteness.[59] Given the history of pseudoscientifically informed representations of the Irish working class as "black," particularly during the mid to late nineteenth century,[60] this relatively new conception of Irishness as "pure" white reveals the shifting definitions of Irishness in U.S. culture during the past hundred years or less. Negra reminds us in the introduction to this volume that "Irish" was once a socially stigmatized ethnic category. Taking up where the Know Nothings left off, the Ku Klux Klan, alongside other anti-Catholic and anti-immigrant organizations of the nineteenth century, were among those doing the stigmatizing. As Jody M. Roy notes there was a "striking similarity" between the Supreme Order of the Star-Spangled Banner (Know Nothings) and groups like the Klan.[61]

However, contemporary white supremacist groups capitalizing on the popularity of Irishness have seemingly purged this ethnic identity of its religiosity (although the same cannot be said for 1980s and 1990s U.S. mainstream media portrayals of the troubles, which insisted on framing every event within a Protestant/Catholic paradigm). Irishness, so long inextricably linked with Catholicism, has been divested of this association in the unlikeliest of places (which might help account for the curious arrangement of flags behind the white supremacist leaders in the photo on the Stormfront site). The connotative transformation of Irishness from black to white has both inspired new uses for this identity and impacted the overreporting of Irish ancestry in late-twentieth-century America. As Dominique Bouchet notes: "Ethnicity has become a way of reacting to social change, whereas it was formerly more a way of avoiding it. It is no longer the articulate expression of conformity to inherited unambiguous principles but the creative claim to nonintegration in a multicultural and rapidly changing society."[62]

Given the popularity of all things Irish throughout and beyond the 1990s, it is no surprise to see a wide variety of groups attempting to capitalize on its fashionableness. As the merchandise available at mainstream Irish/Celtic-themed festivals indicates, the commodification of Irishness within white supremacist communities although a relatively new trend is a fast-growing one. Perry contends that "in dramatic ways, hate groups threaten to extend their impact beyond the immediate membership."[63] Appealing to Irishness as a form of whiteness is an effective method for doing this. Irish cultural studies cannot afford to ignore the dangerous possibilities of these increasingly mainstream practices.

Turning Green: "Ancillary" Consumers of Irishness

Despite the fluidity of ethnic categories today, identifying with
a particular ethnic group becomes the home base, a point of
orientation that serves to satisfy the yearning to belong.
—Marilyn Halter, *Shopping for Identity* (2000)

The third group consuming Irish-themed culture—what I call "ancillary" audiences/users—is comprised mainly of white, suburban, middle- and upper-middle-class Americans who make little or no claim to Irish ancestry but rather appear motivated to invest in it by the recent mainstream popularity of all things Irish. Consider the following setup on *While You Were Out*, one of the countless home-makeover television shows broadcast on The Learning Channel in 2002. An upper-middle-class, white, suburban "stay-at-home mom" (Lisa Curtis) living in North Carolina wants to surprise her husband by inviting the *While You Were Out* team to make over their backyard and patio in a style her husband will love— as an Irish pub. As the show develops, it is revealed that the soon-to-be-surprised husband (Chuck Curtis) is of Czech ancestry and cannot even lay claim to the Irish American moniker. Moreover, Lisa is unable to account for her partner's fascination with this particular ethnicity.

TERESA (host): What would be your ideal for this space?
LISA: He and his brothers, his two brothers and his father have been

planning a trip to Ireland and Scotland for, gosh, years but um . . .
I being sort of selfish said hey you and I need to go on a nice vacation before you go on this big trip with your brothers and I thought
we'll bring a little piece of Ireland here for him.

TERESA: Well why Ireland, is he Irish himself or . . . ?

LISA: He's not Irish, he's not Irish at all.

PETER (designer from England): I know Curtis is Irish.

LISA: See, I didn't even know that.

PETER: You didn't know?

LISA: He's Czechoslovakian.

TERESA: In Ellis Island, a lot of names become Curtis — Curtislawski,
Curtistein, you know what I'm saying?

(Laughter)

LISA: He might not even know so you're going to shock him.

PETER: Oh, good.

With the transformation complete the host Teresa Strasser summarizes
the project: "All I can say is 'cheers.' In the last forty-eight hours the *While
You Were Out* team has transformed this conventional Charlotte backyard into a colorful Celtic outdoor pub for Chuck to enjoy with friends.
Garden designer Peter Bonsey has given the Curtis family a piece of old
Ireland rich in texture and tradition. There's a fabulous lion-head foun-
tain, inventive barrel seats, a colorful pub sign ["Molly Malone"], and a
whole new façade of faux stone to complete this inviting and Irish pub
garden that would make anyone green with envy." A replica of the Blarney
stone (constructed of high-density foam), a glass-encased Irish dancing
costume, and a putting green complete the Emerald Isle look. Chuck arrives home and the show's host asks him what is it about Ireland that he
finds so appealing:

> TERESA: So what is it about Ireland and Irish pubs?
>
> CHUCK: I guess the history of beer probably.
>
> (Laughter)

This ethnic-tinged domestic makeover prompts several observations.
First, when Irishness is performed in suburban backyards (where are the
comparable German or French backyard makeovers?) we can safely assume that it occupies a solidly mainstream position in U.S. culture. Sec-

ond, the inability of the Curtises to articulate their attraction to Ireland is suggestive of Negra's hypothesis in the introduction to this volume that contemporary Irishness has an "everything and nothing quality." As is the case with other ancillary consumption scenarios, in this *While You Were Out* segment there is a peculiar tension at play between similarity and specialness. On the one hand Lisa and Chuck employ Irishness to distinguish themselves within their suburban community while concomitantly aware that they are part of a broader (and thus accepted) cultural trend on the other.[64]

A quick glance at two examples from my pilot study on consumers of Irish-themed culture also points to this "everything and nothing" quality of Irishness amongst ancillary consumers. The first is that of a thirty-four-year-old midwestern college math teacher, bookkeeper, and mother who listed her ethnic origins or ancestry as German. She maintains that although "being born on St. Patrick's Day is the only thing Irish about me . . . I do have a special affection for Ireland" and admits that "there is something about Ireland that seems to call to me even though I am not of Irish descent." A second participant, a twenty-five-year-old midwestern college student, listed her ethnic origins or ancestry as American (and it is unclear what she means by this term) and German, noting: "[On St. Patrick's Day] we always get together with my mom's side of the family and have a St. Patrick's Day dinner (even though we're of German descent)." Further, she is "excited that Irish culture has become so popular in America. I love it! I feel like I'm part of something really special."

Perceptions of specialness and uniqueness are frequently articulated when Americans describe their feelings about Ireland. But in the case of ancillary audiences that specialness is policed, ensuring such differentiation does not violate broader suburban norms. At one moment in the *While You Were Out* episode, Lisa expresses concern that the makeover may be "too much" for her neighborhood. For ancillary consumers Irishness is closely related to wider, often conflicting, suburban ideologies that champion conformity alongside illusory conceptions of "American" individuality. As M. P. Baumgartner notes, "suburbs are strikingly homogenous by urban standards, a feature of their social organization painstakingly maintained by a variety of techniques, including zoning laws."[65] Baumgartner further observes that "middle-class people tend to be socially anchored only loosely into their atomized and shifting networks of associates. Their high rate of mobility from place to place means that bonds between persons are frequently ruptured and replaced with new and equally temporary ones, so that relationships often have short pasts and futures."[66] Although ancillary audiences do not have ancestral ties to Ireland, their claims and articulations of Irishness often function as a cultural antidote to such suburban realities.

In recent years ancillary consumers have also been fueling the Irish-themed merchandise boom. In 1999 Enterprise Ireland fretted that Irish-themed stores "attract an ethnic customer to the exclusion of the mainstream customer market. Either the merchandise does not appeal to non-ethnic customers or the appearance and ambience of the store suggest to non-ethnic consumers that it is not for them. It raises the question as to whether Ethnic Stores are overlooking the large mainstream consumer market that might well be interested in quality merchandise such as crystal, tableware, apparel, etc. that can be sold on its own merit, irrespective of its Irish connection."[67] Three years later this marketing deficiency had been addressed. In 2002 Enterprise Ireland noted that "there has been an increase in Irish American customers, a sizeable decline in Other Celtic[68] customers and *a 40% increase in customers with no Irish or Celtic connections.*"[69] In this short period not only do we see more Irish Americans buying more Irish-themed products, but now more ancillary audiences express attraction to Irishness and demonstrate consumption behaviors that relate to this attraction. Perhaps this helps account for the presence of $80 mohair throws, photo frames, and Grateful Dead t-shirts, which seem to have no connection to Ireland at all, in the Creative Irish Gifts spring 2004 catalog. The number of Americans claiming Irish ancestry actually decreased by 5 million between 1990 and 2000, indicating that ancillary audiences play a much larger role in the Irish-themed consumption boom than is typically acknowledged.[70]

Festivals are particularly lucrative venues in which to sell Irish-themed goods. Thirty-six of the fifty states have had at least one Irish festival in the last five years, and a majority of those host such events annually.[71] In the same period an additional thirteen states have had at least one "Celtic" festival (including an Irish dimension).[72] Hawaii was the only state for which I could find no record of Irish or Celtic festivals, but their official

1. T-shirts on sale at the 2003 IrishFest in Milwaukee promote a flexible, recombinant sense of Irishness. (Photo by the author)

tourist website does list an annual St. Patrick's Day parade.[73] Predictably such festivals attract sanctioned and even deviant audiences but ancillary consumers can also be found at these events. Indeed the massive popularity of such festivals is the direct result of successful appeals to wider non–Irish American audiences. As Halter notes, festivals are "examples of cultural forms grounded in economic interests."[74] One of the major motives driving the proliferation of Irish/Celtic festivals is the opportunity for vast financial rewards for the organizers, the vendors, and the city hosting the event. The Milwaukee IrishFest bills itself as the "largest and best Irish cultural event in North America."[75] T-shirts on sale at this event in 2003 appealed (presumably) to Americans of Italian, German, and Polish descent as well as Irish (see figure 1). In fact practically the entire U.S. white population was accounted for in this display. Although implied, the absence of *American* on these shirts is also significant. The caption accompanying the "stars, stripes and shamrocks shirt" in the spring 2004 Creative Irish Gifts catalogue announces "you *can* have it both ways!" As do "my country, my heritage" t-shirts that serve as "eloquent testimonials to your patriotism and your heritage" in the same catalogue.

It seems that one can conveniently claim Irish ethnicity alongside American allegiance. But nonwhite groups are rarely if ever allowed similar identity alignments. Would American be read as a tacit constituent element on a t-shirt configuring Jamaican or Nigerian ethnicities? As Mary Waters notes, "aside from all of the positive, amusing, and creative aspects to this celebration of roots and ethnicity, there is a subtle way in which this ethnicity [Irish] has consequences for American race relations."[76] Although, as noted, ancillary audiences have little or no known Irish (or Celtic) connections, as is the case with both sanctioned and deviant consumers, they remain a predominantly white audience.

Conclusion: My Big White Irish Wedding

In 1999 Michael McNicholas, Enterprise Ireland's senior vice president of consumer products, declared "the overall potential of Irish goods in the USA has yet to be fully tapped."[77] Despite a generally ailing economy, by 2004 the U.S. Irish-themed goods market was still developing, helped in part by the growing trend of Irish-themed weddings. Members of NACBA argue the increasing popularity of wedding kilts rather than tuxedos is helping fuel recent sales as Irish-themed retailers vigorously attempt to break into the lucrative U.S. bridal market. The Irish-themed wedding in the final episode of Fox's reality television show *My Big Fat Obnoxious Fiance* — watched by an estimated 21 million people — is one example representative of this argument (proud of their Irish ancestry, the brothers of the featured bride Randi Coy had long promised to wear kilts at their sister's wedding).[78]

The seemingly limitless Irish-themed goods market is a clear indication that connotations of Irishness in U.S. popular culture have undergone some radical transformations in the last decade. Fervent consumption habits, institutional help, identity crises, new subcultural trends, the rise of the Internet, and an increasingly volatile culture of race in America (fueled especially by white fears of becoming a minority group) have all played a part in this metamorphosis. As a result new uses of Irishness are constantly being devised by a variety of groups attempting to capitalize on its mainstream popularity. Participation by sanctioned, deviant, and ancillary audiences in a variety of Irish-themed cultural practices from tattooing to shopping indicates the distinctions between these groups are less stable than a first glance might suggest. Not only do these audiences often engage in similar practices, but they can also increasingly be found doing so in the same geographical spaces, most notably at Irish-themed festivals. More significantly, however, sanctioned, deviant, and ancillary groups are connected through race. Richard Dyer notes that "race is . . . never not a factor, never not in play."[79] While it is (or ought to be) a truism to say that most Irish- and Celtic-themed events in the United States are overwhelmingly white, the contemporary consumption of Irishness has become a critical stage on which U.S. racial ideologies are performed. Given its high consumer demand, Irishness in the United States will likely be "sold out" for the foreseeable future.

Notes

Many thanks to Anne Tarrant and her colleagues at NACBA and Enterprise Ireland for their generosity of time and spirit at the NACBA trade show; to Ruari Curtin, also of Enterprise Ireland; and to Kate Kelty Naples at Creative Irish Gifts. Thanks also to the participants in my exploratory pilot study on Irish American identity and popular culture. Special thanks are reserved for Diane Negra for being a great editor and inspiring mentor.

1. See for example Grant McCracken, *Culture and Consumption: New Approaches to the Symbolic Character of Consumer Goods and Activities* (Bloomington: Indiana University Press, 1988); and Neva R. Goodwin, Frank Ackerman, and David Kiron, eds., *The Consumer Society* (Washington, D.C.: Island Press, 1997).

2. Marion Casey, "Ireland, New York and the Irish Image in American Popular Culture, 1890–1960" (Ph.D. diss., New York University, 1998) details the merchandizing of Irishness in the United States in earlier eras.

3. For more on early examples of Irishness in U.S. popular culture, see Marilyn Halter's *Shopping for Identity* (New York: Schocken Books, 2000).

4. Ibid., 198.

5. Elizabeth C. Hirschman, "American Jewish Ethnicity: Its Relationship to Some Selected Aspects of Consumer Behavior," *Journal of Marketing* 45 (1981): 105.

6. Ibid.

7. Juliet B. Schor, *The Overspent American: Upscaling, Downshifting, and the New Consumer* (New York: Basic Books, 1998), 59.

8. Enterprise Ireland, *Helping Irish Companies to Grow Profitably in World Markets*, 2004.

9. "NACBA's mission is to facilitate communication among businesses involved in

Celtic retailing in the USA and Canada and to develop and implement programs of value to its members," <http://www.celticbuyers.com/about.htm>.

10. Evidence for this is culled from NACBA's newsletter *Seanchai* and my own observations and interactions at the Celtic Marketplace Trade Show in Lombard, Illinois, September 2003.

11. Enterprise Ireland, *1999 North American Irish Stores Report*, 1999, 1.

12. Enterprise Ireland, *Irish Stores in North America Research Update for 2002*, 2002, 3.

13. Ibid., 23.

14. Ruari Curtin, vice president for consumer products at Enterprise Ireland (New York office), telephone conversation with author, 20 June 2003. Curtin noted in relation to Irish-themed merchandise on QVC that "no other country has two days fully dedicated to products made from that country."

15. Kate Kelty Naples, letter to author, 10 April 2003.

16. Creative Irish Gifts 1987 catalogue.

17. Ibid.

18. Although today, with the troubles off the front pages and the rise of Celtic Tiger respectability, this group has been subsumed within the broader and more sanctioned Irish American audience.

19. And if you have an obviously Irish first or surname, chances are that you are on one of the so-called "ethnicated mailing lists" which catalogue companies use. "We rent or purchase mailing lists from other catalog companies. We also rent or sell our lists, as well. Much research is done beforehand. Naturally, we only rent lists having an Irish theme. Many lists 'segment' or break down lists according to categories, for example, ethnicity. If it is Irish, we buy it. Eighty percent of catalog shoppers are women, so we prefer them and often purchase 'generic' lists of women only. Some lists segment even more precisely, such as by first name. If the names are Molly, Kate, Bridget, etc., we always buy them." Naples, letter to author.

20. Caroline K. Lego et al., "A Thirst for the Real Thing in Themed Retail Environments: Consuming Authenticity in Irish Pubs," *Journal of Food Service Business Research* 5, no. 2 (2002): 19.

21. Kent Grayson and Radan Martinec, "Consumer Perception of Iconicity and Indexicality and Their Influence on Assessments of Authentic Market Offerings," *Journal of Consumer Research* 31, no. 2 (2004): 299.

22. Lego et al., "Thirst for the Real Thing," 67.

23. Ibid., 64.

24. Halter, *Shopping for Identity*, 66.

25. Naples, letter to author.

26. Ibid.

27. Ibid.

28. Sam Binkley, "Kitsch As a Repetitive System," *Journal of Material Culture* 5, no. 2 (2000): 142.

29. As Jim Collins rightfully accuses much cultural studies of doing these days in his study *High-Pop: Making Culture into Popular Entertainment* (Methuen, Mass.: Blackwell, 2002), 14.

30. Nicholas Garnham and Raymond Williams, "Pierre Bourdieu and the Sociology of Culture: An Introduction," in *Media, Culture and Society: A Critical Reader*, edited by Richard Collins et al. (London: Sage, 1986), 116–30.

31. Outside Irish American communities, perhaps both lapel pins and bowling shirts connote equally garish identity badges, however, within that community, they signify distinctly different class characteristics. For example, lapel pins are now accepted signifiers of elite and middle-class Irishness as one must at the very least own a lapel in order to wear a lapel pin. This, of course, implies that one must also possess upper-class respectability. In contrast, bowling shirts are imbued with a clear sense of working-class culture. Not only is one proud to bowl (bowling, as Paul Fussell has suggested, is to be found at the rather low end of the ball game spectrum — golf, croquet, etc. being "high ball") one is equally proud to proclaim that affiliation in public (rather like the function of the suit in middle-class and elite settings). My argument is that these class distinctions are irrelevant in the sense that both signs (pins and bowling shirts) operate as distinct announcers of one's Irishness although they clearly function in different class environments. See Paul Fussell, *Class: A Guide Through the American Status System* (New York: Touchstone Publishers, 1992), 112–13.

32. Binkley, "Kitsch As a Repetitive System," 145.

33. Enterprise Ireland, *1999 North American Irish Stores Report*, 37.

34. Aside from the obvious sentimentalism, what was additionally intriguing about these comments is that more than half of the above participants had visited Ireland during the last six years.

35. As Peter K. Lunt and Sonia M. Livingstone note, "hitherto, very little research has explored the meanings of objects. For all the social sciences, the relations between people have been considered paramount and research has been slow to recognize the social nature of people's relations with objects." *Mass Consumption and Personal Identity: Everyday Economic Experience* (Buckingham: Open University Press, 1992), 65.

36. Barbara Perry notes that "consistent with the shifting demographics (that is, increasingly middle-class membership) and sophistication of the hate movement is an increasing willingness to take advantage of the Internet as a tool for both recruitment and unification." *In the Name of Hate: Understanding Hate Crimes* (New York: Routledge, 2001), 174.

37. Brian Levin, "Cyberhate: A Legal and Historical Analysis of Extremists' Use of Computer Networks in America," in *Hate and Bias Crime: A Reader*, edited by Barbara Perry (New York: Routledge, 2003), 363.

38. <http://www.stormfront.org>, accessed 12 March 2004.

39. Ibid.

40. The official government of Northern Ireland version does not have a Union Jack in the top left-hand corner.

41. Clem McCartney and Lucy Bryson, *Clashing Symbols?: A Report on the Use of Flags, Anthems and Other National Symbols in Northern Ireland* (Belfast: Queen's University Press, 1994), 21.

42. Abby L. Ferber, "Constructing Whiteness: The Intersections of Race and Gender in US White Supremacist Discourse," in *Hate and Bias Crime: A Reader*, edited by Barbara Perry (New York: Routledge, 2003), 353–54.

43. Matthew Hathaway, "Musicians Unknowingly Play for White Supremacists at Recruitment Event," *St Louis Post-Dispatch*, 28 November 2003, C1.

44. <http://www.nationalvanguard.org/story.php?id=1170>, accessed 12 March 2004. Incidentally the "young girls in Irish costumes" continue to occupy a prominent place in the photo display of the event on the National Alliance's website, even though the dancing school and teachers were quick to distance themselves from the group on learning of the alliance's ideology from the Irish consulate. One teacher in particular has repeatedly asked the organization to remove pictures of her dancers from the National Alliance website. Almost two years after the event, the teacher remains unsuccessful in her efforts.

45. <http://natvan.com/pub/021404.txt>, accessed 12 March 2004.

46. Perry, *In the Name of Hate*, 165.

47. Margo DeMello, *Bodies of Inscription: A Cultural History of the Modern Tattoo Community* (Durham, N.C.: Duke University Press, 2000), 137.

48. <http://www.adl.org/hate_symbols>, accessed 10 March 2004.

49. <http://www.dc.state.fl.us/pub/gangs/prison.html>, accessed 13 June 2004.

50. Susan Benson, "Inscriptions of the Self: Reflections on Tattooing and Piercing in Contemporary Euro-America," in *Written on the Body: The Tattoo in European and American History*, edited by Jane Caplan (London: Reaktion Books, 2000), 238; DeMello, *Bodies of Inscription*, 49.

51. DeMello, *Bodies of Inscription*, 202.

52. <http://www.irishecho.com/newspaper/printable.cfm?id=13564>. According to the website for *Irish Echo*, it is "the USA's most widely read Irish American newspaper."

53. <http://www.splcenter.org/intel/intelreport/article.jsp?sid=139>, accessed 12 March 2004.

54. <http://www.turnitdown.com>, accessed 12 March 2004.

55. <http://www.hpa.org>, accessed 12 March 2004.

56. <http://www.panzerfaust.com>, accessed 12 March 2004.

57. Ibid.

58. <http://www.panzerfaust.com/catalog/jewelry.shtml>, accessed 12 March 2004.

59. I am not suggesting that "Celtic" and "Irish" are equivalent terms or identities. However, among the audiences analyzed in this study the two are repeatedly conflated, and this is especially the case among deviant consumers.

60. See for example L. Perry Curtis Jr., *Apes and Angels: The Irishman in Victo-*

rian Caricature (Newton Abbot, England: David and Charles, 1971); Dale T. Knobel, *Paddy and the Republic: Ethnicity and Nationality in Antebellum America* (Middletown, Conn.: Wesleyan University Press, 1986); or Noel Ignatiev, *How the Irish Became White* (London: Routledge, 1995).

61. Jody M. Roy, *Rhetorical Campaigns of the 19th Century Anti-Catholics and Catholics in America* (Lewiston, N.Y.: Edwin Mellen Press, 2000), 199.

62. Dominique Bouchet, "Marketing and the Redefinition of Ethnicity," in *Marketing in a Multicultural World: Ethnicity, Nationalism, and Cultural Identity*, edited by Janeen Arnold Costa and Gary J. Bamoosy (Thousand Oaks, Cal.: Sage, 1995), 90.

63. Perry, *In the Name of Hate*, 137.

64. In the 2000 census approximately a fifth of the white population claimed Irish or Scotch-Irish ancestry.

65. M. P. Baumgartner, *The Moral Order of a Suburb* (New York: Oxford University Press, 1988), 10.

66. Ibid., 91.

67. Enterprise Ireland, *1999 North American Irish Stores Report*, 36.

68. As noted earlier, although obviously not the same, the conceptual categories "Irish" and "Celtic" are more often than not conflated in contemporary U.S. mainstream culture.

69. Enterprise Ireland, *Irish Stores in North America Research Update for 2002*, 9, emphasis added.

70. From 44 million in 1990 to 39 million in 2002.

71. Alabama, Alaska, Arizona, California, Colorado, Connecticut, Delaware, Florida, Georgia, Illinois, Indiana, Kentucky, Maine, Maryland, Massachusetts, Michigan, Minnesota, Missouri, Montana, Nebraska, New Jersey, New Mexico, New York, North Carolina, Ohio, Oklahoma, Oregon, Pennsylvania, Rhode Island, Tennessee, Texas, Vermont, West Virginia, and Wisconsin.

72. Arkansas, Idaho, Iowa, Kansas, Louisiana, Mississippi, Nevada, New Hampshire, North Dakota, South Carolina, South Dakota, Utah, Virginia, Washington, and Wyoming.

73. <http://www.gohawaii.com>, accessed 17 May 2004.

74. Halter, *Shopping for Identity*, 102.

75. <http://www.irishfest.com/festivalinfo/index.htm>, accessed 8 November 2003.

76. Mary C. Waters, *Ethnic Options: Choosing Identities in America* (Berkeley: University of California Press, 1990), 156.

77. Enterprise Ireland, *1999 North American Irish Stores Report*.

78. According to Fox the "almost bride" of the show, Randi Coy, is "planning to use some of her winnings to take her family on a trip to Ireland for her dad's upcoming 50th birthday," <www.fox.com/bigfat>, accessed 17 June 2004.

79. Richard Dyer, *White* (London: Routledge, 1997), 1.

MARIA PRAMAGGIORE

"Papa Don't Preach":
Pregnancy and Performance in
Contemporary Irish Cinema

I n *The Snapper* (1993), Sharon Curley (Tina Kellegher), pregnant and drunk, sings "Papa Don't Preach" for her friends at a Dublin karaoke pub. Sharon impersonates Madonna — popular music's most egregious bad girl — by performing a song that underscores the film's interest in teen pregnancy, family, Catholicism, and Irish working-class culture. As a pregnant woman making a spectacle of herself by channeling the blatantly sexual Madonna, Sharon is a figure of fascination for onlookers. But later, when the identity of the prospective father becomes common knowledge, Sharon loses her cultural cachet. Although she spins a tale of a romantic tryst with a Spanish sailor, the members of her close-knit community learn that the sexual liaison involved the middle-aged father of one of Sharon's friends. When they begin to treat her as a brazen Jezebel, they seem to be punishing Sharon for consorting with an earthly patriarch rather than the heavenly father or the equally intangible pirate of her fantasies. Whether glorified through a pop-star performance or vilified as the emblem of sexual impropriety, Sharon's pregnancy initiates a social crisis that unfolds in bodily, domestic, and public spaces.

Based on the second novella in Roddy Doyle's Barrytown trilogy, *The Snapper* emphasizes the social character of women's sexuality.[1] The film shares this fascination with a number of recent Irish films that openly explore the previously taboo subject of unauthorized pregnancy, including *Hush-a-Bye Baby* (1989), *December Bride* (1990), *The Visit* (1992), *Blessed Fruit* (1999), *The Playboys* (1992), *A Man of No Importance* (1994), *Circle of Friends* (1994), *The Most Fertile Man in Ireland* (1999), and *The Magdalene Sisters* (2003).[2]

In *Cinematernity*, Lucy Fischer argues that, in the cinema, maternity always involves a crisis. By contextualizing problem pregnancies as *social* crises, these recent Irish films reject the generic codes of the maternal melodrama, a classical Hollywood formula revived and/or reinterpreted in contemporary films such as *Fatal Attraction* (1987), *Baby Boom* (1987), *Mermaids* (1990), *The Hand that Rocks the Cradle* (1992), *Little Women* (1994), *The River Wild* (1994), *One True Thing* (1998), and *Stepmom* (1998).[3] These Irish problem-pregnancy films move beyond the individual, psychological focus of the maternal melodrama to challenge traditional Irish notions of women's sexuality. In doing so, they also raise important questions about the relationship between Irishness and postmodernity.

The films emphasize sexuality and reproduction partly because they are responding to specific events that took place in Ireland during the 1980s and 1990s that involved public discussion of divorce, abortion, contraception, and homosexuality. Yet, in the process of addressing contemporary debates, the films intervene in a powerful tradition of representation that casts the nation of Ireland as a woman, reconsidering that iconography from a postmodern perspective.

The often comical trope of the problem pregnancy thus signifies a profound national crisis. These films use the discourse of pregnancy and maternity to speak to the painful and promising renegotiation of Irish tradition, and more specifically, the reformulation of an Irish national identity that was for many decades shaped by the Catholic Church, the institution that dominated public and private matters. As Irish cultural theorist Luke Gibbons has stated, a number of contemporary Irish films are "charged 'family romances' [that] themselves operate politically, as alternative national narratives to the official discourse of faith and fatherland."[4] These alternative national narratives coalesce around the figure of the improperly pregnant woman, who, because of nationalist traditions linking woman and nation, functions as the focal point and lightning rod for the larger community.

Like other Irish commodities exported during the Celtic Tiger boom of the 1990s — the now-ubiquitous Irish pub and the pulsating strains of

1. Papa (Colm Meaney) doesn't preach, even when the public pregnancy of his daughter Sharon (Tina Kellegher) instigates a community scandal in Stephen Frears's *The Snapper* (1993). (Courtesy Photofest)

Riverdance are two examples—these films simultaneously market Irishness for global consumption and express a host of social, economic, and political anxieties. They address the change and dislocation arising from Ireland's economic and social integration with Europe, its rapid economic growth (which reversed a century-long trend of out-migration), and its experiences with globalization (in 2004, Ireland's was named the world's "most globalized" economy).[5]

As several problem-pregnancy films suggest, however, the impetus for reexamining Irish national identity derives from Irish tradition itself, and, more specifically, from the Irish theatrical tradition. In this essay I focus on two problem pregnancy films—*The Playboys* and *A Man of No Importance*—that link problem pregnancy and the Irish theatrical tradition. Set in 1957 and 1963 respectively, the films portray a prelapsarian Irish Republic teetering on the brink of the 1960s, a decade whose symbolism cannot be overstated. Each film depicts the plight of a young Irish Catholic woman who becomes pregnant outside of marriage and is involved in theatrical productions. The two films not only suggest that pregnancy is a performance, they also treat it as a metaphor for various scandalous forms of identity that threaten the hegemony of traditional Irish Catholicism. *Playboys* and *A Man of No Importance* link the Irish theatrical tradition and the liminal state of pregnancy to the postmodern idea that gender, national, sexual, and racial identities are performances.

Sexual Politics and the 1980s: "A Lousy Decade for Irishwomen"

Irish problem-pregnancy films of the 1980s and 1990s acknowledge the public and political character of female sexuality and use fiction to reframe the divisive rhetoric that accompanied heated debates. During these decades, issues related to sexuality and reproduction were constantly in the public eye because of several court cases involving unmarried pregnant women, two abortion referenda (1983 and 1992), two divorce referenda (1986 and 1995), and discussions regarding the relaxation of laws restricting the availability of contraception.

In several instances, these court cases involved personal tragedies that played out on an international stage. In 1983, Joanne Hayes was accused of and confessed to giving birth to a baby who washed up on the beach in Kerry, but it was later discovered through DNA testing that she was not the infant's mother. She was then accused of killing that infant and her own child, who died at birth. In 1984, Ann Lovett, pregnant at fourteen, gave birth to a child that died at a statue of the Virgin Mary in Granard. In 1992, the X case (involving a fourteen-year-old girl who had been raped and sought an abortion in England) made international headlines as the Irish High Court sought to prevent the girl from leaving the country. After numerous demonstrations, the court subsequently overturned the decision on appeal, which led to the second abortion referendum.[6] Making reference to this series of events, Irish feminist Nell McCafferty called the 1980s a "lousy decade for Irishwomen."[7]

The broader historical backdrop to these explosive events derives from another traumatic birth: the establishment of the Irish Free State in 1922 after the War of Independence with Britain. Whereas earlier Irish nationalist movements included Protestants and Catholics in the ideal Irish nation, the treaty that ended the war and partitioned the island established a Catholic nation in the south, one in which the church's dominance over matters of sexuality and reproduction was formalized in law. The Censorship of Publications Act of 1929 prohibited books advocating contraception, the 1935 Criminal Law Amendment prohibited the sale and importation of contraceptives, and the constitution of 1937 included articles that officially endorsed as a national goal the woman's confinement in the domestic sphere.

The dominance of the Catholic worldview in all matters public and private, including sexuality and reproduction, is reflected in the constitution. Article 41.3 banned divorce, and article 41.2 stated, "by her life within the home, woman gives to the state a support without which the common good cannot be achieved" and pledged, "the State, shall, therefore, endeavor to ensure that mothers shall not be obliged by economic necessity to engage in labor to the neglect of their duties in the home."[8] Historian Jenny Beale underscores the ideological underpinnings of article 41 by pointing to the slipperiness of its language. The woman of the first sentence is conflated with the mother of the second, so women and mothers become synonymous.[9]

Most of these laws remained in effect until the 1970s, when, in response to European Community directives, a series of reforms removed the special status of the Catholic Church, struck down the marriage bar that had prevented married women from working outside the home, and implemented equal-pay legislation. It is important to recognize the ongoing tension between tradition and modernization inherent in this progressive project, however. In 1979, in the midst of these reforms, Pope John Paul II visited Ireland, galvanizing traditional Irish Catholics with a speech urging the preservation of tradition in family matters. As the pope's visit made evident, the equation of woman and mother became a focal point for religious and national debates.

The problem-pregnancy films of the 1980s and 1990s thus reflect deep fissures in Irish culture and express them through a heightened attention to women's bodies. In *Playboys* and *A Man of No Importance*, problematically pregnant women create controversy. Their pregnant performances force the community to question the conflation of woman and mother, challenging the stability of the maternal body through which the nation has defined itself.

The Irish Nation as a Woman:
Visions and Revisions

Because problem-pregnancy films such as *Playboys* and *A Man* foreground a community's response to a woman's unauthorized sexuality, they intervene in a long national tradition of representing Ireland as a woman. According to C. L. Innes, by the late nineteenth century, "two female images had become potent social, political, and moral forces in Catholic Ireland—the images of Mother Ireland or Erin, and the Mother of God, often linked through iconography to Mother Church."[10] Virgin Mary apparitions at Knock in County Mayo in 1879 solidified the power of the post-famine "devotional revolution" during which the Catholic Church became Ireland's principal religious and secular institution.[11] Later, legendary Celtic women warriors and the figure of the *Shan Van Vocht* (an old woman celebrated in nationalist ballads of 1798 and referred to as Mother Ireland) inspired Irish Literary Revival writers such as W. B. Yeats and those who instigated the War for Independence with the Easter Rising in 1916. I would argue that, in a similar vein, contemporary revisions of powerful Irish women—from a 1985 incident in Cork where onlookers reported that statues of the Virgin Mary had moved, to the feisty women characters in problem-pregnancy films—use the body of the woman/mother to animate the postmodern moment of renegotiating the relationship between Irishness and Catholicism.

An influential documentary film—Anne Crilly's *Mother Ireland* (1988)—examines this representational rhetoric directly. Crilly considers the way that Ireland has been represented as a woman whose French and Spanish allies helped her fight colonial rule and as an old woman who urged her sons to sacrifice their lives for her. Crilly refuses to relegate these images to the past, arguing, "the same debates were still going on in the 80s as were going on at the end of the last century, around the suffragette issue, about feminism and nationalism."[12] Crilly also points out that, increasingly, the image of Ireland as an unspoiled Colleen has replaced that of Mother Ireland as a means of enticing business and tourism during the pre–Celtic Tiger economy of the 1980s. Crilly's observation underscores secular trends in the Republic that challenge traditional Irish Catholicism.

While Crilly's work approaches the nationalist rhetoric that combines woman/mother with the Irish nation in a direct manner, fictional problem-pregnancy films critique this tradition through playful narratives of scandal (*The Snapper*, *The Playboys*, and *A Man of No Importance*) and scathing melodramas that indict Catholic dogma and practices (*The Magdalene Sisters* and *Hush a Bye Baby*). *The Playboys* and *A Man of No Importance* use the pregnant woman to embody the tension between traditional and postmodern notions of Irish national identity.

Both films are set during the late 1950s, a moment on the cusp of the 1960s whose symbolism cannot be overstated. The 1960s is widely understood as a decade of profound social transformation in which Ireland reversed its traditional insularity (maintained through World War II) and initiated a shift to the increasingly urban and international Republic of the 1970s, 1980s, and, especially, the 1990s.[13] The films underscore the concept of a contemporary postnational transition by displacing their stories of gender and sexual dissent (which seem to emerge directly from the debates of the 1980s) to the earlier period of the 1960s. By resituating current concerns within the zeitgeist of the 1960s — a decade typically seen in retrospect as having made a favorable contribution to Irish modernization — *Playboys* and *A Man* frame the intensely divisive (and sometimes tragic) cultural politics of the 1990s with a hopeful, progressive vision.[14]

The films exhibit another temporal peculiarity. In foregrounding pregnancy as performance, they adopt the rhetoric of plural identity associated with discourses of Irish postcoloniality and postnationality that arose at the end of the twentieth century, not during the 1950s. In other words, these films retroactively apply notions of Irish postmodernity to the midcentury period in which the films are set.

Irish Postmodernity and Identity as Performance

Playboys and *A Man of No Importance* slyly locate the dissolution of a traditional Irish Catholic identity in the 1950s, a chronological midpoint between the nationalist-inspired Irish Literary Revival of the 1890s and the postnational Irish Economic Revival of the Celtic Tiger 1990s. Although their primary target is Catholic dogma, the films pursue a secondary line of critique by drawing on postcolonial and postmodern theories of identity as performance. They express Irish cultural studies perspectives that examine Ireland's experiences of colonization in light of British racial taxonomies, and reframe the Irish diaspora in the context of American racial politics. These perspectives also encompass arguments regarding ethnic and sexual diversity within an Ireland no longer seen as monolithic.

A brief mention of recent work linking Irish theatricality to identity politics will have to suffice for the purposes of this essay. In terms of the racial politics of the Irish diaspora, U.S. labor historian Noel Ignatiev and Irish cultural critic Fintan O'Toole both have characterized Irish performativity in the American historical context as a process of becoming, not being, white. O'Toole and Eric Lott characterize early-twentieth-century Irish immigrants through their identifications with indigenous others, sometimes theatricalized in literal practices of blackface minstrelsy. O'Toole discusses a selective identification process wherein the Irish identified with Indians but not with African Americans: "The identification of Irish and Indian, set free of its moorings in fear of the forest, became playful, theatrical and a badge of pride. The same did not happen in relation to the identification of Irish and blacks, because, after all, there were real blacks in New York and Chicago, and the Irish were often in direct competition with them."[15]

In the view of these and other scholars, whiteness was a racial attribute the Irish sought to acquire. The work of scholars like L. P. Curtis argues for the notion that the Irish were racialized subjects in the context of British colonialism. As elaborated in my analyses below, *The Playboys* echoes this discourse of colonial identification by asserting a connection between Irish experiences under British rule and African American experiences of slavery in North America. In a somewhat different vein, *A Man of No Importance* proposes an internal Irish diversity with respect to religion and sexuality. The film uses tropes of identification and performance in relation to queer identities and seeks to establish an Irish tradition of sexual dissidence. In so doing, the film prefigures queer scholarship in Irish Studies, including that of Lance Pettit and Éibhear Walshe.[16]

The Playboys and *A Man of No Importance* unsettle the female iconographies that loom large in the conceptual and historical foundation of the Irish nation. They reach into the past to reconsider Irish theatrical and religious traditions from a postmodern vantage point. Their protagonists, Tara McGuire (Robin Wright Penn) and Adele Rice (Tara Fitzgerald), do more than challenge Irish Catholic ideologies regarding gender. As they flout the notion that the only sexuality compatible with Irishness is marital heterosexuality, they also call into question the homogeneity of the Irish nation in terms of race, gender, and sexuality.

These films evoke social crises because women pose a public threat to the sanctity of virginity and the sacrament of marriage. As the challenge to tradition coalesces around these women, they function as the prostitute does in the work of James Joyce, as analyzed by Clair Wills. Joyce's prostitute threatened the bourgeois Catholic state because she moved freely within the public sphere, resisting her proper positioning in the private domestic realm.[17] The prostitute denies the masculine presumption to the public domain. In *The Playboys* and *A Man* publicly pregnant women assume their rightful, public place in any attempt to refigure national identity in a postnational era.

In these films, the pregnant woman evokes not only the fragility of the public/private divide (because her condition makes sexuality visible), but by self-consciously performing pregnancy in defiance of social norms, she implies that national, religious, and gender identities are less stable than they appear. As a multiple and split subject, she acts as an emblem of the underlying indeterminacy of all identities. These instabilities are crystallized in the trope of the theatrical that dominates both films.

The Playboys: Theatrical Pregnancy

Tara McGuire in *The Playboys* and Adele Rice in *A Man of No Importance* are women who transgress borders (between public and private, north and south, and Ireland and England). They embody resistance to Catholic bourgeois codes in a period that coincides with Ireland's emergence from postwar isolation and its rapprochement with Europe. Moreover, the films use pregnant performances to highlight internal fissures in concepts of national, gender, and sexual identity rather than assuming the challenge to tradition comes from "external" sources alone.

In Gillies MacKinnon's *The Playboys*, a traveling theatrical troupe in 1950s county Cavan wreaks as much havoc on the traditional village as

2. The romance between Tara (Robin Wright Penn) and Tom (Aidan Quinn) is tinged with biblical allusions and postcolonial politics in *The Playboys* (1992). (Courtesy Photofest)

does villager Tara McGuire, who refuses to name the father of her out-of-wedlock baby boy. The opening sequence depicts the crisis of Tara's pregnancy as theater: The members of her small village witness firsthand her challenge to Catholic orthodoxy. Tara's water breaks in a copious manner in the midst of a church service, so her baby's birth upstages the solemn performance of the Catholic Mass.

Themes of performance and dissembling are woven throughout the film, as Tara refuses to name the baby's father, innocently smuggles goods across the border between Northern Ireland and the Republic, and falls in love with one of the actors, Tom Casey (Aidan Quinn). Their relationship develops on public property: the fact that their "private" lives are on display for all to see is made clear in two scenes. In the first, Tara and Tom make love in the players' trailer, which is parked in the middle of the town green, rocking the vehicle for all to see. In the second, the community appreciates the blessed and blasphemous aspects of Tara's holy family, formed by the coupling of Tara with a man who is not her son's father, at the village hay pitching: Tom, Tara, and her son ride in on a donkey and Tara wears a blue shawl. As important to the film's performance aesthetic as the self-conscious framing of this updated "Jesus, Mary, and

Joseph" tableau is the panning shot across the face of the villagers as the family rides in.

In addition to performing her pregnancy and maternity in ways that reject the Catholic virgin-maternal, Tara's name also underscores the film's interest in performance. *Tara* invokes certain historical and metaphorical connections between Ireland and the U.S. South that reach fruition in a live performance of *Gone With the Wind*. Tara's name evokes two geographical sites of national trauma: she may be named for the Hill of Tara, the location of precolonial Irish glory, or for the O'Hara plantation, locus of the neocolonial glory of the Irish who immigrated to the U.S. plantation south.

Framing the scene in which Tara's baby's paternity is revealed to the villagers, the irrepressible players stage a production of *Gone With the Wind*, the 1939 Selznick production that has just reached this provincial town's movie theater.[18] The history of this film's Irish reception is an important element of *The Playboys'* challenge to Irish Mariolatry. *Gone With the Wind* was not screened in the Republic of Ireland when it was released because the official film censor, James Montgomery, required so many cuts that the distributor withdrew it. Ironically, Montgomery vigorously objected to the childbirth scene![19] Thus, while the state of maternity was formally recognized within the Irish constitution, the embodied processes of becoming a mother—sex and childbirth— were deemed obscene.

The performance of *Gone With the Wind* might easily be dismissed because of its anarchic humor. The actors improbably recreate the Civil War story as a musical immediately after they and the villagers see the film. Tom, who has not seen the film, must quickly assume the "role" of Clark Gable (which he plays as John Wayne), and characters call out for their entrance cues from the wings. But the performance lampoons pieties regarding the U.S. Civil War, combining *The Playboys'* interest in performances of gender with a postmodern perspective on Irishness and racial performance.

The incursion of American popular culture marks historical relationships and commonalities between Irish and African American cultures through experiences of enslavement and anticolonial civil wars. In the players' staging of *Gone With the Wind*, Mammy, a role undertaken by the preeminent player (Milo O'Shea) in blackface drag, questions the logic of fighting for the South in the Civil War because it will merely secure the "freedom to be slaves" (a phrase that rhymes with James Connolly's phrase describing Irish women prior to the War for Independence as the "slaves of slaves"). The performance privileges Mammy's incisive critique of the plantation melodrama over the trials of the putative heroine, who is reduced to a blubbering ninny. The player connects histories of resistance in a performance that is, finally, incoherent and indeterminate; for example, it might be argued that the scene cites Irish agrarian resistance societies like the Ribbonmen and Whiteboys, composed of men who adopted female dress.[20] It also may refer to the history of minstrelsy in the United States, in which Irish performers donned blackface.

Regardless of its somewhat unfocused pastiche, the performance proposes a connection between Irish and African American people, through the postcolonial concept of internal colonization, where the colonial (and postcolonial) subjects are assumed to have internalized the logic of the colonizer. Mammy also exposes an important contradiction of both the Irish and African American experiences with civil war: their lingering legacies of lack of freedom and economic opportunity, despite official rhetoric to the contrary.

At first glance, *Gone With the Wind* appears to be the quintessential American film, recounting the essential American conflict — the Civil War. Yet this narrative and its visual accompaniments are clearly transformed by the Irish context, where a civil war and sectarian conflict resulting from colonization has bifurcated the nation irrevocably. And the film's staged parody reminds viewers that the characters in the plantation economy of the American story, the O'Haras, are in fact Irish immigrants who ultimately face the traumas of civil war and racist economics despite the fact that they emigrated.

Furthermore, Mammy narrates this version of *Gone With the Wind*, focusing the theatrical dynamism and focalizing the moral complexity of the players' romp. The scene happily dispenses with conventions of race and gender to produce a carnivalesque misreading of the epic tale of the American South. In doing so, the film participates in an assault on a classical text of Irish whiteness.

A useful comparison might be drawn between *The Playboys* and *The*

Wind Done Gone, writer Alice Randall's parodic 2001 novel, written from the perspective of an African American woman named Cynara, who is the daughter of Mammy and Planter (Scarlett O'Hara's father). The heirs to Margaret Mitchell's estate brought suit against publishing house Houghton Mifflin, arguing the "unauthorized derivative work" infringed on the copyright of the original novel.[21] But John Sitter, a literary scholar who filed a declaration in the case, argued that the novel relates events "from a perspective unseen in *Gone With the Wind. The Wind Done Gone* thereby is able to analyze questions of race, gender, power, and powerlessness, more penetratingly through its creation of a character who is more broadly thoughtful than most of the characters in *Gone With the Wind*."[22]

Even more salient to this discussion is Sitter's citation of a moment in the novel that overturns the easy identification of the Irish immigrant with whiteness: "in *Gone with the Wind*, much is made of Scarlett's father's attachment to the land being due to the fact that he is Irish, while in *The Wind Done Gone* his love of the land 'has something African in it.' This is a poignant detail, evoking the attachment that the slaves had to their homeland and their pain at being taken from it."[23] Here the O'Haras' fierce attachment to home (Tara in the original, Tata in Randall's novel) is best understood through African eyes as the postcolonial lament of the unwilling émigré.

Freedom has often been figured as emigration to America in Irish cinema and literature, and *The Playboys* is no exception. Tom Casey embodies the freedom and opportunity offered by emigration. One source of his attractiveness is his claim that he has been to America and even better, to the American West: California. But, in another performance that debunks myths, Tom's American sojourn is revealed to be a lie. In reality, he spent three months in jail serving time on a bigamy charge for his brother, a rejection of Catholic doctrine regarding sexuality as well as a satirical swipe at the romantic view of America as a land of opportunity. In fact, at the film's conclusion, Tara leaves the village with Tom to go not to America, but to Dublin.

Finally, the absurd conjunction of theater and cinema does more than reveal a desire to reflect on colonialisms and civil wars through a raucous mixing of Irish drama and American film cultures. Theater is a critical metaphor for Irish national identity because of its historical associations with the nationalist politics of the Abbey Theatre and the theatricality of Catholic ritual. But the film does not propose that modern media such as film and television have eclipsed the theater (which is linked to authentic Irish tradition). Instead, the Irish theater is shown to be a thriving form that can creatively respond to the challenge posed by new technologies. The film privileges neither the traditional Irish theater nor the later, American, technological advances. They coexist and interpenetrate, suggesting that Irishness involves adaptation and creative response.

The unpredictable irreverence of adaptation and creative response are evident throughout the film when formal performances are interrupted by public theatrics, as in the opening scene when Tara's water breaks during Mass. Much later, in the midst of the players' tour de force, Tara's sister disrupts the performance by running screaming into the tent to announce that Sergeant Hagerty (Albert Finney), a bureaucratically powerful but not well-liked policeman, has kidnapped Tara's son. Hagerty, a specter of the parochial, paternalistic authoritarianism of De Valera's Ireland, threatens to appropriate the future, but he fails.[24] The secret of the child's paternity is revealed during a melodramatic exchange, equal to any in *Gone With the Wind*: humiliated by Tara's rejection, a drunken Hagerty returns the child. Shortly thereafter, Tara, Tom, and her son leave on the back of a motorcycle.

Throughout the film, Tara performs a socially improper pregnancy and maternity by refusing to name the sergeant as the father, by refusing his offers of marriage, and by publicly creating a new holy family. By connecting Tara's pregnancy to religious and theatrical performances, the film exposes the incongruities at the heart of the Irish Catholic reverence for the Virgin Mary and forwards a notion of gender and national identities as inherently performative. That performativity embraces racial identity as well. The film re-deploys blackface in an attempt to link Irish Catholic and African American experiences of colonization. As it redefines Irish national identities as irreverent, postcolonial, diasporic performances, *The Playboys* flaunts its opposition to De Valera's ideal: rural, insular, Catholic Ireland.

A Man of No Importance:
Performing Sexual Difference

In *A Man of No Importance*, a pregnant performance exposes the gap between narrow concepts of Irishness as understood and legislated by Catholicism and the actual diversity of Irish identities. The film features Albert Finney as Alfie Byrne, a closeted gay Dublin bus conductor whose love for Oscar Wilde compels him to cast his ever-faithful passengers in amateur productions of Wilde's work.[25] Like *The Playboys*, the film is set around 1960. Unlike the former film, though, *A Man* portrays an urban Irish community defined by the insularity of the previous decades that is, nevertheless, capable of generating dissent from within.

Questions of Ireland's internal diversity are central to the film; the performance of Alfie Byrne's pregnant rising star, Adele Rice (Tara Fitzgerald), and Alfie's fondness for Oscar Wilde situate sexual pluralism at the center of discussions about Irishness in historical and contemporary contexts. Because Wilde was Anglo-Irish, and Alfie and his passenger-performers are Catholic, Alfie's infectious admiration for the playwright asserts that Irish artists and national heroes (often one and the same) need not be Catholic or heterosexual. Here the reference to the Irish theatrical tradition asserts the fact that nonnormative subjectivities—here, sexual outlaws—have been a part of the modern Irish nation and the postmodern Irish diaspora.

Alfie selects Adele, a young newcomer to his bus route, to star in Wilde's *Salome*. He encourages his unwilling driver friend, Robert (whom he refers to as Bosie, the name of Wilde's lover), to play the role of John the Baptist. In this arrangement, Alfie's creativity and sexuality merge: he constructs a romantic triangle in which he identifies with Adele as Salome and is able to project Robert as an object of his desire. In keeping with his repressed sexuality, he idealizes Adele as an ethereal princess rather than a sexual temptress as he prepares her for the role.

Frequent rehearsals draw Alfie and Adele together as director and protégé and they become friends. But the local authorities become uneasy about the play's content. Thanks to Alfie's landlord, who reports the use of unsavory language (the word *virginity*) to the parish council, rehearsals are brought to a halt.[26] Alfie visits Adele's boarding house and finds her having sex with John, a man she admits does not love her, and he is both confused and crushed. Alfie abandons his idealized vision of Adele as Salome and recognizes that while Adele is able to enact the sexually subversive aspects of Salome off-stage, he has never done so himself. Moreover, Adele is pregnant, which causes a public outcry. As a public scandal, her pregnancy performs her sexuality for the community.

Alfie's disillusionment with Adele is replaced by his growing desire to perform his sexuality, as Adele has done. Early in the film, Alfie visits the local gay bar and leaves soon after being noticed by several young men. But after Adele's revelations surface, he takes to the street dressed as Oscar Wilde. Rather than living vicariously through the performances of others — Wilde, Salome, Adele — Alfie performs as a gesture of coming out. He returns to the gay bar, but he is lured into an alley and beaten. The event is made public, bringing forth recriminations from Alfie's sister. Alfie defends himself by claiming that, although he is now a target of public outrage as a homosexual, he has in truth never known the love of another man. As he has learned, by literally assuming the mantle of gayness in his performance as Wilde, Alfie's desires have become public property.

Adele's and Alfie's performative transgressions embody outlaw sexualities that are suppressed within the majority-Catholic Irish republic because they serve neither marital nor reproductive purposes. Their sexual perversities, however, carry far different consequences. The folly of sexual woman (Adele and Salome) and man (Alfie) are not treated as identical affronts to convention. Adele decides to immigrate to England, which indicates the impossibility of her position in Catholic Ireland. She and Alfie part friends. By contrast, Alfie's community of bus riders welcomes him back the day he returns after his public trauma. He is reunited with his young friend, Robert, who acknowledges Alfie's homosexuality and his own heterosexuality, and finally agrees to play the role of John the Baptist.

Alfie's and Adele's parallel performances diverge: there is no place for Adele to enact her sexuality, her pregnancy, or her maternity in Ireland, despite the legal and religious obsession with women as mothers. She is purged from her Irish Catholic village, from Dublin, and from the nation. Adele's path can be read as a cautionary reminder of the state's continuing interest in and control over maternity. Like the fourteen-year-old pregnant victim of incest in the much publicized X case, Adele cannot find what she needs "at home." By contrast, the Dublin community accepts Alfie as one of their own, perhaps because he is a man, or because he pays homage to the tradition of Irish theater, securing his position within the nation despite his aberrant sexuality. At any rate, the conjunction of Adele's pregnant performance and Alfie's gay performance confirms the fact that the film is as interested in the way Irishness was redefined during the 1990s as it is in the decade of the 1960s. In its citation of Wilde, *A Man* attempts to inscribe a tradition of Irish sexual dissidence into postmodernity and refuses to represent modern Irish history as the ossification of Catholic convention.[27]

Pregnant performances in *The Playboys* and *A Man of No Importance* do more than simply challenge the Irish Catholic view of women's sexuality—as embodied in the figures of Virgin Mary and Salome—as a lingering symbol of an outmoded nationalism in need of redefinition. The films also link the destabilization of gender conventions to theatricality, which connects these postmodern critiques to modern Ireland at the same time that they challenge essentialist concepts of national, gender and sexual identities. Through pregnant performances, *The Playboys* and *A Man of No Importance* express concerns about gender, sexuality, and postcoloniality that emerged from contemporary debates, although they displace these concerns to midcentury Ireland. In foregrounding performativity, the films assert an Irish perspective on postmodernity through a tradition of identification and theatricality, challenging the idea that Ireland can only react to historical forces, rather than function as a source of aesthetic and intellectual innovation.

Notes

1. The two other novellas in the trilogy were also made into films: *The Commitments* (1991) and *The Van* (1996).

2. I refer to these films as Irish, although other film scholars, such as Kevin Rockett, have classified them as British films, or British/Irish films, or Irish-themed films. See *Still Irish: A Century of the Irish in Film* (Dublin: Red Mountain Press, 1995). I embrace the slipperiness of these national classifications—that is, I have no quarrel with any of these designations—because, as I argue in this essay, the films themselves pur-

vey a troubled national identity through a now-global commercial form that makes it increasingly difficult to identify national products. Furthermore, Irish film production has become pluralized in the context of the creative and financial hybridity of the EU (the end results are sometimes derogatorily referred to as Euro-pudding). So I resist the desire for taxonomical neatness, since any strict rules for such designations are unsatisfactory, whether based on content, sensibility, and/or production concerns (ranging from location shooting to writing, directing, and acting). The Irish Film Industry Committee itself remained somewhat noncommittal in the late 1960s as it contemplated creating an indigenous industry: "Following the example set in recent Canadian legislation, we took as a working definition of an Irish feature film one made in Ireland with a significant Irish creative, artistic and technical content." *Report of the Film Industry Committee* (Dublin: Stationery Office, 1968), 11. I choose the term *Irish film* here mainly because the films self-consciously perform Irishness for international audiences (a strategy that treats the enormous Irish diaspora as a market) while expressing anxieties about the meaning of Irishness that clearly arise from events in Ireland in the past two decades.

3. For discussions of the maternal melodrama in classical Hollywood cinema, see E. Ann Kaplan's *Motherhood and Representation: The Mother in Popular Culture and Melodrama* (New York: Routledge, 1992) and her article "The Case of the Missing Mother: Maternal Issues in Vidor's *Stella Dallas*," in *Issues in Feminist Film Criticism*, edited by Patricia Erens (Bloomington: Indiana University Press, 1990): 126–36; Linda Williams, " 'Something Else besides a Mother': *Stella Dallas* and Maternal Melodrama," in *Issues in Feminist Film Criticism*, 137–62; and Lucy Fischer, *Cinematernity* (Princeton: Princeton University Press, 1996). In general, the melodramatic formula, which relies heavily on chance elements and heightened emotions, has been used to foreground women's sacrificial maternal subjectivity rather than to offer any overt social critique.

4. Luke Gibbons, "On the Beach," *Artforum International* 3, no. 2 (19992): 13.

5. National Public Radio, "Talk of the Nation," story on Globalization Index, 1 April 2004.

6. For further information on these cases, see Emily O'Reilly, *Masterminds of the Right* (Dublin: Attic Press, 1988); Ailbhe Smyth's collection, *The Abortion Papers Ireland* (Dublin: Attic Press, 1992); and Nell McCafferty, *A Woman to Blame: The Kerry Babies Case* (Dublin: Attic Press, 1985). There were national and international repercussions of the abortion debate because Irish policy involved the European Community and vice versa, as the question of disallowing an Irish woman to travel within the EC (e.g., to England) to have an abortion was part of the discussion.

7. Quoted in Elizabeth Butler Cullingford, "Seamus and Sinead: From 'Limbo' to 'Saturday Night Live' by way of *Hush a Bye Baby*," *Colby Quarterly* 3, no. 1 (1994): 46.

8. Quoted in Jenny Beale, *Women in Ireland: Voice of Change* (Bloomington: Indiana University Press, 1987), 7.

9. Beale, *Women in Ireland*, 7.

10. C. L. Innes, *Women and Nation in Irish Literature and Society, 1880–1935* (Athens: University of Georgia Press, 1994), 41.

11. The term *devotional revolution* comes from Emmit Larkin's now-famous 1972 essay, "The Devotional Revolution in Ireland, 1850–75," *American Historical Review* 77, no. 3 (1972): 625–52. The church's special status became increasingly troubled during the 1980s due to scandals that encompassed allegations of the physical and sexual abuse of children as well as the inhumane treatment of women and children at unwed mothers' homes and orphanages, including Castlepollard, Goldenbridge, and the Gloucester Street Laundry. Peter Mullan's 2002 *The Magdalene Sisters*, a fiction film based on Mullan's viewing of a documentary about these practices, depicts these abuses.

12. Interview with Anne Crilly, Women's Education, Research, and Resource Center (WERRC) Interview Project, University College, Dublin, 28 May 2004, <http://www.tallgirlshorts.net/marymary/anne.html>.

13. The First Programme for Economic Expansion, implemented by Taoiseach (Prime Minister) Sean Lemass, is credited with opening the economy to foreign investment after decades of Irish Free State policies of economic independence and wartime neutrality. In addition, membership in the UN (1956), application for EEC membership (1961), and the Second Vatican Council "were seen by many as ushering in a welcome, outward-looking attitude in Irish life," according to Luke Gibbons. *Transformations in Irish Culture* (Cork: Cork University Press, 1996): 77. John Cooney, in *The Crozier and the Dail: Church and State 1922–1986* (Cork: Mercier Press, 1986), calls the 1960s a "watershed" in Irish history. Both also consider Irish television (Radio Telefis Eireann or RTE), chartered in 1961, to be "a focus and stimulator of much of this new revolution" (Cooney, 83).

14. It's no coincidence that the IRA was quiescent during this period, after having lost a brutal border war in the late 1950s. The films avoid the political and economic questions related to Irish Republicanism entirely, focusing instead on social and cultural issues.

15. Fintan O'Toole, *The Lie of the Land: Irish Identities* (London: Verso, 1997), 64. See also Eric Lott, *Love and Theft: Blackface Minstrelsy and The American Working Class* (New York: Oxford University Press, 1993).

16. See Lance Pettitt, *Screening Ireland: Film and Television Representation* (Manchester: Manchester University Press, 2000); and "G(ay)uiness is Good For You," *South Atlantic Quarterly* 91, no. 1 (1996): 205–212; and Éibhear Walshe, ed., *Sex, Nation and Dissent in Irish Writing* (New York: St. Martin's, 1996).

17. Clair Wills, "Joyce, Prostitution and the City," *South Atlantic Quarterly* 95, no. 1 (1996): 91.

18. See Donal ó Drisceoil, *Censorship in Ireland, 1939–45: Neutrality, Politics and Society* (Cork: Cork University Press, 1996) for an account of the Republic of Ireland's insularity during World War II. Chapter 2, " 'Neutral at the Pictures," discusses the amendment of the 1923 and 1930 Censorship of Films Acts by article 52 of the Emer-

gency Powers Order of 1939, which broadened significantly the censor's latitude in rejecting a film. Montgomery's successor, Richard Hayes, banned Charlie Chaplin's *The Great Dictator* in 1940 (35–36).

19. Ibid., 35.

20. The Whiteboys dressed in white smocks; see Luke Gibbons's essay "Identity Without a Centre," in *Transformations in Irish Culture*, 134–47.

21. "Summons and Complaint," Suntrust Bank v. Houghton Mifflin, 16 March 2001, <http://www.houghtonmifflinbooks.com/features/randall_url/pdf/Summons_and_Complaint.pdf>. See also "*The Wind Done Gone*: Questions and Answers about this Dispute," <http://www.houghtonmifflinbooks.com/features/randall_url/qandas/shtml>.

22. John Sitter, "Declaration," 28 March 2001, <http://www.houghtonmifflinbooks.com/features/randall_url/pdf/Declaration_John_Sitter.pdf>.

23. Ibid.

24. The term "De Valera's Ireland" has come to signify the conservative, agrarian, and Catholic values promulgated by Eamon De Valera, the leader of the anti-Treaty forces during the Civil War and the politician who dominated politics and culture in post-Independence Ireland, as party leader of Fianna Fail (1926–59), as taoiseach (1922–48), as the leader of two governments in the 1950s, and finally in the largely ceremonial capacity of president (1959–73).

25. Finney's character is based on Michael MacLiammoir, an actor, writer, and stage designer associated with the Gate Theatre in Dublin from the 1930s to the 1970s. He was also a publicly acknowledged gay man who interpreted Oscar Wilde in a one-man show titled *The Importance of Being Oscar* (1963) and wrote about his connections to Wilde in a memoir entitled *An Oscar of No Importance* (1968). English-born, MacLiammoir's real name was Alfred Willmore. According to Éibhear Walshe, MacLiammoir "kept his beauty alive (Dorian-like) with paint and powder, and his face was a familiar, exotic sight on the streets of Dublin . . . as he grew older, his ever more persistent attempts to remain glamorous and star-like were remarkably successful and helped him to achieve the status of a public figure" (*Sex, Nation and Dissent*, 11). MacLiammoir and his lover, Hilton Edwards, founded the Gate Theatre in 1928 and "presented the first Irish production of Wilde's *Salome* (Wilde was to be an emblematic figure in MacLiammoir's creative life)" (12) See Walshe's "Introduction: Sex, Nation and Dissent" (1–15) and "Sodom and Begorah, or Game to the Last: Inventing Michael MacLiammoir" (150–69).

26. It may be coincidental, but film historians consider the use of the term *virginity* in *The Moon is Blue* (1953) a watershed moment in the decline of the Hollywood Production Code.

27. Clair Wills argues that James Joyce not only brought "advanced European modernity to bear on Irish culture, but also [inscribed] a dissident Irish dimension onto modernity itself" ("Joyce, Prostitution and the City," 79).

STEPHANIE RAINS

Irish Roots: Genealogy and
the Performance of Irishness

In contemporary Irish America, genealogical research is a widely
popular cultural practice, and genealogical interest is a recurring
theme in popular representations of Irish America's cultural contact
with Ireland itself. These genealogical fictions include tourist advertising,
feature films, and memoirs. Within these texts, the prevalence of genealogical discovery as either a motivation or a resolution for diasporic contact with Ireland suggests the centrality of family history to the performance of ethnicity for Irish America.

Consideration of genealogy as an element of Irish American ethnic
performance leads directly to a questioning of the ways in which diasporic communities within the United States imagine themselves, as well
as their relationship to other ethnic or racial groups. Diasporic genealogy, as a popular practice of history, articulates very precisely the often
troubled nexus between individual or family identities and broader eth
nic identities. In particular, ideologies of ethnic or racial delineation and
hierarchies of exclusion are thrown into sharp relief by the specifics of
actual lines of descent and interrelationship. This essay will therefore examine ideologies of family history within the context of their relationship
to those broader concepts of ethnic, racial, or national histories. Changes
to the practice of history itself are central to the rise of genealogical research as a popular cultural practice and a mode of ethnic performance.
This is especially true for a diasporic group such as Irish Americans,
whose inscription into traditional narratives of history has been marginal. Thus, it is necessary to examine the important links between new

modes of historical practice and the popular practices, such as diasporic genealogy, which they have engendered.

As a cultural practice, genealogy is distinguished by its uncentered nature—it has developed and is operated largely by disparate alliances of amateur and otherwise unconnected individuals and organizations whose sole link is their interest in the practice itself. This does not mean, of course, that its practice is not ideological in nature, especially with re-gard to the ideology of ethnic-identity performances which are revealed by the specifics of its practice. For Irish America, one of the most im-portant elements of this ideology, as mentioned above, is the intercon-nection between ethnic history and ethnic identity. The centrality of this issue to the entire contemporary genealogy industry is evident from the industry's very origins, which place genealogical practice firmly within the arena of American racial and ethnic politics.

In 1976, as the United States celebrated its bicentennial, one of the nation's all-time best-sellers was published. The social and cultural im-pact of Alex Haley's *Roots* was enormous, and extended well beyond the African American community for whom it had the most explicit appeal. David Chioni Moore describes how the book sold more than 1.5 million hardback copies in its first eighteen months, "was translated into twenty-four languages, and sat atop *The New York Times* non-fiction best-seller list for more than five months beginning in late November 1976." As a result of its television serialization the following year, "seven of the ten most-watched television shows in United States history were episodes of 'Roots.' Over the course of those nights, some 130 million Americans, or nearly three in five, and of all races and ethnicities—indeed more than 100 million of whom must statistically have been white—had seen some or all of the show."[1]

One of the more obvious interethnic—and cross-racial—effects of the book and television series was the huge increase in interest in geneal-ogy and family history. This was a rising trend which predated *Roots*, was clearly linked to other social changes within and beyond the United States, and had already been demonstrated by the popularity of other nar-ratives, such as the film *The Godfather* (1972), which focused attention on the foundation of the Italian diaspora in the United States. However, the role of *Roots* as both a catalyst for and symbol of the genealogy industry is clear. This was signaled early on by Haley himself, in an interview with the *New York Times*, in which he agreed that "whites too may become interested in their genealogy. The book's theme is universal in terms of lineage, heritage and the common concern with oral history." Going on to discuss his initially tentative communications with the contemporary descendants of the slave-owning Murray family discussed in *Roots*, Haley insisted that eventually "there was a sense of acceptance, of realizing that [their] pasts were intricately knotted with one another's . . . It also points out the fact that there are very few of us who are ethnically pure."[2]

The particular appeal of *Roots* to diasporic Americans, including Irish Americans, was immediately understood by the travel industry, which responded rapidly. In 1977, Continental Airlines launched a discount-fares promotion under the slogan "Take Our Routes to Your Roots," and by 1978 advertisements for Aer Lingus in the Irish American press presented a map of Ireland in which place-names had been replaced with local family names under the heading "This Is Your Ireland."[3]

Following the phenomenal success of *Roots* in the mid-to-late 1970s, a number of other texts with particular significance to Irish Americans appear to have taken on specific meaning in terms of the diaspora's increased interest in their preemigration ancestry. Survey respondents questioned about their consumption of Irish-interest culture had read books such as Cecil Woodham Smith's *The Great Hunger*, Tim Severin's *The Brendan Voyage*, and Thomas Flanagan's *The Tenants of Time*.[4] Leon Uris's 1976 novel *Trinity* was by far the most popular of these texts, with 50 percent of all informants in one study reporting that they had read it.[5]

Although, unlike *Roots* itself, *Trinity* is not explicitly concerned with the tracing of origins, and is strictly fiction, as opposed to Haley's controversial "faction," the connections made between the two texts, at least within the Irish American population, are striking. *Trinity*, which details the effect of the Irish troubles from the famine to 1916 on several generations of a Catholic Ulster family, was also a success on a scale comparable to *Roots*, spending thirty-six weeks at the top of the *New York Times* bestseller list in 1977.[6] The significance of this novel to Irish America can be seen not only in its sales figures, but also in the nature of the spin-off events it spawned.[7]

1. Aer Lingus advertisement for "roots tourism" (1978).

Critical reception of *Trinity* followed a similar pattern to that of *Roots*. The mainstream reviews (particularly those appearing in the Irish American press) it received on its publication were highly enthusiastic. One reviewer even claimed, "This is a classic. As a matter of fact, I would choose to call it a masterpiece, for it is truly a work of art."[8] The book's middlebrow success, however, like that of *Roots*, appeared to result in a lack of interest among more scholarly critics. And in the few cases where it has received scholarly attention, it has been attacked, again like *Roots*, for its fictionalization of historical fact. The writer Eilís Dillon, speaking of Leon Uris and Thomas Flanagan in 1981, argued that they "were so inaccurate in their facts that they have scarcely justified their incursion into the history of another country than their own. Taking liberties with history in fiction seems to me somewhat unprincipled but you will be told that Scott did it. One wonders if that justifies it."[9]

James A. Cahalan, in his assessment of the Irish historical novel, reserves particular contempt for *Trinity*, again based on its historical, social, and literary inaccuracies. Reflecting Dillon's disapproval of Uris's nationality, Cahalan refers pointedly to *Trinity*'s obvious appeal to Irish American (rather than Irish) readers, and then goes on to recount the fact that during his fatal hunger strike inside Long Kesh Prison in 1981, Bobby Sands memorized the entire novel and recited it to fellow inmates over an eight-day period. Citing the partisan nature of the novel, he argues that "the Irish writer cannot escape the nightmare of history, nor could Bobby Sands escape *Trinity*. Thus has fiction pathetically influenced life: not only is history relived in the historical novel; the historical novel resounds in history . . . in its inaccurate, twisted view of history it is a very long way indeed from the moderate Sir Walter Scott or, for that matter, from the partisan but conscientious Irish writers."[10]

It is outside the scope of this essay to explore the literary merits of historical fiction. However, the sustained rise in interest in genealogy during the late twentieth century in fact reflects several genuinely radical shifts in both historical and social conceptions of memory and identity; and these shifts have particular relevance for the Irish American diaspora.

The diaspora had, of course, shown interest in tracing their genealogy back to "the old country" prior to the mid-1970s. As in other social groups, this activity has precedents dating back at least to the end of the nineteenth century. However, both the extent of and motivation for this practice began to change significantly after the cultural sensation of *Roots*, which heightened levels of interest and made actual research in genealogy an accepted feature of the cultural landscape.

Genealogy and Historical Discourse

Roots has always received an ambivalent response from professional historians. In one of the few scholarly articles to deal with the novel, Chioni Moore, after commenting on the scarcity of academic engagement with the book, proposes that the reasons for this critical silence are not only the discomfort of historians with Haley's use of "faction," but also the unease of literary critics with "the novel's decidedly middlebrow status."[11] Chioni Moore goes on to argue, "Yet another and partly connected reason for *Roots*'s critical non-existence may be that most scholars, particularly those many on the Left, have been uncomfortable with the unchallenging character of the book's politics . . . *Roots* situates American crimes of race all comfortably in the past, and when the family's narrative stops in about 1921, one is left with an American success story in the classic mold."[12] Thus, the book was rejected by the Left for being middlebrow and politically unchallenging, even as it was vilified by representatives of the political Right such as Nancy Reagan and David Duke for being inflammatory and vicious.[13]

Significantly, the contemporary fascination with family history, and its perceived relevance to personal and group identity, has received attention which follows a similar pattern to the reception of *Roots*. Frequently described (but rarely analyzed) by newspapers and magazines, this fascination is only occasionally remarked on in more scholarly publications.[14] On those occasions, it often appears to be assumed that amateur genealogists, like the novel which was often their inspiration, pursue an agenda alien to both the Left and Right of the contemporary-history academy. The pattern of rejection for the family-history phenomenon is generally that traditionalist historians are suspicious of the "amateur" nature of these investigations, while more radical proponents of the discipline reject the implied ideology of an emphasis on the "family."

The suspicion with which family history is regarded, particularly by the Left, is illustrated by Eric Hobsbawm's description of "a more familiar form of genealogy, that which seeks to buttress an uncertain self-esteem. Bourgeois parvenus seek pedigrees, new nations or movements annex examples of past greatness and achievement to their history in proportion as they feel their actual past to have been lacking in these things."[15] This formulation suggests a useful reading of the activities of many genealogy "scholars" through Freud's analysis of the "family romance," in which the subject rejects their actual lineage in favor of a fantasy parentage of greater status.[16]

For the Irish American diaspora, rather than for the Irish in Ireland, there is however the experience of emigration to consider when examining the motives behind genealogical interest. This experience, whatever its ultimate material gains for many, was a further removal from a culturally significant narrative of connection between generations as well as from their physical localities. This feature of the Irish diaspora's (and other diaspora's) appetite for tracing distant ancestors back "home" has been recognized by David Lowenthal, who admits that "quests for roots reflect this trauma; heritage is invoked to requite displacement."[17]

The Irish genealogy service of the National Library in Dublin, newly redesigned in 1998, received 10,000 visitors in its first year, 40 percent of whom were from the United States. A professional researcher working for the National Library's service was quoted as saying that "prosperous families in the US often want to know how their ancestors lived and are extremely pleased to hear they were famine emigrants living in extreme poverty with lots of children, because it shows how far they have come."[18]

In 1998, the *Irish Times* reported that "the number of 'roots tourists' ha[d] more than doubled in the last 10 years and in 1996 over 70,000 visitors spent £30 million in Ireland while tracing their family history."[19] Research on genealogy has also become one of the most popular uses of the Internet, with a huge proliferation of dedicated sites and 160 million messages passing through RootsWeb, one of the more established websites, in just one month in 1999.[20] Another indication of the level of enthusiasm for the subject has been the growth of specialist genealogical computer programs available to researchers, including the highly complex Master Genealogist and the Millennia Legacy Family Tree, designed to complement the database of the Mormon Church of the Latter-day Saints, themselves major contributors to the increased levels of access to genealogical information.

However, significant as they are, the improvements to the accessibility of records relating to Irish American (and other ethnic groups') family history is not, in itself, a sufficient explanation for the scale and enthusiasm with which such research has been undertaken, particularly in the period following *Roots*. Just as significant, in fact, have been the major theoretical shifts which have occurred within the history academy itself, and which have both reflected and enabled not only practical developments such as cataloguing of the necessary categories of historical information itself, but also the reevaluation of the entire process of making history.

The publications of *Roots* and *Trinity* in the mid-1970s coincided with the institutionalization of radical forms of historical practice pioneered during the 1960s. These included oral history, local history, history workshops, and folk histories. These new practices varied according to context and ideology, but shared an intention to open up the parameters of historical knowledge to include those categories of information, experience, and perspective which had not been sufficiently recognized by traditional, and "national," histories. Historians engaged in this type of work have been characterized as wanting to "democratize not just the content of history (adding the stories of African Americans, industrial workers, immigrants, women, and gays) but also its practice; they wanted to turn audiences into collaborators."[21]

Within the Irish context, Kevin Whelan, a historian who has himself made a considerable contribution to the area of local and localized history, has argued that these radical forms of historical practice have offered an invaluable method of reassessing Irish national and, crucially for our purposes, international history, by offering an alternative to revisionist/nationalist arguments. "With its diverse micro-narratives, local history acted as a defense mechanism against both the ruthless totalizing claims of historical meta-narratives and against the rootless blandness of mainstream Anglo-American consumer culture."[22] It is within this developing recognition of the value of micronarratives that the surge of interest in family history must be understood; within this context, genealogy, performed largely by amateurs tracing their own ancestral origins, can be understood as the smallest possible unit of such micronarratives.

If the methods and values of traditional history concentrated on the activities and perspectives of not only elite social groups and individuals, but also on the pursuit of a "national" history, the majority of emigrants and their descendants were, in effect, doubly excluded from this narrative. Not only were the original emigrant founders of most diaspora families, generally speaking, members of the largely undocumented and unconsidered working classes, but the fact of their migration meant that their life histories could not (or would not) be encompassed within the framework of any one national history. This would appear to be particularly true in the Irish and American examples, as from the late nineteenth century onwards, each nation, albeit for different reasons, placed a strong emphasis on the establishment of a distinct and coherent national history which frequently sought to downplay the significance of outside influences in the interest of nation building. This is not to claim that the narrative of emigration/immigration was not given attention in historical studies of either Ireland or the United States; rather that the twin processes were studied as discrete and unconnected events whose significance related largely to their impact on the national body politic either left behind or entered into.

For the diasporic communities whose ancestors made these journeys, however, the process was a single and indivisible event, albeit one open to multiple meanings. Moreover, the experience of simultaneously leaving one home and establishing a new one which characterizes the beginnings of all diasporas was, in effect, a foundational narrative for the communities of the emigrants' descendants, and as such is of essential importance to the establishment and circulation of both individual and group identity. This was precisely the kind of project which traditional historical practice was unable and unwilling to provide for such communities.

Historical Narrative and Narrative History

At this point, it is useful to consider the role played by narrative itself in the processes by which the Irish American diaspora constructs and circulates its group memories and identities. It is here that the connections between history and narrative, as well as between narrative and collective memory, emerge; and here, also, that the crucial role of narrative construction within the pursuit of family history in particular is clarified.

The use of narrative within historical discourse is a highly contested area. Theorists such as Hayden White have argued that historical narrative acts to "subsume" individuals within the established system of social relations. Other commentators have suggested that narrative formulations allow for historical discourse to operate within the "universal" patterns of storytelling, thus remaining tangible to nonprofessionals.[23]

Issues of narrative and storytelling are particularly pertinent in the arena of the forms of history which developed during and after the 1960s. Oral and folk histories, in particular, have a heavy reliance on rediscovering and recuperating narratives "from below," often through the use of individual and small-group storytelling.

The construction of historical narrative requires a process of forgetting through selection, as well as remembrance; although the extent to which this was acknowledged within the traditional historical academy is debatable at best. John Frow illustrates this essential point in his discussion of "repetition and forgetting," in which he posits the metaphor of reversibility against the traditional historical trope of retrieval. Within this model, therefore, it is recognized that because the past itself does not exist, its reconstruction is necessarily produced under the conditions of the present. Frow argues that "rather than having a meaning and a truth determined once and for all by its status as an event, its meaning and its truth are constituted retroactively and repeatedly; if time is reversible then alternative stories are always possible . . . Forgetting is thus an integral principle of this model, since the activity of compulsive interpretation that organises it involves at once selection and rejection . . . memory has the orderliness and teleological drive of narrative. Its relation to the past is not that of truth but of desire."[24]

What this recognition suggests, therefore, is that the theoretical contests over historical narrative described above are actually discussing two very different kinds of narrative. The subsuming narrative of mystification criticized by White appears recognizable as the historical construction which does assume a "meaning and truth determined once and for all by its status as an event," as well as one in which the crucial process of selection and rejection is not recognized—a deceptively ideological act, as White argues. With reference to the memories of the Irish American diaspora, the categories of historical narrative which "subsumed" individuals within their systems of social relationship creation were those of "national narratives," whether of Ireland or the United States, which sought to examine the impact of emigration and immigration on nation-building projects, without reference to the levels of meaning such narratives had within the lives of their main players, the diaspora themselves.

By contrast, the construction of micronarratives which work with, and make room for, the complex personal narratives of those most affected by the creation of the diaspora seems more analogous to the approach favored by theorists anxious to allow a recognizable voice to groups subsumed by traditional macronarratives. It is important to remember that these micronarratives are not merely derived from inviting different people to tell them—in effect, from the masses rather than the elite. Instead, they are the construction of different kinds of narrative, with different concepts of time, space, and events. In his discussion of the concept of collective memory, Paul Connerton introduces the issue of oral and folk histories, arguing that oral historians have discovered the difficulty of persuading interviewees to organize their life histories into chronological narrative form. Connerton argues that this difficulty occurs because such an approach is primarily the form of an elite who are able, through their positions of public-sphere privilege, to see their own histories as synonymous with the "objective" history of institutions. In contrast, "when oral historians listen carefully to what their informants have to say they discover a perception of time that is not linear but cyclical . . . The basic cycle is the day, then the week, the month, the season, the year, the generation."[25] The connection Connerton makes here between the construction of microhistory narratives and the use of cyclical, rather than linear, time is clearly reflected in the actual practices of those engaged in researching their family histories, and has far-reaching consequences which in many ways belie the critique of genealogy as being conservative and purely nostalgic.

The concept of a diasporic national home, with all the powerful nostalgic associations it contains, becomes particularly complex for a diaspora which has reached its second, third, or even fourth generation since emigration. Such is the case for the Irish American diaspora by the period of this discussion. While, of course, America was still receiving, and would continue to receive to the present day, many first-generation immigrants, well before the 1970s there was established a substantial Irish American population who had no firsthand experience of Ireland, and in particular no experience of postindependence Ireland. The negotiation of such Irish Americans' relationship to Ireland therefore becomes one dominated by the concept of a home nation which is not only elsewhere, but which is not directly and personally remembered. It is this moment at which Ireland becomes, for the majority of the world's population who identify themselves as Irish, a home understood through the consumption of narrativized images — principally those of film and tourism — rather than firsthand memory or experience.

Family History and Ethnic History

It is outside the scope of this article to consider fully the social changes which had occurred immediately before the 1970s within America. However, it is worth noting that members of "old stock" immigrant groups such as Irish America had moved rapidly from ethnically based urban and working-class environments into "Americanized"' suburban and nascently middle-class neighborhoods, and were engaging in what has been termed "generation-skipping" through education and economic success.[26]

This reflects one of the principal points of discussion among later theorists of this subject; whether ethnic identification could survive the social movement of members of the group from the predominantly working-class, communally organized, ethnic neighborhoods out into the middle-class suburbs. In the case of Irish Americans, this debate was explicitly raised by Lawrence J. McCaffrey in 1976, when he claimed that "Irish America exists in a cultural nowhere. The trip from the old city neighborhoods to the suburbs has been a journey from someplace to no place. It is probably too late to save the Irish, but their experience may help other ethnics to learn to cherish cultural heritages that are priceless and irreplaceable."[27]

By the end of the 1970s, however, it had become apparent that the Irish Americans, like other diasporas, had not lost their sense of collective memory and identity in the way McCaffrey suggested. The ever-increasing interest in genealogical research among Irish Americans was increasingly reflected in the occurrence of genealogical fictions in popular cultural narratives. Typically, these narratives featured an Irish American's search for his cultural identity through an examination of his ethnic heritage; this search usually involved a visit to contemporary Ireland.

The theme of the Irish American's "return" to Ireland, most likely for the first time, had already been a central feature of many of the tourist promotional films produced in the 1950s and 1960s, such as *O'Hara's Holiday* and *The Irish in Me*. These had been marked by the extent to which, unlike travelogue films produced for other markets, they relied on narrativization.[28]

The Irish in Me, made in 1959, deals explicitly with the subject of the Irish American diaspora who have no direct knowledge of Ireland. It is heavily narrativized, centering on the story of Sheila, a twelve-year-old Irish American girl traveling over not only to meet the grandfather she has never seen before, but also the nation to which she "belongs." The film, which is narrated by her grandfather, follows Sheila from her arrival at Shannon Airport through an exploration of Dublin alongside her grandfather, and then on a journey into the country to meet her extended family.

The film's narrative is used to explore the meaning this journey and the meeting with her extended family has for Sheila. She is shown making friends and exploring the countryside with Sean, a boy of similar age from her family's village. After a day in which Sheila climbs trees and splashes in rivers, her grandfather's voice-over declares, "Deep in the heart of Ireland, Sheila becomes in spirit what she is in heritage—an Irish girl come home to the land of her forefathers. She cannot give a name to the thing she feels in her heart—it might be called pride, or a love of country. To Sheila is it a nameless joy—a feeling of belonging with the Irish boy Sean. There is deep contentment . . . and then the summer is gone. It is time to return home . . . She takes Ireland with her."[29] So for Sheila the experience of Ireland is one of spiritual homecoming, rather than "mere" touristic

2. Irish American Sheila arrives in the land of her forefathers in *The Irish in Me* (1959). (Irish Film Archive)

3. Irish American Sheila discovers her sense of belonging in *The Irish in Me* (1959). (Irish Film Archive)

pleasure. And indeed the narrative of the film itself almost obstructs the process of tourism which it is designed to promote, through its concentration on the fictional characters and their relationships. *The Irish in Me*, in fact, through its engagement with Sheila's selective inheritance of Irish culture, is recognizing and screening the act of negotiation between diasporic memory and contemporary reality which is an essential part of the Irish American visitor's experience of Ireland.

The same motivation would appear to be in evidence in *O'Hara's Holiday*, another 1950s promotional film aimed at Irish Americans, when the eponymous hero, a New York policeman, visits Ireland for the first time, to have a "damn good holiday," but also to trace his family. It is not made clear whether he has any particular knowledge of his family's place of origin, but he is shown near the beginning of the film making inquiries in the Kenmare area, although to no immediate avail. Later on, however, after enjoying his holiday (and acquiring a fiancée), O'Hara almost literally stumbles across his Irish family in a village he travels through on the way to Shannon Airport for his return flight. Making it clear that this development is the best possible end to his holiday, O'Hara promises to return again to Ireland in the future, bringing with him "lots of little O'Hara's" to continue the family line.[30] The distinctive use of narrative within material designed for the later-generation Irish American diaspora, as well as the important place of family origins within that narrative, point again toward the role of collectively inherited memory and identity within such communities.

The nature of that collective memory, for a second- or third-generation Irish diaspora, is significant within the context in which it is generated and reflected in their contact with Ireland itself. By the nature of cross-generational cultural transmission, much of the understanding and experience of Irish Americans' Irish identity is necessarily through the medium of narrative, be it filmic or literary. This process is even more pronounced in the diasporic "recollection" of Ireland (as distinct from their diasporic Irish identity within America) for those generations who have never previously been there. In the twentieth century and for Irish Americans in particular, while a considerable amount of their cultural identification would have come from narratives within their community, they would also have acquired an extensive exposure to images of Ireland, primarily through the medium of film. Further, it is clear that this narrativized process of family and ethnic identification had become particularly central to the cultural practices of those later-generational Irish Americans who had also experienced the impact of the enormous social changes in the United States following World War II. One of the distinguishing features of late-twentieth-century ethnic-performance techniques such as genealogical research, however, is the extent to which the hybridity of ethnic identities in the United States became recognized and even celebrated within popular practice.

Genealogy and Ethnic Hybridity

A number of primarily sociological surveys and studies of white ethnicities in the United States were also carried out from the 1980s onwards, in an effort to discover the reason for such ethnic identities' persistent survival across several generations. A study conducted in 1984–85 by Richard Alba on ethnic identification among white Americans questioned 524 randomly selected residents of the "Capital Region" of New York State. With respect to interest in and use of family background as part of identity construction, however, Alba found, when asking respondents about the importance of their family's ethnic history, that "noteworthy in this respect [was] the desire of many of [his] respondents to trace their genealogical roots . . . That history, however, is not ethnically exclusive; it is something that can be appreciated by others from different ethnic backgrounds."[31] Alba highlights the issues of social mobility, intermarriage, and geographical dispersion as having had a considerable effect on concepts of ethnic identity among later-generation white Americans, in ways that may have had a direct effect on the popularity of family history.

Alba also discusses ethnic hybridity, which was to become a dominating feature of later studies. He notes that with increasing intermarriage, many white Americans "are largely free to identify themselves as they will."[32] This process is particularly relevant to Irish Americans, who, in Alba's study, were some of the most ethnically mixed respondents.[33] Other studies conducted throughout the 1990s have paid great attention to this development, often allying it to Gans's theory of "symbolic ethnicity."[34]

The element of choice in the adoption of their ethnic identity by contemporary Irish Americans was the central topic of another major study conducted within white European diasporas in the 1990s by Mary C. Waters.[35] Her study was deliberately designed to test the individual and collective cultural identities of now–middle-class suburban diaspora members. It started from the understanding that such respondents have made their ethnic affiliations largely as a matter of choice, and set out to examine the ways in which this actually operates in terms of the transmission and performance of cultural practices. Waters examines the crucial differences between the ethnic choices available to white Americans and those available to African Americans (whatever the complexity of their ancestral origins), grounding her discussion in the history of U.S. law on racial identification, as well as in the politics of passing as white or of giving recognition to white ancestors who may have been slave owners. This discussion not only echoes Chioni Moore's examination of the selective genealogy of Alex Haley's *Roots* (which largely ignores the author's white ethnic heritage), but is also of great relevance to the issue of historical Irish American positioning in the social and racial hierarchies of American society.

Waters's findings are unusually well illustrated in the film *The Nephew* (1998).[36] The film concerns the arrival on an island off the west coast of Ireland of Chad, a black Irish American teenager. Following the death of his emigrant mother in New York, he is coming "home" to his mother's country to live with her estranged brother; the film's narrative centers around the revelation and resolution of the estrangement which caused Chad's mother to leave Ireland.

The Nephew's handling of its central theme—the issue of Ireland's nonwhite diaspora—is indicative of how politically sensitive this topic still remains. Having placed race at the center of its story, the film then appears to go to great lengths to avoid facing the contradictions inherent to its own subject matter; the few scenes in which Chad's race is mentioned are truncated, and the dialogue is often unconvincingly styled so as to discount this issue as a factor in plot developments. In one of the most telling early scenes regarding Chad's cultural adaptation into island life, for example, he and his uncle attend a neighbor's funeral and wake. This is his first introduction to most of the local population, none of whom had known of his ethnic origins before his arrival. The islanders are shown giving communal sanction to Chad's Irishness at this funeral, during a scene in which he is prevailed on to sing during the wake. To their surprise, he sings a mournful ballad in Irish, and as he continues, the stunned silence gradually changes to a chorus of other voices joining in. When the song is finished, Chad is asked, "Who in the name of God taught you that?" He replies, "You may find it hard to believe . . . but I'm Irish." From this early point on in the film, Chad's ethnic choices are rarely questioned again—an implausible narrative decision which neglects this sensitive issue in favor of foregrounding the resolution of a troubled romance blighted by a family-based feud.

Leaving aside the effect this has on the narrative coherence of the film itself, such decisions are highly revealing of the extent and limitations of ethnic-identity representation for later-generation immigrant groups in the United States at the end of the twentieth century. Writing of the white (and partly Irish) ancestry more or less passed over in *Roots*, produced nearly twenty years earlier than *The Nephew*, Chioni Moore points out that "one would have been stunned, for example, to have found Haley's ancestral discursus beginning with a fully genealogically defensible sentence: 'Early in the spring of 1750, in the village of Ballyshannon on the upper end of Donegal Bay, a manchild was born to Paddy and Mary O'Reilly.' As a matter of day-to-day reality in the United States, the general dynamic of ethnic choice is divided very strictly by colour."[37] However, *The Nephew*, despite its structural flaws as a text, usefully demonstrates both the changes as well as the consistencies in popular imaginings of such mixed ethnic and family history since its earlier representations in *Roots*.

Another — deliberately comic — example of the very real levels of conscious and unconscious choosing of ethnicity by later-generation American immigrant groups is provided in *The Matchmaker* (1997), in which Marcy, assistant to U.S. Senator McGlory, is sent to Ireland to discover his genealogy in order to attract the Irish American vote in Boston for his reelection.[38] By the end of the film Marcy has failed, despite her best efforts and the cheerfully fraudulent assistance of the locals in the senator's "home" village of Ballinagra, to find any of the senator's ancestors. At this point, during a scene in which the narrowly reelected senator, wearing a plastic green hat, assures his supporters that "it's a great day for the Irish," his father admits to Marcy that their family was originally from Hungary. "The real name was something like Mikelós . . . McGlory is an Ellis Island name, you know the kind of thing, the U.S. is full of them. And, er, as a Democrat living in Boston, I may have played up the Irish thing just a wee bit." *The Matchmaker*'s story of the expediency of Irish ethnicity for politicians may have derived some of its inspiration from the rumors surrounding President Reagan's visit to Ireland in 1984.

During that trip, he was taken on a highly publicized visit to his "ancestral village" of Ballyporeen, in county Tipperary. Ballyporeen had been selected as the birthplace of Reagan's Irish ancestors based on an entry in the parish register—a piece of genealogical documentation which came under increasingly satirical scrutiny by the press.[39]

Reginald Byron's 1999 sociological study was also concerned with ethnic hybridity and choosing among the later-generation diaspora. It was conducted entirely in the Albany, New York, area, among more than 700 randomly selected later-generation Irish Americans, and is highly suspicious of the levels of cultural or personal meaning attached to ethnicity by respondents whose ancestry is mixed, and whose knowledge of Ireland or Irish history is not detailed. He goes so far as to produce statistical tables outlining the likely percentage of Irish ancestors belonging to the later-generation diaspora according to generational cohorts, therefore linking ethnic identity to bloodlines in a manner suggestive of many earlier approaches to the subject.[40] The element of choice regarding ethnicity for such Irish Americans is then explicitly related to the rise of multicultural policies (particularly within the national school system) in contemporary U.S. society. Byron argues, "Nowadays, in the interests of even-handed, egalitarian multiculturalism, American schoolteachers not uncommonly ask children to say what they 'are' (not merely to say what their immigrant ancestors' origins were a century ago), forcing them to identify with an ethnie [ethnic group], no matter how irrelevant such a question might be to the child's circumstances."[41]

Overlooking the essential contradiction inherent in much of his attack on such enforced quasi-racial identification being based on equally deterministic arguments about ethnic inheritance, Byron goes on to question the validity of diaspora members' attachment to their ethnic heritage, arguing, "Our informants' parents and grandparents looked to the future, to the day their children and grandchildren would attain the American Dream . . . Multiculturalism has brought about a new kind of project and has opened up a bourgeoning [sic] market in politicized and manufactured heritage: both have produced essentializing myths."[42]

In Byron's study, 65.1 percent of respondents had attempted to learn about their genealogy. Another popular filmic representation of Irish American genealogical interest within a multicultural American society, which suggests a different reading from Byron's of multicultural recognitions of ethnicity and genealogy in the classroom, is *This Is My Father* (1998). The film shows particular sensitivity toward the emotional motivations for, and consequences of, the search for family lost during the disjuncture of emigration.[43] The story focuses on history teacher Kieran Johnston and his journey from Illinois to Ireland in search of his parents' history. It takes place in three separate but irretrievably intertwined locations of time and space: contemporary America, contemporary Ireland, and a narratively reconstructed Ireland of the past. In this way, the search for the central character's personal history is framed through a narrative which is cyclical and cross-generational in its shadowing and mirroring of past and present events.

Particularly illuminating are the film's opening and closing sections, which respectively represent Johnston's motivations for his quest back to Ireland and the consequences of his discoveries for his sense of personal and social identity. The film opens in his classroom in Aurora, Illinois, where a pupil is completing her presentation to the group of a family-history project set by Johnston. Her implausible account of a self-aggrandizing genealogy, which makes unsubstantiated references to heroes of the American Revolution, the king of Norway, and Eric the Red is a sharply drawn example of the traditionally criticized family-romance fictional account of roots.[44] It acts as a catalyst for a bitter outburst from Johnston, who declares, "I'm not interested in your family tree, and I really don't want to know who you think you might be related to. I do want to know your family's history as it relates to the twentieth century." He then goes on, after a mild confrontation with an African American student regarding the relevance of his teaching, to relate the statistically predicted life expectancies and demographic projections for the class as a whole. After listing what proportion of them can expect to go to college, as well as what proportion will, statistically, spend time in prison, he concludes with the projection that only two out of the class are likely to "achieve some sort of financial stability." The bleakness of these predictions is also reflective of the fractured social relationships among both the multicultural students and their teacher, and is immediately followed by scenes introducing Johnston's lonely and fractured family life. His Irish mother has been silenced from telling her own story in the most literal sense, having been left unable to speak following a stroke. She is being cared for by Johnston's sister, a single mother who is struggling to bring up her teenage son. Of this section of the film, Martin McLoone has commented that "the framing story, set in the Chicago suburb of Aurora, is shot in muted browns, suggesting the lack of color and excitement in the lives of these troubled and anxious Irish-Americans."[45] Indeed, the opening scenes appear to reflect many of the concerns voiced during the 1970s regarding the loss of Irish American identity within the "lace curtain" suburbs of a city formerly characterized by inner-city Irish neighborhoods.

Into this situation, however, *This Is My Father* also introduces the added complications of the multiculturalism of the contemporary United States; Johnston's history class is one of noticeably mixed ethnicity, and the African American pupil who challenges the relevance of his teaching is clearly hinting at their ethnic differences as a source of this perceived lack of connection between them. The fact that these establishing scenes of contemporary American society among later-generation immigrants take place within a history classroom is in itself significant, as the national curricula of U.S. history and social studies have been the embattled locus of ideological disputes concerning multiculturalism, often played out through the almost universal family-tree projects — directly inspired by *Roots* — set for schoolchildren.[46]

At the end of the film, after he has undertaken his journey to Ireland, the story returns to Johnston's history class. The camera pans back from a close-up on the photograph which prompted the search, to reveal that it is being passed from hand to hand by the now silent and attentive group of students as they listen to Johnston recount the story of his family history which the audience has just seen. McLoone suggests that "above all, the photograph symbolizes an encounter between Ireland and America that is ambivalent and elliptical as it has resonated down the years."[47] The indicated change in the nature of the relationship between Johnston and his pupils, from distrust and alienation to sympathy and shared emotions, is clearly intended to suggest that the discovery of his origins has resulted in more than one kind of resolution. Not only, the film implies, has Johnston acquired a more secure sense of personal identity from the knowledge of his family history, but this factual and emotional knowledge has also allowed for a bridging of the social barriers of alienation between himself and his pupils, even those whose family and ethnic backgrounds are apparently very different from his own.

Another genre of increasing popularity which deals with Irish American narratives of identity and communal memory is the memoir of individual Irish Americans' search for the historical basis of their family background. These memoirs are often a hybrid form, part autobiography, part family history, part travelogue, and they typically document the authors' Irish American childhoods, often describing extended adulthood visits to Ireland to research the roots of their ethnic identities.[48]

One of the most sensitively traced of these family memoirs, Richard White's *Remembering Ahanagran: Storytelling in a Family's Past*, is an exploration, by a professional historian, of the complex relationship between history and memory. White approaches this issue through a comparison of the congruencies and ellipses between the stories of Ahanagran, in county Kerry, told by Sara, his first-generation immigrant mother, with the archival evidence and documentation of his family and their move to the United States.

White also discovers other important differences between himself and his extended family in Ireland, ones which are based less on his position as a professional historian, and more on his own and his mother's positions as members of the diaspora returning to the homeland which their relatives have never left. Recounting a fruitless attempt by himself and Sara to persuade her brother Johnny to recall particular events in their past, he explains, "He knows all he needs to know of the place in which he lives. He has lived here his whole life, and what he doesn't know he doesn't think has hurt him."[49] However, such an organic and unstructured relationship to the past, even, or perhaps especially, to one's own past and that of one's family, is unavailable to those who have the disjuncturing experience of emigration embedded in that past. This suggests some interesting possible explanations for the striking interest displayed by the Irish diaspora in their roots, an interest which is not always mirrored by their relatives who stayed in Ireland.

What differs between Ireland and Irish America, therefore, is the need for the many and obvious gaps in this historical and geographical knowledge to be filled; this is the motivation which provokes Lowenthal's description of the diaspora as "heritage hungry." And the difference between the two groups is, predominantly, one of context. The disjuncture, and indeed trauma, experienced by the generation who left Ireland was most strikingly manifested in the removal of context for the knowledge and memories which they had of their group identities. By contrast, those who remain in the landscape and community which provides context to those memories have less "hunger" for the inevitably missing details of their narratives. As Richard White noted of his uncle, "for Johnny, what is forgotten remains forgotten and best left undisturbed. The past around him is past enough."[50] For those whose personal history contains the rupture of emigration, however, the lack of context for the memories which do remain seems to provoke a need to fill in the gaps and elisions between those memories. The hunger of which Lowenthal speaks, rather dismissively, is indeed a real longing; but one which is better characterized as being for a complete narrative whose unity of detail might provide a consolation for the lack of organic context in which to place it. Again Freud's family romance appears an appropriate metaphor for this process; rather than conjuring up a fantasy lineage, however, the members of the diaspora seem more to desire an impossibly accurate lineage in order to compensate for the lack of a recognizable setting against which to place the group memories which constitute their identity.

The connections between genealogical investigations and the contributions of repetitive, cyclical narratives toward the formation of diasporic group identities are therefore clear. In a closing chapter which reflects the final scenes of *This Is My Father* to a remarkable degree, White describes the assignment he habitually sets for his university history students: "They are to take their family—a person, a generation, people from several generations—and explain how their lives intersected with major developments or trends in American history. When the assignment works, they see the lives of their ancestors and relatives as part of larger currents... The flaw in the assignment, I have gradually come to realise, is that I identify the past exclusively with history and history with the kind of work that I do: academic history."[51] What White is arguing here is that in contrast to his approach to the subject as a professional historian, his students, like his mother, have "made memories where [he] seek[s] history"; and he concedes that "history has its own weaknesses that memory can uncover and probe."[52]

Conclusion: Roots and Networks

It appears that the growing interest in family origins and history among Irish Americans over the second half of the twentieth century was a practice indicative of many more radical and socially significant projects than the middlebrow and conservative nostalgia it has been predominantly associated with. Indeed, the genealogical industry seems, on closer inspection, to be a symbolic practice which is the principal mode of popular engagement with the genuinely far-reaching social, cultural, and ideological changes of the era.

Underlying the individual enthusiasms for discovering Irish personal origins and family stories is the highly contested ideological ground of personal and ethnic history and identity for later-generation Irish Americans. The common dismissal of genealogical practice by commentators and the frequently unquestioning fervor of its practitioners represent two deeply divided schools of thought on the place and role of ethnicity itself in American society.

As I have outlined, the criticisms of renewed interest in family history are most frequently contained in the work of social scientists engaged in investigations of the parallel interest in ethnic origins. These criticisms position such ethnic identification as being either a conservative attempt to disengage with wider social connections and movements,[53] or as being inherently inauthentic due to its apparently symbolic nature among the largely middle-class and suburban exponents of the practice.[54]

With respect to the charges of conservatism, it is clear that many of these assumptions stem from genealogy's late-nineteenth-century and early-twentieth-century formations, as opposed to its contemporary manifestations. And while it obviously cannot be denied that individual motivations for undertaking family research may indeed still be conservatively nostalgic, professional genealogists note that most researchers are no longer hoping to discover elite ancestries, and are actively interested in the social conditions experienced by their forbears.[55] Equally importantly, as discussed above, many saw their activities as being inclusive rather than exclusive.⁵⁶ The more prevalent charge of inauthenticity, in that most Irish Americans expressing an interest in their backgrounds no longer lead lives necessarily structured by that cultural inheritance, requires a more detailed refutation.

The historical development of contemporary interest in ethnic origins arose from the rejection of the melting-pot thesis of earlier social and political scientists studying immigrant groups' maturation in the United States. That thesis had supposed that the process of Americanization presumed to occur with the simultaneous passing of generations and achievement of upward social mobility would eradicate all interest in and practice of ethnically identifiable traits and histories. However, the evidently growing enthusiasm for roots research among later-generational immigrant groups challenges this supposition. Those studies which have tended (to greater or lesser extents) to dismiss this trend for ethnic identification in American society have, following Gans's formulation of the concept of symbolic ethnicity, tended to do so on the continued assumption that later-generational immigrants, particularly those who are largely middle class and suburbanized, cannot have a "genuine" connection to their family's previous national or ethnic history due to their current social status.

This approach to contemporary genealogical research shows, through its own methodology, a continuing though often unstated reliance on the basic tenets of the melting-pot thesis in its equation between economic or temporal change and formations of group identity and history. It also, crucially, relies on dubious cultural concepts of authenticity in determining which groups of Irish Americans' ethnicities are authentic and which groups' are not. By its own methodological assumptions, this approach implies that only those who experienced the particular social and economic conditions of certain Irish neighborhoods in American cities during the late nineteenth century and the early twentieth can claim authentic Irishness. This highly prescriptive implied definition is clearly flawed in itself, but also fails to take into account the different patterns of later immigration. Irish immigration into the United States continued throughout the later twentieth century, albeit on a smaller scale than that of earlier decades, and therefore the creation of the later-generation

Irish diaspora is an ongoing project; contemporary second- or even third-generation Irish Americans may easily be descended from immigrants who arrived after the social impact of World War II on Irish inner-city neighborhoods. It should also be remembered that contemporary first-generation Irish immigrants are arriving in the United States from a considerably more culturally and ethnically heterogeneous Ireland than previous generations of new arrivals. The ways in which their ethnicity structures and dictates their social and cultural practices is potentially symbolic even before they have left Ireland, let alone once they are a part of American society.[57] Critics of contemporary interest in family history (and the interest in ethnic history which it often indicates) are therefore, through the typically exclusive device of authenticity, potentially denying the Irishness of even first-generation contemporary immigrants. It can therefore be argued that a much less prescriptive and predetermined perspective on the levels of meaning attached to ethnic and family identification needs to be brought to the analysis of survey respondents' assertions on this subject. Such a perspective would avoid the obscuring development of hierarchies of cultural authenticity determined according to social and economic positioning. The ideological assumptions of the roots industry, however, also need to be analyzed with greater critical awareness. Without denying the very real meaning its practice represents to those involved, as well as the wider implications it has for the interrelationships of America's different ethnic groups, there seem to exist largely unexplored contradictions at the heart of genealogical research.

The reasons why Irishness is so often the ethnicity "chosen" do require careful interrogation, especially in light of Waters's insightful analysis of the racial ideologies underlying some aspects of this choice. The extent to which Irishness may be seen as offering a relatively comfortable version of whiteness—as an ethnicity which is incontestably white when convenient, but which also allows for the claiming of historical narratives of oppression and exclusion—may well be an important consideration in its popularity among those of mixed white ethnicity.[58] At the same time, it is often evident that most later-generation Irish Americans are of mixed ethnic origin, and those investigating their family history are choosing their researched ethnicity with full knowledge of, and often equal interest in, their other ancestry. This is reflected in their responses to surveys such as those cited above, in which recognition is given to their complex ethnic associations. It is clear that the choosing of one predominantly cited background, such as Irishness, does not require, for the majority of the very large number of people involved, a rejection of their other ethnicities. Indeed, it is in this way that popular practice appears to have avoided some of the methodological exclusiveness expressed by scholarly researchers. In the light of these contradictions, it is perhaps important to maintain the distinction between, on the one hand, the choosing of an ethnic identity, and on the other, the pursuit of genealogical research as a cultural practice. While the former contains considerable space for the choice of Irishness as a comfortable version of whiteness, the latter actually undermines the concept of such ideological comfort due to its inherent revelation of the mixed ethnicities of most participants.[59]

Precisely because of the inclusive and complex ethnic reality recognized in popular expressions of interest in Irish roots, however, it seems necessary to reassess the underlying ideology of rootedness, as manifested in genealogical research. This concept of the root as a seminal source for diverse but interrelated later developments is one profoundly embedded in many forms of cultural and scientific discourse. The limitations of such a metaphor have been highlighted previously, as in Chioni Moore's call for a discussion of Haley's work in terms "not about roots but about routes; trajectories, paths, interactions, links."[60] Such a theoretical position is compatible with the wider perspective of postcolonial and postmodern diaspora theory, recognizing as it does the dangers of assumptions of purity in cultural construction. It is also compatible with the theoretical explorations of Irishness within that postcolonial and postmodern discourse; these have tended to emphasize the difficulties of canons of authenticity as linked to purity and monocultural origins.[61]

The resulting challenge, in academic discourse, to concepts of cultural or genetic roots, in favor of webs or networks, is clearly in accord with the practical approaches of popular genealogy, in which diaspora groups such as mixed-descent Irish Americans negotiate their hybrid identities and histories without, for the most part, cultural difficulty. As Catherine Nash has argued, "genealogy, despite its easy co-option in essentialist versions of identity, may provide a way of beginning the task of understanding the complexities of subjectivity and social location, and of rethinking identity as neither fixed and essential, nor endlessly fluid and freely self-fashioned, and an always incomplete inventory of the self."[62] What appears to have occurred, in fact, is a dislocation between practice and terminology in the pursuit of family history. While the language of genealogy remains anchored by the rooted tradition of *O'Hart's Irish Pedigrees* or *The Origin and Stem of The Irish Nation*, the practice has, by necessity, accepted the inapplicability of concepts of rootedness, and has moved toward new, if largely unarticulated, models of webs and networks.

Notes

1. David Chioni Moore, "Routes: Alex Haley's *Roots* and the Rhetoric of Genealogy," *Transition* 64 (1994): 6.

2. "A Talk with Alex Haley," *New York Times*, 26 September 1976.

3. *Chicago Irish American News*, 18 April 1978.

4. Reginald Byron, *Irish America* (Oxford: Oxford University Press, 1999), 117–18.

5. Ibid., 260.

6. *Chicago Irish American News*, October 1977, 10.

7. In October 1977, for example, a Trinity Ireland Festival was held at the Woodfield Shopping Mall in Schaumberg, Illinois. Organized around a promotion of both *Trinity* and *Ireland, A Terrible Beauty*, the book of photographs and text about Ireland jointly produced by Uris and his wife while he was writing the novel, this event was advertised as "an arts, culture and entertainment festival." *Chicago Irish American News* October 1977, 10.

8. Tommy McGuigan, *The Irish World and American Industrial Liberator and Gaelic American*, 26 June 1976, 13.

9. Quoted in James M. Cahalan, *Great Hatred, Little Room: The Irish Historical Novel* (Dublin: Gill and Macmillan, 1983), 193.

10. Ibid., 202.

11. Chioni Moore, "Routes," 8.

12. Ibid.

13. Ibid., 7.

14. A recent exception to this is Catherine Nash, "Genealogical Identities," *Environment and Planning D: Society and Space* 20 (2002): 27–52. Nash's nuanced reading of popular genealogical practices usefully considers the specifically diasporic enthusiasm for family-history research.

15. Eric Hobsbawm, *On History* (London: Weidenfeld and Nicholson, 1997), 21.

16. Sigmund Freud, "Family Romances," in *The Standard Edition of the Complete Works of Sigmund Freud*, vol. 9, edited by J. Strachey (London: Hogarth Press, 1953). In this essay, first published in 1909, Freud describes how, once a child's initial wor-

ship of its parents is diminished by the reality of their individual flaws, "the child's imagination becomes engaged in the task of getting free from the parents of whom he now has a low opinion and of replacing them by others, who, as a rule, are of a higher social standing" (238–39). Family history, therefore, was already, by the beginning of the twentieth century, associated with nostalgia. This association has continued to the present, as illustrated by Raphael Samuel's reference to "Freud's 'family romance,' the child's rejection of real-life parents in favor of imaginary and more glamorous others—a recurring fantasy which seems very germane to the current enthusiasm for family history, and the discovery of 'roots.'" Raphael Samuel, *Theatres of Memory*, vol. 1, *Past and Present in Contemporary Culture* (London: Verso, 1994), 374.

17. David Lowenthal, *Possessed by the Past: The Heritage Crusade and the Spoils of History* (London: Free Press, 1996), 9.

18. "National Library Service Expects to Welcome 10,000th Visitor," *Irish Times*, 29 June 1999, 8.

19. "A Sheep-Stealer in the Family," *Irish Times*, 3 August 1998, 6.

20. David Jackson, "How To Program Your Family History," *Time*, 19 April 1999, 58–59.

21. Roy Rosenzweig and David Thelen, *The Presence of the Past: Popular Uses of History in American Life* (New York: Columbia University Press, 1998), 4.

22. Kevin Whelan, untitled entry in *The Oxford Companion to Local and Family History*, edited by David Hey (Oxford: Oxford University Press, 1996), 242.

23. For a detailed discussion of this debate, see Alex Callinicos, *Theories and Narratives: Reflections on the Philosophy of History* (Cambridge: Polity Press, 1995). Callinicos compares the condemnation of historical narrative by theorists like Hayden White with Alasdair MacIntyre's assertion that "narrative history of a certain kind turns out to be the basic and essential genre for the characterisation of human actions" (54).

24. John Frow, *Time and Commodity Culture: Essays in Cultural Theory and Postmodernity* (Oxford: Clarendon Press, 1997), 229.

25. Paul Connerton, *How Societies Remember* (Cambridge: Cambridge University Press, 1989), 20. Connerton draws extensively on the classic theories of collective memory formulated by Maurice Halbwachs. Halbwachs's work itself crucially emphasizes the importance of family groups in the production of lasting collective memories, pointing out that despite the individual differences of perspective within a family group, "it is not because memories resemble each other that several can be called to mind at the same time. It is rather because the same group is interested in them and is able to call them to mind at the same time that they resemble each other." Maurice Halbwachs, *On Collective Memory* (Chicago: University of Chicago Press, 1992), 52.

26. Lawrence J. McCaffrey, *The Irish Diaspora in America* (Bloomington: Indiana University Press, 1976), 158–59.

27. Ibid., 178.

28. Stephanie Rains, "Home from Home: Diasporic Images of Ireland in Film and

Tourism," in *Irish Tourism: Image, Culture and Identity*, edited by Barbara O'Connor and Michael Cronin (Clevedon, England: Channel View Publications, 2003), 196–214.

29. *The Irish in Me*, dir. Herman Boxer, Universal International Color/Dudley Pictures Corporation, 1959.

30. *O'Hara's Holiday*, dir. Peter Bryan, Tribune Films. Although the exact date of the film is unknown, the Irish Film Archive classifies it as dating from the 1950s, and the film's visual clues strongly support this classification.

31. Richard Alba, *Ethnic Identity: The Transformation of White America* (New Haven: Yale University Press, 1990), 315.

32. Ibid., 295.

33. Ibid., 47. Of the old-stock European immigrants in Alba's study, 82 percent of those with Irish ancestry were of mixed ethnicity, compared to 46 percent of Italians and 64 percent of Poles. Only the Germans and the Scots, at 88 percent and 90 percent respectively, were more likely to be of mixed ancestry than the Irish.

34. Herbert Gans, "Symbolic Ethnicity: The Future of Ethnic Groups and Cultures in America," *Ethnic and Racial Studies* 2 (1979): 1–20.

35. Mary Waters, *Ethnic Options: Choosing Identities in America* (Berkeley: University of California Press, 1990), 155–64. See also Noel Ignatiev, *How the Irish Became White* (New York: Routledge, 1995).

36. *The Nephew*, dir. Eugene Brady, Irish DreamTime/World 2000 Entertainment, 1998.

37. Chioni Moore, "Routes," 15.

38. *The Matchmaker*, dir. Mark Joffe, Polygram/Working Title, 1997.

39. See Gene Kerrigan, "Waiting For the Sheriff," *Magill*, May 1984.

40. Byron, *Irish America*, 146.

41. Ibid., 290.

42. Ibid., 295.

43. *This Is My Father*, dir. Paul Quinn, Filmline International/Hummingbird Communications, 1998.

44. The film *The Last of the High Kings* contains a similar example of the parodying of unlikely genealogical claims. The mother of Frankie, the central character, claims the family is descended from the Irish high kings. See note 16 for a discussion of such uses of genealogy. *The Last of the High Kings*, dir. David Keating, RTE/Parallel Films/Nordisk, 1996.

45. Martin McLoone, *Irish Film: The Emergence of a Contemporary Cinema* (London: British Film Institute, 2000), 190.

46. The popularity of this classroom exercise in U.S. history curricula has been highlighted by respondents to a number of studies on ethnicity. See Byron, *Irish America*, 128, as well as Rosenzweig and Thelen, *Presence of the Past*, 179–81. For a discussion of the incorporation of the Irish famine into U.S. state curricula, see Catherine M. Eagan's contribution to this volume.

47. McLoone, *Irish Film*, 194.

48. Alice Carey, *I'll Know It When I See It: A Daughter's Search For Home in Ireland*, (New York: Clarkson Potter, 2002); Joan Matieu, *Zulu: An Irish-American's Quest to Discover her Roots* (Edinburgh: Mainstream, 1998); Maureen Waters, *Crossing Highbridge: A Memoir of Irish America* (Syracuse: Syracuse University Press, 2001); Richard White, *Remembering Ahanagran: Storytelling in a Family's Past* (Cork: Cork University Press, 1999).

49. White, *Remembering Ahanagran*, 43.

50. Ibid., 44.

51. Ibid., 271.

52. Ibid., 272.

53. See Rosenzweig and Thelen, *Presence of the Past*.

54. See Alba, *Ethnic Identity*; and Byron, *Irish America*.

55. David Hey, *Family History and Local History in England* (London: Longman, 1987), xi–xii.

56. Alba, *Ethnic Identity*, 315.

57. For a useful discussion of the position of 1980s Irish immigrants in the United States, see Mary P. Corcoran, *Irish Illegals: Transients Between Two Societies* (London: Greenwood Press, 1993), as well as Ray O'Hanlon, *The New Irish Americans* (Dublin: Roberts Rinehart, 1998).

58. Diane Negra explores Irishness as a "comfortable" version of whiteness in her introduction and essay in this volume.

59. In this context, the actual practice of genealogical research offers the potential for family histories such as the one cited above by Chioni Moore, in which an African American's genealogy begins in Ballyshannon.

60. Chioni Moore, "Routes," 21.

61. See Luke Gibbons, *Transformations in Irish Culture* (Cork: Cork University Press, 1996); David Lloyd, *Ireland After History* (Cork: Cork University Press, 1999); and Colin Graham and Richard Kirkland, eds., *Ireland and Cultural Theory: The Mechanics of Authenticity* (New York: Macmillan, 1999).

62. Nash, "Genealogical Identities," 46.

LAUREN ONKEY

Ray Charles on Hyndford Street:
Van Morrison's Caledonian Soul

I heard the voice of America

Callin' on my wavelength

Tellin' me to tune in on my radio

I heard the voice of America

Callin' on my wavelength

Singin' "Come back, baby, come back."

— Van Morrison, "Wavelength"

On 30 November 1995, President Bill Clinton made a historic visit to Northern Ireland, the first sitting U.S. president to do so. The Clinton administration had been heavily involved in the peace-process negotiations, and the president's visit signaled American interest in the future of Northern Ireland.[1] He landed in Belfast, gave an address at Mackie International engineering plant, made stops on the Shankill and Falls roads, traveled to Derry for a speech at Guildhall Square, and ended the day back in Belfast for a Christmas-tree lighting ceremony outside city hall in front of a crowd estimated at 80,000. Clinton was preceded on stage by Van Morrison, who was dressed in the Blues Brothers outfit he so often sported in the late 1990s, captured on the cover of his 1997 album *The Healing Game*: black fedora, sunglasses, suit coat, and tie. His band included a three-piece horn section and the singer Brian Kennedy. They played two songs from Morrison's most recent album, *Days Like This*: "No Religion," a remarkable choice given the setting ("There's no religion here today"); "Days Like This," a song that became an anthem of the peace process; and the set-closing "Have I Told You Lately That I

Love You," which he dedicated to "Bill and Hillary." The crowd waved American flags as they watched Morrison and waited for the president.

"Van the Man," as he was introduced, was by this time one of the most recognizable Irishmen in the world, and certainly one of the most famous Belfast natives. But the Irishness Morrison had on display that night was different from his New Age Celticism or collaborations with the Chieftains. This was an Irishness deeply connected with America and black music: on the day when he represented hopes for new Northern Ireland identities to the world, Morrison's soulful sound and awkward look signified the profound and ambiguous impact of African American music on Irish culture. Morrison's singing demonstrated his lifelong facility with rhythm and blues and soul music. His look, though, couldn't help but to evoke the politics of white appropriation of black music and black authenticity. One might be tempted to see him as one of Roddy Doyle's Commitments, trying on soul music because the Irish are "the niggers of Europe," and then moving on to country music when soul didn't fit. But Morrison has never been accused of such inauthenticity.

The appearance with Clinton signifies the complex and sometimes contradictory interchange of Irishness and blackness in Morrison's work: Morrison left Northern Ireland in the late 1960s and has always avoided Northern Irish politics but agreed to play at this important political event; he is considered quintessentially Irish, but he is recognized for playing "black" music; he considers fame antithetical to his traditionalist approach to Irish and black music but had become one of Ireland's biggest celebrities of the Celtic Tiger 1990s. To be sure, Van Morrison created a musical identity through black music—but can such an identity challenge sectarian Irishness? The kind of Irishness marketed by Guinness, Aer Lingus, and the Irish Tourist Board? Irishness as what Diane Negra calls in the introduction to this volume "a reliable form of whiteness"?

Declarations of black identity by the Irish or Irish Americans usually depend on essentialized notions of both blackness and Irishness; the point of making the alliance is to suggest that both groups share access to an authentic identity distinct from a dominant culture. The New York rock/rap/*ceili* band Black 47 and the Northern Irish Civil Rights Association of the late 1960s used such essentialism to create political alliances based on a belief in shared oppression. In another branch of this trope,

1. In the late 1990s, Van
Morrison sported a look
that evoked the soul music
era of the mid-1960s — and,
unfortunately, the Blues
Brothers.

best exemplified by U2's film *Rattle and Hum* (1988), blackness is evoked
to access primal expression of authentic emotion, to legitimize the Irish
as Celtic soul brothers. This forges a purportedly unproblematic link with
African Americans: the Irish have been oppressed, and therefore soul and
rhythm and blues are appropriate vehicles for Irish musicians. As Bono
put it, "I was called a 'White Nigger' once by a black musician, and I took
it as he meant it, as a compliment. The Irish, like the blacks, feel like outsiders."[2] Playing music with African Americans became a way for a band
like U2 to define themselves as an authentic alternative to prepackaged
bands created by record companies, to stage a racialized sincerity. But
such identifications can reinscribe African Americans as noble savages,
naturally more in tune with truth and soul than whites who have "pro-
gressed" into postmodernity. In this process, the Irish can use African
Americans as a tool to become authentically Irish, to get in touch with
their authentic suffering, or their precolonial ethnic authenticity; but the
definition of Irishness that emerges is as retrograde and limiting as depicting blacks as noble savages.

The convergence of Van Morrison's facility with black musical styles
and his exploration of Irishness in the second half of his career challenge the construction of a natural Irish/African American affinity in

productive ways. His Irishness is a hybrid, urban identity that bears the mark of transatlantic crossings at its root; it is created out of the migrancy of Irish people and of American culture, especially African American music. Echoing Paul Gilroy's *Black Atlantic*, Hazel Carby argues that "black routes and roots, passages and origins, are constantly interwoven with the migratory histories and cultures of other peoples whose own 'routes and roots' are sometimes carried by and sometimes expressed through political and cultural vessels marked as black."[3] Morrison grew up in Belfast steeped in African American music, so, strangely, his exposure to black music began at home. After a stint with an Irish show band, Morrison formed the blues band Them in the mid-1960s, and then, after moving to the United States in 1967, went on to a successful solo career in the 1970s with music rooted in rhythm and blues. Throughout these years he rarely wrote about Ireland or marked his work as Irish. In the 1980s, he created a more self-conscious Irish identity in his work; he became "One Irish Rover" with an "Irish Heartbeat" on a "Celtic Excavation" for the "Celtic Ray," and experimented with traditional Irish music for the first time.[4] But memories of the impact of black music on his formative years in Belfast dominated the best music of this return to Irishness.

Morrison's work suggests that the relationship between blackness and Irishness can be a modern, transatlantic, and creative one that provides alternatives to fixed identity rather than one that reinscribes colonial, racist stereotypes. In the 1991 BBC special "One Irish Rover," as footage of the Irish landscape dissolved into footage of a Louisiana bayou, Morrison said in a voice-over, "Blues sounded natural, like the most natural thing I'd ever heard . . . I mean in retrospect it is a bit strange . . . to think, well . . . here I am and what have I got to do with this culture? This is still early days, I mean I was ten, eleven maybe at the time . . . I felt I could relate to these words. Somehow it told me something about my own life." Unlike U2 or Black 47, Morrison does not define or claim knowledge about African Americans because of his Irishness; in other words, he does not make a claim to black authenticity by declaring his Irishness. Morrison creates an imaginative, affective, "authentic" connection to black music through dialogue with radio and records rather than the rhetoric of shared suffering, thereby mixing his definition of both Irishness and blackness.

Colin Graham contends that "authenticity has affected the basic discourses of Irish culture and identity politics in its prevalence, and has thus attained a status near to that of shared currency."[5] Building on Jacob Golomb's notion of historic authenticity as the "loyal" utilization and recreation of the past of one's people, Graham argues that "authenticity relies on the ability to 'utilize' and culturally employ such 'loyalty'—authenticity is thus constantly a cultural, textual phenomenon, defining, recreating and projecting. Authenticity may resist definition, but its materiality in textuality is undeniable."[6] The United States plays a key role in consuming and producing "the authenticity of Irishness."[7] The relentless tide of Irish emigration to the United States and the influence of American postwar popular culture in Ireland, especially in cinematic and musical form, account for America's powerful imaginative role in contemporary Ireland. This may also explain why the Irish have often been drawn to America, and not to other formerly colonized societies, for metaphors and images to describe their experience of colonialism.

In describing the fluid, "intertwined" relationship between Ireland and America, Fintan O'Toole argues that "the notion of America itself is an Irish invention, the notion of Ireland an American invention. When we step into this divide, we step into, not an open space, but a hall of mirrors."[8] In the 1950s and 1960s when Morrison was growing up, America represented modernity, freedom, and license as an alternative to provincial, poor, unhip Ireland. But American blues, rhythm and blues, rock and roll, and soul music can also represent roots and authentic, antimodern alternatives to a hypercapitalist disposable modernity. Through constant transatlantic crossings, black music can simultaneously offer a flexible, modern identity that is not bound by tradition, and, paradoxically, a set of authentic roots.

Van Morrison's work both embraces and exemplifies these double meanings. In his memories of listening to Morrison as a youth in Belfast, for example, Martin McLoone remembers feeling excited that Northern Ireland could be on the same stage as American blues towns: "What Morrison's success meant for me was the thrill of witnessing the periphery take centre-stage—of hearing Sandy Row, Fitzroy, Belfast (and Dublin) being invoked in a space normally reserved for the likes of Memphis, Galveston and all those famous points along Route 66."[9] McLoone argues

that Morrison's "art is an art of the periphery, which soaks up the influences of the centre, adapts these to its own designs and then presumes
to offer them back to the centre in a wholly unique form."[10] Of course,
Leadbelly and John Lee Hooker were not "central" in American culture
in the 1950s when Morrison first heard them; in fact, when he first came
to the United States, he was surprised that the blues and rhythm-and-
blues music he grew up with was not better known. In the Irish American
hall of mirrors, music from the margins in American culture — i.e., towns
peripheral to financial, political, and media centers — can be received in
Ireland as "central." Morrison created an America dominated by African American music and musicians who were not sufferers or primitives.
Morrison was not offering up an essentialized Irishness or blackness; he
was offering a hip Irishness, where Sandy Row is a stop along Route 66,
and where Route 66 was the center of America.

Morrison's extraordinary performance of "Listen to the Lion," on *St.
Dominic's Preview* (1971) enacts his desire for and challenge to authentic
roots. The song has a slow, soft, folkish sound. But as he often does, especially in live performance, Morrison breaks away from singing words.
Moaning, scatting, and chanting in a long ending to the song, Morrison
repeats the lines "And we sailed, and we sailed, and we sailed, and we
sailed . . . Away from Denmark, way up to Caledonia . . . And we sailed . . .
All around the world. . . . Looking for a brand-new start." The "we" are
Celtic people, who end up, by the end of the song, in America: "And we
sailed/Way up from the Golden Gate/Way up to New York City." The lion
is Morrison's voice, his inspiration, which is released to find a brand-new
start in America.

Like many rock critics of the 1970s, Greil Marcus explained Morrison's
skill at rhythm and blues and blues by making "natural" links between the
Irish and African Americans. But Marcus heard a much more confusing
and creative cultural exchange than most. In a famous 1975 description
of Morrison, Marcus quotes Irish tenor John McCormack on what makes
a good singer: "You have to have the yarrrrragh in your voice," which
Marcus hears in "Listen to the Lion."

Certain themes have emerged in Morrison's music, from album to
album: an attempt to come to grips with his existence as an Irish-

man, whose homeland is in flames, who lives safely, if not peacefully, in America; a corresponding will to discover or recapture a mythical homeland, "Caledonia," or Scotland, the place from which his ancestors originally came, ages ago; an attempt to shape and communicate a sense of freedom.

Morrison is heir to a tradition of mysteries, and he knows it. He is a Celt, and at least a spiritual descendant of the Irish prelate St. Brendan, who set out from Ireland 1500 years ago and who, according to legend, reached America itself, and perhaps founded a colony, which disappeared. So there may be a sense in which Morrison can understand that he was always an American (could have been, was meant to be); that his place in America is fated, even if it is unsettled, as he stretches out toward that mythical Caledonia, even believing, sometimes, that in a long and intricate manner, the blues came not from Africa, but from Scotland. That here came from there, that there are no divisions, that all parts of himself are, somehow, linked. Yet this is not a belief, it is a possibility.[11]

Marcus gets carried away with his Celticism in linking Morrison with St. Brendan, but he makes the very important observation that the Irish American relationship in Morrison's work is a site of creative hybridity where the idea of authentic or pure cultural identity becomes ludicrous, impossible to trace, a hall of mirrors. Marcus describes homeland as a place created in some space between Ireland and America, in the idea between the two, in the relationship between Irish, English, and African music. Marcus uses the phrase "here came from there," with the knowledge that the location of here and there is always changing. Blackness and Irishness reflect each other in Morrison's career, where here and there, authenticity and roots, are always shifting.

In a 1972 interview, Morrison reflected on the importance of American influences in Belfast: "See, Belfast is not like England, even though it's a part of Great Britain. It's got its own trip going. The American influences are stronger than the English influences because of all the Irish who have immigrated to the United States in the last few generations. Like all my relatives lived in Detroit and Toronto, places like that."[12] Morrison almost joined them. His father went to Detroit in the early 1950s hoping to find steady work and send home for his family: "He went to check things out. Later he was supposed to bring the rest of the family over but it didn't work out. He did send me some American clothes, but the other kids were jealous of them."[13]

Morrison was born of Protestant parents in Bloomfield, a working-class neighborhood of East Belfast, in 1945. His father worked as an electrician at the Lagan docks. Belfast's large port brought black music to the city; Gerald Dawe describes "the afterglow in Belfast of the 1950s left by the many American troops, including black GIs, who had been stationed throughout the north. Having brought with them not only bubble-gum and cigarettes, but their own styles of music and dance, they took over the floor of ballrooms such as the Plaza (built in 1942) with, for Belfast, an uncharacteristic flamboyance and glamour."[14] Morrison's father, George, loved jazz and accumulated an extensive jazz, gospel, and blues record collection. As a result, young Van first heard Leadbelly, Mahalia Jackson, and Duke Ellington in his own home. In many interviews over the years, Morrison has recalled the excitement of going record shopping with his father on Saturday mornings to find these magical recordings. He also absorbed the sounds of Irish folk music like the McPeake family and John McCormack.[15] His mother's family was very musical, hosting regular weekend sings that included songs like "Star of the County Down" and "She Moved Through the Fair," which he later recorded.

Morrison has suggested that Belfast had a uniquely mixed musical environment. In a 1970 interview, American folksinger Happy Traum asked him, "How does someone from Belfast get into American country blues?" He responded, "We get it both live and from records. Memphis Slim has been in Belfast; Jesse Fuller, Champion Jack Dupree, John Lee Hooker's been there. They've got folk clubs and rock clubs there, but it's got nothing to do with the English scene. In fact, I'd go so far as to say it doesn't have much to do with the Irish scene either, it's just Belfast. It's got its own identity, it's got its own people . . . it's just a different race, a different breed of people."[16] Morrison also absorbed American music through Radio Luxembourg and Voice of America radio, which broadcast into the United Kingdom.[17] American music must have been both normal and exotic to Morrison—normal because it was a continuous presence in his house, but exotic because it was from such a different world from what Dawe calls "the conservatism and civic priorities of Belfast in the mid-to-late 1950s."[18] His interest wasn't shared by his friends, since no one else had the access to black music that he did.

Morrison fell in love with Leadbelly records very early on, and later enjoyed the popular versions of his songs such as "Rock Island Line" and "Goodnight Irene" by Lonnie Donegan, who sparked the skiffle craze in England and Ireland in the late 1950s.[19] In the liner notes to *The Skiffle Sessions*, a 2000 album that Morrison recorded with Donegan, Morrison wrote, "Given the geographical distance between me and my heroes, skiffle arrived where and when I needed it. It was too good to be true. What had once been an eccentric taste in American folk-blues was now a popular hit. Music was the common denominator and skiffle provided a bridge between what I had always been listening to and what everyone else was suddenly discovering." Unlike many of his generation, who first got turned on to American music through early rock-and-roll hits, Morrison's most powerful musical influences were pre–rock and roll: "When I joined my first rock & roll band, I was still listening to blues and progressive R&B and jazz. I never saw rock & roll as the whole picture."[20]

After a series of small local bands, Morrison's first serious professional work was as part of the Monarchs, an Irish showband, from 1960 to 1963. Showbands dominated Irish popular music at this time, both north and south. They always included a horn section and usually had eight or ten members who wore matching suits, developed set dance routines, and specialized in copying the pop hits of the day as well as sentimental Irish numbers.[21] The showband repertoire usually featured a lot of country and western, and could include numbers as different as Johnny Mercer's "Fools Rush In," Johnny Cash's "I Walk the Line," and the Beatles's "I Want to Hold Your Hand." As Brian Hogg suggests, they " 'were peculiarly Irish, a tumble of pop tunes and sentimentality, a frantic dance music playing the hits, but in its own honed style of racket mixed in [with] rural sweetness.' "[22] In addition, as Alan Clayson describes, the showbands played Irish songs such as "The Rose of Tralee," "Delaney's Donkey," and "The Outlawed Raparee."[23] In *Isle of Noises: Rock and Roll's Roots in Ireland*, Mark Prendergast argues that showbands "dominated every town and city in Ireland . . . With their vast resources they controlled the dissemination of popular music throughout the country."[24] Morrison remembers the professionalism that the showbands displayed: "They did comedy, right, they did top ten, they did jazz, they did impersonations—you know it was a very professional show. It wasn't just like a matter of guys like doing steps and wearing suits. It was a couple of levels above that."[25] Showbands are most often remembered as a symbol of how uncool Ireland was in the early 1960s. Success in a showband demanded that musicians copy and imitate. Phil Lynott, the late guitarist and lead singer of Thin Lizzy said, "Showbands have destroyed some of the country's finest musicians."[26] Bob Geldof calls them "crap, the desert years" and "typical Paddydom" in *From a Whisper to a Scream*, a 2001 documentary on the history of Irish rock and roll. Morrison could not fully develop his interest in blues and rhythm and blues in such an Irish context.

However, because the showband circuit included trips abroad, it provided a conduit to black music that built on Morrison's experience with records and radio. The Monarchs gave Morrison an opportunity to travel outside of Northern Ireland to England and Germany and to meet Americans who could teach him more about the music he loved. The showbands were put through their paces in Heidelberg, Frankfurt, and Cologne, playing multiple sets every night to demanding audiences that included many American GIs. Most importantly for Morrison, the German trip gave him the chance to meet African Americans who knew the music he had heard only on records and the radio. Monarch George Jones remembered their time in Heidelberg as central to Morrison's development: "For the first time in his life he had met American coloured GIs who dug soul, blues and all the music that he was weaned on. Van drifted away every day to get near coloured guys who talked the same language as him. He suddenly became a big influence on The Monarchs. We started playing all this soul music in the clubs of Germany and we really began to like it."[27] In a 1998 interview, Morrison described the experience in religious terms: "I remember when I was in Germany with the Monarchs meeting this GI called Lee. He played guitar and sang with us one night. He did 'Stormy Monday.' And he had this record player in the hotel and he played all this Bobby Bland stuff. I don't like talking in biblical terms but it was like the road to Damascus. It was a real eye-opener."[28]

It's typical of Morrison's story that he meets Lee in Germany—not in the Mississippi Delta, or in Chicago. His "authentic" experience with black music comes about because of modern, transatlantic movement that crosses national and ethnic boundaries. This encounter, as Jones suggests, pushed the band toward playing more R&B, and made the showband scene back in Ireland seem even more untenable. Showbands were particularly popular in rural areas and certainly would not have allowed Morrison to explore the music that most excited him. While the Monarchs provided Morrison important professional training and a chance to travel, they were ultimately limiting and provincial—they were, in short, too Irish.

Morrison left the Monarchs and formed the band Them in 1964. Them played regularly at the Maritime Hotel in College Square North in Belfast. Billy Harrison, an early guitar player in Them, remembers, "The Maritime Hotel became a place that people made pilgrimages to. It became the fount of blues learning in Ireland."[29] The British blues craze brought artists like Little Walter, Sister Rosetta Tharpe, Roosevelt Sykes, Sonny Terry & Brownie McGhee, Muddy Waters, and Otis Spann to the United Kingdom in the early 1960s, and many touring acts included Belfast on their circuit. The explosion of the Beatles had opened the door to pop groups, but Them specialized in contemporary blues and rhythm and blues in the style of British bands such as the Rolling Stones, the Animals, John Mayall's Bluesbreakers, and the Yardbirds. Live and on record, they covered contemporary, urban black music like Bobby "Blue" Bland's "Turn on Your Love Light," and his arrangement of "Stormy Monday"; Ray Charles's "I Got a Woman"; Chris Kenner's "Something You Got"; James Brown's "Out of Sight"; Jimmy Reed's "Bright Lights Big City" and "Baby What You Want Me To Do"; and John Lee Hooker's "Don't Look Back" and his arrangement of "Baby Please Don't Go." There was always an element of mimicry in the British blues boom—bands initially copied original versions note for note—but the bands also honored American bluesmen and brought them a new audience. Them gave Morrison a chance to respond to the sounds he'd heard as a child. Them broke from the conservatism of the showband scene in their sound, attitude, and dress, shunning the pop hits of the day and matching suits. Morrison describes their sound as a challenge to the popularity of the Beatles:

2. Them, pictured here in early 1965, abandoned the matching outfits of the Irish showband era for a scruffy style that reflected their blues-based sound. (Courtesy Michael Ochs Archives.com)

"The R&B movement over here was actually an antiestablishment stance against the Beatles. This is something that didn't happen in America. It was against that silly image . . . When it started it had nothing to do with rock. It was actually against the rock/pop movement."[30] Gerald Dawe remembers that when he was growing up in Belfast, "Morrison's voice, Them's music, dress and mannerisms were guaranteed to satisfy a feeling for rebellious self-assertion."[31] Them represented a hip, liberating, urban Irishness that was inextricably linked with America. Their set lists were entirely American music plus original songs; they did not play any of the Irish kitsch songs of the showband era.[32] The band was very popular in Belfast, but they found a less welcome reception in the more rural areas of Northern Ireland, where the crowds wanted the showbands. Billy Harrison: "Once you get out into the country, forget it . . . We were OK in places like Lisburn and Newtownards, but you got to remember that the country in Ireland is still the country . . . The biggest industry in Cookstown is bacon, sausages, pig-farming. We played the town hall. They were used to showbands. They were not ready for an R&B group . . . Groups to [these people] meant the Shadows, clean cut guys doing steps and all this."[33] The crowd threw pennies at the band, and at the end of the show Morrison said, "Goodnight, pigs," causing a riot. As Eric Wrixson, the original keyboard player in the band, put it, "In the early sixties there was an incredibly huge gulf between Belfast and every other city in Northern Ireland."[34]

Them thrived in the period of the 1960s just before the troubles ignited. The period of Them's rise is usually considered one of relative peace, or as John Darby describes it, of "an absence of overt conflict" characterized by a focus on "economic expansion."[35] The IRA offensive of 1956–62 had failed largely due to a lack of support, and the 1963 retirement of Unionist stalwart Lord Brookeborough as prime minister and the election of the more moderate Terence O'Neill also suggested more tolerant times. Some observers have suggested that Them reflected these new possibilities. Tom Nairn argues that Morrison's work evokes the years just before 1968, "when youngsters on both sides of Ulster's religious divide discovered a musical liberation culture which could take them away from . . . the old parochial grouses of their respective extended families."[36] Dawe argues that "the Maritime . . . provided a chance for kids of every religion and none to get together. Such thoughts would have been far from the minds of those at the time, however; all that mattered was the music. For many working-class kids, seeing students look like 'beatniks' would have had a greater effect on them than wondering about what church they went to."[37]

But nationalism and Unionism were still firmly in place. Thomas Hennessey describes the 1950s and early 1960s as a "cold war" in Northern Ireland, which "remained a fundamentally divided and sectarian society. Differences between the two communities pervaded all aspects of society."[38] Billy Harrison observes that musicians could defuse traditional tensions between Protestants and Catholics, but only temporarily: "When you get into music and you're playing, the guy's a musician. There's no mention of what religion he is. He's only what he is, as regards the music. [But] there was always the Catholic area and the Protestant area, which you couldn't always walk through safely if you were of the wrong persuasion."[39] Morrison has said very little about sectarian conflict over the years, and when he has commented, he remembers a youth outside of it: "This was before all that bigotry got really big. Everybody was just too busy getting on with what they liked to do and what they're interested in, there was no time for that. The people that I grew up with, my peer group of that time, wasn't into that stuff. They were into sharing ideas, you know they had energy and they were like interested, they saw a bright future. All that changed later on."[40]

Them's "blackness," then, is associated with a challenge to — or at least an escape from — sectarianism. At their best, they offered alternatives to fixed ideas of Protestant/Catholic identity through their focus on American blues. Them's musical blackness was different from the overtly nationalist assumption of blackness expressed by the Northern Irish Civil Rights Association in 1968.[41] The band's assertion of the centrality of black music and their right to play it without defensiveness or explanation was not rooted in the rhetoric of shared oppression or tied to nationalist aspirations. Them signified liberation, modernity, a celebration of transnational and transatlantic youth culture, and perhaps subtly, therefore, a challenge to essential Irish identities.

While Them might have been very hip at home, the band members were still considered Paddys in England. For a time, the band was based in London, and band members recall their Irishness counting against them. John Wilson, a drummer in one of the later incarnations of Them, said that the English music business treated them like they were "idiots from Ireland."[42] In a 1993 interview, Morrison said, "I can remember in the '60s, to be from Ireland was a disadvantage . . . For instance, to be in London and be Irish, you were fucked. Now it's cool, it's hip . . . I was in London in the '60s and it was like, Fuck you, we don't want to know. We were ostracised. Even if you were a rock star! You were just Paddy."[43] Their thick Northern accents didn't help make the band members more accessible. Outside of Ireland, Irishness put limits on the kind of new identity that playing blues and rhythm and blues offered at home.

After a series of lineup changes and conflicts with managers and producers, Them broke up in 1967, and Morrison headed to America to record as a solo act. There were few opportunities to pursue a professional rock music career in Ireland, and so Morrison did what so many Irish people of his generation did and left Ireland for America. At a time when rock and roll became rock and psychedelic experimentation dominated the scene, Morrison stayed grounded in rhythm and blues and soul. But he also developed an original style that mixed R&B, folk, blues, and jazz, holding it all together with his unusual and powerful voice. Craig Werner argues that straight imitation was the weakness of the British blues movement: "The Brits were least interesting when they came closest to realizing their goal of authenticity. They sounded best when they quit worrying about how John Lee or Muddy or the Wolf . . . did it. Not that the straight imitations sounded bad. They just didn't amount to much in the way of response.[44]

During his live shows in the first half of the 1970s with the Caledonian Soul Orchestra (whose name was both Celtic and a nod to Louis Jordan's 1945 hit "Caldonia (What Makes Your Big Head So Hard)"), he continued to cover R&B songs; he regularly performed Willie Dixon's "I Just Wanna Make Love to You," Ray Charles's "I Believe to My Soul," and Bobby Bland's "Ain't Nothing You Can Do." Morrison could write hits with a conventional verse-chorus structure (the R&B "Jackie Wilson Said" or the jazzy "Moondance" are good examples), but he also wrote more impressionistic, free-form songs that pushed at the boundaries of pop music. Yet with the arguable exception of *Astral Weeks*, he never indulged in the era's excesses of concept albums and free-form jamming. As a result, his music challenges the growing split in the late 1960s and early 1970s between white rock musicians as "artists" and black musicians as more primitive (or natural) entertainers. The politics of his music were never much of a concern for Morrison, however. He moved to the United States at a time of race riots and splits in the counterculture over race, but such social upheaval never entered into his music, and he stayed out of the limelight in rural retreats like Woodstock, New York, and Marin County, California. Yet his music asserted a deep connection with African American culture.

Werner describes the importance of connections to ancestors in "the gospel impulse" of black music: "The gospel impulse half remembers the values brought to the new world by the men and women uprooted from West African cultures: the connections between the spiritual and material worlds; the interdependence of self and community; the honoring of the elders and the ancestors; the recognition of the ever-changing flow of experience that renders all absolute ideologies meaningless."[45] Morrison honored his musical ancestors by mastering R&B forms and by weaving references to African American music and musicians into his lyrics.[46] In "Astral Weeks" (1968), the opening track to his landmark album of the same name, Morrison sings to a woman: "If I ventured in the slipstream/Between the viaducts of your dream/Where immobile steel rims crack/And the ditch in the back roads stop/Could you find me?" The song has no chorus; its jazz structure, propelled by acoustic bass and guitar, conveys a mood of longing and mystery. And then Morrison drops in a reference to his childhood hero Leadbelly: "There you go/Standin' with the look of avarice/Talkin' to Huddie Ledbetter/Showin' pictures on the wall." The reference to Leadbelly—if the listener can pick it up, if the listener knows that Huddie Ledbetter is Leadbelly—amplifies the blues in the song ("Ain't nothin but a stranger in this world/I'm nothing but a stranger in this world/got a home on high"), and makes the singer into a character in the poetic landscape. In "These Dreams of You" (1970), a more conventional R&B song, Ray Charles roams the singer's strange dreams: "And Ray Charles was shot down/but he got up to do his best/a crowd of people gathered round/to the question answered 'yes.'" In more literal songs, he calls up soul singer Jackie Wilson's spirit to describe his love in "Jackie Wilson Said (I'm in Heaven When You Smile)" (1972) and in "The Eternal Kansas City" (1977) he transforms the city into a kind of mecca where pilgrims will come: "Train down to St. Louis/Get me there alright/Over to the city there, you know that one/Where the farmer's daughter digs the farmer's son/Dig your Charlie Parker/Basie and Young/Witherspoon and Jay McShann/They will come." Such a compendium of knowing references required specialized knowledge about the history of black music, which directed listeners away from Morrison and back to his musical ancestors.

Morrison also celebrated the effect of black music in a series of songs about the power of radio and its ability to transmit the mystical power he felt when he first heard black music. Radio is a transmission source for both authentic ancestors and a medium that provides the potential for creating a new sort of authenticity. He turns on the radio to soothe the young girl dying of tuberculosis in the haunting blues song "TB Sheets," (1967); in "Caravan" (a 1937 Duke Ellington song title) from *Moondance* (1970), the radio becomes a conduit for the singer and his lover to communicate: "Turn up your radio and let me hear the song/Switch on your electric light/Then we can get down to what is really wrong," and the song ends with insistent shouts of "radio! Turn it up!" In "Wavelength" (1978), he uses the image of the radio as a metaphor to describe communication between himself and his lover, and between himself and America. He "hears the voice of America calling me home" on the radio, fusing the idea of home with the black music he heard on Radio Luxembourg and the Voice of America networks; "home" isn't Ireland, but hearing black music in Ireland.

Morrison's complex and unconventional engagement with black music led critics to praise his "authentic" playing of black music. His brand of R&B and cover versions of R&B music have been widely received as genuine—i.e., Morrison is not accused of parodying, ripping off, or simply copying black artists, as evidenced by a 1972 review in CREEM magazine that carried the headline "Soul Brothers: Al Green, Sly Stone, Van Morrison."[47] Dave Marsh's assessment of Morrison is typical of the time: "He now seems less like a great white R&B singer than like one of the very few rock artists who has invented a personal emotional equivalent of the blues."[48]

But critics in the 1970s attributed Morrison's facility with black music to an Irish essentialism that had little to do with Morrison's Belfast culture or any image he promoted; their Ireland represents "ancient beliefs" and spirituality. In the early 1970s, Tom Donahue (record producer and manager at KSAN-FM, San Francisco, considered the founder of FM radio), remarked, "He's got the voice and lyrics that remind you of generations of hard times and misery and that kind of black Irish soul."[49] Lester Bangs attributes the "darkness" of (Protestant) Morrison's lyrics to "a truly Irish literary sense of doom and fear (the same terror as epiphany found in James Joyce, and probably just about as rooted in Catholicism)."[50] Reviewing 1974's "TB Sheets" in *Melody Maker*, Michael Watts wrote that Morrison's "poetic muse wings its way amongst the Gaelic mysteries, and lends his music a rare, unspecified eloquence quintessentially Irish."[51] This rhetoric was taken to its extreme in a 1978 *Rolling Stone* interview where Jonathan Cott read Morrison a line from Ernest Renan's "The Poetry of the Celtic Races" describing the Celts as having a "realistic naturalism . . . a love of Nature for herself, a vivid feeling for her magic, commingled with the melancholy a man knows when he is face to face with her, and thinks he hears her communing with him about his origin and his destiny" and then asks, "Do you feel close to that?" Cott continues to push some "Celtic" interpretations of songs: "In a song like 'Slim Slow

Slider' the image of the woman riding a horse white as snow seems to be connected to the Celtic symbol for clairvoyance and death." Morrison replies with his characteristic resistance to interpreting his own songs: "I thought the song was about Ladbroke Grove."[52]

During this period, Morrison rarely made reference to Ireland in his song lyrics, and did not draw on Irish musical styles. But his ability to sing R&B was made sense of as a product of his Irishness, an Irishness that had little to do with the postwar East Belfast where Morrison grew up. His distinctiveness could be explained only as a product of a stereotype, like Leadbelly wearing a chain-gang suit or urban blues musicians coming to England for the first time and being forced to play rural, country blues to satisfy the audience's expectations for the authentic expression of primitive artists. To American audiences and critics who bought into this image, Morrison could be a conduit to an authentic, mysterious, ethnic Irishness that had guilt-free connections to African Americans.

In the 1980s, Morrison began to write more explicitly about Ireland, and experiment with traditional Irish music, a process that began with a trip he took to Cork and Killarney in October 1973. Much of his 1974 album *Veedon Fleece* was written on the trip, and reflected a fascination with the Irish landscape in songs such as "Fair Play" and "Streets of Arklow." By the late 1970s, after he'd moved to England, he seemed to feel both compelled and free to explore Ireland, especially Irish literature and music, and he performed in Belfast in 1979 for the first time in twelve years. In various interviews in the 1980s and early 1990s, Morrison talked about his interest in Ireland as a way to discover the traditions of Irish culture that were either uninteresting or unavailable to him when he was growing up, using ideas of roots and authenticity to explain his interest. Morrison told an interviewer in 1982 that he didn't really "rate" Irish music when he was younger. "I think," he said, "it can be dangerous to not validate the music of where you're from, for anybody . . . For me it's traditional. I'm a traditionalist. I believe in tracing things back to the source and finding out what the real thing was, and how it changed."[53] In 1985 he told Bill Flanagan, "You live in a lot of different places and it gives you a broader perspective on life in general. One becomes very cosmopolitan. But there's a big part of me that's just strictly involved with Ireland . . .

I think at a certain point you become a citizen of the world but you belong to a certain place. So I'd say I'm a citizen of Europe and America but I belong to, specifically, Ulster."[54] Morrison was both returning to the sounds and traditions of his personal history, and creating a place for himself in a larger Irish tradition that he did not know much about. He used Irishness, and its generic association with tradition, as an antidote to what he saw as the excesses of the materialist pop-music world.

His interest in Ireland coincided with intense spiritual exploration, as he experimented with Christian mysticism, Scientology, and Cyril Scott's ideas on the healing power of music.[55] But his interest also seemed affected by his time in America. Gerry Smyth argues that Ireland's "strong cultural and political links with America" produced an "intense trans-Atlantic cultural traffic in which images of 'home' were exchanged and distorted."[56] And as Morrison began to reconnect with Ireland, and to create a self-consciously Irish identity for himself, he began to write about the place of black music in his memory of growing up in East Belfast as much as he did about poets and rural landscapes that are more stereotypically coded as Irish. Black music is then simultaneously the conduit to the world outside Ireland, and the conduit back to Ireland. These songs were an extension of his earlier work about the power of black music but now they tied black music very specifically to his articulation of his Irish memories.

As part of Morrison's exploration of Irishness, he developed literary interests, especially in Irish writers. He told Victoria Clarke of the *Irish Post* in 1992 that when he was at school, "there wasn't one book by any Irish writer" so he had no exposure to Irish literature until later in life.[57] In 1991, he participated in a Channel 4 television show, "Coney Island of the Mind," where he talked with Northern Irish poets Seamus Deane, Michael Longley, Gerald Dawe, and John Montague about how their native landscape had shaped their work. Morrison stated that he discovered that his previous "unconscious" moves were part of the Irish literary tradition. "I wanted to find out where I stood and what tradition I came from. Well, eventually, I found out that the tradition I belong to is actually my own tradition. It was like getting hit over the head with a baseball bat." This discovered tradition is an invented authenticity, and it sounds remarkably similar to the "natural" connection he claimed with black music. Morrison included references to writers such as Yeats (he even set "Crazy Jane on God" and "Before the World Was Made" to music),[58] William Blake, James Joyce, John Donne, Oscar Wilde, Dylan Thomas, Seamus Heaney, and Arthur Rimbaud in much the same way as he had made reference to black artists in the 1970s. He had already treated black musicians like great writers and poets, so treating poets as subject matter for rock or R&B songs seemed quite in concert with his earlier moves.[59]

An important characteristic of Morrison's Celticism is that he embraces a Celtic vision across the British Isles. He is as interested in English Romantic poets as he is in things specifically Irish; he has also repeatedly evoked Avalon, the burial ground of King Arthur and the site of Jesus's mythical visit to England. Morrison has been reluctant to talk about a more inclusive Celticism, however, because of its political implications; he has always avoided talking about politics in Northern Ireland. In 1985 Bill Flanagan asked him, " 'The British Isles are so divided, so different. Coming from Ulster you must be especially sensitive to that. Yet when you sing, "Ireland, Scotland, England and Wales/I can hear the mothers' voices calling 'Children, children' " (in 'Celtic Ray'), you put forth a vision of one place, one people.' 'Well, I wouldn't want to get into that kind of territory. But . . . it's just basically a Celtic invocation. There's nothing political about it.' "[60] In 1987 he told *Q*: " 'Celtic' is a loaded word nowadays, it's politically loaded. Many people do not want to acknowledge the broad Celtic vision."[61] As he has throughout his career, Morrison avoided talking about specific political divisions in Northern Ireland, even as he was doing things that were politically coded; as a Belfast Protestant, for example, he was associating himself with a nationalist literary tradition.

"Summertime in England" from *Common One* (1980) exemplifies Morrison's use of blackness and Irishness in a spiritual vision. The album cover features a photo of a man, possibly Morrison, in a cap and walking stick, walking up a hill; the border around the photo is a rusty brown, suggesting the rural simplicity fetishized by the Romantic poets, and the singer in the song, who could be a tourist in the Lake District, asks, "Did you ever hear about Wordsworth and Coleridge, baby?" and "Can you meet me in the country/In the summertime in England?" After a funky, bass-driven opening, the song shifts to a slower, gospel beat and the lyrics move from the real to the mystical: the singer hears "the gospel music/The voice of Mahalia Jackson came through the ether."

Morrison had first heard Jackson from his father's record collection, but his memory of her is a deeply spiritual one. He has said in several interviews that her music is some of the first that he remembers hearing. In a 1982 interview, he recalled that he first felt a "feeling of wonder" when he heard her voice.[62] Of course, Jackson was not an obscure figure; in addition to her popularity as a gospel singer, she had a weekly CBS radio show in the 1950s that exposed her to a wide audience. She was also a leader in the civil rights movement of the 1950s and early 1960s and sang at the 1963 March on Washington. Morrison's nod to her in "Summertime in England" can be read as a response to her effect on him as a child rather than an appropriation of her spirituality; she evokes both mystical spirituality and his daily life in Belfast. One might be tempted to argue that Morrison elevates Jackson to the poetic pantheon of Yeats, Wordsworth, and Blake, but given his pattern of referencing black musicians, it might be more accurate to say that his newfound interest in literature inspires him to elevate poets to the spiritual level of Mahalia Jackson. When he shouts, "I want to go to church right now and pray," we are reminded that Morrison's exploration of Irishness, spirituality, and poetry was, from the start, in dialogue with the magic he had always heard over the radio. Over the years, Morrison has made "Summertime in England" a highlight of his live performances, adding references to Seamus Heaney, W. H. Auden, Allen Ginsberg, Dylan Thomas, and D. H. Lawrence to the mix. But *Common One* did not receive positive reviews in the rock press. While critics had always been comfortable with Morrison's claim to black music, they were less comfortable with his overt poetic persona.

Morrison's exploration of Irishness and spirituality—as well as the negative reception of *Common One*—coincided with his rejection of the rock industry. In many interviews in the early 1980s, Morrison distanced himself from rock, and juxtaposed it with "real" music and music as a healing force. Ireland became the symbol of this healing in his lyrics and sound. *Beautiful Vision* (1982) featured "Celtic Ray," Morrison's declaration of a Celtic spirit; the Celtic Ray mixes the mystical/religious imagery of a spiritual mother who calls all home ("All over Ireland, Scotland, England, and Wales/I can hear the mothers' voices calling 'Children, children, come home children . . .' I've been away from the Ray too long") with temporal, hoary images of a coal man and a fishmonger. "Irish Heartbeat" from *Inarticulate Speech of the Heart* (1983) romanticizes "home" and the return to an Irish family, using a traditional-sounding melody: "Oh won't you stay/Stay a while with your own ones/ Don't ever stray/Stray so far from own ones/'Cause the world is so cold/ Don't care nothing for your soul/That you share with your own ones." Morrison combined this romanticism with New Age sounds that were becoming popular in the early 1980s. Synthesizer and trumpet player Mark Isham played on *Common One, Beautiful Vision*, and *Inarticulate Speech of the Heart* and he brought the soft-jazz sounds that characterized his work on the Windham Hill label and many successful film soundtracks. *Inarticulate Speech of the Heart* featured several innocuous instrumentals ("Connswater," "Celtic Swing") a style that Morrison pursued in "Evening Meditation" on *A Sense of Wonder* (1985) and "Celtic Excavation" on *Poetic Champions Compose* (1987).

Connell and Gibson argue that the "natural" sounds of New Age music construct a primitive Irish identity: "Irish ambient music often incorporated uilleann pipes, and Scottish music the bagpipes. Natural sounds (an explicit conjunction of indigenous peoples as 'natural') contributed to the primitivist fantasies of tranquility, timelessness and human interactions with nature. Relaxation and spiritual healing were the anticipated consequences."[63] Natasha Casey points out the frequency with which "Irish," "Celtic," and "New Age" are conflated, and notes the appeal of this inoffensive Irishness to American audiences: "Irish music in its American mainstream variety can be located in the respectable (see apolitical) genre of world music where artists such as Enya, The Chieftains, and Mary Black thrive."[64] Morrison's new music perpetuated the belief in Ireland's natural spirituality, although his most New Age album, *Inarticulate Speech of the Heart*, was one of his least successful. For others, however, the association between Ireland and a soothing, rejuvenating New Age Celticism proved to be a goldmine. Enya, the former singer for the innovative Irish folk band Clannad, released her first solo album, *The Celts*, in 1986. The album, the soundtrack for a six-part BBC series on Celtic peoples, was an unexpected hit, which paved the way for the phenomenal success of *Watermark* (1988). Her beautiful, ethereal vocals and the lush soundscapes evoked a vague spirituality that could be incorporated easily into a variety of settings in need of Irish authenticity, most notably the soundtrack to the Irish immigrant fantasy film *Far and Away* (1992).

Morrison's self-consciously Irish period culminated in an album of traditional Irish music with the Chieftains, *Irish Heartbeat* (1988). Morrison described the project as sonic exploration: "I started meditating and doing sounds, and seeing what I could do with my voice when I was meditating. That led me more into listening to Irish folk music and Scottish folk music and the drone, the pipes and all this sort of stuff."[65] The album featured Morrison's vocal experiments, where he sometimes imitated instruments or simply growled. Paddy Maloney of the Chieftains heard "traditional west of Ireland keening" in Morrison's wordless vocal stylings.[66] The album featured numbers that had been favorites of Morrison's mother, like "The Star of the County Down," "I'll Tell Me Ma," and "Marie's Wedding," as well as a remake of "Celtic Ray" in a more traditional style, transformed from the version on *Beautiful Vision* to include uilleann pipes, fiddle, tin whistle, and bodhran.

The *Belfast Telegraph* reviewer attacked the record, writing that if Morrison sang his version of "My Lagan Love" at a party in Belfast, people would leave early, and that his interpretation of "Raglan Road" would cause "trouble in the Dublin pubs."[67] Morrison brought some of his R&B style to traditional songs, and as a result, *Irish Heartbeat* was not well-received by traditional music fans. Derek Bell of the Chieftains attributes the criticism to Morrison's soul-style singing: "From the purist's folk point of view it's grotesque . . . I mean no purist is going to sing things like 'She Moved through the Fair,' repeating 'our wedding day' three times. That's an element of soul music. The repetition and jazz-like style of words for the sake of emphasis . . . It has nothing to do with our tradition at all . . . and the folkies don't like it."[68] The sense of authenticity Morrison generated with black music may have hindered his ability to "authentically" claim access to such overdetermined expressions of Irishness as the familiar songs on *Irish Heartbeat*.

However, not everyone considered *Irish Heartbeat* inauthentic. The album was reviewed very well in the rock music press and was a top-twenty hit on the UK pop charts. Dawe cautions against seeing *Irish Heartbeat* as an especially important work: "in his music Morrison invokes too many cultural influences to warrant raising the Chieftains collaboration above all others or to suppose that his sense of cultural identity is synonymous with an Irish nationalist conception."[69] Although Morrison occasionally collaborated with the Chieftains in the 1990s, *Irish Heartbeat* proved to be a sideline in his career rather than a final return home. The albums that followed did not show further interest in Irish traditional music.

Some of Morrison's music of the 1980s appeals to the desire for Ireland as a mystical and therefore safe source of ethnic authenticity. But the bulk of his work continued to fuse blackness and Irishness in an unusual and challenging way. He continued to cover American black music on record and in concert; for example, he covered Ray Charles's "If You Only Knew" on *A Sense of Wonder*, and juxtaposed it with the Irish instrumental "Boffyflow and Spike" by the band Moving Hearts. For Morrison, blackness and Irishness are inseparable rather than comparable. In a trenchant critique of the politics of *Riverdance*, Hazel Carby argues that by juxtaposing ethnicities but presenting them as discrete cultures, the music-and-dance revue implies that different ethnic groups have a history unique to each:

> The effect is to establish a common reference system of human suffering while securing discrete divides between groups of peoples. It is in this sense that the cultural and aesthetic politics of *Riverdance* imagine and present Irishness for global consumption as the story of one successful ethnic group among many, an Irishness to be understood within the frame of reference of multiculturalism. This multiculturalism is now predominantly digested within the frame of reference of corporate images like that of Benneton or Coca-Cola, a combination of numerous discrete cultures each with its own folk forms and roots . . . This global culture without history, I would argue, affirms the importance of national cultural boundaries in the face of their combination into large, corporate controlled, political and economic international entities, like the new Europe, while at the same time denying the internationalism of its peoples and cultures whose actual histories

have been messily intertwined into social, political and economic relations that consistently crossed and recrossed racial and ethnic boundaries and which are embodied in miscegenated cultural forms rather than ethnically pure folk cultures.[70]

Because blackness and Irishness are sonically and thematically tangled at the root of his work, Morrison avoids the *Riverdance* problem of depicting the Irish as one successful ethnic group among many. Even when Morrison is consciously exploring Irishness, he does not — or cannot — separate his relationships with Irishness and black music as distinct experiences. When he returned to Irishness, he did not treat it like an "ethnically pure folk culture," but as an identity understood through black music.

The most compelling music of Morrison's "Irish" period explores his early years in Belfast. Although he had occasionally made reference to Belfast before, in the 1980s he began writing very specifically and positively about his childhood with what Tom Nairn calls "almost unbearable nostalgia."[71] The songs celebrate a return to Ireland via memories of reaching outwards from Belfast to America via black music; his miscegenated ancestors, his "old ones," therefore, are both Irish and black. McLoone argues that Morrison offers "cherished memories of his roots but they are also moments of transcendence — memories of escaping from these roots."[72] Remembering Hyndford Street means remembering what drew him away from Hyndford Street. In "Cleaning Windows" from *Beautiful Vision* (1982), Morrison uses a funk rhythm to tell the story of his early job cleaning windows with his partner Sam. Morrison had left the Orangefield School at fifteen years old, and after unsuccessful jobs as an apprentice fitter at a structural-steel engineering company, a typical trade job for working-class Protestant boys, and in a meat-cleaning factory, he began cleaning windows in his neighborhood. The song infuses the joy and pride of working and making money — "What's my line?/I'm happy cleaning windows . . . I'm a working man in my prime/cleaning windows" — with memories of his work as a musician: "I was blowing saxophone on the weekend/in that down joint" and hearing blues music in his home: "I heard Leadbelly and Blind Lemon/On the street where I was born/Sonny Terry, Brownie McGhee/Muddy Waters singin' 'I'm a

Rolling Stone.'" Morrison here constructs a joyful youth infused with black music; he associates the music with his home and street, thereby making black music an essential element of home.[73] The ballad "Got to Go Back" from *No Guru, No Method, No Teacher* (1986), mixes the expected sentimental Celticism about the importance of returning home to Ireland ("Got my ticket at the airport/Well I guess I've been marking time/I've been living in another country/That operates along entirely different lines/Keep me away from porter or whiskey/Don't play anything sentimental, it'll make me cry") with his memories of listening to Ray Charles at school: "When I was a young boy/Back in Orangefield/I used to gaze out/My classroom window and dream/And then go home and listen to Ray sing 'I believe to my soul' after school/Oh that love that was within me/You know it carried me through." By using an image of transatlantic communication to create an image of "home," Morrison defines black music as both modern and traditional, exotic and homespun.

Morrison returned to the image of radio, but he now gave it a specifically Irish context. In "Wavelength" the radio called him home to America; in "In the Days Before Rock and Roll" from *Enlightenment* (1990) Morrison collaborates with Belfast poet Paul Durcan, whose 1988 essay on Morrison "The Drumshambo Hustler" argued that Morrison's work should be on required reading lists for the Irish Leaving Certificate Poetry Curriculum: "no Irish poet since Kavanagh had produced poetry of the calibre" of thirty Morrison songs.[74] Durcan and Morrison trade verses — Durcan reads, Morrison sings — combining the literary Irishness Morrison had been cultivating and fusing it with his memories of the power of black music. The song memorializes the time before rock and roll, when Morrison was absorbed by radio. It opens with an image of trying to tune in Radio Luxembourg and Armed Forces Network on the radio: "I am down on my knees/At those wireless knobs/Telefunken, Telefunken/And I'm searching for/Luxembourg, Luxembourg,/Athlone, Budapest, AFN,/Hilversum, Helvetia/In the days before rock 'n' roll." Morrison even makes radio-static noises on the record, echoing the static at the opening of "Wavelength," and Georgie Fame's organ part is in Morse code, three dots and three dashes.[75] The radio is a bridge to an outside world: "Fats did not come in/Without those wireless knobs/Elvis did not come in/Without those wireless knobs/Nor Fats, nor Elvis/Nor

Sonny, nor Lightning/Nor Muddy, nor John Lee." Morrison calls out for them: "AFM stars of Jazz/Come in, come in, come in, Ray Charles/Come in, the high priest." Ray Charles, the high priest of music, is here the Celtic Ray, integral to Morrison's memories of Belfast.

Hymns To the Silence (1991) brought all of the strands of the Irish period together — including their contradictions — in a masterful performance. Morrison juxtaposes gospel, poetry, traditional Irish music, jazz, and rhythm and blues in his most complex exploration and creation of his Irishness. The album featured bleak, black-and-white photographs of Hyndford Street empty of people. The songs wallow in authentic images of home and roots, especially musical roots, but ultimately suggest the impossibility of ethnically fixed origins. This is best illustrated by Morrison's version of "I Can't Stop Loving You," backed up by the Chieftains; the song was made famous in 1962 by his R&B hero, Ray Charles, but was a hit on the American country charts. Irish and black music are equally available signifiers of authenticity, but that authenticity is multifarious and impure, a mix of R&B, country, and traditional Irish sounds. Throughout the album, Morrison trades in an authenticity of interdeterminate, multiple sources that productively frustrates the desire for ethnic or national purity. In "Take Me Back" he wants to be taken back "to when the world made more sense," a spiritual moment when he understood God, or "the light," but he explains the feeling by associating it with "the golden afternoon when we sat and listened to Sonny Boy blow." The album also features two gospel songs, "Just a Closer Walk With Thee" and "Be Thou My Vision," songs that Morrison would have heard going to Church of Ireland or Jehovah's Witness services with his mother.[76] He sings a traditional rendition of "Just a Closer Walk With Thee" featuring organ and choir, and then, at the moment when a preacher might launch into a sermon, Morrison weaves in remembrances of his youth:

> See me through days of wine and roses
> By and by when the morning comes
> Jazz and blues and folk, poetry and jazz
> Voice and music, music and no music
> Silence and then voice

Music and writing, words
Memories, memories way back
Take me way back, Hyndford Street and Hank Williams
Louis Armstrong, Sidney Bechet on Sunday afternoons in winter
Sidney Bechet, Sunday afternoons in winter
And the tuning in of stations in Europe on the wireless
Before, yes before it was the way it was
More silence, more breathing together
Not rushing, being
Before rock 'n' roll, before television
Previous, previous, previous
See me through, just a closer walk with Thee

Returning to a nostalgic sense of home means turning to urban, sophisticated uptown music, such as Hank Williams, Louis Armstrong, and Sidney Bechet, for the inspiration of memory. Morrison expresses nostalgia and longing for silence, yet he has equal fondness for raucous, urban American music on the radio; even at his most sentimental, he reaches outside of Belfast.

"On Hyndford Street" from the same album also uses the idea of return (the opening line is "Take me way back") and collects details from a number of his songs over the years, including "Cyprus Avenue" from *Astral Weeks*. Morrison reads the words over synthesized pipe sounds played by Derek Bell of the Chieftains.

Hyndford Street, Abetta Parade
Orangefield, St. Donard's Church
Sunday six-bells, and in between the silence there was conversation
And laughter, and music and singing, and shivers up the back of
    the neck
And tuning in to Luxembourg late at night
And jazz and blues records during the day
Also Debussy on the third programme
Early mornings when contemplation was best
Going up the Castlereagh hills
And the cregagh glens in summer and coming back
To Hyndford Street, feeling wondrous and lit up inside

With a sense of everlasting life
And reading Mr. Jelly Roll and Big Bill Broonzy
And "Really The Blues" by "Mezz" Mezzrow
And "Dharma Bums" by Jack Kerouac

This is both a rural and urban vision, combining Morrison's time in the hills and listening to the radio and records when he is home. The pipes give it a recognizable Irish sound, but that is clearly mixed with the black music celebrated in the lyrics.

The last three lines, however, bring us back to the hall of mirrors that is Morrison's relationship to blackness. Here, Morrison remembers not only listening to black music but reading about it; the reference to "reading" Jelly Roll Morton and Big Bill Broonzy suggests that Morrison had tracked down Broonzy's autobiography *Big Bill's Blues*, which was published in London in 1955, and Alan Lomax's 1949 biography of Morton, *Mr. Jelly Roll*, revealing both his passion for the music and his distance from it. Jack Kerouac, whom Morrison also mentions reading in "Cleaning Windows," had an infamous obsession with African Americans, best summarized in this passage from *On the Road*: "At lilac evening I walked with every muscle aching among the lights of 27th and Welton in the Denver colored section, wishing I were a Negro, feeling that the best the white world had offered was not enough ecstasy for me, not enough life, joy, kicks darkness, music, not enough night."[77] "Mezz" Mezzrow also expressed this desire to be black. Mezzrow was a white jazz clarinetist and saxophonist in the 1920s and 1930s, and published a popular memoir, *Really the Blues*, in 1946. Mezzrow fashioned himself as the ultimate hipster and jazz insider. Indeed, Norman Mailer modeled his concept of the white negro on Mezzrow.[78] Mezzrow's and Kerouac's desire for blackness created an exotic, racist blackness for young readers like Morrison to emulate. When Mezzrow leaves reform school as a teenager, he makes a commitment to be black: "I not only loved those colored boys, but I was one of them—I felt closer to them than I felt to the whites, and I even got the same treatment they got . . . By the time I reached home, I knew that I was going to spend all my time from then on sticking close to Negroes. They were my kind of people. And I was going to learn their music and play it for the rest of my days. I was going to be a musician, a Negro musician, hipping the world about the blues the way only Negroes can."[79]

There's no doubt that Mezz Mezzrow was comfortable among African Americans, and he did significant work in promoting African American musicians (although he was not a good musician himself). But as Gayle Wald argues, "even the sincerest emulation of the qualities with which one invests an Other is not itself necessarily free of self-interest; certainly in Mezzrow's case, it is not free of the objectifying or exoticizing proclivities endemic in the sort of racist representation that, in other contexts, he would have vigorously repudiated."[80]

Morrison's unironic reference to Mezzrow and Kerouac—as we have seen, Morrison name checks only those he admires—questions the politics of his "authentic" use of blackness. He has created a dignified "black" identity in the rhythm of his music, the phrasing of his singing, and his vast knowledge of and respect for black music. But Mezzrow and Kerouac remind us that just because Morrison has avoided the politics of the appropriation of black music does not mean that his work is exempt from those politics. So when he takes the stage in his Blues Brothers outfit, we must consider the status of any "Irish" appropriation of "blackness." I suggest that the crucial difference between Morrison and Kerouac and Mezzrow (and, for that matter, Bono in his *Rattle and Hum* phase and the Commitments), is that Morrison doesn't lay claim to defining black identity—he doesn't use blackness like a commodity he owns, that he can sell to counter his own anxieties. It is often in that love or desire for blackness that blackness is essentialized and made primitive. His humility and desire for musical communication and response is no small matter given the history of white appropriation of black music. Morrison's relationship with black music is more subtle, deeper, and simply more respectful, but it does not exist in a vacuum. It can be used to signify the very simplistic multiculturalism I am suggesting it challenges, in part because Morrison cares little for clarifying the politics of his music.

Which brings us back to Morrison's appearance with President Clinton. Was he chosen to appear because he was a safe, apolitical choice? If so, then is the potential challenge of his music diluted and absorbed by more popular and mainstream versions of Irishness where his blackness becomes an easy multiculturalism? Morrison is now an Irish celebrity; his late-1990s romance with former Miss Ireland Michelle Rocca made him a regular feature in the tabloids, and his legal battles over repairs on his home are covered in the *Irish Times*. Although he is hardly a political figure, he has lent support to some high-profile causes besides the Clinton visit: he marched in Dublin for the divorce referendum in 1995, and contributed a new version of "The Healing Game" to *Across the Bridge of Hope* to raise money for the Omagh Fund in 1998, set up to support victims of the bombing in Omagh, Northern Ireland, that killed twenty-nine people. Except for occasional one-off performances, Morrison has not pursued his experiments with traditional Irish music or New Age music since the 1980s.[81] Morrison's high-profile Irishness has coincided with his most overt exploration of blues, jazz, and R&B in a series of albums of cover songs. *How Long Has This Been Going On* (1995) is an album of primarily jazz covers; *Tell Me Something: The Songs of Mose Allison* (1996) is a tribute to and a collaboration with Allison, the American blues and jazz piano player and songwriter; *The Skiffle Sessions* (2000) is a collaboration with Lonnie Donegan and Chris Barber, two English skiffle stars; and *You Win Again* (2000) is a collaboration with country singer Linda Gail Lewis, featuring country and early songs by Hank Williams, Fats Domino, and Bo Diddley. These rather tame albums—entertaining but not particularly original—coming at a time of highly marketable Irishness, may mean that Morrison's provocative mix of Irishness and blackness can be comfortably appropriated into a safe Irish ethnicity, especially for Irish Americans. But at its best, and taken as a whole, his work reminds us that "miscegenated cultural forms" can offer alternatives to national and corporate definitions of Irishness. He has always sung—or growled—right past these contradictions, creating and claiming affective connections across cultures. Turn it up.

Notes

1. Sinn Fein President Gerry Adams said of Clinton's visit: "It was probably the first popular event that could bring together the hopes and expectations that had been opened up by the cessation of the previous August." Trevor Birney and Julian O'Neill, *When the President Calls* (Derry: Guildhall Press, 1997), 139.

2. Paul Hewson, "The White Nigger," in *Across the Frontiers: Ireland in the 1990s*, edited by Richard Kearney (Dublin: Wolfhound Press, 1988), 190.

3. Hazel Carby, "What Is This 'Black' in Irish Popular Culture?" *European Journal of Cultural Studies* 4, no. 3 (2001): 326.

4. "One Irish Rover" appeared on *No Guru, No Method, No Teacher* (Polydor, 1986); "Irish Heartbeat" on *Inarticulate Speech of the Heart* (Polydor, 1983); "Celtic Ray" on *Beautiful Vision* (Warner Brothers, 1982); and "Celtic Excavation" on *Poetic Champions Compose* (Mercury, 1987).

5. Colin Graham, " '. . . maybe that's just Blarney:' Irish Culture and the Persistence of Authenticity," in *Ireland and Cultural Theory: The Mechanics of Authenticity*, edited by Colin Graham and Richard Kirkland (London: Macmillan, 1999), 9.

6. Ibid., 11.

7. Ibid., 23.

8. Fintan O'Toole, "Meanwhile Back at the Ranch: Images of Ireland and America," in *The Lie of the Land: Irish Identities* (New York: Verso, 1997), 33.

9. Martin McLoone, "From Dublin up to Sandy Row: Van Morrison and Cultural Identity in Northern Ireland," *Causeway* 1, no. 3 (summer 1994): 42.

10. Ibid.

11. Greil Marcus, "Van Morrison," in *Rolling Stone Illustrated History of Rock and Roll*, rev. ed., edited by Jim Miller (New York: Rolling Stone Press, 1980), 322.

12. John Grissim Jr., "Van Morrison: Blue Money & Tupelo Honey," *Rolling Stone*, 22 June 1972, 37.

13. Quoted in Brian Hinton, *Celtic Crossroads: The Art of Van Morrison* (London: Sanctuary Publishing, 1997), 19. In "Choppin' Wood" from *Down the Road* (Polydor, 2002), Morrison tells the story of his father's time in America, which left him dissatisfied when he returned home: "And you came back home to Belfast/So you could be with us like/You lived your life of quiet desperation on the side/Going to the shipyard in the morning on your bike/Well the spark was gone but you carried on."

14. Gerald Dawe, *The Rest Is History* (Newry, Northern Ireland: Abbey Press, 1998), 34.

15. "The McPeakes were a well-known Belfast family with a large repertoire of folk songs. Francey and Francis McPeake, father and son, were also accomplished uilleann pipers. The family had a unique style of harmony singing accompanied by uilleann pipes, not an instrument used for this purpose. In the fifties they were visited by song collectors like Peter Kennedy from BBC radio, and by Pete Seeger who filmed them in Belfast in 1953." Nuala O'Connor, *Bringing It All Back Home: The Influence of Irish Music* (London: BBC Books, 1991), 127.

16. Happy Traum, "The Interview," *Rolling Stone*, 9 July 1970, 31.

17. Until the creation of Radio One, a station dedicated to broadcasting pop music, in 1966, the BBC broadcast very little pop music. Radio Luxembourg broadcast an English-language program every night for five to six hours, featuring a lot of American pop and R&B music. As a result of their success, many pirate radio stations were set up that broadcast from ships outside territorial waters, such as Radio Caroline. See John Hind and Stephen Mosco, *Rebel Radio: The Full Story of British Pirate Radio* (London: Pluto, 1985).

18. Dawe, *The Rest Is History*, 35.

19. See Patrick Humphries, *The Lonnie Donegan Story 1931–2002* (London: Virgin Books, 2004); and Michael Dewe, *The Skiffle Craze* (London: Planet Books, 1998).

20. Van Morrison, interview by Paul Lewis, *Now Dig This*, December 1991, 22–26, <http://www.harbour.sfu.ca/~hayward/van/van/html>.

21. For a history of the showbands, see Vincent Power, *Send 'Em Home Sweatin': The Showband Story* (Dublin: Kildanore Press, 1990).

22. Quoted in Clinton Heylin, *Can You Feel the Silence? Van Morrison: A New Biography* (Chicago: Chicago Review Press, 2003), 30.

23. Alan Clayson, *Call Up the Groups! The Golden Age of British Beat 1962–67* (Poole, England: Blandford, 1985), 168.

24. Mark J. Prendergast, *The Isle of Noises: Rock and Roll's Roots in Ireland* (New York: St. Martin's, 1987), 11.

25. *From a Whisper to a Scream: The Living History of Irish Music*, dir. David Heffernan, Winstar Video, 2001.

26. Hinton, *Celtic Crossroads*, 27.

27. Ibid., 31.

28. John Kelly, "Interview with Van Morrison," *Irish Times*, 11 April 1998.

29. Steve Turner, *Van Morrison: Too Late to Stop Now* (New York: Viking, 1993), 44.

30. Bill Flanagan, *Written in My Soul* (Chicago: Contemporary Books, 1986), 375.

31. Dawe, *The Rest Is History*, 47.

32. A rehearsal set list, probably from 1966, shows how much soul and R&B the band was playing; first set: "Night Train"/"Midnight Hour"/"Let the Good Times Roll"/"Gloria"/"Here Comes the Night"/"Help Me"/"Boom Boom"/"Half as Much"/ "Baby Please Don't Go"/"I'll Go Crazy"; second set: "Stormy Monday"/"Turn on Your Love Light"/"Little Girl"/"Mystic Eyes"/"Good News"/"Stand By Me"/"After It's Too Late"/"Ain't Nothing You Can Do." Turner, *Van Morrison*, 73.

33. Heylin, *Can You Feel the Silence?* 92.

34. Ibid., 79.

35. John Darby, "The Historical Background," in *Northern Ireland: The Background to the Conflict*, edited by John Darby (Belfast: Appletree Press, 1983), 23.

36. Tom Nairn, *Faces of Nationalism: Janus Revisited* (London: Verso, 1997), 158.

37. Dawe, *The Rest Is History*, 44–45.

38. Thomas Hennessey, *A History of Northern Ireland: 1920–1996* (New York: St. Martin's, 1997), 115.

39. Heylin, *Can You Feel the Silence?* 77–78.

40. Niall Stokes, "What's Wrong with This Picture?" *Hot Press*, 28 October 2003.

41. See Brian Dooley, *Black and Green: The Fight for Civil Rights in Northern Ireland and Black America* (London: Pluto Press, 1998).

42. Heylin, *Can You Feel the Silence?* 114.

43. Victoria Clarke, "The Hardest Thinking Man in Showbiz," *Q*, August 2003, 60.

44. Craig Werner, *A Change is Gonna Come: Music, Race & The Soul of America* (New York: Plume, 1999), 87.

45. Ibid., 28

46. See Michael Dunne, "Tore Down a La Rimbaud: Van Morrison's References and Allusions," *Popular Music and Society* 24, no. 4 (2000): 15–29.

47. Many other rock critics have made similar statements emphasizing Morrison's authentic ability with R&B; Lester Bangs writes, "One of the amazing things about Morrison is that he took these natural artistic proclivities and made them work in the context of black American R&B and white British pop music, with no loss of integrity." Liner notes to *Them Featuring Van Morrison* (Parrot BP 71053-4, 1972); Craig Werner describes Morrison as "awash in blues and gospel spirit" (*A Change Is Gonna Come*, 81).

48. Dave Marsh, "Van Morrison," in *The New Rolling Stone Record Guide*, edited by David Marsh and John Swenson (New York: Random House, 1983), 345.

49. Grissim, "Van Morrison," 36.

50. Bangs wrote a superb essay on Morrison's 1968 album *Astral Weeks* in *Stranded: Rock and Roll For a Desert Island*, edited by Greil Marcus (New York: Random House, 1979).

51. Quoted in Hinton, *Celtic Crossroads*, 167.

52. Jonathan Cott, "Van Morrison: The *Rolling Stone* Interview," *Rolling Stone*, 30 November 1978, 52.

53. O'Connor, *Bringing It All Back Home*, 127.

54. Flanagan, *Written in My Soul*, 377.

55. See Cyril Scott, *Music: Its Secret Influence Through the Ages* (London: Rider and Co., 1950).

56. Gerry Smyth, *Space and the Irish Cultural Imagination* (New York: Palgrave, 2001), 170.

57. Quoted in Hinton, *Celtic Crossroads*, 304.

58. "Before the World Was Made" was released on *Too Long in Exile* (1993); "Crazy Jane on God" was recorded for *A Sense of Wonder* (1985), but the Yeats estate did not grant permission for the song to be used. It was eventually released on *The Philosopher's Stone* (1998), a collection of previously unreleased studio tracks.

59. In "You Don't Pull No Punches But You Don't Push the River" on *Veedon Fleece* (1974), Morrison mixes his passions for mystic poets and soul music in the image of "William Blake and the Eternals, oh standin' with the Sisters of Mercy," suggesting Blake fronting a big soul revue, with female backup singers.

60. Flanagan, *Written in My Soul*, 377.

61. Quoted in Hinton, *Celtic Crossroads*, 260.

62. Turner, *Van Morrison*, 149.

63. John Connell and Chris Gibson, *Sound Tracks: Popular Music, Identity and Place* (New York: Routledge, 2003), 203.

64. Natasha Casey, "*Riverdance*: The Importance of Being Irish American," *New Hibernia Review* 6, no. 4 (2002): 14.

65. Quoted in Heylin, *Can You Feel the Silence?* 415.

66. Ibid., 416.

67. Ibid., 418.

68. Ibid., 418.

69. Dawe, *The Rest Is History*, 44.

70. Carby, "What Is This 'Black'?" 330.

71. Nairn, *Faces of Nationalism*, 157.

72. McLoone, "From Dublin up to Sandy Row," 42.

73. The street imagery comes up again in "The Street Only Knew Your Name" from *Inarticulate Speech of the Heart* (Polydor, 1983) — previously recorded in 1975 — where he describes the street as key to a sense of identity: "Your street, rich or poor/You should always be sure of your street/There's a place in your heart, when you know from the start/And you can't be complete without a street."

74. Paul Durcan, "The Drumshanbo Hustler," *Magill*, May 1988, 56.

75. Fame told an interviewer, "You always used to get that Morse code interference on the radio when you'd be trying to tune it in, you'd pick up the ships. It was all completely out of time, but it fitted." Hinton, *Celtic Crossroads*, 297.

76. Morrison's father did not attend church but his mother was something of a spiritual seeker. For the best account of his mother's religious background, see Heylin, *Can You Feel the Silence?*; and Turner, *Van Morrison*.

77. Jack Kerouac, *On the Road* (New York: Penguin, 1956), 180.

78. See Norman Mailer, *The White Negro* (San Francisco: City Lights Books, 1957).

79. Mezz Mezzrow, *Really the Blues* (New York: Random House, 1946), 18.

80. Gayle Wald, "Mezz Mezzrow and the Voluntary Negro Blues," in *Race and the Subject of Masculinities*, edited by Harry Stecopoulos and Michael Uebel (Durham, N.C.: Duke University Press, 1997), 119.

81. For example, he recorded "Tá mo Cleamhnas Déanta" with the Chieftains (*Éist: Songs in their Native Language*, 1998); "Shenandoah" with the Chieftains on the soundtrack to *The Irish in America: Long Journey Home*, 1998; and a new version of "St. Dominic's Preview" on *Sult: Spirit of the Music*, a broadcast from the Irish-language TV station TnaG, now known as TG Ceathair.

MARY McGLYNN

Garth Brooks in Ireland, or,
Play That Country Music, Whiteboys

In 1997, Ireland's GDP expanded nearly 11 percent, its largest growth rate during the boom known as the Celtic Tiger. That year, Ireland's relative purchasing power exceeded the EU average, meaning that its citizens experienced a higher standard of living than the average European consumer.[1] Unemployment was for the first time lower than in the EU.[2]

In the same year for which these figures would suggest a prosperous, thriving nation, Garth Brooks sold more albums in Ireland than any other human being.[3] That May, Brooks sold out in Croke Park in Dublin three nights in a row. Three months later, on 7 August, 800,000 Garth Brooks fans converged in New York's Central Park, a crowd rivaling those that turned out to see the pope in 1995 and the Dalai Lama in 2003. Although New York City did not itself have a country music radio station anymore, devotees in concert t-shirts easily recognized each song by its opening notes, singing along and dancing, whether they watched live or on one of the closed-circuit televisions set up for overflow crowds. According to Nielsen, a further seven million viewers watched the live concert on HBO, the network dramatically pairing the New York and Dublin tour stops on billboards that read "One Man, Two Nations," creating an image of Garth Vader, the imperial destroyer.

Country, a musical genre more identifiably "American" than any other, flourished in Ireland throughout the twentieth century, even as that music itself evolved.[4] Brooks first hit the Billboard charts in 1989, at a time when country music barely registered on the American cultural consciousness, but by 1996, 42 percent of all American radio listeners tuned in to country—70 million people.⁵ Brooks's songs, which draw on rock and pop influences, depict a world of fun-loving people who aren't afraid to let their softer sides show, people happy with the simple pleasures in life, a change from earlier country lyrics of betrayal and heartbreak. In his reviving—and reshaping—of country music, Brooks outsold Elvis, Michael Jackson, and Billy Joel, sitting second only to the Beatles in all-time album sales.⁶ Both his message and his particular style of music hit a chord (so to speak) in the United States and in Ireland, raising the question of what kinds of shared sensibilities in the two cultures Brooks gave expression to.

The ease with which Garth found a niche in Irish pop culture speaks to the cross-fertilization of U.S. and Irish cultures, suggesting that each national self-image was reinforced by his persona; his popularity tells us about how Ireland constructs both itself and the nation to which it has exported so many citizens. This intertwining of U.S. and Irish cultures begins as far back as their shared colonial status under the British Empire, their shared gene pool via massive immigrations beginning over 300 years ago and still in motion, and, in the twentieth and twenty-first centuries, their mutual constitution of one another via cultural depictions and products. While the most widely circulating images of Irishness in the United States lean toward luck, loquacity, and liquor, and Irish sketches of the American character involve brashness, cash, and bustle, each nation has relied on the other as a repository of a variety of conflicting and overlapping images. As Fintan O'Toole would have it, "America and Ireland represent not opposites, not a dialogue of modernity and tradition, but a continual intertwining in which far from Ireland being the past and America being the future, America can constitute Ireland's past and Ireland can invent America's future. When we deal with this relationship, we are dealing not with something final and closed, but with something obsessive, repetitive, continually unfinished, all the time renewing itself in old ways."⁷

The Irish journalist Olivia O'Leary remarked on her BBC program in 1999 that "poor, Gaelic, Catholic Ireland has . . . an unholy interest in making money and a level of US investment so massive that some people call it the 51st state."⁸ Contrary to O'Toole's formulation, O'Leary's characterizations of both the United States and Ireland in this remark draw

1. The Irish embrace of Garth Brooks in the 1990s worked to set aside earlier images of Ireland in favor of a prosperous modernity and transatlantic commonality.

on long-standing (and diametrically opposed) stereotypes, of Ireland as the land of saints and sages, and of America as the land of opportunity, noting the massive change in Ireland's economic fortunes in the 1990s. Beginning the decade as one of the poor country cousins of the European Union, by the mid-1990s Ireland had the fastest-growing economy in Europe, due in large part to American investment. By 1999, Oliver O'Connor would observe that "over 25 per cent of US manufacturing investment in the EU is in the Republic. Nearly half our exports are by US multinationals. The US is our largest single source of investment, with more than 500 companies employing more than 74,500 people, that is, 70 per cent of those employed in IDA-supported companies and about 7.5 per cent of total private sector employment."[9] The growing American industrial presence translated directly into prosperity for a large percentage of the Irish population.

While cultural observers bemoan the apparently uncritical absorption of American elements into Irish daily life, economists and the public at large see at least two sides to such perceived contamination. Historically, Ireland linked politics and religion, as epitomized by the primness and patriotism of its first president, Eamonn De Valera; now, as Conor McCarthy identifies it, the faith in modernity is dominant in contemporary Irish public life. McCarthy critiques this faith for inaccurately polarizing nationalism and modernity and for its sanguine view of the processes of modernization: "Modernisation theory envisages this process as taking place largely smoothly . . . in a consensual manner."[10] Indeed, a Republic citizenry wary of the claims of nationalism over the last thirty years has welcomed American products as emblems of the mastery of modern life, as evidence of progress from the perceived backwardness of the De Valera days.

What the public endorses through wearing clothes from the Gap and Ralph Lauren, economists have embraced through interpretations of Ireland's economic growth that credit open markets and foreign investment, faulting circumscribed ambitions and inward-looking nationalism for the series of setbacks to prosperity that came in the wake of each earlier (and always short-lived) economic boom. Philip O'Connell differentiates the late eighties interpretations of Ireland's ongoing economic weaknesses, suggesting that the "culturalist interpretation" of Joe Lee looks to "factors inherent to the society: Analyzing the divergent interpretations generated by scholars in the late 1980s of Ireland's (then) ongoing economic weakness, Philip O'Connell identifies two general paradigms, one attributing economic travails to external factors such as Ireland's peripheral geographic and economic positions, with the other seeing internal causes. O'Connell casts the latter viewpoint as a "culturalist interpretation," which explains Ireland's listless economy via "factors inherent to the society: national institutions which reward mediocrity, an inability to harness intellectual resources, and failings of national character and identity."[11] Other commentators look to external factors such as Ireland's peripheral geographic and economic positions. According to J. Peter Clinch, Frank Convery, and Brendan Walsh, once the country left behind its "bad economic policies — the continuation of protectionist trade policies into the late 1950s and irresponsible fiscal experimentation in the late 1970s . . . it was well positioned to attract foreign direct investment from the booming US economy and quickly, if belatedly, catch up with the world's richest countries." If a new national mindset had been responsible for a weak economy, it was replaced by an outlook perceived to be less Irish and therefore more financially savvy.[12] As Ireland's economic fortunes have improved (declining slightly as the Internet-era Celtic Tiger proved unsustainable), repeated self-investigation in the Irish press has revealed anxiety about the Americanization of the nation, from outrage over O'Leary's remarks to concerns about the "steady diet of mediocre American culture" offered on television.[13]

This importation of American culture in Ireland, for all its current pervasiveness, reverses centuries of cultural dissemination in the opposite direction. Throughout the settling of North America and the early decades of the United States, Scottish and Irish immigrants came to the American South to work as overseers on plantations or as small farmers on the ever-expanding frontier. As these regions came to be associated with poverty and backwardness, so did their music—the bluegrass, hillbilly, and folk tunes that evolved in part from Celtic immigrants. Certainly the racial tensions that permeate(d) politics and culture in the South underlie much southern music as well, growing as it did out of interwoven racial traditions. At the end of the nineteenth century and the beginning of the twentieth, for instance, early aficionados of American folk music feared the eclipse of the folk tradition by modernization, equating folk with Anglo-Saxon origins: "The Anglo-Saxon rural peasantry was presumed to be disappearing, through urban migration, adjustment to industrial occupations, increasing literacy, and intermarriage with outsiders, and this meant the disappearance of the purest forms of American folklore."[14] The faith in the South as "a repository of traditional values" is one element that remained constant through the variety of manifestations that southern music adopted throughout the twentieth century.[15] Another recurring feature was the effort to incorporate and resolve two seemingly contradictory elements of the frontier lifestyle—the individualism and self-reliance of the pioneer, the cowboy, and their descendants, and their love of the land, and by extension, the nation.

Country music was not the only genre that grew out of southern traditional music, but its recurrent popularity since its inception as country and western marks it as a crucial articulation of American values and norms. Again, these principles have often been contradictory; country embraced both the hillbilly uprightness of the Carter family and the rough edges of Hank Williams and honky-tonk. According to the 2003 BBC documentary *Lost Highway*, as the recording industry took shape in Nashville, part of what country was seeking to escape was its "juke joint" reputation of drunkenness and sensuality. Moreover, country-western performers, as early as the 1930s, dressed in western garb to conceal the music's lower-class background. Gene Autry, for example, performed early on in a suit, but it wasn't until he donned a cowboy hat that he made it big: in his article subtitled "From Hillbillies to Cowboys," Peter Stanfield argues that performing in a dress suit spoke too directly to a "man desperately trying to escape the confines of his class. [But] where the suit failed him, the stetson saved him: as a cowboy, Autry transcended any notion of class."[16] The myth of the West firmly and convincingly recapitulates the land-of-opportunity rhetoric that the United States has always used to elide its own class distinctions; furthermore, in the wake of the Great Depression, it was soothing to evoke a prelapsarian West and its "comforting symbolism of independence."[17] "In the 30s, part of the cowboy's appeal was that he carried none of the overt race or class consciousness of the hillbilly or his white trash cousin, yet through deed and action he supported the concept of Anglo-Saxon superiority whilst being incontestably American in origin."[18] Bill Malone suggests that the cowboy was "a latter-day Anglo-Saxon knight."[19]

As rock and roll and the cultural revolution of the sixties came to dominance, country music saw a decline. The squeaky-clean image proffered by Nashville was out of step with the national appetite and its conception of the South, which was better affirmed by such southern rock groups as the Allman Brothers Band and Lynyrd Skynyrd. More traditional in their sound, "outlaw" singers like Waylon Jennings and Willie Nelson modernized country, paradoxically, by reintroducing the "rebellious, untamed, even countercultural aspects" of cowboy culture.[20] *Urban Cowboy* and crossover successes like Barbara Mandrell and Kenny Rogers boosted the popularity of clean-shaven country—what Richard A. Peterson refers to as "soft shell" country.[21] But by the late eighties, country suffered the likes of such songs as Hank Williams Jr.'s "If The South Woulda Won." With defiantly retrograde lyrics ("If the South woulda won we woulda had it made . . . We'd put Florida on the right track, 'cause we'd take Miami back and throw all them pushers in the slammer . . . I'd have all the cars made in the Carolinas and I'd ban all the ones made in China"), country music revealed too blatantly the racial politics and economic anxieties of those not privy to the eighties boom. Working-class whites concerned about the direction of the nation found kindred spirits in country, which ended up sinking back into its lower-class associations, no longer the Ozarks but the trailer park. Hank Williams Sr. might have had to don a cowboy hat to lose lower-class resonances, but Hank Williams Jr. signifies the lower class in much the same getup. The fact that the costume was basically unchanged over the span of fifty years pointed out the conservatism underlying country music by the 1980s and evoked an image of an "independent, unsophisticated, and tough creature" known as the "Confederate male."[22]

Yet, by the late nineties, the Country Music Association awards were being televised in prime-time network slots. Country Grammys used to be given out during commercials, but in 2004, Allison Krauss, winner of the award for best country instrumental performance, performed during the show. More tellingly, at the 2004 People's Choice Awards, which rely on Gallup poll data to determine America's favorites, five of the nine nominees in "Favorite Musician" categories (male performer, female performer, and group or band) hailed from the country charts. In its rise to prominence, new country seems to many traditionalists to have compromised the very qualities that gave it an identity distinct from other forms of popular music. "Country music, once the voice of a distinct minority in America—working-class Southerners—had become the voice of the new American majority: middle-class suburbanites. No longer about one particular place, country music had become about *every* place."[23] Yet *Lost Highway* argues that Garth Brooks is born of the same rejection of Nashville as such antiestablishment country musicians as Dwight Yoakam and Ryan Adams. Because he breaks out of rigid forms, Brooks is seen even by some within country's counterculture as part of the rebellion. But Brooks's revolution places country alongside pop, making room for Shania Twain and the Dixie Chicks; his insurgency takes on rock and roll rather than remaining distinct from it. Trisha Yearwood suggests in *Lost Highway* that Brooks builds on the legacy of Kiss and glam rock: "He took the barriers of country music and he busted them . . . he turned the show part into a show and kept the music country." Indeed, Brooks has been known to smash guitars, rock star–style, and in 2000, his all-time album sales surpassed 100 million copies, making him the best-selling solo artist ever. No longer the dowdy country cousin, contemporary country represents a major economic and cultural force.

Reaction to this force is vehement at times: the most popular of what are disparagingly called "hat acts," Brooks has been labeled plastic for his costume of Stetsons and super-starched shirts and for his slick publicity machine.[24] Most interviews refer to the fact that he has a degree in marketing; that a country star went to college at all is no longer a notable detail. And indeed, when his first album was released, Brooks shrewdly secured a whole year's promotion budget. His portrait of the South is of the technologically progressive Sun Belt, his shows known for their high-tech special effects. He walks through fire onstage, flies over the crowd, and wears a cordless microphone. While old country music evoked images of the West to conceal its undesirable southernness, contemporary country is no longer ashamed of the South; that is to say, contemporary country has redefined the south as modern, suburban, and middle class.

How much did country shake its image, and how much did America return to country's values, to the values of the Old West, and of the old westerns? As Bruce Feiler argued in 1996, country is "much more clearly about core American values than anything coming out of Seattle or New York in the last ten years [creating] one of the most vivid examples of America's reigning backlash against its own culturally liberal past."[25] Feiler aptly identifies the way that country music's rise has paralleled a resurgence in conservatism in the United States and emphasizes that today's lyrics, if they mention social issues at all, focus on the domestic—spousal abuse, alcoholism, etc. In suggesting that country used to have a more political edge he downplays its trajectory of upward mobility. The change isn't in the scope, a move from social to personal—as the valorization of the individual has remained a constant through all of country's manifestations—but in attitude: before, if you were supposed to stand by your man or walk the line, it was a hard-edged, painful, gutsy thing to do, what Barbara Ching and others term "hard country" and Erwin Panofsky would characterize as "hard primitivism."[26] New country wants you to stay with your spouse, too, but it's supposed to feel natural and right, and it's part of a larger picture of national conformity. The individual used to be an outcast at some level, but now, we're all individuals in pretty much the same way.

The idea that country lyrics have universal meaning, "the bland insistence that the music represents us all,"[27] seems like a harmless enough cliché about lyrics that often appear innocuous in themselves, but there are gender, class, and racial subtexts at play that make the personal political. "In order to reconcile America's democratic ideals with the politics of indirect exclusion, conservatives have contested previously dominant cultural codes and liberal assumptions related to the pursuit of racial equality," Amy Ansell argues, suggesting the emergence of a new racism that "operates on the basis of ideas such as individual rights and color blindness, denying that it is a theory about race at all, its principles all the while serving to justify the retreat from racial justice in thought and policy."[28] In part by putting distance between itself and openly racist groups, it is "a new form of racism that operates without prejudice, and even without the category race. It is a new form of exclusionary politics that operates indirectly and in stealth via the rhetorical inclusion of people of color and the sanitized nature of its racist appeal."[29] While there is no reason to assume that Brooks himself is a racist, his songs and persona delineate an America of individuals and draw on the rhetoric of Ansell's new Right, reinforcing the image of a tolerant, postracial society. " 'We Shall Be Free,' one of his [Brooks's] concert anthems, is a message of tolerance said to have been written after he witnessed the Los Angeles race riots."[30] In casually relying on the term "race riots" in interviews, Brooks endorses a reading of the 1992 disturbances that distances people without a "race problem" (i.e., white people, who show "tolerance") from the uncontrolled other.

Brooks's song makes a treacly, sincere pitch for free speech, freedom of religion, and general social justice, concepts widely seen as desirable. He echoes Martin Luther King Jr., stating that we shall be free "when the last thing we notice is the color of skin/And the first thing we look for is the beauty within," advocating a society that has moved beyond constructions of race: "when there's only one race and that's mankind." In hailing a colorblind society, Brooks opens up a space for those who would like to move beyond questions of race now. As Ansell alleges, "the new racism is couched within, not against, America's civil religion, taking on the vocabulary of equal opportunity, color blindness, race neutrality, and above all, individualism and individual rights."[31] Similarly, Feiler seeks to explain the absence of black country performers and audiences by suggesting that "country music has become yet another example of a widening racial gulf in American culture . . . its voluntary segregation."[32] This explanation disavows any racist intent and instead emphasizes the free choice of individual black and white consumers to have different cultural preferences.

Indeed, the lyrics to "American Honky-Tonk Bar Association," one of Brooks's rowdier tunes, make explicit how he conceives of his audience, as "the hardhat/Gunrack, achin'-back/Over-taxed, flag-wavin', fun-lovin' crowd," a series of characterizations that speak to a lower middle-class, nonurban, Republican mindset. Coded reference is made to race when the song complains about the way that "your dollar goes to all of those/Standing in a welfare line." Where earlier country songs would assume the perspective of less affluent Americans, Brooks's lyrics repeatedly locate him and his audience in the mainstream middle class, promoting what Feiler calls "fanfare for the reconciled," an acceptance of the status quo. Thus the power of lines like "and as she [the speaker's ex-girlfriend] walked away and I looked at my wife/And then and there I thanked the good Lord/For the gifts in my life." The song is called "Unanswered Prayers" and accepts the less sexy way life has turned out, rejoices in the path more traveled by. The Brooks canon repeatedly reaffirms its core values of monogamy, religion, and family. Country lyrics today, and Brooks's especially, are geared not to the loner of the Old West but to bedroom communities and family values, the message being to accept what you have, love God, and drink less in the collective universal suburb of American mass culture. If the Old West and country music were about isolated outcasts, the new West and its new soundtrack, Garth Brooks, are about isolated "incasts." Mainstream values have become insular, advocating the values, even the nobility, of individual conformists.

One of Brooks's most popular songs, "Friends in Low Places," crystallizes the social values of new country: "Blame it all on my roots/ I showed up in boots/And ruined your black-tie affair." The narrator's background—his roots—is implicated in his inappropriate behavior, while the "black-tie affair" comes across as artificial and pretentious. The narrator occupies a middle ground, neither roots nor black tie. He refers to "that ivory tower/That you're livin' in" and the way that he can get just as high as this lofty tower with a few drinks. The woman he appears to address here is figured as upper-class and immobile, whereas the male narrator can move from group to group.[33] On the live album, Brooks has his fans sing the final verse, in which the narrator asks his ex-girlfriend to "kiss my ass." Brooks himself is silent here, introducing the audience by saying he's going to let his "friends in low places sing." This is Garth: he's no snob, not "big on social graces," avoids the "ivory tower"; but he's also not in the low places personally. He's willing to associate with the lower class but is really in a middle place himself. Country is trying to move away from its working-class background, but still willing to use it as a challenge to the intelligentsia.[34] The in-betweenness has particular resonance in the way that Brooks figures his audience as the friends in low places, inviting the crowd to sing with just that invocation. In an interview whose transcript is included on the Planet Garth website, Brooks says that the audience participation gives those in the crowd the chance to be "the person they always wanted to be. Hell they're up there center mic and stage and it's them that sang it, it ain't me. I can't hear myself, they're all just singing the words and they take over the song and it's theirs," crucially at the moment that it is most crude. By displacing the lower-class elements of his lyrics onto his fans while maintaining an accessible vernacular, Brooks (regardless of his actual economic position) asserts his own space in a middle class that draws on the ethos of southern white conservatism.

How the Irish Became Country

It is this compromise—between upward mobility and working-class roots, between pop and country, between the myth of the West and the lifestyle of the suburbs—which makes Garth Brooks such a comfortable fit for so many Irish fans. By contrast, contemporary Irish pop music is likely to articulate concepts and claims counter to suburban family values: When U2's Bono disrupted the Grammy telecast in 1994, announcing that he intended to "fuck the mainstream," Garth Brooks followed up with a speech taking offense at this pledge. "The message I would send to the youth is not to screw up the mainstream . . . but work with it to make it what you want." Brooks employs the rhetoric of inclusion, using the idea of the mainstream as a way to attack the supposed cultural elite, a position that found easy acceptance in Ireland. At the time of his greatest popularity in the American imagination, Garth outsold Celine Dion and even U2 in Ireland. To better understand Brooks's popularity in Ireland, it is necessary briefly to trace the history of country music and the ethos of the Old West there.

At the dawn of the twentieth century, Ireland was in the midst of a cultural revival and nationalist resurgence, with Celtic flutes and harps and fiddles popularized for the urban middle classes. By the 1920s, as Ireland became a nation once again, its borders closed to many outside influences, the biggest signs of American culture in many villages were the empty houses of the recently emigrated. But the Ireland envisioned at this time by De Valera was to be especially pious, and so the traditional dances held in homes and at crossroads were banned as immoral and bookshelves were relieved of the impropriety of Joyce and Beckett.[35] By the mid-forties, big band music was ascendant, legally sanctioned by the government and priests alike in a way that *seisúns* of traditional music were not. As a consequence, groups known as showbands began to tour the Irish countryside, covering big band and early rock music tunes so that locals could dance in chaste, acceptable forms. Young people gathered in dancehalls, men on one side of the room, women on the other, the performances upholding a reputation for moral innocence, temperance, and good, clean fun. Because "the slick, sophisticated, highly polished sounds of the best showbands were difficult to emulate . . . [whereas] country music was simple and almost anyone could play it,"[36] a hybrid genre known as country and Irish emerged, its apex coming as over 700 touring bands entertained rural communities nationwide in the mid-sixties.[37]

While purists decried the supposed degeneration from the showband to country music, both showbands and the country-and-Irish scene appeared to their fans to offer access to the sort of glamour that had long been alien to the Irish countryside. Now derided as tacky and derivative, in the "ballad boom" of the sixties these musicians epitomized a blend of local and international cultures, often taking names that linked them to the emergent sounds in Britain and the United States: the name the Plattermen echoed the doo-wop group the Platters; the Polka Dots evoked the Ink Spots. In translating this music onto an Irish scene, performers by default rendered it white, a fact made racially charged by such band names as the Dixies, for a band from Cork.

The reference to Dixie evokes the American South, but it was far more common in Irish culture in the 1960s for references to the United States to be to the Old West. Romantic portrayals of the American West entered the Irish imagination via country music, cowboy novels, and western films. The eastern coast of Ireland, and Dublin in particular, has long been perceived as the site of colonialism, modernity, and stuffy propriety, while the west, the more remote the better, has represented Celtic Ireland, vital, bawdy Ireland, authentic Ireland. The American West and the Irish one were seen as similar in origin and mindset, both resisting the encroachment of external, urban forces of modernization and capitalism. The two Wests were seen in Ireland as interchangeable, both affirming lawlessness, an antigovernment attitude, and a deep, organic connection to the land. Throughout the midcentury decades, Ireland looked to its own past and America's, overlapping them in a romanticized myth: the immigrant roots of Jesse James were emphasized in Ireland, all the western motifs working together to reinforce the notion of the West as something that both nations experienced and understood—Ireland doubly, via its participation in America's West as well as in its own.

In the face of these overlaps and appropriations, Luke Gibbons has made a very convincing argument about the differences between the two Wests: while the American West is about individualism, he argues, the Irish West is figured as collective.[38] The best way to see this is to compare films about the two Wests—1952's *The Quiet Man*, say, whose rich American hero returns to Ireland to integrate into what appears to be a warm, vibrant rural Irish farming community, versus *Shane* (1953), whose American hero helps farmers then rides off alone. To Gibbons, this distinction between the collective and the individual overrides all the surface similarities of the two Wests.

While Gibbons's reading of the individual in the western usefully throws the Irish West into contrast, a further modification is required. Throughout the genre, though many heroes disappear into the sunset or die for their cause, Douglas Pye has argued that the tension between settlement and wilderness is not resolved in favor of isolation as often as

Gibbons might suggest. Rather, "the hero's in-between position enacts a battle between the pulls of isolation and separateness and of relationship and community, a conflict which can have no definitive resolution."[39] Pye goes on to suggest that as the western evolves, and particularly as its post-war optimism is replaced by Vietnam-era anxiety, the troubled, flawed loner becomes the emblematic hero.

Perhaps a burgeoning sense of individualism, borne of resistance to the collectivism of nation and religion, explains why through the 1950s and 1960s, western films were so eagerly consumed in Ireland, reenacted by little Irish boys the same as little American ones. Recent criticism and fiction has sought to reveal the impact of American cultural products on Irish communities at the time; the protagonists of both Roddy Doyle's 1993 novel *Paddy Clarke Ha ha ha* and Patrick McCabe's 1992 novel *The Butcher Boy* are obsessed with the Old West.[40] Paddy's access comes via the television version of the old western *The Virginian*, which offers images of happy couples in a way that his home life cannot. *The Butcher Boy* likewise shows the wistfulness behind 1950s and 1960s consumption of American popular culture; the social outcast Francie Brady's happiest memories are of "John Wayne moments" in his life. To the small boy with little grasp of reality, Wayne represents not an American past, but his own past, which turns out to be as illusory and unrecoverable as the West of Wayne movies: as reality closes in on him, a mental hospital for the criminally insane looming, he says that "the tie [I wore] was real John Wayne style but I says there's to be no more about John Wayne or any of that, that's all over. Everything's changed now it's all new things."[41] Like the singing cowboys of the 1930s, Francie sees a western identity as a way to escape the confines of his class status; his reading of the western also locates it in the past.

John Ford himself—of Irish birth and a self-proclaimed bilingual (another cultural invention)—suggested that the Irish have a particular affinity for westerns: "Who better than an Irishman could understand the Indians, while still being stirred by the tales of the US cavalry? We were on both sides of the epic."[42] What Ford suggests here is that Ireland's colonial heritage and nationalist conflicts prime its citizens to read the western onto their own lives. Fintan O'Toole uses the term *Irish Indians*—the savages of Europe cross the ocean and find themselves the cowboys.[43] *Into the*

West (1992) treats this issue with subtlety, as Elizabeth Butler Cullingford has pointed out, characterizing the Irish as both cowboy and cavalry, and the travelers as cowboy and Indian. While the two young heroes of the film, members of the ostracized caste of Irish Travellers, cast themselves as cowboys in their efforts to free a horse from a succession of corrupt owners, "the film tests and gradually discredits [this] assumption," instead highlighting the racist treatment the boys receive from the settled Irish, a move that inverts the long-standing association of the Irish with nonwhite peoples and instead renders them white oppressors.[44] Of equal significance is how the film "emphasize[s] the fact that . . . the travelers and their horses are anachronisms."[45] The community viewing the world through the lens of the western is, like the genre, displaced to the past.

While the west of Ireland moved into modernity, the memory of its past was kept alive by those in Dublin and even more via emigrants. Those who had left behind a primitive rural economy came to idealize it as authentic and unchanging, romanticizing their homeland. Much as American country had temporary urban success in the 1930s with displaced southerners longing for the heartland, country programming that failed in Mayo still drew huge audiences in Dublin: "country-and-western music imported into Ireland from America is itself not so much an aspect of modernity as of nostalgia, a part of the dynamics of memory and displacement . . . When Irish people yearn for America they may not yearn for an America of the present but an America of the past . . . The Irish country people in the city wanted to listen to country-and-western because it reminded them of their past, and that image of the past was American."[46] As the Irish economy improved, country music came to be seen by the younger generations as "for the old folks," for those in country and farming communities. Country music came to embody authenticity and the past, Irish and American elements merging.

Garth in Ireland

While listeners in earlier decades sought nostalgia from their country music, Brooks's contemporary audiences seem to seek out songs that speak to their everyday lives, both in the United States and in Ireland. Yet Brooks's own construction of Ireland relies on precisely this sort of wistfulness for a bygone era. In a telephone news conference to promote a 1998 NBC special, "Ireland and Back," covering his 1994 tour of Ireland, Brooks distanced himself from pop music: "The singer, who has been criticized by some traditional country fans, said he 'appreciates the respect we get from pop and rock,' but added, 'let's face it, there's not that much cutting-edge look to our stuff . . . Make no mistake, I never want to be anything other than country music.' "[47] While in other circumstances Brooks is less absolute in his allegiance to country, his denial of his pop heritage occurs in an Irish context, intimating his own construction of Ireland and country music as shared sites of tradition. Brooks said he was "impressed" by Ireland because "as soon as you get there (it's) so comfortable . . . your fists become unclenched, your defenses aren't up."[48] Various interviews also emphasize Brooks's Irish roots—his mother's grandmother, it seems, is from county Cork, and Brooks suggests that his mother and the Irish people share "an undying spirit of hope—anything is possible," precisely the sentiment he articulates in his 1995 song "Ireland." His assertion of Ireland as a repository of traditional values in the song dovetails with the account of it as his mother's homeland in casting the nation as a site of authenticity.

But Brooks's music is "real" in another way as well. The way that the music of Garth Brooks resolves conflict between high and low, urban and western, is suggestive of an Irish understanding of and simultaneous wariness of a postcolonial stance. In 1991 Jimmy Rabbitte could claim that Ireland was "a Third World country" in the film version of *The Commitments* (set during the economic downturn and unemployment of the eighties), echoing a decade of debate about Ireland's status; books about the Irish economy at that time bore such titles as *Ireland in Crisis: A Study in Capitalist Colonial Underdevelopment* (1986), *Facing the Unemployment Crisis in Ireland* (1993), and *The Irish Disease and How to Cure It: Common-Sense Economics for a Competitive World* (1995).[49] Almost overnight, however, the book titles have changed—*From Famine to Feast* (1998) and *Bust to Boom?* (2000)—and the GDP is growing at a healthy rate—the quick turnaround creating a doubleness of status in much the way that whiteness and postcoloniality can, making the western a compatible form and the ethos that Brooks's music in particular appeared to represent reassuring.[50] Not only did America embody contradiction and compromise, but Brooks's music reads such doubleness as, to rework Diane Negra's formulation, "a set of tropes about what white masculinity looks like and is."

Beyond the embrace of in-betweenness lies another layer of Brooks's appeal—recall Ford's dictum about experiencing both sides of the epic. Richard Laytie and Christopher T. Whelan noted that in Ireland "between 1987–94 growth was observed predominantly in the professional and managerial class with a corresponding decline in the manual sector. As a consequence it is among the latter that we observe a striking increase in upward mobility and proportionate decline in downward mobility."[51] Taken in conjunction with the relative prosperity of Irish consumers and the across-the-board increase of Irish educational attainment, what we saw emerging in Ireland in the mid-1990s was a middle class of a size and character radically different from what came before it. Class begins to be measured more by economic factors than social ones—that is, income matters more than profession. Moreover, the middle class now outnumbers those above and below it, and country music is seen now as their soundtrack, what is often called in Ireland "middle of the road" music. Such music is cast by its fans and marketers as in step with mainstream values not understood by the educated and privileged. One suggestion that the intelligentsia is out of touch came from Senator Donie Cassidy, in making an application in 1999 to launch a country music station in Ireland, when he remarked that "the people in the Dublin 4 area do not know what is happening in the world of country music and Irish recording artists."[52]

O'Toole wrote in 1984 about the spate of ranch-style houses beginning to appear on rural roads, arguing that their mentality demonstrated a "perfect compromise between consumerist individualism and the desire to stay put in your own place, between the new values and the old."[53] More recently, Hugo Hamilton has commented on the "Dallas style architecture which has sprung up all across the country," mentioning country music as well in his catalogue of "anything that moved us away from the stifling post colonial atmosphere of the 1950s."[54] The American-style homes, all of frontier-style design, like the American music of Brooks, reveal an Irish middle class comfortable with American ideals and values. In patterning themselves on the American middle class, Brooks's Irish listeners embraced a modernity with conservative racial and cultural politics. As Conor McCarthy suggests, the assumption that the "move from tradition to modernity is socially, economically and politically positive and progressive" relies on a self-congratulatory belief in an enlightened present.[55]

Such a shift in class dynamics is suggestive of why Ireland likes Garth Brooks. But why he likes Ireland also factors in his popularity there, and reasserts the question of which nation imaginatively constitutes and configures the other. On the Planet Garth website, fans are able to enter reviews of concerts they attended in Brooks's world tour. Steven Walsh describes "something special" the front of the crowd at Croke Park was invited to do in 1997: "Garth was filming 'The River' for his new live album and video and wanted to ride on the crowd on top of our outstretched hands . . . He asked us not to take his hat or his mic. and to stay off his zipper region.:-) We carried him out into the crowd . . . He said he trusted the Irish crowd enough to do it and said he wouldn't have been able to do that anywhere else."[56]

There's an understood shared value system at work here, in which Brooks senses safety within an Irish culture long known for its sexual conservatism and the ethnically desirable crowd intuitively grasps Brooks's own understanding of sexual propriety. Kevin McCarthy of Dublin writes that "at one point . . . the crowd began to sing an Irish football song . . . GB just stood back and for a few minutes we entertained him. His eyes told his true feelings. GB was home."[57] The blend of American and Irish cultures occurs simultaneous to Brooks's positioning as spectator. The mutual admiration of Brooks and his Irish fans manifests itself in his casting of them as performers. As O'Toole has suggested, "exile makes things that are unconscious—language, gesture, the accoutrements of nationality—conscious. It makes the exile a performer . . . [Performance] involves, for the Irish in America, playing the white man and remembering the Indian that is left behind . . . an essential image of the doubleness of the exile's condition."[58] Brooks's performance recasts the Irish audience in the same light as Irish Americans at the same time as it repositions him as at home in Ireland.

The reference to home is especially interesting in this context. If Brooks's lyrics relocate the locus of American culture in the modern-

2. Garth Brooks safely surfs the crowd at Croke Park, Dublin, in June 1997.

ized but traditional South, he has found a similarly comforting homeland in Ireland. In interviews Brooks has stated that his song "'Ireland'
is totally just a fantasy," though he also discusses the importance of the
nation as the first place he realized that his music was accepted outside
of the United States.[59] Brooks hails from Oklahoma, but in "Ireland" he
speaks the thoughts of an Irish immigrant dreaming of home (with its
"rolling fields of green and fences made of stone") the night before he
dies in an Alamo-esque battle, pitting "forty against hundreds/In someone else's bloody war."[60] Ireland here represents history, noble fighting—
a lost cause, men outnumbered, horses. The song constitutes Ireland as
the site of the past, of chivalry and individual bravery. For Brooks, Ireland
represents values similar to those which country music represents for his
Irish listeners, each party constituting the other as the repository of values
their current economy no longer allows them the luxury of indulging.

Coda

While Brooks announced his retirement in 2000, he remains a visible
pop-culture figure as his music still receives airtime and he has not

withdrawn from advertising endorsements. Brooks's 2003 biography on Country Music Television was its highest-rated broadcast ever, evidence that he remains popular with the public. Further indication of his enduring status came with the critic- and fan-voted lists of the top 100 country music songs ever. Fourteen years after its original release, the "better to have loved and lost" ballad "The Dance" came in at number one for fans and number fourteen for critics, with "Friends in Low Places" ranking number six on both lists. Brooks's high-profile romance with country star Trisha Yearwood has kept his image current as well, as has his "Be You. Do what you do" Dr. Pepper campaign.

A southern brand now marketed nationally, Dr. Pepper epitomizes the recuperation of the South and the relocation of the essence of American culture there. The Brooks commercial draws on the themes of a lost rural past, using a down-home backdrop of a dusty country general store to advocate the consumption of the soft drink as a method of distinguishing oneself from others. The individual is elevated at the same time as uniqueness is revealed to be something that can be acquired through purchase of a mass-produced product, a message in keeping with that of the isolated incasts populating Brooks's songs throughout his dominance in the nineties. Like those content with their wives and friends in low places, the ideal Dr. Pepper consumer sees himself as a matter-of-fact nonconformist who happens to be fairly conventional.

The Planet Garth website reports that since his retirement, Brooks "has moved back to Oklahoma to help his ex-wife, Sandy, raise the couple's three daughters. Brooks said that while he misses the life he knew of performing and recording music, his new life as hands-on dad is even better."[61] While Brooks's divorce might seem to contradict the family-values cant of such songs as "Unanswered Prayers," it can also be seen as further alliance with his listeners, who are subject to the same pressures on their marriages, and Brooks continues to perform fatherhood appropriately by remaining amicable with his ex-wife and taking part in childcare, masculinity intact because he is still cast as the helper rather than the primary caretaker. Meanwhile, Brooks's rocker alter ego, Chris Gaines, has also achieved success in Ireland, to the point that Irish boy band Westlife, itself the apotheosis of hyper-produced pop music, covered a Gaines tune, "Lost in You," on their 2003 release *Turnaround*. That same year also saw a conjunction that is suggestive in the context of the increased conservatism in Ireland and the United States signaled by the popularity of Brooks. An increase in negative reaction in Ireland to Eastern European, Asian, and African asylum seekers coincided with a directive specifying that parents of Irish citizens are no longer guaranteed residency, a regulation which paralleled a U.S. policy also designed to restrict undesirable immigrants and suggested that Irish racial politics were moving closer to the American model.

Notes

1. John Bradley, "The Irish Economy in Comparative Perspective," in *Bust to Boom? The Irish Experience of Growth and Inequality*, edited by Brian Nolan, Philip J. O'Connell, and Christopher T. Whelan (Dublin: ESRI, 2000), 21.

2. J. Peter Clinch, Frank Convery, and Brendan Walsh, *After the Celtic Tiger: Challenges Ahead* (Dublin: O'Brien, 2002), 20–21.

3. To be fair, Brooks was beaten for top-seller by a TV-host turkey puppet known as Dustin. The album was called *Unplucked*.

4. One could argue that jazz is equally American, though its racial dynamic paints a different America than country's does, and its acceptance in Europe came from a far more intellectual audience than country's.

5. Bruce Feiler, "Gone Country," *New Republic*, 5 February 1996, 19.

6. The majority of the information here about the country music industry comes from Feiler's "Gone Country" and from the Planet Garth website, <http://www.planet garth.com>.

7. Fintan O'Toole, *A Mass for Jesse James: A Journey through 1980s Ireland* (Dublin: Raven Arts Press, 1990), 133.

8. Brendan Glacken, "An American State of Being," *Irish Times*, 30 August 1999, 14.

9. Oliver O'Connor, "Time to Think of America," *Irish Times*, 27 August 1999, 55. The IDA is the Irish Government agency that secures foreign investment.

10. Conor McCarthy, *Modernisation, Crisis and Culture in Ireland, 1969–1992* (Dublin: Four Courts Press, 2000), 15.

11. Philip J. O'Connell, "Sick Man or Tigress? The Labour Market in the Republic of Ireland," in *Ireland, North and South: Perspectives from Social Science*, edited by Anthony F. Heath (Oxford: Oxford University Press, 1999), 216.

12. Clinch, Convery, and Walsh, *After the Celtic Tiger*, 22.

13. Mary Corcoran, "Strong Sense of Locality in the Cyber-Village," *Irish Times*, 9 August 2003, 14.

14. Bill C. Malone and David Stricklin, *Southern Music/American Music*, rev. ed.

(Lexington: University Press of Kentucky, 2003), 29. Malone sees the Anglo-Saxon theory of southern culture as more pervasive than the "Celtic thesis," which he calls "a view of more recent vintage" that argues for Scots, Irish, and Welsh antagonism as the roots of the "South's unique culture." Both hypotheses identify similar traits in southerners and seek to account for the interest in "white southern purity" (183 n. 14).

15. Ibid., 29.

16. Peter Stanfield, "Country Music and the 1939 Western: From Hillbillies to Cowboys," in *The Book of Westerns*, edited by Ian Cameron and Douglas Pye (New York: Continuum, 1996), 23.

17. Stanfield, "Country Music and the 1939 Western," 24.

18. Ibid., 25. See Diane Negra's discussion of the way that a common whiteness used to be used to constitute nation; clearly this incarnation of the cowboy was a part of that homogenization. "The New Primitives: Irishness in Recent US Television," *Irish Studies Review* 9, no. 2 (2001): 229–39.

19. Malone and Stricklin, *Southern Music/American Music*, 30.

20. Ibid., 87.

21. Richard A. Peterson, *Creating Country Music: Fabricating Authenticity* (Chicago: University of Chicago Press, 1997).

22. Barbara Ching, *Wrong's What I Do Best* (Oxford: Oxford University Press, 2001), 80.

23. Bruce Feiler, *Dreaming Out Loud: Garth Brooks, Wynonna Judd, Wade Hayes and the Changing Face of Nashville* (New York: Avon, 1998), 38.

24. *Hat act* suggests a singer's ability to look good in a hat is his most important attribute and that the substance of his music has been sacrificed to a generic style. Many such performers were one-hit wonders, but the term has been applied to such chart-toppers as Clint Black, Tim McGraw, Toby Keith, and Alan Jackson.

25. Feiler, "Gone Country," 20.

26. Luke Gibbons draws effectively on Panofsky's terminology (from *Meaning in the Visual Arts* [Chicago: University of Chicago Press, 1983]) in "Synge, Country and Western," one of the major inspirations for this essay. In *Transformations in Irish Culture* (Notre Dame, Ind.: University of Notre Dame Press, 1996).

27. Ching, *Wrong's What I Do Best*, 4.

28. Amy Ansell, "The Color of America's Culture Wars," in *Unraveling the Right: The New Conservatism in American Thought and Politics*, edited by Amy Ansell (New York: Westview Press, 1998), 174.

29. Ibid., 175.

30. Kathy Sheridan, "King of Country," *Irish Times*, weekend supplement, 17 May 1997, 1.

31. Ansell, *Unraveling the Right*, 175.

32. Feiler, *Dreaming Out Loud*, 248.

33. A burly former athlete who describes his background as "oil-field trash,"

Brooks holds a B.A. in business from Oklahoma State University; country's audience is often educated as well, with a higher percentage of college- and postgraduate-educated listeners than rock or urban contemporary (Feiler, "Gone Country," 19).

34. Brooks has complained that people view country as "redneck music — the voice of right-wing, even racist, America," a view which he counters by suggesting that "what they really dislike, yet would never dare say it, is the class of people country music is singing about." Joe Jackson, "Urbane Cowboy," *Irish Times*, 21 August 1992, 10.

35. De Valera was American born, curiously, and thereby one of the first of the returning immigrants; this move in reverse becomes increasingly significant statistically as well as culturally as a key feature of the Celtic Tiger.

36. O'Toole, *Mass for Jesse James*, 102.

37. Don Bennett has written about the differences in the lyrics of American- and Irish-generated country songs, pointing out that themes of female infidelity, for instance, were downplayed in Ireland, where the music had an even more conservative bent than in the United States. Brooks seems to represent the synthesis of both strains. Bennett's work appears in Chris Curtin, Mary Kelly, and Liam O'Dowd, eds. *Culture and Ideology in Ireland* (Galway: Galway University Press, 1984).

38. Gibbons, "Synge, Country and Western," 24.

39. Douglas Pye, introduction to *The Book of Westerns*, 14.

40. Roddy Doyle, *Paddy Clarke Ha ha ha* (London: Secker and Warburg, 1993); and Patrick McCabe, *The Butcher Boy* (New York: Delta, 1992).

41. McCabe, *Butcher Boy*, 168–69.

42. Quoted in Richard Maltby, "A Better Sense of History: John Ford and the Indians," in *The Book of Westerns*, 34, from Tag Gallagher, *John Ford, The Man and his Films* (Berkeley: University of California Press, 1986), 341.

43. O'Toole, *Mass for Jesse James*, 136.

44. Elizabeth Butler Cullingford, *Ireland's Others: Gender and Ethnicity in Irish Literature and Popular Culture* (Notre Dame, Ind.: University of Notre Dame Press, 2001), 180.

45. Ibid., 182.

46. O'Toole, *Mass for Jesse James*, 132–33. Similarly, country transformed itself as its audience and practitioners moved to the northern cities so that "listeners could wallow in nostalgic reverie for a lost agrarian past whilst effacing the pejorative connotations attached to such a past by the urban middle-classes." Stanfield, "Country Music and the 1939 Western," 23. In both nations and times, listeners are already physically and temporally displaced from country's supposed locus.

47. Don Rhodes, "Garth Brooks Special Focuses on Ireland," Reuters, 1 March 1998. Rather than release a pop album under his own name, Brooks created a rock-star persona named Chris Gaines to be a vehicle for his top-forty longings. At the same time, reviews of all of his albums tend to make distinctions between the tradi-

tional country songs and the pop arrangements, suggesting that he has embodied old country and new country all along.

48. Ibid.

49. *The Commitments*, dir. Alan Parker, Beacon Communications, 1991; Raymond Crotty, *Ireland in Crisis: A Study in Capitalist Colonial Underdevelopment* (Dingle, Ireland: Brandon, 1986); Kieran Kennedy, *Facing the Unemployment Crisis in Ireland* (Cork: Cork University Press, 1993); Cathal Guiomard, *The Irish Disease and How to Cure It: Common-Sense Economics for a Competitive World* (Dublin: Oak Tree Press, 1995).

50. Michael Littleton, ed., *From Famine to Feast: Economic and Social Change in Ireland, 1847–1997* (Dublin: Institute of Public Administration, 1998); Brian Nolan, Philip J. O'Connell, and Christopher T. Whelan, eds. *Bust to Boom? The Irish Experience of Growth and Inequality* (Dublin: ESRI, 2000).

51. Richard Laytie and Christopher T. Whelan, "The Rising Tide and Equality of Opportunity: The Changing Class Structure," *Bust to Boom?* 104–5.

52. Eibhir Mulqueen, "Cassidy Puts Case for Country Music," *Irish Times*, 19 April 1999, 18. Dublin 4 is the best-known postal code in Ireland and has come to be seen as synecdochic for the cultural elite.

53. O'Toole, *Mass for Jesse James*, 109.

54. Hugo Hamilton, "Ireland—The Snug of Europe," *Irish Times*, 29 June 1996, 12.

55. McCarthy, *Modernisation*, 15.

56. <http://www.planetgarth.com/reviews.dublin.html>, accessed 2 March 1999.

57. Ibid.

58. O'Toole, *Mass for Jesse James*, 136.

59. <http://www.octopusmediaink.com/GarthBrooks.html>, accessed 2 March 2003.

60. "Ireland," lyrics by Garth Brooks, Stephanie Davis, and Jenny Yates.

61. <http://planetgarth.com/>, accessed 17 September 2003.

AMANDA THIRD

"Does the Rug Match the Carpet?":
Race, Gender, and the Redheaded Woman

It takes a redheaded woman to get a dirty job done.

—Bruce Springsteen, "Redheaded Woman"

You'd find it easier to be bad than good if you had red hair.

—Anne Shirley, in Lucy Maud Montgomery's *Anne of Green Gables*

I've just arrived and the pub is crowded and noisy. It's the usual Wednesday night crowd of university students downing pints. I'm standing at the bar trying to spot my friends. I've just washed my long auburn hair and it's down. Some guy next to me is buying a beer. I can feel him staring. He tries to make conversation and I send him the not-interested vibe. But he's persistent. He tries again and I shrug him off, anxiously searching the crowd for a familiar face. He pauses. I can feel him searching for a pickup line that will work. I brace myself. And then it comes . . .

"So . . . does the rug match the carpet?"

I give him my best drop-dead look and walk away. I then spend the rest of the night inventing sassy comebacks.

This incident, which took place almost ten years ago, is what first got me thinking about the ways that redheaded women are constructed in English-speaking cultures. Anglo cultures understand redheaded women in a very particular, ambivalent set of ways, largely as a consequence of the English colonization of Ireland and the subsequent racialization of the Irish. Historically, England's colonial project in Ireland, a form of colonialism which entails the subordination of a group that is, as Luke Gibbons puts it, both "native" and "white," has been complicated by the lack of a readily available visible marker of difference by which to construct the Irish as other and as subaltern.[1] As Anne McClintock, quoting Clair Wills, notes, "the difficulty of placing the pale-skinned Irish in the hierarchy of empire 'was . . . the absence of the visual marker of skin color difference which was used to legitimate domination in other colonized societies.'"[2]

In the context of a form of colonization where chromatism as a category of difference was not easily deployed to construct the colonial other, red hair became one clear physical marker, among others, of Celtic or Irish difference. As Nira Yuval-Davis states, "every racist construction has at least some dimension of a mythical embodiment of the 'other.' This can relate to any part of the body."[3] In the absence of a difference of skin color, then, red hair was a distinguishing feature within the problematic category of whiteness that enabled the singling out of the Irish and Celts as inferior, and as other, that was necessary in order for English imperial expansion into Ireland to take place. That is, red hair was constructed as one characteristic of Irish otherness—in the colonial imaginary, it signaled their "off-whiteness" or their "not-quite-whiteness." It is this process of othering that overdetermines the construction of redheaded women in English-speaking cultures. Redheads are produced, to use Bhabha's phrase, as "almost the same, but *not quite.*"[4]

Redheaded women have a much more strikingly visible presence in the representational spaces of Anglo cultures than redheaded men. Indeed, while redheaded men are not entirely invisible, the image of the redheaded man doesn't circulate in the same kinds of ways, and with the same kind of sexualized and spectacular prominence, as the image of the redheaded woman.[5] For example, Hollywood has given us an impressive number of iconic female redheads: Nicole Kidman, Lucille Ball, Rita Hayworth, and Bette Midler, to name but a few. On the other hand, redheaded male celebrities are rather more thin on the ground. Redheaded masculinity, it seems, simply does not have the same kinds of currency; it does not evoke the powerful mythologies that female redheadedness does. Red hair on a woman speaks in Anglo cultures, and very loudly at that.

This dichotomy requires that we think through how the category of gender gets deployed in colonial discourse to construct and subordinate the other. Following Anne McClintock's argument, colonialism can be understood as a struggle between competing masculinities in which the discourses of race and gender articulate with one another to produce a framework that serves to legitimate colonial domination of the other. As numerous scholars working in areas that may be broadly defined as post-colonial have implied, but rarely stated outright, the other, whether it be racial, classed, or gendered, is constructed by colonial discourse as a fundamental threat to the project of colonialism. For example, McClintock argues that male imperial discourse is characterized by a recurrent doubling of aggression and megalomania and "an acute paranoia and a profound, if not pathological, sense of male anxiety" toward women.[6] In other words, the gendered discourses of male colonialism produce the figure of woman ambivalently; she is constructed as simultaneously desirable and threatening to colonial order. It is the idea that woman represents a threat to the colonial project that I want to focus on here.

Historically, colonial discourse has deployed the category of gender to feminize the other — to produce the colonized as a feminine other. Traditionally, postcolonial theorists have emphasized the ways that this process of feminization produces the other as passive, weak, and in need of the moral guidance of the colonizer. While this line of argument is worthwhile, and has been a necessary part of understanding the processes by which colonizers have achieved the subordination of the colonized, it's important to consider the ways that the racial other, through the process of feminization and the subsequent association with woman-as-threat, gets constructed as a threat to colonial power. In the colonial context, discourses of race and gender work to mutually inscribe one another, resulting in the production of the racial other as feminized threat. More than this, and simultaneously, in inserting the racial other into the representational order as feminized threat, the interplay between the discourses of race and gender works to contain that threat. These discourses call the other-as-threat into being, and in doing so, operate to manage that threat. The feminization of the racial other thus legitimates the colonial subjection of the other by mobilizing the prior order of rigidly defined gender relations underpinning male imperialism. This in turn serves to protect the male colonial project from the threat of the other.

Despite the popular perception that colonialism is dead and buried, the colonial representational order, based on processes of othering, continues to overdetermine the construction of identities in the (post)colonial era, albeit in a modified form. In the contemporary context, in places like Australia, England, and the United States, popular discourse systematically relegates the experience of colonization to the past. However, as Richard Dyer suggests in his account of Western cultural constructions of whiteness, the racialized structures of thinking that characterized the colonial worldview continue to persist in the postcolonial context. Speaking of the contemporary Western world, Dyer notes that "racist thought . . . is part of the cultural non-consciousness that we all inhabit."[7] In other words, the persistence of racist thought in postcolonial cultures evidences a process of colonial othering at play within the contemporary representational economy.

In English-speaking postcolonial societies, then, in the context of the historical colonization of Ireland by England, the redheaded woman becomes a site where the racial and gendered productions of colonial otherness intersect. The image of the female redhead represents a synthesis of woman (the colonial gendered other) and Irishness (the English colonial racial other). It is for this reason that she is constructed ambivalently in Anglo cultures, as at once desirable yet threatening. Signifying both womanness and Irishness, the redheaded woman embodies the feminine sexualized threat of the Irish racial other.

As I have noted, in colonial cultures the discourses of race have historically been mobilized to mark the colonizer as superior and therefore legitimately dominant. In English-speaking postcolonial cultures, however, whiteness has been experiencing a crisis in legitimacy since at least the 1970s. This has become particularly acute in postcolonial contexts in which, in conjunction with the speaking of subaltern histories, there has been a shift toward producing subjectivity through the prism of identity politics. Whereas previously whiteness was invisible to the extent that it was a marker of privilege, increasingly, in certain contexts, whiteness has become a highly visible category of difference with strong pejorative connotations. Thus, whiteness, within the economy of postcolonial identity politics, is an increasingly problematic signifier.

In this context, some critics have suggested that Irishness has gained discursive currency as a "safe" version of whiteness — or "enriched white-ness," as Diane Negra puts it — displaying the necessary subaltern cre-dentials that derive from a history of colonial otherness and circulating transnationally in essentialized and commodified forms. Irishness thus offers a way of performing whiteness with legitimacy.[8] However, in the repackaging of Irishness as a form of "nonproblematic" whiteness within dominant culture, what is remarkable about the ways that Irishness is deployed in current contexts is that the subaltern, and often threaten-ingly subversive, history of Irish otherness, rather than being disinterred, disappears. Increasingly Irishness circulates as a signifier of middle-class comfort, old-fashioned values, nostalgia, and harmless joviality. In this sense, Irishness operates to restore legitimacy to (at least part of) the category of whiteness.

The process of encoding Irishness as a restorative form of whiteness depends on the sublimation, and therefore the containment, of the more sinister and threatening dimensions of the history of Irish otherness. One of the ways this sublimation takes place is via a process of displacement of the subversive elements of Irish otherness onto the figure of the red-headed woman. In making this argument, I want to draw attention not only to the ambivalence with which Irishness has historically been con-structed, but also to the contingency of the category of whiteness itself as it circulates within Anglo cultures today. I should clarify here that this essay does not seek to identify the "true nature" of redheaded women. Rather, I am concerned with the female redhead as a discursive con-struct — with the range of ways that female redheadedness articulates as the effect of the play of discourses within Anglo postcolonial cultures.

Red-Hot Women: Anglo Constructions of the Redheaded Woman

It must be said from the outset that flame-haired women are not con-structed in straightforward fashion. Discursively, redheadedness oper-ates in contradictory and often openly conflicting ways. The effect of this is that female redheadedness is regarded with ambivalence in Anglo cul-tures. One of the few commentators on redheadedness in white culture, Grant McCracken, speaking from the point of view of the nonredheaded

1. The incendiary qualities assigned to red hair in Anglo cultures are aptly expressed by the name and marketing of this Australian brand of red-tipped matches. (Courtesy Swedish Match Australia)

(male) majority, says that "red hair has two opposing qualities: appeal and danger" and this means that we are both "attracted and repulsed" by the redhead.[9]

In English-speaking cultures, red hair is talked about as incendiary, and redheads are constructed as fiery, in every sense of the word. Perhaps one of the best examples of this is the use of the stylized cartoon image of the white-skinned redheaded woman used by Redheads, an Australian brand of matches and lighters. However, advertisements for red hair dye also invoke metaphors of heat and combustion. For example, the book on trends in hair color published in association with women's magazine *Marie Claire* encourages readers to indulge in "a dash of tabasco, a sprinkle of ginger, or a head full of fiery flames."[10] As McCracken says, "there is something combustible about that hair."[11] Redheads are hot-tempered, hot-blooded, hot-headed, and hot under the collar. They have flaming passions and burning desire. And, most notoriously, they are hot in bed. These ways of talking about flame-colored hair, and the people who brandish it, are the same ways we talk about anger, temper, and rage, using phrases like *fiery temper* and *burning with anger*.

By contrast, redheads can also be cool as cucumbers: clever, conniving, calculating, cunning, cold-blooded, and in control. In certain contexts they are constructed as highly rational, and as having a strong sense of knowing what they want, along with the determination to carry it out. Nicole Kidman's handling of her divorce from Tom Cruise, for instance, was represented in the media as miraculously levelheaded. Another example is the popular-culture construction of Gillian Anderson, who played Special Agent Dana Scully in the cult television series *The X-Files*, and is famous for her straight red bobs. Anderson has been dubbed the "thinking man's crumpet" in Britain — "a testament to Gillian Anderson's on- and off-camera personae as a woman who is both beautiful and brainy."[12] Further, while Scully's chemically enhanced copper tresses metamorphosed their way through the entire red-inspired spectrum, Scully herself remained hard-nosed, rational, scientific, and fundamentally unflappable throughout the duration of the series, as Anderson was cited by more than one commentator for her "cool" performance style.[13] And more recently Marcia Cross's glossy redheaded character Bree Van De Kamp in the hit program *Desperate Housewives* is at once the epitome of cold composure, control, and cunning manipulation. These characterizations both feed into and are fed by the cultural mythologization of redheads as level-headed and shrewd.

In these incarnations, the female redhead is constructed as always already marginal and therefore problematic, given that she defies Western patriarchal constructions of femininity which position women as fundamentally irrational, passive, and subservient.[14] Her ability to reason constructs her as liminal; a condition which Victor Turner describes as "ambiguous."[15] She is woman/female/feminine, but not quite. And thus the young female redhead often gets portrayed as the tomboy. Preeminent examples are the two Annes of children's popular culture — Anne Shirley of Lucy Maud Montgomery's *Anne of Green Gables* and the redheaded Little Orphan Annie of the popular-culture franchise of the same name, whose quick wits and outspokenness thwart the money-hungry plan of the orphanage director, Miss Hannigan. Here we have articulations of the female redhead's doubly marginal status as both rational and female.

Paradoxically, the female redhead also represents the other extreme of patriarchal constructions of femininity in that she is also constructed as, at least potentially, excessively irrational. In Australia, the redheaded right-wing "people's politician," Pauline Hanson, was often constructed in the media as "crazy," and her policies as "irrational." Troped the "redheaded bushfire," Hanson was subject to media coverage in which her redheadedness was a markedly frequent feature in accounts of her rise to political prominence. Discursively, Hanson's redheadedness systematically operated as shorthand for her impulsiveness and irrationality, and as such constituted one mechanism by which her political agenda could be dismissed. While her solutions to the "problems" of national debt and immigration were indeed simplistic and politically unsound, arguably Hanson was more easily discredited as mad because she was constructed in the mainstream media as the unpredictable and outrageous redheaded woman.[16]

While it can be argued that all women in Western modernity are constructed as the irrational other,[17] redheaded women are constructed as particularly prey to their passions, as the outer limit of women's potential for irrationality. At best they are spontaneous, at worst, impulsive. McCracken asserts that we are fascinated by redheads because they "can marshall energies and a determination the rest of us cannot. On the other [hand] we believe they are pulled helplessly behind runaway impulses, incapable of self-control."[18] Inasmuch as redheads are perceived as constantly on the brink of an outburst, barely controlled, they represent not open hostility, but "a subtle, more social quality of menace."[19] In other words, they are fundamentally unpredictable, constantly threatening to disrupt the smooth functioning of everyday life, constantly about to explode.

This redheaded unpredictability is ambivalently regarded as both a strength and weakness of character. We admire redheads, and yet they frighten us. As McCracken says, "redheads make us nervous because we imagine them ready to give vent to what we keep harnessed. Redheads are what we could be if we could do what we wanted to. Redheads represent our reckless, hot-headed, unconstrained side."[20] Indeed they may well represent the threat of a Freudian "return of the repressed," the threat of the disruption of the rational by the irrational, and thus are regarded with caution and charged with ambivalence.

This ambivalence effect is also produced by the sexualization of the female redhead. As McCracken suggests, "men are simultaneously alarmed but intrigued by redheaded women . . . Redheaded women send a double signal to men. They seem on the one hand to be disinclined to play out traditional gender roles or to act the perfect little compan-

Red alert

2. The redhead, like the Australian actress Nicole Kidman, provokes both alarm and attraction. (Courtesy Headpress)

ion. On the other hand, they promise sensual delights of extraordinary proportions."[21]

In Anglo cultures, redheaded women are constructed as sexy, sensual, seductive, and spontaneous. But redheads are not passive receptacles for male desire; they are active figures of hypersexuality. Take for example, Bruce Springsteen's song "Redheaded Woman," in which he sings: "Well brunettes are fine man / And blondes are fun / [But] it takes a redheaded woman to get a dirty job done." While blondes are "fun," the implication, so poetically put by Springsteen, is that redheaded women will give you the "ride" of your life. As Springsteen says, the redheaded woman "can see every cheap thing that you ever done" because naturally, one presumes, she's already done it.[22] In the context of this eroticization of female red hair the redheaded woman is often featured in fantasies of sexual sordidness.

Partaking in the sensual delights the redhead offers does not come without risks. She represents the sexualized threat of the phallic woman, the strong, sexually aggressive female who invokes the castration anxiety of the vagina dentata. She promises a man an unfathomably good romp, at the expense of the risk of "dismembering" himself. A good example of the circulation of the cultural stereotype of the redhead as phallic woman can be found in Bronwen Walter's account of Irish frontier women in the United States, *Outsiders Inside*. Walter cites the following account to illustrate the ways that Irish women were romanticized in frontier culture: "Flame-haired Kate O'Leary, as tough as she was good-looking, ran a saloon and sporting house in Dodge City. In addition to fighting Indians when she was a girl and shooting dead an overly active cowboy on her doorstep, she was not above keeping order in her establishment with a few well-placed shotgun blasts."[23] Further, the redheaded woman will take you and then dump you before you've had time to find your trousers. A recent issue of *B Magazine* reported the results of a survey into hair color and women's character traits. "Beware the cheating redhead . . . Women who dye their hair red are more likely to cheat on their partners . . . Women who dye their hair blonde or brown are more likely to remain faithful."[24] In this respect then, and in the others that I have outlined, the redheaded woman comes to mark the outer limits of culturally acceptable female behavior.

The key to understanding why redheaded women are constructed ambivalently is an understanding of how redheadedness is racially coded. In English-speaking cultures redheadedness is broadly associated with Celticness but in particular with Irishness. Indeed, the two are often conflated in the current era of high-profile Irishness, to the degree that Irishness has colonized the meanings of Celticness, including the identity signifier of red hair. For example, one redheaded woman I interviewed claimed that, while her heritage is predominantly Scottish, when people ask her about her ethnic origins she almost always emphasizes the fact that she has an Irish grandfather, simply because " 'then it makes sense to them that [her] hair's so red."[25] This assimilation of redheadedness into Irishness is demonstrated again by the screen names used by women participating in the Realm of Redheads online forum; while a few go by names that invoke Celticness, such as CelticRose and CelticFireLady, more choose names that invoke the association of red hair with Irishness, like Irisheyes and IrishGirl.[26]

Similarly, a recent USA *Today* advertisement for *Irish Girls About Town*

3. Newspaper advertisement for Maeve Binchy, Marian Keyes, and Cathy Kelly's shortstory collection, *Irish Girls About Town*, 2003. (Courtesy Simon and Schuster)

by Maeve Binchy, Marian Keyes, and Cathy Kelly makes this connection between Irishness and red hair explicit. The Irish girls of the title are symbolized on the book's cover by a pale-skinned woman lying on a bed of green ivy with her long deep-red locks radiating outwards around her. The pun that accompanies the image—"Paint the town green!"—in substituting the word *green* for *red* in the popular phrase, plays with Western-culture associations of Irish national identity with the green of the shamrock, and Irish racial identity with red hair. In this context, the red hair of the Irish girl signifies her "greenness," her Irishness.

If redheadedness connotes Irishness, and if we consider the positioning of the Irish in the context of English colonization of Ireland, then the ambivalence invoked by the redheaded woman begins to make sense. The English project of colonizing Ireland deployed redheadedness, along with a range of other physical characteristics, to construct Irish otherness, and thereby establish the colonial right to rule.

Redheaded "White Negroes" and Simian Celts

As many commentators have pointed out, thinking about the colonized as members of distinct groups which are constructed as fundamentally other ("them") to the imagined community (the "we") provides the legitimating discourse of the colonial right to rule. As I have noted, in the context of English colonization of Ireland, this construction of otherness, which in the typical case is constituted through the identification of a range of visually discernible physical traits that produce otherness in racial terms, presented a problem for English colonizers. As Gibbons has suggested, when the colonial project turned "to Ireland, the wheel ground to a halt for here was a colony whose subject population was both 'native' and 'white' at the same time."[27] This meant that by the nineteenth century the Irish were regarded ambivalently—as "white" but also as colonial subjects, and therefore necessarily "not white." And so the English set about establishing a racial science—what we now know as "scientific racism"—that would justify the otherness of the Irish "race," and construct them as not quite white.

The tradition of Irish difference goes back at least as far as the Norman invasion of Ireland in the twelfth century. At this time, however, Irish, or rather Gaelic, difference was predominantly conceptualized not in racial terms but in cultural terms, with Gaelic customs and traditions forming the basis of this perceived difference. Ideas about the racial difference of the Irish were circulating as early as the beginning of the fourteenth century, when a growing concern with the perils of the Hibernicization of the "English by blood"[28] saw a number of preventative statutes introduced by the fledgling Anglo-Irish–dominated Irish parliament. In 1366, the Statute of Kilkenny was ratified, forbidding intermarriage, the fostering of children, concubinage, and such between the Anglo-Irish colonizers and the "native" Irish, betraying a preoccupation with the "purity" of bloodlines. George Boyce writes, "The Statute of Kilkenny was the product not of English domination, but of English fear that the tide of their power was ebbing, and of the recognition that the division based on descent was in danger of obliteration."[29] This embryonic form of the English racialization of the Irish coexisted with ideas about Irish cultural difference throughout the medieval era.[30]

By the late sixteenth century, Queen Elizabeth's scheme for the English plantation of Ireland had been abandoned.[31] But the violence of the Irish resistance had firmly impressed on the English colonizers the idea that they were dealing with an unreasonable and barbarous people who were in a lesser stage of civilization — "the wild Irish," as Edmund Spenser called them. Elizabeth's failed attempts to convert the Irish to Protestantism only further reinforced these English perceptions of the Irish. As Boyce remarks, "Catholicism in its Irish form was the badge of the inferior race . . . The whole enterprise [that is, the civilizing mission of plantation] was seen in racial terms."[32] However, it was not until the nineteenth century, when the British Empire got caught up in the momentum of the scramble for Africa, and the emergence of Darwinian thought gave the English colonizers a way of explaining difference in terms of evolution, that the racialization of the Irish approached the status of an institutional "science."

Victorian scientific racism drew on a wide variety of sources, but was perhaps most directly informed by the "healing art" of physiognomy. The Hippocratic School of physiognomy believed that not only an individual's constitution but also their character and temperament could be ascertained via a reading of the facial and other physical features, including the color and texture of the hair, voice, and posture. A healthy and balanced individual exhibited a harmony of the "four moist humours of blood, phlegm, black and yellow bile" in equal proportions.[33] A lack of balance produced physical manifestations of one of the four types into which individuals could be classified; the sanguine, the phlegmatic, the melancholic, and the choleric. As L. Perry Curtis states: "By the early 1800s physiognomical dogma had become part of the popular scientific folklore, and men from all walks of life in every part of Europe relied to some degree on this method of 'seeing through' their neighbours as well as strangers from other lands . . . Physiognomical convictions could be found amongst the most educated and prosperous families as well as among those who believed in 'the evil eye' *or dreaded meeting strangers with red hair on the road.*"[34]

The acclaimed physiognomist James Cowles Prichard, in his treatise *Researches into the Physical History of Man* published in London in 1813, claimed that, among other physical characteristics, red hair characterized the "sanguine" type. To quote Curtis again: "According to Prichard's classification, the sanguine type was marked by reddish hair, blue eyes and a ruddy complexion. The temperament accompanying these features was not only 'acute' but emotional, hedonistic and somewhat irritable."[35] Here we have a concrete example of the historical linkage of redheadedness with bad temper and a lack of emotional control that still circulates in Anglo cultures today. This kind of construction of redheadedness was easily deployed in the context of English colonization of Ireland to situate the Irish Celt as other.

In the imperial climate of the mid-nineteenth century, the emerging science of social Darwinism articulated with the discourses of physiognomy to provide a "science" of racial classification which was appropriated by a keen group of English ethnologists who were dedicated to the project of proving the Irish, along with certain other "races" of the British Isles, inferior. Dr. John Beddoe, for example, founding member of the Ethnological Society in England, invented a scale of Nigrescence that measured "residual melanin in the skin, hair and eyes" in order to establish the proximity of the races of Britain and Ireland to the races of Africa.[36] He concluded that the index rose sharply from east to west, and south to north in Britain, establishing a hierarchy of whiteness in which "the English middle-class male was placed at the pinnacle of evolutionary hierarchy . . . White English middle-class women followed. Irish or Jewish men were represented as the most inherently degenerate 'female races' within the white male gender, approaching the state of apes. Irish working-class women were depicted as lagging even farther behind in the lower depths of the white race."[37] In *The Races of Britain*, published in Britain in 1885, Beddoe concluded that the Irish race had strong connections to the races of Africa: "In the West of Ireland . . . the head is large, the intelligence is low and inhabitants demonstrate a great deal of cunning and suspicion . . . Ireland is apparently the centre of prognathism [the jutting of the lower jaw], most of its lineaments are such as lead us to think of Africa as its possible birthplace; and it may be well, provisionally to call it Africanoid."[38]

One effect of establishing Irish proximity to the "Negroid" races of Africa was the attribution to the Irish of all those characteristics which, in the context of the colonial encounter with the African continent, had been ascribed to the African population. For example, the Irish race was condemned for laziness, low intelligence, and, in particular, base sexuality, drawing on a history of, as Winthrop D. Jordan writes, "English perceptions that integrate sexuality, blackness, the devil and the judgement of God who had originally created man not only 'Angelike' but 'white.' "[39] The conflation of blackness, evil, and base sexuality drew on demonological traditions that had been circulating in the medieval church even before there was any face-to-face contact with black people. In the context of colonialism, these ideas provided a pool of ready-made myths on which to construct racial difference. Constructing Irish difference, its not-quite-whiteness, thus rested only on finding scientific proof of the connections between the genealogies of the black races of Africa, and these "white negroes."[40]

Like Prichard, both Beddoe and, later, Madison Grant, deployed hair color as a characteristic that further enabled the classifying of the Irish as racially other. Beddoe notes that the Irish Celts have hair that is "reddish-brown, red or raven black," and Madison Grant writes that "when the peoples called Gauls or Celts . . . first appear in history, they are described . . . as . . . gigantic barbarians with fair, and very often red hair."[41]

This racialization of the Irish was further compounded by the scientific "discovery" and classification of the great apes of Africa in the mid nineteenth century, filling out the spaces in the diagrammatic tree of man's evolution. The Irish, it was repeatedly said, were much more closely related than the English not only to black people but to the apes of Africa, and this could be scientifically proved, once again, through an application of physiognomical methods. As Murray Pittock puts it, "the identification of the gorilla and the classification of the other great apes in the 1840s provided . . . a fresh impetus in the context of rising nationalism to re-emphasize the ethnic gulf between Irish Celt and Anglo-Saxon. As Punch put it in 'The Missing Link' on 18 October 1862: ". . . A creature manifestly between the Gorilla and the Negro is to be met with in some of the lowest districts of London and Liverpool by adventurous explorers. It comes from Ireland . . . The somewhat superior ability of the Irish Yahoo to utter articulate sounds, may suffice to prove that it is a development, and not, as some may imagine, a degeneration of the Gorilla.' "[42]

By the 1860s, then, English ethnographers had mapped the features of the Irish physique and character, highlighting their simian nature. As Curtis explains, "by the 1860s the 'representative Irishman' was to all appearances an anthropoid ape . . . In cartoons and caricatures, as well as in prose, Paddy began to resemble increasingly the chimpanzee, the orangutan and finally the gorilla . . . a distinctly dangerous ape-man."[43] For example, in Morgan's 1869 cartoon of the Irish Frankenstein, the Irishman is represented as a "human orangutan with the expression of the village idiot."[44] This construction of the Irish as like orangutans is telling with respect to the implication of red hair in Irish racial difference because, of course, the orangutan is red-haired.[45]

As Curtis has argued in *Apes and Angels*, his account of the racialized constructions of the Irish in Victorian caricature: "Many—although by no means all—educated and respectable Victorians regarded the 'native' Irish as belonging to a distinct order of mankind or 'race,' which they called Celtic or Gaelic. Using the loaded word 'race' loosely or inconsistently, these English observers assigned to themselves all those superior qualities that they systematically denied to the Catholic Irish . . . Most respectable Victorians believed in a natural opposition between an Anglo-Saxon 'Us' and a Gaelic or Celtic 'Them,' which was reinforced by the great religious divide between Protestantism and (Roman) Catholicism."[46] The effect of this racialization of the Irish, constructed as it was out of "scientific" claims of Irish proximity both to the black races of Africa and to the great apes, was to discursively produce the Irish as both not properly white and as "a race in decline."[47] But this production of the Irish was highly problematic for the English imperialist. It depended on a disavowal of what the English colonizer might logically conclude when he came into contact with the Irish other, that the skin color of the majority of the Irish population was remarkably similar to, if not the same as, the skin color of the colonizing Englishman. That is, the English colonial male perceived the Irish ambivalently as both white in terms of the color of their skin, and not white, in that colonial knowledge necessarily constructed them as the racialized colonial other.

This produced in the English colonizer an experience of the Irish as representing the horror of the abject.[48] That is, as Julia Kristeva puts it, the horror of that which "disturbs identity, system, order" and is thus expelled from the "self," the "same," but haunts the borders of the subject's identity, constantly threatening to return.[49] For Kristeva the abject is "something rejected from which one does not part."[50] In Kristeva's understanding, the process of abjection is not one of objectification. The abject is not an entirely differentiated other. Rather, the abject is simultaneously same and other, simultaneously within, or a part of the subject, and outside, rejected by the subject. For the white English colonizer, the Irish represented that which is repudiated from within the colonial self by white English colonial identity. As Ania Loomba writes, "in fact, the lack of color difference *intensified* the horror of the colonial vis-à-vis the Irish."[51]

There were attempts to differentiate Irish whiteness from English whiteness. For example, John Beddoe, in his classification of the races of the British Isles, distinguished between different kinds of whiteness, claiming such things as "the Celt's color of the skin rang[es] from a ruddy white to a swarthy hue."[52] We may read these kinds of descriptions as attempts to "color" Irish whiteness—to produce the Irish as "off-white." However, Irish whiteness remained for the English colonizer profoundly unsettling. As Charles Kingsley recounted on return from his first trip to Ireland: "I am haunted by the human chimpanzees I saw along that hundred miles of horrible country . . . But to see white chimpanzees is dreadful; if they were black, one would not feel it so much. But their skins, except where tanned by exposure, are as white as ours."[53] The response of Thomas Carlyle to the problem of the Irish is telling. His answer is to remove their whiteness. He writes, "Black-lead them and put them over there with the niggers."[54]

It is useful to note here that redheaded individuals are commonly also extremely pale-skinned. That is, in Anglo cultures the redhead manifests as hyperwhite, or the embodiment of what Richard Dyer refers to as "extreme whiteness." This is perhaps especially accentuated in a "white" former British colony such as Australia where national identity is frequently configured in terms of blonde hair, blue eyes, and a deep tan.[55]

Hence, in the colonial context, Irish otherness has always been perceived as dangerously unstable. The tenuous classification of the Irish as not properly white, no matter how well justified by scientific discourse, always threatened to unravel, and in the process draw attention to the contingency of English whiteness and of the English claim to supremacy. Furthermore, the resilience of the Republican movement and the often-violent Irish grassroots resistance to colonial rule in Ireland and elsewhere continued to position the Irish as a threat to the English colonizers, and the English industrial class. As such, Irish otherness required constant policing. Indeed, Murray Pittock suggests that, because of the difficulty of distinguishing Celtic groups such as the Irish from the English, the racialization of these groups received the most rigorous attention.[56] It is this sense of the threat of Irishness to the white English male colonial project that attaches itself to redheadedness and underwrites the cultural ambivalence toward it.

If the experience of colonization produced for the English colonizer a sense of the Irish colonial other as the abject, then colonialism responded with a vigorous process of casting the Irish out. Colonial discourses constructed the Irish as "not at home" in Ireland, as strangers who needed to be subject to the discipline of the English colonial regime. The impressions of Friedrich Engels, reflecting on his journey to Ireland in *Ireland and the Irish Question*, shed light on this colonial Irish "not-at-homeness." Engels concluded that the history of English colonialism had left the Irish feeling strangers in their own country. Andrew Hadfield and John McVeagh, paraphrasing Engels, write, "like the land they were living in, the inhabitants of Ireland . . . appeared to Engels as a ruined people . . . which was the legacy of [their] centuries-old colonial history . . . And the ordinary people? Their history has made them feel 'no longer at home in their own country' . . . And for [Engels] there is nobody—colonizer any more than colonized—who can claim a true home in Ireland."[57] This emptied-out colonial territory, this place no one can call home, is inhabited, then, by strangers.

Historically, colonialism has often constructed colonized peoples as strangers who have no claim over the colonized territory.[58] This both legitimates the colonial agenda and operates to contain the threat the other poses to imperial order. However, constructing the colonial other as stranger also produces them as an ambivalently coded threat. As Zygmunt Baumann has noted in relation to Jews—another group of people who disturb constructions of whiteness in similar ways to the Irish colonial subject—the stranger is "ineradicably ambivalent . . . blurring a boundary line vital to the construction of a particular social order or a particular life-world."[59] Producing the Irish white/not white colonial others as strangers thus draws attention to their ambivalent positioning within the English colonial representational order. They are simultaneously same and other, white and not white. Thus, characterizing the Irish as strangers, perhaps paradoxically, accentuates the colonial sense of them as abject—as an ambivalently perceived threat to the racial order imposed by colonialism. If, as I have suggested, colonial Irishness maps onto redheadedness in the postcolonial context, the ambivalent English imperial construction of the Irish other as stranger—as not at home— provides us with a way of explaining why redheads are constructed ambivalently today.

Mapping Ambivalent Irish Otherness Onto the Redhead

It is estimated that natural redheads make up somewhere between 2 and 3 percent of Anglo cultures.[60] As a minority whose difference is comprised of a highly visible physical marker, many redheads report suffering forms of prejudice. Interestingly, redheads often express the experience of this prejudice in terms that mobilize the discourses of racial exclusion that are frequently used by minorities to describe their experience within the homogenous modern nation-state.[61] For example, Mick Hucknall, lead singer of "blue-eyed soul" outfit Simply Red reports on being ginger-haired in the United Kingdom: "I tell you, if there were no blacks in this country, redhead people would get the hassles. We're a serious minority, only something like 3 percent, and you definitely do get picked on at school."[62] Hucknall's discursive line between redheads and blacks highlights one of the ways that racial otherness gets projected onto the redhead. Importantly, the narration of these kinds of experience speaks to the not-at-homeness of redheads in Anglo cultures, their ambivalently constructed strangeness.

If, like the Irish, redheads are not at home in Anglo cultures, it makes sense, then, that the two redheaded Annes of children's popular culture, Anne of Green Gables and Little Orphan Annie, are both orphans. They are both strangers to the communities they find themselves in. The adventures of Anne of Green Gables begin when Anne is sent by the orphanage to live with Marilla and Matthew Cuthbert, much to the dismay of the Cuthberts, who had requested a boy. Charmed by Anne's curiosity and her outspoken manner, the Cuthberts decide to keep Anne. Nonetheless, Anne's at-homeness is always tentative. She remains acutely aware that she is not the little boy the Cuthberts asked for, and with her bright red hair and frank manner, Anne constantly struggles to fit in. She is an "unusual" young woman who demonstrates not only a propensity for "wild imaginings" but also an excessively masculine set of character traits; all things which position her outside the realm of desirable female behavior, and as an outsider to the small community of Avonlea. The narratives of the Green Gables novels thus center on Anne's efforts to feel at home in her new community. Similarly, in the 1982 film *Annie*, Little Orphan Annie is living in an orphanage under the guardianship of the alcoholic Miss Hannigan when she is invited to stay with the millionaire Daddy Warbucks "just for a week" to keep him company. Hers, too, is a story of not fitting in, and of the search for love and a place she can call home.[63] This not-at-homeness of the two redhaired Annes can be understood as discursive projections of Irish not-at-home-ness.

Furthermore, this Irish not-at-homeness also explains why the redhead is easily, and frequently, produced as exotic in Anglo cultures. One might think here, for example, of the English pre-Raphaelite paintings of the mid-to-late nineteenth century such as the London-born Dante Gabriel Rossetti's "Dante's Dream" in which the pale-skinned, titian-haired Beatrice reclines on a lounge, surrounded by her attendants, in a room decorated in sensuous deep reds and scattered with poppies and Oriental ornaments. More recently, the images of Nicole Kidman in her role as Satine in Baz Luhrmann's movie musical *Moulin Rouge* (2001) also play on notions of the exotic. Numerous images of Kidman circulated in the promotion of the film, but one striking example features Kidman, excessively redheaded and pale-skinned, posing in a costume of white ostrich feathers and sequins against the backdrop of the rich interiors of the Parisian nightclub.[64] Equally, the controversial advertisement, banned in the United Kingdom but reproduced in glossy women's magazines such as *Vogue* and *Marie Claire*, for the exotically named perfume Opium juxtaposes the naked body of the red-haired, hyper-pale-skinned model Sophie Dahl against a background of vivid blue satin.[65] Dahl's body, captured in a moment of autoerotic bliss, in combination with her translucent white skin and a head of slightly disheveled but unmistakably red curls, works to emphasize the idea of the exotic that is evoked by the name of the perfume.

Peter Mason describes the exotic as a representational effect "produced by a process of decontextualization and recontextualization."[66] Further, he argues that "the exotic is *never at home.*"[67] According to Wills, "if an utterance, [such as the redhead here] can be grafted onto another context, this means that it has no 'natural' place, never did have."[68] Colonialism has a long history of representing othered peoples as exotic.[69] Indeed the process of rendering the colonized as exotic helps constitute them as other to the dominant we that defines the homogenous nation-state. The exotic, as a representational effect, arguably produces ambivalence. Mason talks about the "emptiness of the exotic, its function as a blank screen onto which a profusion of often *mutually contradictory* representations [can] be projected, resulting in the overcrammed fullness of the exotic."[70] Inasmuch as the redhead signals the latent cultural memory of the Irish as colonial other, it is not surprising that the redhead gets produced as not at home and as exotic.

These constructions of Irish otherness underpin the contemporary cultural currency of redheadedness as a residual marker of Irish difference in postcolonial Anglo cultures. Redheads — particularly female redheads — mark the barely repressed memory of the English colonization of Ireland, drawing unwanted attention to the arbitrariness of the category of whiteness that still underpins constructions of national identity in Anglo postcolonies.

The Threatening Woman and the
Feminization of the Racial Other

Bram Dijkstra argues that nineteenth-century Western modernity was characterized by a cultural undercurrent of misogyny that culminated by the end of the century in an unprecedented and widespread antifeminine sentiment. Over the course of the nineteenth century, women came to represent the embodiment of evil; a sexualized threat to the intellectual development of rational man, and therefore an obstacle on the path of man's progress to spiritual enlightenment. Not surprisingly, Dijkstra attributes the rise of this pervasive cultural mistrust of women in no small part to the very same kinds of intellectual trends that facilitated the racialization of the Irish. Namely, the adoption of the more prejudicial possibilities of evolutionary theory as justification and legitimation of the white male's claim to supremacy in modernity. Dijkstra outlines how nineteenth-century thought constructed man as aligned with the mind and reason, and woman with the body and the material world. In the context of a culture which privileged the capacity to reason as the key to spiritual transcendence, the effect of this binary opposition of man and woman was to construct women as incapable of evolving into higher spiritual beings. Indeed, it was often claimed that the female of the species, far from evolving, was destined to decline ever further. Just as the Irish were configured as a race in decline, that is, "women were fated to grow ever more obtuse in their femininity."[71] Spiritual transcendence in this worldview was strictly a male prerogative.

Indeed, the art, philosophy, and literature of the nineteenth century endlessly recounts this idea, arguing in the process not only that woman was incapable of accompanying the rational male on his quest for spiritual perfection, but that woman hindered the male. Being at a lesser stage on the evolutionary scale, woman simply did not have the intellectual capabilities to gain her entry into the male realm of higher spirituality, and thus constantly tempted man backwards to her safe haven of erotic materiality. In more anxious accounts of the steps man must take to reach spiritual transcendence, women were represented as envious of man's superior capacities for spiritual understanding and as doing everything within their powers to prevent him from reaching his ultimate goal. In this sense, woman represented a threat to the unfolding of man's divine destiny.

Man was thus locked in a struggle between, on the one hand, the temptation of woman that, if not resisted, led him back to his animal state, and on the other, the repudiation of the feminine which propelled him forwards and upwards to spiritual purity. For man, whose destiny for greater spirituality was guaranteed by his intellect, woman embodied the temptations of the material world. In particular, woman, as the locus of reproduction, represented the lure of the flesh. It was thus women's sexuality, woman as the personification of the sins of the flesh and signifier of the moment of original sin, which presented the most profound threat to man's spiritual betterment. As the Viennese sex theorist Otto Weininger put it: "Man possesses sex, her sexual organs possess woman . . . The condition of sexual excitement is the supreme moment of a woman's life. The woman is devoted totally to sexual matters, that is to say, to the sphere of begetting and reproduction."[72] Thus man was admonished to relinquish woman and to free himself of sex. This was no easy task for, "unfortunately, the flesh was weak and woman delicious."[73]

A spiritually advanced society, it was held, was one in which male and female identities were completely separated. In this scenario woman, constructed by masculine discourse as dependent on man, represented a problem for the male on his spiritual path. Inhabiting a discursive space of dependency which constructed her as in need of men to fulfill her base sexual desires, woman was never quite separate from man, always wishing him back to her erotic realm. As Weininger observed, "sexual differentiation is never quite complete."[74] This in turn meant that men were never free of women either. Woman exerted a constant downward pull on man, a pull which, if he surrendered to it, would throw him back to a lesser state of evolution and dash his chances of spiritual transcendence. Le Conte, describing man's journey to a higher spiritual plane, wrote: "In man spirit emerges above the surface into a higher world, looks down on Nature beneath him, around on other emerged spirits about him, and upwards to the Father of all spirits above him. Emerged, but not wholly free—head above, but not yet foot-loose."[75] And so man repudiates woman but he never quite frees himself of her. She constantly beckons, threatening to undo him, a shadow from which he cannot separate himself, and which threatens to engulf him.

We can begin to see here how the otherness of the category of woman articulates in similar ways to Irish otherness within the nineteenth-century English representational economy. Both Irishness and femininity, that is, constitute a threat to hegemonic white masculine order. Woman, like the Irish, for the nineteenth-century modern white male, destined but struggling for spiritual enlightenment, is the abject—that "thing rejected from which one does not part," that which "disturbs identity, system, order."[76] And so, woman is sexualized because her sexualization, her entry into the representational order as sexual threat, constitutes a technology of control. But her representation as sexual threat only increases her abjection. At once desirable and threatening, she is constructed ambivalently.

In the more specific nineteenth-century context of colonialism, the threat of female sexuality is even more acutely felt. As I have already suggested, the colonial right to rule was justified by the discourse of race, generated by the imperialist privileging of evolutionary biology and deployed to establish a hierarchy of races. This means that in the colonial scenario, "racial purity," for which we can read "national purity" and by extension "cultural purity," becomes an ongoing preoccupation for the colonizer. Miscegenation must be prevented at all costs, for miscegenation represents the dilution of the boundaries between the races as they are defined by colonial discourse, and so the dilution of the purity—and supremacy—of imperial culture. The line that divides "us" and "them," colonizer and colonized, must be rigorously and repeatedly drawn. These boundaries are always already blurred, but colonialism, in its anxious need to convince both itself and those it subjects of its right to power, constantly seeks to establish and police an order predicated on the hierarchical division between same and other. It is this order that the figure of woman threatens to undermine. And it is this feminine threat that helps to explain why redheaded women are constructed ambivalently within the postcolonial representational order.

As biological reproducers of the nation, and the group to whom the social and cultural education of youngsters was entrusted under nineteenth-century gender divisions of labor, the onus of maintaining racial, national, and cultural purity in many senses was seen by colonizers to rest with women. While male colonialism consistently disavowed the agency of women, colonial hegemony nonetheless depended on the cooperation of women to reproduce (in both the material and the metaphorical sense) the borders between the racial groups that necessarily intermingled in the context of the colonial encounter. In this pursuit of constructing boundaries between the groups that comprised, and thus ensured the livelihood of, the empire, then, women's sexuality increasingly became one of the explicit objects of the technologies of colonial surveillance. As Anne McClintock suggests, "controlling women's sexualities, exalting maternity and breeding a virile race of empire-builders were widely perceived as the paramount means for controlling the health and wealth of the male imperial body politic, so that . . . sexual purity emerged as a controlling metaphor for racial, economic and political power . . . Body boundaries were felt to be dangerously permeable and demanding continual purification, so that sexuality, in particular women's sexuality, was cordoned off as the central transmitter of racial and hence cultural contagion."[77] Under colonialism, then, the bodies of women became sites where the borders of colonialism were repeatedly rehearsed. This regulation of women's sexuality constitutes one way in which women were understood to mark the limits of Empire.

However, women were also perceived as a persistent threat to this maintenance of sexual, and therefore racial, boundaries. The control of women's sexuality was perceived as dangerously unstable. Women's sexual activities always threatened to escape the watchful eye of male colonialism, producing an anxiety in the male colonizer. Indeed, for McClintock, colonial attitudes toward women, like those toward the racial other, were characterized by an ambivalence. This ambivalence was the product of a recurrent doubling in male colonial discourse; on the one hand "male megalomania and imperial aggression," and on the other "male anxiety and paranoia."[78] That is, the masculine discourses of colonialism produced women not only as the boundary markers of empire, but also as fundamentally threatening to colonial order, which only produced the need for stricter controls over women's sexuality.[79] McClintock notes the myriad English colonial bureaucratic and legislative initiatives directed at the containment of women's sexual and related roles, such as the administrative patrolling of "open or ambiguous domestic relations," "non-productive" women (prostitutes, unmarried mothers, spinsters), and interracial marriage, as well as the rationalization of motherhood and childrearing.[80] Indeed, the extent of colonial surveillance of women's sexuality betrays the dimensions of the threat women were perceived to pose to imperial order. Like the colonial racial other then, the colonial gendered other, that is, woman, was constructed ambivalently.

In colonial fears of the risk woman's sexuality posed to racial purity, we can detect a colonial logic that maps the racial onto the gendered, and vice versa. We can see how the "purity of race" gets bound up with the "sexual purity" of women. In colonial thought, the discourses of race and gender articulate together, mutually reinscribing one another in order to contain the threat to the fiscal and libidinal economy of the imperial state posed by the racial and/or gendered other.

The racialization of the Irish was bound up with a conception of them as feminine. For example, Matthew Arnold, in 1867, claimed that the "Celtic race . . . is an essentially feminine race" which is fascinated by "bright colours," is lacking in "balance, measure, and patience" and which demonstrates a "perpetual straining after mere emotion."[81] As I noted earlier, postcolonial critiques of this process of feminization have traditionally emphasized the ways that such constructions work to produce the racial other as weak, passive, subservient, and disempowered, a critique that addresses just one facet of colonial representations of racial otherness. If we remember for a moment McClintock's observation that colonial discourse is characterized by a recurrent doubling of megalomania and paranoia, and that both women and the Irish have historically been constructed as a threat to colonial order, we can begin to see how the colonial association of the racial other with the gendered other operates to (re)produce the idea of the racial and/or gendered other as threat. Both the racial and the gendered other get produced ambivalently, both as disempowered, and paradoxically, as fundamentally threatening to the colonial project.

As I have been suggesting, women are constructed as a sexual threat to a colonial order that turns on a concept of the purity of races. Similarly, the Irish are constructed as a racial group that threatens the English constructions of whiteness that provide the legitimation of the colonial right to rule. That is, in the context of the English colonization of Ireland, both women and the Irish are produced as other by white male colonial discourse and come to represent the threat of the abject, the horror of that which is simultaneously both same and other. The association of feminine threat with racial threat in the complementary processes of feminizing and racializing the Irish thus operates to reproduce and reinforce Irish otherness and abjection, and hence justify their subordination in the colonial context. Thus it is redheaded women, and not redheaded men, who are produced ambivalently in Anglo cultures, as particularly dangerous, as simultaneously sexually threatening and desirable, and as always only barely in control of themselves.

Conclusion

Gerardine Meaney has suggested that "a history of colonization is a history of feminization. Colonial powers identify their subject people as passive, in need of guidance, incapable of self-government, romantic, passionate, unruly, barbarous — all those things for which the Irish and women have been both praised and scorned."[82] Redheaded women signify both the racial threat of the Irish and the gendered threat of woman, two categories which historically unsettled the category of whiteness so fundamental — yet always only contingent — to the English colonial project in Ireland, "England's oldest colony."[83]

In postcolonial Anglo cultures, the experience of colonization has not been erased from memory. Rather, its residual still circulates in and through culture. As I indicated at the beginning of this essay, the specter of colonization continues to structure so-called postcolonial understandings of the world. The racial and gendered ordering of colonization is written into the representational order of late-capitalist Anglo societies — it underpins the processes of imagining identity, and shapes the range of practices we perform in relation to those imaginings. Colonialism, as Stuart Hall says, "has its histories — and histories have their real, material and symbolic effects. The past continues to speak to us."[84] In the case of Irish otherness, this colonial history does not speak to us directly. Rather it whispers to us in the language of sublimation. In this landscape, the redheaded woman signifies the others that the English white male colonial subject repudiates but from which he can never quite separate himself, those who enable the legitimation of colonial order and simultaneously threaten to destabilize that process of legitimation. The redheaded woman embodies, in other words, the threat of the disruption of colonial order by its others. Signifying both Irishness and womanness, the redheaded woman gets constructed ambivalently in contemporary culture as both desirable and threatening. In the postcolonial context, as we have seen in relation to the figure of the redheaded woman, the displacement of these kinds of colonial anxieties enables Irishness to be produced as a benign form of whiteness—a way of performing whiteness legitimately—within contemporary English-speaking cultures.

Let me return to the incident with which I began this essay—the question of whether or not the rug matches the carpet.[85] This question is fundamentally a question about authenticity. However, not *authenticity* in the sense that it is normally deployed in postcolonial critiques, which entails establishing the credentials of certain individuals who claim to be able to speak on behalf of a colonized group. Rather, this is a question that, in the context of the cultural legacy of English colonialism in Ireland, seeks to establish the authenticity, and therefore the potency, of the threat posed to postcolonial order by the redheaded woman. Red hair calls the question of authenticity into play; it potentially speaks the "truth" of the threat of the other.

Notes

1. Luke Gibbons, "Race Against Time: Racial Discourse and Irish History," *Oxford Literary Review* 13 (1991): 95.

2. Anne McClintock, *Imperial Leather: Race, Gender and Sexuality in the Colonial Contest* (New York: Routledge, 1995), 52.

3. Nira Yuval-Davis, *Gender and Nation* (London: Sage, 1997), 49.

4. Homi Bhabha, "Of Mimicry and Man," in *The Location of Culture* (London: Routledge, 1994), 89.

5. Men's redheadedness, rather, tends to be either produced as "unmasculine," or it is disavowed. In relation to the former, Grant McCracken cites numerous studies that found that "redheaded males were seen as 'very unattractive, less successful, and rather effeminate.'" *Big Hair: A Journey into the Transformation of Self* (London: Indigo,

1997), 126. With respect to the disavowal of men's redheadedness, in Australia at least, redheaded men are often called "Blue." This refers, depending on who you ask, to the color of the eyes most commonly associated with male redheadedness, or to the color which is positioned diametrically opposite red on the color wheel. Regardless which explanation you prefer, this nickname constitutes a disavowal of male redheadedness.

6. McClintock, *Imperial Leather*, 24.

7. Richard Dyer, *White* (London: Routledge, 1997), 7.

8. See Diane Negra's introduction to this collection.

9. McCracken, *Big Hair*, 127.

10. Colours Hair Trends Book, *Marie Claire, Australia supplement*, 2000, 15.

11. McCracken, *Big Hair*, 124.

12. "The X Files Undercover: Gillian Anderson/Special Agent Dana Scully," <http://www.foxhome.com/trustno1/low/behind/b4main.html>, accessed 10 May 2004.

13. See for example "Gillian Anderson," XFRoadRunners (from the Canadian *TV Guide*, "The 51 Hottest Stars on TV Special Issue"), <http://www.xfroadrunners.com/articles/tvguide_sept01.html>, accessed 10 May 2004.

14. There is a significant literature that describes and explains this positioning of women in Western modernity. See for example, Carole Pateman, *The Sexual Contract* (Cambridge: Polity Press, 1988); Genevieve Lloyd, *The Man of Reason: 'Male' and 'Female' in Western Philosophy* (London: Routledge, 1984); and Phyllis Chesler's classic text, *Women and Madness* (1972; reprint, San Diego: Harcourt Brace Jovanovich, 1989).

15. Victor Turner, *The Ritual Process: Structure and Anti-Structure* (Ithaca: Cornell University Press, 1969), 95.

16. For further discussion of Pauline Hanson's redheadedness, see Judy Lattas, "'We Wouldn't Be Dead for Quids': Hansonism, Fascism, Death and Difference," *Oceania* 71, no. 3 (2001): 226–41.

17. See for example Lloyd, *Man of Reason*.

18. McCracken, *Big Hair*, 125.

19. Ibid., 122.

20. Ibid.

21. Ibid., 127.

22. Incidentally, Springsteen also alludes to the rug/carpet preoccupation: "Tight skirt, strawberry hair/Tell me what you've got, baby, waiting under there."

23. Bronwen Walter, *Outsiders Inside: Whiteness, Place and Irish Women* (London: Routledge, 2001), 73.

24. "Juice," *B Magazine*, December 2001, 204.

25. Pippa, interview by author, 18 October 2001. This was one of a small number of unstructured face-to-face interviews I carried out with redheaded men and women in Western Australia. These were primarily generated by a radio talkback interview I did with Verity James for Perth's ABC Radio 720AM. We might also understand Pippa's

claim (above) as an expression of buying into the "discursive currency" of Irish white-ness that Diane Negra argues "authorizes a location and celebration of whiteness in ways that would otherwise be problematic."

26. The Realm of Redheads website can be found at <http://www.realmofredheads .com/>, accessed 14 January 2002. Where the proxies used by participants alluded to national and/or ethnic identity, they referred exclusively to Celticness, and in particu-lar to Irishness. While I want to focus here on the equation of redheadedness with Irishness in the postcolonial symbolic economy, a similar argument could easily be made about Celticness in general, or about other Celtic national identities such as Scottishness.

27. Gibbons cited in McClintock, *Imperial Leather*, 60.

28. J. A. Watt's phrase as cited in D. George Boyce, *Nationalism in Ireland* (London: Routledge, 1982), 30.

29. Boyce, *Nationalism in Ireland*, 31.

30. See Boyce, *Nationalism in Ireland*, 41.

31. Queen Elizabeth is perhaps one of the most visible female redheads of English history. While Elizabethan iconography represents "Astraea" as a redhead, evidence suggests that she was in fact a natural blonde. However, Elizabeth was the proud owner of over eighty periwigs, her favorite colors being saffron yellow and auburn red. See Jean Keyes, *A History of Women's Hairstyles 1500–1965* (London: Methuen, 1967), 11. In her preference for the red-haired wig, Elizabeth was upholding the traditional associa-tion of red hair with English royalty; an association that I suggest undergoes radical change with the rise of scientific racism in the Victorian era. It is productive to reflect on why Elizabeth continues to be immortalized as a redhead today, as opposed to a saffron blonde. The Virgin Queen's power derived in no small part from her public dis-avowal of her femininity, best expressed in her refusal to marry as is emphasized in the film *Elizabeth*, starring Cate Blanchett (dir. Shekhar Kapur, Columbia/TriStar, 1998). This kind of unwomanly defiance of gender norms is now stereotypically associated with the redheaded woman. The present-day canonization of Elizabeth as a redhead privileges her individual rebellion over her role in England's plantation project in Ire-land, thus disavowing the problematic positioning of her female leadership of English male imperialism.

32. Boyce, *Nationalism in Ireland*, 56.

33. L. Perry Curtis, *Apes and Angels: The Irishman in Victorian Caricature* (Wash-ington, D.C.: Smithsonian Institute Press, 1997), 6, emphasis added.

34. Curtis, *Apes and Angels*, 5.

35. Ibid., 10.

36. McClintock, *Imperial Leather*, 52.

37. Ibid., 55–56.

38. John Beddoe, *The Races of Britain* (1885; reprint, Washington, D.C.: Clive-den, 1983).

39. Winthrop D. Jordan as cited in Yuval-Davis, *Gender and Nation*, 50.

40. The term *white negroes* was coined by Gustave Molinari in 1880. See McClintock, *Imperial Leather*, 52.

41. Beddoe, *Races of Britain*. Madison Grant was a leading North American eugenicist of the early twentieth century who warned against the "dangers of miscegenation" in *The Passing of the Great Race*, first published in 1916. See Madison Grant, *The Passing of the Great Race*, <http://www.africa2000.com/XNDX/madgrant2-06 .html>, accessed 14 January 2002.

42. Murray G. H. Pittock, *Celtic Identity and the British Image* (Manchester: Manchester University Press, 1999), 52.

43. Curtis, *Apes and Angels*, 2.

44. Ibid., 49.

45. This association of Irishness and redheadedness with orangutans appears to still circulate today. One of my informants tells me that his sons call their redheaded Irish friend "Ranga," short for orangutan.

46. Curtis, *Apes and Angels*, xi.

47. Pittock, *Celtic Identity*, 71.

48. With reference to understanding the Irish as representing the abject for the English colonizer, McClintock runs an interesting argument that deserves further elaboration, but which, for reasons of space, cannot be undertaken here. McClintock calls for an understanding of colonialism in terms of a "situated psychoanalysis." She argues that "under imperialism . . . certain groups [such as the Irish] are expelled and obliged to inhabit the impossible edges of modernity . . . Abject peoples are those whom industrial imperialism rejects but cannot do without . . . The abject returns to haunt modernity as its constitutive, inner repudiation: the rejected from which one does not part." *Imperial Leather*, 72.

49. Julia Kristeva, *Powers of Horror: An Essay on Abjection* (New York: Columbia University Press, 1982), 4. The abject, for Kristeva, is at its most powerful when it is rejected from within the self. She writes, "The abject . . . is experienced at the peak of its strength when that subject, weary of fruitless attempts to identify with something on the outside, finds the impossible within." *Powers of Horror*, 5.

50. Ibid., 3.

51. Ania Loomba, *Colonialism/Postcolonialism* (London: Routledge, 1998), 109.

52. Beddoe, *The Races of Britain*.

53. Charles Kingsley as cited in Loomba, *Colonialism/Postcolonialism*, 109.

54. Thomas Carlyle as cited in Pittock, *Celtic Identity and the British Image*, 71.

55. For Dyer, in contemporary Western cultures extreme whiteness is perceived ambivalently by the white majority. He writes: "Extreme whiteness coexists with ordinary whiteness: it is exceptional, excessive, marked. It is what whiteness aspires to and also . . . fears . . . Extreme whiteness thus leaves a residue, a way of being that is not marked as white, in which white people can see themselves." *White*, 222–23, emphasis

added. Dyer's formulation of extreme whiteness as a residue that terrorizes ordinary whiteness can be understood as describing the contemporary perception of extreme whiteness as abject. It is precisely this notion of abject extreme whiteness that often gets attached to the redhead in Anglo cultures today. In the postcolonial construction of the redhead as the embodiment of extreme whiteness, then, we have the articulation of an abject whiteness that parallels the abjection of Irish whiteness, a problematic, disturbing, and contested whiteness, in the era of English colonialism.

56. Pittock, *Celtic Identity and the British Image*, 70.

57. Andrew Hadfield and John McVeagh, eds., *Strangers to That Land: British Perceptions of Ireland from the Reformation to the Famine* (Gerrards Cross, Buckinghamshire: Colin Smythe, 1994), 24.

58. For example, English colonials declared the territory now known as Australia as *terra nullius*. Effectively, this legal definition constructed the Australian continent as void of human life and its indigenous Australians as (nonhuman) "strangers." For further discussion, see Australian historian Henry Reynolds, *The Other Side of the Frontier: Aboriginal Resistance to the European Invasion of Australia* (Ringwood: Penguin, 1982).

59. Zygmunt Baumann, *Modernity and Ambivalence* (Cambridge: Polity Press, 1991), 61.

60. McCracken, *Big Hair*, 125.

61. This appears to be particularly acute in the school playground. A number of redheads living in the United States, the United Kingdom, and Australia report being ostracized at school. See <http://www.realmofredheads.com/>, accessed 14 January 2002.

62. "Roussette," August 2001, <http://www.realmofredheads.com>. The construction of Simply Red's music as "blue-eyed soul" positions it as a substantially whitened version of this traditionally black popular-music form. However, the band is named after its redheaded vocalist. As such, if red hair connotes the "not-quite-whiteness" of Irish ethnic identity, then this "blue-eyed soul" is only partially, or incompletely, "white." This positions Simply Red in the same liminal space between the construction of "white" and "black" identity that Irishness occupies.

63. Indeed, while ostensibly the narrative of the film version of *Annie* (dir. John Huston, Columbia/Tristar, 1982) tells us a story about Depression-era America, there is a subtextual narrative about the English colonization of Ireland. Red-haired orphan Annie can be read as representing the untamed, undisciplined Irish colonial subject. The film's plot revolves around a struggle for ownership of Annie between red-haired Miss Hannigan (the uncivilized, feminized Irish) and Daddy Warbucks (the English male colonial state). Warbucks's name signals both the paternalism of the colonizer, and the military/industrial nexus of modern colonial states. He eventually wins over, and in the process, tames the wild red-haired orphan and assimilates her (albeit perhaps tentatively) into white civilized domesticity. We can read this story as a projection

of English colonial fantasies about the conquest of the Irish. While the film replicates many of the original comic strip's features, the film's subtext may be attributed in part to the influence of director John Huston — the American director who, in order to evade what he described as the "moral rot" of U.S. culture, emigrated to Ireland in 1952 where he continued to live for the following twenty-three years (obtaining citizenship in 1964). Peter B. Flint, "Obituary: John Huston, Film Director, Writer and Actor, Dies at 81," <http://www.nytimes.com/learning/general/onthisday/bday/0805.html>, accessed 8 June 2004.

64. See the photographs by Annie Leibowitz in Jonathan Van Meer, "The Wildest Party," *Vogue Australia*, January 2001, 124–37.

65. This image can be found at <http://shop.store.yahoo.com/solissf/nasodaadba.html>, accessed 8 June 2004. This advertising image "accounted for a third of all complaints about poster advertising" in England in 2000. Interestingly, "the second most complained about advert was for gas supplier Npower, which featured a ginger-haired family accompanied by the words: 'There are some things in life you can't choose.' " See <http://ad-rag.com/179.php>, accessed 8 June 2004. My thanks to my friend, Amanda Cinanni, who drew my attention to the Opium advertisement and the controversy it caused.

66. Peter Mason, *Infelicities: Representations of the Exotic* (Baltimore: Johns Hopkins University Press, 1998), 6.

67. Ibid., 6, emphasis added.

68. D. Wills as cited in Mason, *Infelicities*, 9–10.

69. See Yuval-Davis, *Gender and Nation*.

70. Mason, *Infelicities*, 3, emphasis added.

71. Bram Dijkstra, *Idols of Perversity: Fantasies of Feminine Evil in Fin de Siecle Culture* (New York: Oxford University Press, 1986), 219.

72. Weininger as cited in Dijkstra, *Idols of Perversity*, 219.

73. Ibid., 223.

74. Ibid., 219.

75. Le Conte as cited in Dijkstra, *Idols of Perversity*, 217.

76. Kristeva, *Powers of Horror*, 4.

77. McClintock, *Imperial Leather*, 47.

78. Ibid., 26.

79. For McClintock, this doubling of paranoia and megalomania is most neatly expressed in Jan Van Der Straet's drawing [1575] of Vespucci's "discovery" of America. McClintock writes, "In the central distance of the picture, between Amerigo and America, a cannibal scene is in progress. The cannibals appear to be female" (26). For McClintock, this drawing encapsulates not only the power of the male colonizer but also the male colonial fear of women. The figure of the Gaelic cannibal is prevalent in early colonial representations of the Irish. In particular, it is Irish women who are singled out as cannibalistic, illustrating the ways in which English colonialism of Ire-

land was characterized by "paranoia and megalomania" toward women. For example, Fynes Moryson alleged that during the famine of the 1590s, "many honest gentlemen living in Newry can witness that some old women of those parts, used to make a fire in the fields, and divers little children driving out the cattle in the cold morning, and coming thither to warm them, were by them surprised, killed and eaten." Cited by Norah Carlin, "Ireland and Natural Man in 1649," in *Europe and Its Others*, vol. 2, edited by Francis Barker et al. (Colchester: University of Essex, 1985), 99–100.

80. McClintock, *Imperial Leather*, 47–48.

81. Matthew Arnold as cited in Pittock, *Celtic Identity and the British Image*, 67, 65.

82. Meaney as cited in Yuval-Davis, *Gender and Nation*, 53.

83. Tamara L. Hunt, "Wild Irish Women: Gender, Politics and Colonialism in the Nineteenth Century," in *Women and the Colonial Gaze*, edited by Tamara L. Hunt and Micheline R. Lessard (New York: New York University Press, 2002), 49.

84. Stuart Hall as cited in Loomba, *Colonialism/Postcolonialism*, 182.

85. James Bond asks a similar question of Tiffany Case when he first meets her in the film *Diamonds Are Forever* (dir. Guy Hamilton, MGM, 1971). He asks the seemingly blonde Tiffany, "Do the collars match the cuffs?" Tiffany subsequently reveals that underneath her blonde wig, her hair is actually red. In the context of my discussion of the meanings of red hair here, then, Bond might be understood to be quizzing Tiffany about her authenticity on two counts.

GERARDINE MEANEY

Dead, White, Male: Irishness in
Buffy the Vampire Slayer and *Angel*

The closing decades of the twentieth century saw a definitive and rapid shift in the characterization of the vampire in fiction, film, and television. Vampires ceased to be figures of invasive otherness and became creatures so like ourselves that they largely lost their villain status and became the heroes of increasingly postmodern, amoral horror. It is in the context of this evolution that the appearance of a guilt-ridden Irish vampire with a soul in the genre-defining cult TV shows, *Buffy the Vampire Slayer* (1997–2003) and *Angel* (1999–2004), needs to be understood. This essay will examine the function of Irishness in these series as both an exemplary, assimilable white foreignness and as a site of displacement of the difficulties of white identity within postmodern popular culture. It takes as its starting point Richard Dyer's observation that a key component of the cultural construction of whiteness is its construction not just as a norm, but also as the opposite of color, the opposite of race. "The invisibility of whiteness as a racial position in white (which is to say dominant) discourse is of a piece with its ubiquity."[1]

Numerous articles have analyzed the marginalization and sometimes quite literal demonization of racial others in *Buffy the Vampire Slayer*.[2] Mary Hammond has more recently argued that the series embodies a "nightmare vision of a world power beset by anxieties about faith, morality, and the future and in need of a reinterpretation of its immigrant past."[3] My primary object here, however, is an interrogation of the discourse of whiteness and the deployment of Irish ethnicity within that discourse in these series.

The extraordinarily rapid and prolific academic exegesis of *Buffy* is largely centered on the question of whether the circulation of images of female empowerment in postmodern popular culture constitutes subversion or co-option. A focus on the heroine's masculine counterpart poses acute questions about race and ethnicity for readings which seek to emphasize the subversive and progressive effects of current "quality television." In the character of Angel, progressive and regressive elements co-exist, and his Irishness is only occasionally foregrounded, interwoven for the most part in the back-story that connects the series to other texts, other genres, other histories. Yet his Irishness is both a series of ironic quotations of a particular ethnicity and a persistent displacement of the problem of whiteness. In his interaction with a plethora of outsiders, vampires, nice white girls, and, above all, racial others, the character performs an uncanny likeness of a traditional American hero. But that performance is camp, ironic, and laced with intertextual references which draw attention to the constructedness of the image and even its ideological purpose. Angel's characterization nods knowingly to psychoanalytical, postcolonial, and queer readings of vampire fiction.

Irishness, Masculinity, and Race

The Irish filmmaker Bob Quinn declared some years ago that "Ireland has long been a figment of the American imagination."[4] The function of that particular figment and its status as a product of imagination is increasingly complex and ambivalent. In mainstream Hollywood representations of Ireland in the late 1990s, the metonymic relation of Irishness to terrorism receded.[5] The link between Irishness and the past became dominant, but also stripped of its previous negative political connotations. The association of Irishness with a lost rural idyll in U.S. popular culture can be traced back to the silent productions of the Kalem Company between 1911 and 1916. Its identification with a form of masculinity threatened by industrial society and recoverable through ethnicity and a return to pastoral values has been a key element of U.S. representations of Ireland since the paradigm-setting Irish American fantasy of Ireland, *The Quiet Man* (1952).

As Luke Gibbons points out, "not least of the paradoxes of *The Quiet Man*'s undisputed status as the emblematic representation of the Irish on the screen is that while it has garnered accolades from directors as diverse as Spielberg and Scorsese, for others it is the bane of Irish cinema."[6] Gibbons persuasively argues that the film needs to be understood as a self-reflexive and critical pastoral and "that its romantic evocation of Ireland is not meant to be taken for real, anymore more than its beguiling surface tranquility."[7] Those Irish filmmakers and critics who so deplore it may not be the naive proponents of narrative authenticity that this formulation makes them seem, however. As Gibbons's study of the film itself demonstrates, *The Quiet Man* "became virtually a master narrative in Bord Failte's (Irish Tourist Board) promotion of Ireland abroad, especially for the American market."[8] The Irish dislike of the film may be rooted in unease with the figmentary status of Ireland, initially produced as a cultural commodity and ethnic resource for tourist consumption, then as magnet for inward investment by multinational corporations. The film marks the simultaneous erasure and fetishization of Ireland's history and locality, the advent of Ireland as simulacrum of the object of another's desire. At the heart of this is the paradox that Ireland is sold as that which cannot be sold, as a place where relationships with persons and place cannot simply be reduced to transactions between commodities and where gender, familial, and communal relations have an authenticity or atavism (inflections vary) lost in contemporary society.

In *The Quiet Man*, the ultimate American conservative hero, John Wayne (as Sean Thornton), recovers his manhood by becoming Irish. Sean Thornton is unable to fight after killing an opponent in the boxing ring. He leaves America and returns to his mother's cottage in Innisfree. There he falls in love with and marries Mary Kate Danaher (Maureen O'Hara). Before the marriage can be truly realized, however, he must claim her dowry, in other words reunite his economic and familial roles. To do this he must also fight again, this time his brother-in-law for his wife's socially symbolic dowry, rather than an anonymous opponent for simple cash. Finding his place in a rural Irish community restores to him the meaningful masculine role of which the commodification of his body and bravery in the boxing ring had deprived him. Irishness then offers a mode of masculinity which is out of place in industrial and postindustrial societies, but also a narrative of containment of that masculinity within a romantic role.

Whatever the critical subtext of Ford's film, both U.S. popular culture and the Irish tourist industry for many years appropriated its Technicolor rural Ireland as a nostalgic emblem of lost traditional family values and gender roles, acted out in idyllic rural settings.[9] The emigrant's complex of desire, anger, and loss of homeland was transformed into a profitable fantasy of return and plenitude. In contrast, contemporary Irish and, increasingly, Irish American, representations of the Irish past almost overwhelmingly identify it with deprivation, family dysfunction, perverse or repressed sexuality, sexual violence, class conflict, and, in general, buried trauma. As this analysis of *Buffy the Vampire Slayer* and *Angel* will show, this dual identity of Ireland as a site of the idealized family and the failure of that family extends the functions of Irish characters in certain types of popular narrative. Moreover, the identification of Ireland with what could be termed gothic family narrative is deployed in both series to criticize precisely those family values and heroic masculinities with which Ireland continues to be associated in the mainstream media.[10]

Vampires, Anachronism, and Ireland

The horror genre depends to a large extent on dramatic anachronism: ancient horrors are unearthed by modern building work, ghosts of the past are activated by present traumas, past traumas eternally repeat themselves. In the romantic figure of the vampire Angel, introduced in *Buffy the Vampire Slayer*, this link to the past is quite literal. Flashbacks over several seasons of *Buffy* and *Angel* show the vampire's human life in eighteenth-century Ireland, his career as the evil vampire Angelus, and the gypsy curse which restores his soul and eventually compels Angel to engage in an heroic crusade to atone for the crimes of Angelus. More than two centuries old, this vampire signifies an anachronistic form of masculinity. When Angel rejects the advances of one of the many young women he heroically rescues, she mocks his antiquated sexual vocabulary. "Make love? What century are you from?" ("Untouched," *Angel*, season two).

The identification of this outmoded masculinity with his Irishness is reinforced in narrative terms by the use of an Irish accent in the flashbacks setting up back-story for his character. This Irish accent is moreover used only in pre–twentieth century settings. In the second episode of season two, "Are You Now or Have You Ever Been?" (which undertakes a remarkable exploration of the horrors of racism and McCarthyism in 1950s Los Angeles), Angel not only has an American accent, but the costume design deliberately invokes his identification with an American icon of troubled masculinity, James Dean. The selective use of the Irish accent identifies Irish ethnicity predominantly with the vampire's human origins as Galway-born Liam and with his demonic alter ego Angelus, at least until Angel becomes a father in season three.

The ambivalence of the recurrent romance narrative of Buffy and Angel is compounded by the double nature of the male romantic lead, whose split between good and evil is characterized by his double identity as the romantic hero, Angel, and his alter ego, Angelus. The labyrinthine gypsy curse establishes that Angel will turn into Angelus if he experiences one moment of true happiness. Consequently when he sleeps with Buffy, he returns to evil and becomes a quite different, even opposite, character. This has been identified by the show's writers repeatedly as a metaphor for the virgin heroine's fear of sexuality and an extreme fictional representation of a regular teenage experience, but it also indicates a horror of male sexuality embedded in the narrative.

The prohibition on sexual fulfillment also makes the sexual identity of Angel's character ambivalent. The narrative repeatedly presents the hero with sexual opportunities he is forced to decline. In consequence he is constantly under pressure to define his sexuality negatively, against other's interpretations that he is castrated ("Guise Will Be Guise," *Angel*, season two) or, repeatedly, gay. Intriguingly, Joss Whedon, the creator of both series, quotes the Irish filmmaker Neil Jordan in the DVD commentary for the first episode of the spin-off: "When sex is impossible, everything becomes sexual." The establishment of the male lead as an impossible object of desire, eternally desiring and losing the heroine, undoubtedly explains some of the popularity of *Buffy* with a female audience in the 18–34 age group. It presents this knowing and media-literate audience with a postmodern romance which it can ironically enjoy on the basis that it is premised on the impossibility of its fulfillment.

The impossibility of the romance between Buffy and Angel falls into the category of "defining narrative enigma or puzzle" crucial to the narrative world of *Buffy the Vampire Slayer*.[11] Elizabeth Krimmer and Shilpa

Raval have argued that this condition of impossibility, crucial to the conjunction of love and death in Western romance narratives, is crucial to the way in which "*Buffy* maintains audience interest by deploying a strategy of narrative deferral."[12] The logic of frustrated-but-endless desire is actually the logic of consumption of the show's pleasures as well as an element of narrative. The cult fan desires and is promised, through merchandizing, fan magazines, and the Internet, intimate involvement in the ideal community, which is another recurrent feature of cult TV series. Fan interaction online is such that to an extent postmodern cult television does actually meet this demand for community, but only virtually. There is a constant excess of desire for involvement — in a narrative which would offer a fully realized identity — beyond the satisfactions offered by the cult series itself. The persistence of this desire is the very condition of fandom, stimulating the appetite for more shows, more behind-the-scenes gossip, more websites. Critical readings of vampire texts have often identified the emergence of the vampire in popular fiction with the emergence of fear of unbridled consumerism. In *Buffy* sexual desire becomes at least in part a metaphor for consumer desire.

In this context the role that Angel's Claddagh ring plays in the second and third seasons of *Buffy* is significant (and that significance is deepened by the fact that copies of the Claddagh ring are "the most popular item on the Buffystore website").[13] The ring is at first all that Angel has left of "my people, before I was changed" ("Surprise," part 1, *Buffy*, season two), next all that Buffy has left of him ("Anne," *Buffy*, season three), and finally the medium of his return, though with the blight of impossibility still on their relationship. The ring signifies his Irishness as a lost identity, but also as the promise of fulfillments beyond the narrative bounds of the series. Underlying the narrative role of the ring is the logic of fetishism, which also underlies the relationship between the show's fans and its merchandise. Both ethnicity and fandom are a complex matter of investment in the right accessories.

The romantic fantasy in *Buffy* is, typically for female gothic, potently fused with a paranoid one, but here given an extraordinarily puritan twist. Sex will instantly convert the romance narrative into a horror one. (Interestingly a similar narrative twist is evident in the ur-text of postmodern television, *Twin Peaks* [1990–91], where the detective is pos-

1. In *Buffy the Vampire Slayer* and *Angel*, David Boreanaz's "vampire with a soul" expresses stereotypical Irish Catholic guilt in an eroticized white male body. (Courtesy Movie Market)

sessed by the evil spirit he has pursued after his only night of passion in twenty-four episodes.) Postmodern horror films, such as the *Scream* trilogy (1996–2000) and *Cherry Falls* (1999), often mock earlier horror films' retributive violence against sexually active characters.

The pivotal role of the loss of virginity in the collapse of a romance narrative into a horror one in *Buffy* season two is more complex. It is played with all the pathos that the soap-opera strand in the series can muster, focusing on the young girl's confusion and hurt. This story arc also has elements of the rape-revenge fantasies in which postfeminist female warriors have some of their origins.[14] Buffy has to become tough enough to kill Angel, and casting her as the innocent young woman whose love is scorned by the (centuries) more experienced Angelus more than legitimizes her violence. A scene where he mocks her reluctance to kill him ends with Buffy kicking him in the groin, defusing the emotional narrative with comic violence, but also demystifying and reducing male potency. Despite this moral narrative, however, evil Angelus also represents a release of that potency from the strictures of romance. Angelus is both released by and a release from the tormented longing which characterizes the romance of Angel and Buffy.

Angel's outmoded but attractive masculinity initially functions as a supplement to the contemporary version of femininity embodied in Buffy. The male lead is morally ambiguous, foreign in origin, and American in accent, so old he is technically dead, yet a focus of dangerous sexuality. The female hero is by contrast spectacularly and often humorously (post)modern.

Families, Nations, and Vampires

The ethnic, moral and sexual duality established for the character of Angel in *Buffy* is repeated in the spin-off series where he takes over the heroic title role. From the start of the series, the character is resolutely identified with the ultimate stereotype of American masculinity, the loner private eye established in countless films noirs. Audiences were simultaneously reminded in season one of his Irish roots, in a series of flashbacks establishing his origin and history. The flashback narrative also includes the character of Liam, the human who became these vampiric alter egos. This Irish narrative is extraordinary for a number of reasons.

Buffy attracted considerable comment for its very positive representation of a female-headed, single-parent family.[15] In contrast the Angel narrative represents the traditional family in terms of violently destructive patriarchy. Elizabeth Cullingford has identified the persistence of the story of Cuchulainn and his killing of his son, Conlaoch, in contemporary Irish film.[16] The work of Yeats and Synge establishes the centrality of violence between fathers and sons in the canon of the Irish theater, but it is repeated in a number of crucial films establishing the definition of contemporary Irish film, including *The Field* (1990) and *Michael Collins* (1996).[17] This trope of violence between fathers and sons emerges unexpectedly and with disturbing violence in the representation of Angel's origins. It is his father's rejection of Liam which is ultimately responsible for his transformation into a vampire, and when he returns from the dead his first act as Angelus is to devour his family. Moreover this parricidal narrative recurs in Angel's relationship with his own son, Connor. The apparent victory of the Oedipal figures in these contemporary American narratives is only superficially in contrast to the more pessimistic Irish narratives. Both fathers prove ultimately to be undefeated. The fatally dysfunctional patriarchal family is like Angel himself, familiar yet other, anachronistic yet persistent, uncanny.

The trope of Irish innocence is ironically employed. Liam is vulnerable to the vampire Darla's seduction, not because of his violence, sexuality, or drinking, but because despite these he is innocent of the ways of the world. When he encounters her under Galway's Spanish Arch she tells him she is from "around," but implies a knowing cosmopolitanism. He replies, "I've never been anywhere" before falling into her devouring embrace ("Becoming," part 1, *Buffy*, season two). Both the acting and costume design reinforce the contrast between her ironic knowledge and his wide-eyed unawareness of the danger.

The use of the Spanish Arch as the scene of Liam's transformation into Angelus, though it is hardly a detail which would be recognized by most of the series' viewers, introduces the dual characterization of Angel's Irish past. As an Irish American he is an assimilated immigrant, but he is also originally European. The arch commemorates trading relationships which link Ireland with old Europe rather than the New World. In her very thorough analysis of stereotypes of Irishness in Buffy and Angel, Donna L. Potts reads this scene as complicit with an Irish American fantasy of Ireland as innocently preindustrial:

> The implication in the afore-mentioned scene is that Liam's acceptance of Darla's offer to see the world ("Becoming," Part 1) results in the loss of his soul, and in turn, that the price the Irishman pays for going global is his very soul—a notion that Yeats would readily have embraced, and that Americans even in the twenty-first century still cling to. Their devotion to the images of quaint Irish peasants and wholesome Colleens, their love tinged with nostalgia for Celtic kitsch such as Irish cottage music boxes that play sentimental Irish tunes, dish towels emblazoned with Irish blessings, and even handcut pieces of Irish turf, is much too alive for them to gracefully accept a globalized, fully wired Ireland emblematized by the comparatively baleful

image of the Celtic Tiger. Darla, incidentally, is an American from the Virginia colony, reminding us that globalization is tantamount to Americanization.[18]

In important ways, however, the character of Liam is not assimilable to stereotypes of Irish American identity. This is certainly not the story of decent working people made good. *Angel* is very specific about Angel's middle-class identity as a merchant's son. The corporate attorney Lindsay justifies his own devil's bargain with the evil law firm Wolfram and Hart by recounting his poor-white-trash origins, scorning Angel's moral high ground as a middle-class luxury. "What were you? Merchant's son . . . couple of servants before you ate them?" Angel's reply — "Only the one" — echoes his own very middle-class contempt for his father's pretensions when the old man accused him of attempting to corrupt "the servants" ("Blind Date," part 1, *Buffy*, season one) Angelus rather than Angel carries the traditional association of vampires with an outdated European aristocracy, but the consequent identification of Angel's back-story as a European one inflected by class preempts the mainstream rags-to-riches element in his American identity. It could be argued that this merely overlays a stereotype of Ireland with one of Europe, but the casting of the Irish vampire in a Byronic mode has interesting implications for his deployment as a form of white ethnicity.

The representation of the Irish family in *Angel* subverts the promotion of traditional family values and the sentimentalization of tradition in many mainstream representations of Irish ethnicity. Both the patriarchal family and tradition as such are repeatedly presented in both *Buffy* and *Angel* as the source rather than the remedy for evil. Liam's violent father, beating and scorning his son for his "whoring" is in marked contrast to Buffy's mother, who, confronted with the fact that her daughter has slept with a much older man, admonishes her for "a serious error of judgment," but nonetheless supports and comforts her. The former family gives birth to the evil Angelus, the latter the heroic Buffy. Moreover, the family pattern which produced Liam/Angelus/Angel is echoed and mirrored in an array of dysfunctional patriarchal families encountered in his spin-off series. The "Prodigal" episode draws analogies between Angel's past and that of an L.A. police detective, Kate. Like Angel,

Kate has suffered from the inadequacies of a domineering and judgmental parent. Kate's father is presented as an old-fashioned uniformed policeman, an Irish American stereotype. He is very much one of the boys, and she identifies her choice of career as an attempt to get his attention by becoming one of those boys herself. Kate's father is soon discovered to be corrupt and is killed by vampires as a result of his dealings in the underworld. Like Angel's relation with his father, Kate's is constructed in tragic terms. Her father's corruption is motivated by an attempt to provide for her, but he can never express affection for her. Traditional masculinity, then, is presented as at best disabled and inadequate, particularly in its crucial paternal role. At worst it is downright abusive.

Both series provide numerous examples of the evils implicit in the traditional family. In *Buffy*, one of the most interesting late additions to the "team," the white witch, Tara, has been convinced by her family that the powers she has inherited from her mother are demonic. This lie endangers both her relationship with her lover, Willow, and the safety of the group. The new ties which Tara has formed—her love affair with Willow and her membership in the group of friends which supports Buffy—provide her with a base from which to challenge her repressive and condemnatory biological family. In "Untouched" in season two of *Angel*, a young woman's psychokinetic abilities are revealed to be rooted in rage against her father's sexual abuse. Like Tara, she finds enough support in the community of outsiders surrounding Angel to confront and transcend her past.

These storylines work on the basis of an identification of the family with trauma and the group with recovery. They are therapy narratives in many respects, but the representation of the patriarchal family as in itself a trauma from which therapeutic recovery is necessary is recurrent and significant. Lynne Segal, commenting on the vilification of changes in family structures in the mainstream U.S. media, has analyzed the way in which abuses which were intrinsic to traditional family structures are now displaced onto the breakdown of those structures: "Even the evils of paternal incest and domestic violence . . . are discarded for the evils of fatherlessness in the tendentious social science discourses of David Papenoe or David Blakenhorn . . . Mysteriously, these pathologies of abuse which feminists identified as part of the warp and weave of traditional, male-dominated family patterns have been rethreaded to appear as *themselves* the product of family breakdown."[19]

Angel's parricidal narratives challenge that process, representing the traditional family as a locus of horror. In doing so the series counters the rampant deployment of Ireland as a scene of nostalgia and family values and draws on elements in contemporary Irish cultural production (particularly the films of Jim Sheridan and Neil Jordan) which have crossed over to the American mainstream.[20] Irishness in the series is cultural shorthand both for the traditional family and for its implicit violence. The flashbacks to Galway offer both a mode of exploring that family and of displacing the critique of it onto another, related culture.

Sidekicks and Teams, Ethnicity and Race

The Irishness of Angel is linked, then, with dangerous male sexuality, tragic familialism, doom at the hands of the past, and a redemption narrative, which promises that the new world will eventually allow him to become unambivalently the hero. It also allows him to function as a pivot in the complex of national and racial identities which comprise the group that forms around the initially singular hero. In the first series this included an Irish half-demon named Doyle, who started out as comic relief and became a much darker figure, tormented by guilt at his betrayal of his demon kin. Doyle was played by the late Irish actor Glenn Quinn, but his Irishness is not specifically accounted for in any of the narratives relating to him. It appears not to have been an element in the original script, but a consequence of the casting. Quinn apparently first auditioned with an American accent and then suggested that he try the character in his native Dublin one.[21]

The identification of this hard-drinking, gambling, and dangerous-living half-demon as Irish does more than rehearse national stereotypes. Doyle functions as a link between the hero and the "powers that be," higher beings who offer Angel a chance of redemption if he fights on the side of good. These powers communicate with the hero through Doyle, who suffers painful and prophetic visions. Doyle's prophetic gift is also a curse and, it is implied, a punishment. The most developed element in Doyle's characterization is his guilt for the past, by which he is haunted,

2. *Angel*'s ensemble cast represents a complex web of ethnic, racial, and gender identities. (Screen capture)

despite an apparent preoccupation with present pleasures. In this sense Doyle was related to the Irish narrative in *Angel* irrespective of casting. Doyle is initially deeply ashamed of his demon side, revealing it to Cordelia only at his death, for example. This shame at his own nature has cost him his marriage and is at the root of his guilt. Because of it, he failed to answer an appeal for help from his demon relatives who have been slaughtered as a result of his negligence.

Doyle, then, is ashamed of his origins and ashamed of being ashamed. He is also an alcoholic. His long monologue in the first episode of season one of *Angel* serves multiple functions. It summarizes Angel's back-story and sets up the narrative premise of the new series. It establishes the tone of the series, setting both horrific and romantic events shown in flash-back in the context of Doyle's witty and ironic understatement. Doyle's speech also establishes the theme of addiction at the heart of the narra-tive. Doyle's speech lectures Angel on the dangers of remaining cut-off from social interaction: if he forms no bonds with people then his longing for their blood will prove ultimately irresistible. The motivational speech is punctuated, however, by Doyle's search for drink in Angel's apartment, continued as they go out to the local liquor store, and completed as Doyle starts to drink from a bottle in the street.

The analogy of vampirism and addiction is now fairly commonplace in the horror genre. Abel Ferrara's 1995 cult vampire film was called *The Addiction*, for example. The analogy is usually with drugs not alcohol, however. Doyle's drinking, his visions, and his guilt, his combination of humor and horror, make him a liminal figure, half-human, half-comedian, half-hero, but also a figure for the hero's liminality. When Doyle learns enough from his mission to recover himself, he fulfils his new heroic role by dying in Angel's place, the character having completed its function in establishing moral and psychological ambivalence as the territory of the series. Doyle also establishes Irishness as haunted, compulsive, and yet redeemable.

The character of Doyle was replaced as Angel's sidekick by Wesley, a comically inept English would-be hero, who also became gradually darker and more dangerous. A series of English antitheses or doubles shadows the development of Angel in both *Buffy* and *Angel*. The antitheses include both Wesley and Buffy's "watcher," Giles, who functions as her father surrogate. Both of these characters are closely identified with stereotypically traditional English values, including a high degree of repression and propriety and a combination of effectiveness in surprising and critical situations with ineffectualness in relatively everyday ones. Angel also has a very different English alter ego in the punk vampire, Spike, who at first represents all that Angel once was. Later Spike becomes Angel's double, first as a rival for Buffy's affection, later for his heroic status (Spike also turns from evil to troubled good).

Angel's twinning with a variety of English characters maps out a series of interlinked forms of ethnic and masculine identity. Wesley, Giles, and Spike either fail to fulfill or exceed masculine ideals of heroism, restraint, or romance. They are contrasted with the female members of the team, whose development is more even: Cordelia progresses from valley girl to visionary to demon and Fred from demented victim to scientific expert. The emergence of a team rather than a series of sidekicks was marked by the inclusion of the only major African American character in either series, Charles Gunn, introduced as leader of a group of street kids defending themselves against vampires in the meaner streets of Los Angeles in "War Zone" in season one.

Angel veers dramatically between liberal and conservative representations of race. It includes a mixed-race couple in Gunn and Fred, which is still rare on U.S. television, but the relationship is always framed by a white rival for the white woman's affections. The series acknowledges its unease with the presentation of an African American character in a subservient role, and Gunn challenges Angel's leadership in plot terms and his own sidekick status through a series of ironic asides. Both Doyle and Wesley seek to emulate Angel's heroic masculinity, in Doyle's case with tragic yet redeeming effects, in Wesley's with comic but ultimately life-enhancing ones. But Gunn is the only viable alternative hero in the series.

The teaser in the episode when Gunn is first introduced draws glaring attention to this. Whedon's remarks on his original inspiration for *Buffy* are much repeated in both fan and critical responses to the show: "It was pretty much the blond girl in the alley in the horror movie who keeps getting killed . . . I felt bad for her . . . She was fun, she had sex, she was vivacious. But then she would get punished for it. Literally, I just had that image, that scene, in my mind, like the trailer for a movie—what if the girl goes into the dark alley. And the monster follows her. And she destroys him."[22] The opening scene in "War Zone" reverses this scenario of the white girl imperiled and then triumphing over "dark" forces. A young and apparently vulnerable African American woman is shown hurrying through a run-down and deserted part of Los Angeles. A high angled shot locating these streets below the freeway gives the impression of a look beneath the surface of the city. In this subterranean world the girl is prey. A series of unattributed point-of-view shots, the staple of so many horror scenes like this, establish she is being watched and followed. Four white men emerge from the shadows behind her. Then she turns into a blind alley and turns to face them. The nature and meaning of the scene is immediately changed by the look in her eye. In a direct parallel to the *Buffy* scenario, the girl becomes hunter not hunted.

However, this girl's role is not that of the slayer/leader. She eventually fights, but she is primarily bait drawing the vampires into a gang of street fighters led by her brother, Gunn. The camera pans upward slowly, from the vampire's point of view, from Gunn's boots to his black clothes. Given that this is a precredit sequence in Gunn's first episode and there have been no cutaway shots establishing that Angel is elsewhere the expectation that the face confronting the vampires will be Angel's is inevitable. When instead the panning shot ends with a close-up of Gunn's face, he responds to the vampire's, "You!," with "Why? Who else were you expecting?"

From the start, then, Gunn is established as well able to fill the heroic role in his own right, a point he repeatedly makes himself. The episode even ends with his declaration that he won't need Angel's help, while Angel acknowledges he might need Gunn's. The insertion of the latter's face where the audience had expected Angel's vampire-pale one draws attention to the importance of sharp contrasts of black and white in the costume and set design. Gunn's street clothes and attitude are often the key element in disrupting the retro look of the series and as such are crucial to maintaining its postmodern play with genre and style. The series ultimately integrates Gunn into the position of subsidiary team player with an unease often displaced in irony.

Gunn's development as a character is explicitly linked to rejection of his old allegiances to a predominantly African American community in order to function within a new overwhelmingly white one. He is initially tormented by divided loyalties, but gradually becomes more integrated into the central team. The crisis point in the narrative of Gunn's divided loyalties comes early in season three, in "That Old Gang of Mine." Gunn discovers that without his leadership his old gang has moved from self-defense to mindless violence against demons. When Gunn was first introduced in season one, he had apparently been on the verge of just such a transformation himself. What he regards as his failure to protect his sister undermines his certainty and appetite for danger, however. His subsequent alliance with Angel is portrayed by his old gang as "moving on up" and selling out. Consequently, Gunn is unable to reason with or restrain them. The gang falls under the influence of a demagogue demon hater who is presented as both racist (against demons) and a kind of rarefied essence of television African American gang member. "That Old Gang of Mine" is indicative of the way in which ironic inversions — African-

American youth as the perpetrators of racist violence against harmless demons—can implode into very old and regressive patterns. Introduced as a "bunch of kids" fighting evil and defending themselves, Gunn's old friends are presented in this episode as violent, unstable, unreasonable, resentful of the hard-earned advancement of others, and unamenable to ethical consideration or just leadership.

Precisely because the issue of race is raised in *Angel*, race threatens to destabilize the show's postmodern, knowing, and self-reflexive relationship with the private-eye and horror genres. The use of the Los Angeles location, so strongly identified with racial conflict in the public consciousness, as opposed to the fictional middle-class Sunnydale, opens up fissures in the hyperdiegesis of the "Buffy-verse." *Angel*'s Irish masculinity as anachronism is important in papering over those cracks. The sexual rivalry between Wesley and Gunn erupts into violence in an episode ("Spin the Bottle," season four) where the characters are magically returned to their teenage selves. Angel, reverting to the persona of a young eighteenth-century Irish man (or, rather, what contemporary television might imagine that to be) encourages the fight, expressing support for "the slave" and remarking, "The English have it coming to them." The scene disassociates whiteness and dominance and deflects the past of slaveholding onto the comical English character. Moreover, Irishness is invoked to identify a different white masculinity, rebellious and innocent of the history of colonial power.

Post–September 11

Irishness has been crucially deployed, particularly in post-9/11 America, in the articulation of white, working-class, male identity. The media mobilization of this identity as heroic has become both a mode of erasure of the trauma of helplessness in the face of such catastrophe and a rhetorical strategy for the casting of consequent U.S. foreign policy as a mode of plucky defense by ordinary Americans. In this context, the emergence of an Irish American superhero in a series on prime-time television is not surprising. Rather more so is the difficulty that *Angel* had in finding a secure programming slot. Even before the announcement that the fifth season would be the series' last, it was often rumored to be on the verge

of cancellation, not apparently because it did not have a sufficient audience, but because the WB did not know where to put it. The series was
originally scheduled directly after *Buffy the Vampire Slayer*, aiming to retain that series' older viewers post-watershed and with its male hero to
secure a stronger male audience than the postfeminist heroine could attract. *Buffy*, however, departed to rival network UPN. Without that lead-
in, *Angel* was repeatedly moved around the scheduling, at one stage immediately following the saccharine family values series, *Seventh Heaven*,
in a problematic pairing. Both *Buffy* and *Angel* have been repeatedly condemned by "family," Christian, and parents' groups in the United States.
(*Angel* also fell foul of the Independent Broadcasting Authority when
it was screened in the UK and *Buffy* is routinely cut for early evening
broadcast by the BBC.[23]) Meanwhile, the WB became preoccupied with a
middle-of-the-road/"family" market.

The difficulty of scheduling *Angel* casts interesting light on Nancy San
Martin's work on the role of the "meso" narrative context in the ideological structure of U.S. television. San Martin has analyzed in detail the
role which scheduling and advertising play in the "particular conflation
of sexuality, race and citizenship [which] has refashioned weeknight network broadcasting . . . how identificatory practices and identities . . .
are programmed and narrativised in 'must see TV.' "[24] San Martin argues
that programs are fitted together in a structure which contains sexuality
within an overarching "heteronormative structure and racial difference
within the presumption of white identity as an unmarked category of
racial identity."[25] *Angel*, far more than *Buffy*, has presented difficulties for
this containment strategy.

The difficulty in absorbing *Angel* into this structure does appear to
have intensified after September 11, just as the series itself appears to
have become darker and more apocalyptic. Angel's performance of Irish
American identity became more problematic at a time when that identity
was being deployed in the mainstream media as a form of heroic masculinity at the heart of U.S. recovery from the trauma of September 11.
The precise point at which those events started to impact on the writing
and production of the show has been identified by Tim Minnear in his
DVD commentary on season three, where he recalls having to sit down on
the day of the attacks and finish a scene in the episode "Billy." The epi-

sode paradoxically focuses on a form of violence repressed within modern Western society. "Billy" deals with the possibility of a "primordial misogyny" which the half-demon and half-human Billy is capable of releasing in every man he touches. While he leaves a trail of destruction in his wake, neither Angel, because he is not human, nor Gunn, because he figures out how the infection works, ever fully express this misogynistic violence. Instead it is the repressed, polite Wesley who embarks on a rampage through the hotel in pursuit of Fred, his reticent infatuation transformed into sexual assault and violence. On the one hand, primordial misogyny appears to be strongest in the "whitest," most middle-class male. On the other, expressing it primarily through this character makes it a mainstream, "normal" aspect of masculinity. Presenting the African American character as too clever to be ruled by atavism is deliberately reversing racial stereotypes; presenting him as unrepresentative of the masculine norm is not.

This episode epitomizes the concern with the repressed, with sexuality and violence, and with relations between the sexes that characterizes both series, and it employs the unexpected reversals of traditional identities characteristic of postmodern horror. The series thereafter takes a different turn, however. In a manner quite at odds with most cult shows, it introduces a set of biological family relationships that supersede loyalty to the working group. Angel, once the prodigal son, becomes a father. His son is the result not of his old romantic liaison with Buffy but of a one-night stand in the previous season with his "sire," the vampire Darla, which he describes as an expression of "absolute despair." This is by no means a reassertion of family values over the negotiated and chosen aspects of group loyalty usually emphasized in cult TV. On the contrary, this birth is so unlikely and so downright wrong that Angel initially fears his heroic duty is to kill both Darla and the baby she is carrying. The child is linked from the first news of its conception with an oncoming apocalypse—the advent of death, not new life. This impossible reproduction echoes a vital theme in Richard Dyer's exploration of the cultural construction of whiteness.

Dyer's analysis of contemporary culture traces both the twentieth-century technology of whiteness (the centrality of the illumination of the white face in the development of photography and film lighting, for example) and the persistence of nineteenth-century imperialist associations of whiteness with spirit, will, and dominance over the body that have long outlasted their original Christian significance. Integral to this, Dyer identifies dissociation between whiteness and life (and a terror of others' fertility and vitality). The fear that whiteness may be either too pure or too feminized to reproduce itself is fused with the emptiness and absence which also define whiteness. (Interestingly, in her exploration of female violence in *Buffy the Vampire Slayer*, Lisa Parks describes the whiteness of the characters as a "void" onto which both fear and desire can be projected.)[26] Horror, Dyer argues, precisely because it has no cultural authority, "is a cultural space that makes bearable for whites the exploration of the association of whiteness with death."[27] The vampire myth is deeply implicated in that exploration:

> The idea of whites as both themselves dead and as bringers of death is commonly hinted at in horror literature and film . . . It is at the heart of the vampire myth. The vampire is dead but also brings death. Because vampires are dead, they are pale, cadaverous, white. They bring themselves a kind of life by sucking the blood of the living, and at such points may appear flushed with red, the color of life . . . Just as the vampires' whiteness conveys their own deadness, so too their bringing of death is signaled by whiteness — their victims grow pale, the color leaves their cheeks, life ebbs away . . . The horror of vampirism is expressed in color: ghastly white, disgustingly cadaverous, without the blood of life that would give color. All of this is so menacing that it is often ascribed to those who are not mainstream whites — Jews, South East Europeans (Transylvania in *Dracula* and its derivatives), the denizens of New Orleans (Anne Rice's *Vampire Chronicles*). Horror films have their cake and eat it: they give us the horror of whiteness while ascribing it to those who are liminally white.[28]

Elsewhere Dyer refers to Irishness as another form of liminal whiteness.[29] Almost any marker of ethnic, sexual, or social difference can be utilized to create a distance from "pure" whiteness which can be exploited in this way.

It is not coincidental that the Irish American Angel manages to reproduce in the 2002 season. It is even more noteworthy that the only sexual coupling that does produce (human) offspring in either series is that between the (un)dead and archaic Angel and Darla. The link between this white birth and death is initially dramatized in two scenes involving Darla. The first is the scene which reveals her pregnancy ("Heartthrob," season three), the second the point where she gives birth ("Lullaby," season three). Seated at the bar of a Costa Rican taverna, she gets information from and then feeds on a sleazy middle-aged man. It is only after she has killed him and gets up from the bar that the viewer sees she is pregnant. Her tight-fitting red dress and her presence in the bar provides a very strong contrast with the "normal" significance of her pregnant form.

Darla is initially desperate to be rid of the pregnancy, but the fetus appears to be able to violently repel any interference. Eventually, in a parody of a discarded mistress, Darla returns to Angel to confront him with the result of their relationship. Their encounters are violent and antagonistic until Angel realizes that not only does this prospective child have a soul, but also that Darla despite herself has come to love it. Darla is never entirely domesticated: she still poses a threat to Cordelia, for example, and her pregnancy seems to exacerbate her appetite for human blood. She remains close to the monstrous, abject mother who figures so prominently in contemporary horror.[30] Her body is designed to deal death, not give birth. Darla eventually resolves her protracted pregnancy by staking herself and disappearing into dust, leaving the infant freed not only from her body but all maternal influence ("Provider," season 3).

This maternal annihilation is a common and disturbing feature of contemporary popular culture, though usually (even more disturbingly) aimed at a younger age group.[31] For example, Harry Potter's mother has sacrificed herself to save him, and the same pattern recurs in Disney's *Ice Age* (2002) and *Finding Nemo* (2003). In *Angel*, the mother's acknowledgment of her own inappropriateness for the maternal role and consequent death establish the hero as sole parent. The strange circumstances of the child's birth leave the male members of the group around Angel uneasy, though Cordelia, for whom Angel is developing an attraction, provides the role of social and safe mother. In a scene which foregrounds the way in which fatherhood makes safe Angel's dangerous sexuality, a close-up of a sleepy Angel and Cordelia feeding the baby from a bottle pulls out to reveal the three are on the bed in his room, the baby positioned between the two adults changing the significance of the location from sexual possibility to comfortable domesticity.

Angel's domestication is linked with a resurgence of Irish ethnicity. He calls his son Connor and even puts the baby's name down for the University of Notre Dame. This Irish family is threatened from the start, though, by an old English enemy, Holtz, a vampire hunter who is identified as a nineteenth-century victim of Angelus and Darla, but who owes a great deal to Vincent Price's Witchfinder General in characterization and costume.[32] Angelus and Darla slaughtered Holtz's family, and the latter has been frozen in time waiting for the chance to revenge himself on them. Holtz's Germanic name, English past, religious certainty, and visual coding as Puritan represent a very different kind of America from the one represented by Angel's heroic redemption narrative. Angel's emergence as a different kind of man, his loss of Cordelia to a rival, and his increasing investment of his identity in his relation to his child are shadowed throughout the rest of season three by Holtz's desire for holy vengeance.

At one point, Angel's old adversaries, Wolfram and Hart, contrive to doctor the animal blood on which Angel normally subsists with traces of his son's blood. From "Mr. Mom," as another parent calls him, he becomes an intoxicated and frighteningly elated shadow of his old self: "The vampire's bite, so evidently a metaphor for sexuality, is debilitating unto death, just as white people fear sexuality if it is allowed to get out of control (out from under the will) — yet, like the vampire, they need it. The vampire is the white man or woman in the grip of a libidinal need s/he cannot master. In the act of vampirism, white society (the vampire) feeds off itself (his/her victims) and threatens to destroy itself."[33] The addiction metaphor is never far from the surface in *Angel*. When it is introduced in the story arc concerning Angel's relation with his son, it raises the possibility of a masculinity too libidinal to be safely contained in fatherhood and also displaces this fear of a masculinity incapable of nurture onto a very old and stereotypical association of Celtic wildness, drunkenness, and excessive and irresponsible fertility. Angel's role as a father brings his Irishness back to the forefront of the narrative, because Irishness itself seems to bring fatherhood into question.

The relationship between Angel and Connor continues to be tinged with danger. Holtz eventually does manage to steal the child, abetted by the other English character, Wesley, who has become convinced by a false prophecy that Angel will destroy his son. This part of season three, where two English characters, each entirely convinced he has right on his side, conspire to destroy the lives of the hero and his son was produced and partly broadcast when the United States was at war in Afghanistan with Britain as its foremost ally. Holtz is identified with retributive violence which has become evil in itself, however just his original cause. Wesley, who has simply misjudged the situation and mistrusted his friend, becomes a character who is denied forgiveness in a storyline where Angel echoes Holtz's obsession with revenge for the loss of his children and tries to smother Wesley in the hospital. "Horror is licensed to deal with what terrifies us partly by giving it free reign for the safe length of a movie, partly by being low, dismissible and often risible, partly by providing happy endings in which the horror is laid to rest."[34] *Angel* deals with the dehumanizing effects of retributive violence at a time when direct engagement with the issue in the public sphere in the U.S. media was severely curtailed. It does so at a safe distance from American identity, however, predominantly through the figure of Holtz (Angel does not, in the end, kill Wesley).

Angel does not offer any happy endings in this season, broadcast in 2002–2003, however. Angel loses his son to Holtz twice. The latter takes Connor, raises him in a hellish alternate dimension, and renames him Stephen, which, as Angel points out, "is a fine name. But it's not Irish." Stephen/Connor returns after two episodes as an angry teenage boy who has learned to hate his un/natural father. The relationship between Angel and Connor goes through a number of dramatic crises in seasons three and four. Season three culminates in a battle at the sea's edge, which ends with Connor imprisoning his father in a steel box and sinking him to the bottom of the sea. This closing episode initially promises the traditional happy ending, which will put all the unbearable angst and dread back behind the safe and silly boundaries of horror's generic conventions. Angel's son fights to defend his father against an attack and rejects his new, English name, reverting to Connor. Cordelia returns and discovers that she reciprocates Angel's feelings. The two are due to meet for the first time after she acknowledges this when Connor intervenes. He follows his father out to the cove where he is due to meet Cordelia and reveals that he still completely identifies with Holtz's hatred of Angel.

The sequence of events which bring them to the edge of the ocean to fight is hugely contrived. It is also reminiscent of one of the definitive scenes in Irish theater: Cuchulainn's battle with his son in Yeats's *On Baile's Strand*. Given the parricidal emphasis of the Irish component of Angel's story in previous series, this reference serves to reinforce his ethnicity and the link with fatal familialism. This exclusive father-son bond, premised on the mother's irrelevance, is presented as murderous and distinctively Irish. It is linked with a revitalized and vigorous white masculine identity that is both inevitably doomed and apocalyptic. Like the patriarchal family, it is doomed to failure, but its failure is catastrophic on a global scale. Connor's birth, it transpires in the next season, is a harbinger of an odd apocalypse. His Oedipal narrative continues its catastrophic course when he sleeps with Cordelia and impregnates her with the incarnation of a goddess/demon called Jasmine. Jasmine's storyline draws heavily on the apocalyptic elements within fundamentalist Christianity. Consequently the series draws attention to the similarities between all forms of religious certainty, particularly their propensity toward totalitarianism.

In another of those reversals and displacements characteristic of postmodern horror, Jasmine is both a god capable of bringing universal peace, and a devil who needs to devour a steady minority of the faithful daily to survive. In its ironic equation of religious certainty with the end of personal freedom and the salvation of the many with the ritual sacrifice of the few, season four appears to offer both a bleak and subversive vision. The fact that this god/demon is played by an attractive African American woman blunts its cutting edge somewhat, however. On the one hand, this female divinity is the opposite of the patriarchal god: on the other hand, she is close to the patriarchal conjunction of darkness, female power, and racial difference as devilish. Her minion rains fire from the sky in a portent of apocalypse that is also a reminder of September 11. Season four of *Angel* registers a sense of apocalyptic nightmare and appears to lose its social and political coordinates as its hero ultimately loses his son in the confusion.

Angel finally resolves his relationship with his son by ending it at the end of season four, making a devil's bargain to work for Wolfram and Hart in order to secure his son's complete loss of all memories of his parentage and to substitute a secure grounding in a very conventional American family. The latter is significantly also a much more feminine one. As well as a conventionally happy father, Connor is endowed with a mother and two sisters. Angel, by contrast, is left alienated, a corporate employee in an evil empire, childless, and unsure of his heroic role. At a time when Irish American identity was being produced as life affirming and heroic in the face of catastrophe, *Angel* presents it as catastrophic in itself, playing out outmoded roles of masculinity and heroism, inadequate to securing the future in its paternal role, puzzled and alienated but dependent on corporate power. In season five, *Angel* initially sought to attract wider audiences, with more stand-alone episodes and less complex narrative, a process parodied in the hero's uneasy relationship with his new employers. Angel's Irish background became irrelevant at the point of his assimilation into corporate America.

Conclusion

In *Buffy the Vampire Slayer*, Angel epitomized a proximate otherness, too close for comfort yet ultimately too different to comfortably embrace. This proximity was possible precisely because he was not racially distinct. Both *Buffy the Vampire Slayer* and *Angel* repeatedly draw attention to the roots of vampire mythology in a white, Christian, middle-class culture. Part of the series' humor lies in the anachronistic and sometimes absurd persistence of primal elements within that mythology in the complex context of postmodern and multicultural popular culture. Willow, for example, wonders what her father would think of "Ira Rosenberg's only daughter nailing crucifixes to her wall." The crucifixes go up just the same, and the witty aside draws attention to a fundamental aspect of *Buffy*'s relationship to its audience. It can ironically deconstruct the universalizing truth claims of Christianity, or indeed the dominant cultural values of white America, but it nonetheless has to work within narrative conventions premised on those cultural dominants. Both *Buffy* and *Angel* ground themselves in an overwhelmingly white middle-class context while ironically drawing attention to the limitations and implicit absurdities of that context. This in itself is not enough, however, to allow the articulation of other identities in any sustained way which would change or challenge the hyperdiegetic elaboration of deconstructed identities (of gender, race, ethnicity, or class).

Angel deploys stereotypes of Irishness, but it also subverts them. Angel originated as the feckless son of a merchant, not a poor dispossessed peasant. He came to America, seeking a new un-life, in despair rather than hope. He is a romantic hero who represents dangerous sexuality but can have no sex life. He is a father whose best legacy to his son is obliteration of his parentage. Hungry, addicted, impotent, desiring, he is a white "dark soul." His Irishness is, rather like the shows in which he appears, both mainstream and at odds with the mainstream. While *Angel* may have struggled to find a place in the schedule, its central character is highly symptomatic of the time in which it was produced: his past Irish, present American, and future most uncertain.

Notes

1. Richard Dyer, *White* (London: Routledge, 1997), 3.

2. See for example, Kent A. Ono, "To Be a Vampire on *Buffy the Vampire Slayer*: Race and ("Other") Socially Marginalizing Positions on Horror TV," in *Fantasy Girls: Gender in the New Universe of Science Fiction and Fantasy Television*, edited by Elyce Rae Helford (Lanham, England: Rowman and Littlefield, 2000), 163–86; and Lynne Edwards, "Slaying in Black and White: Kendra as Tragic Mulatta" in *Fighting the Forces: What's at Stake in Buffy the Vampire Slayer*, edited by Rhonda V. Wilcox and David Lavery (Lanham, England: Rowman and Littlefield, 2002), 85–97.

3. Mary Hammond, "Monsters and Metaphors: *Buffy the Vampire Slayer* and the Old World," in *Cult Television*, edited by Sara Gwenllian Jones and Roberta M. Pearson (Minneapolis: University of Minnesota Press, 2004), 147–64.

4. Bob Quinn, "Contemporary Irish Cinema Supplement," *Cinéaste* 24 (1999): 73.

5. See Gerardine Meaney, "The Devil's Own Patriot Games: Ireland and the Hollywood Action Movie," in *Representing the Troubles*, edited by Éibhear Walshe and Brian Cliff (Dublin: Four Courts Press, 2004), 79–92.

6. Luke Gibbons, *The Quiet Man* (Cork: Cork University Press, 2002), 3.

7. Ibid.,12.

8. Ibid., 91.

9. Ireland as a resource for the recovery of lost gender roles remains a popular

trope. See Diane Negra, "Irishness, Innocence, and American Identity Politics before and after September 11" in this volume.

10. See Margot Gayle Backus, *The Gothic Family Romance: Heterosexuality, Child Sacrifice and the Anglo-Irish Colonial Order* (Durham, N.C.: Duke University Press, 1999).

11. Matt Hills, "Defining Cult TV: Texts, Intertexts and Fan Audiences" in *The Television Studies Reader*, edited by Robert C. Allen and Annette Hill (London: Routledge, 2004), 513.

12. Elizabeth Krimmer and Shilpa Raval, " 'Digging the Undead': Death and Desire in *Buffy*," in *Fighting the Forces: What's at Stake in Buffy the Vampire Slayer*, edited by Rhonda V. Wilcox and David Lavery (Lanham, England: Rowman and Littlefield, 2002), 160.

13. Miranda Banks, "Costume Design and the Production of Heroic Femininity" (paper presented at Console-ing Passions Conference, New Orleans, La., June 2004).

14. Carol Clover, *Men, Women and Chainsaws* (London: BFI, 1992); Jacinda Read, *The New Avengers; Feminism, Femininity and the Rape-Revenge Cycle* (Manchester: Manchester University Press, 1999).

15. See, for example, A. Susan Owen, "Vampires, Postmodernity and Postfeminism: *Buffy the Vampire Slayer*," *Journal of Popular Film and Television* 27, no. 2 (1999): 24–31. For a contrary view of the representation of motherhood in the series, see J. P. Williams, "Choosing Your Own Mother: Mother-Daughter Conflicts in *Buffy*," in Wilcox and Lavery, *Fighting the Forces*, 61–72.

16. Elizabeth Butler Cullingford, *Ireland's Others: Gender and Ethnicity in Irish Literature and Popular Culture* (Cork: Cork University Press, 2001).

17. See Cheryl Herr, *The Field* (Cork: Cork University Press, 2002); and Cullingford, *Ireland's Others*, 231. For her discussion of *Michael Collins*, Cullingford draws on Jordan's production diary, where he describes De Valera as a father to Collins who becomes another defeated Oedipus in this reading.

18. Donna L. Potts, "Convents, Claddagh Rings, and Even the Book of Kells: Representing the Irish in *Buffy the Vampire Slayer*," *Studies in Media and Information Literacy Education* 3, no. 2 (2003), <http://www.utpjournals.com/jour.ihtml?lp=simile/issue10/pottsx1.html>.

19. Lynne Segal, "Only Contradictions on Offer," *Women: A Cultural Review* 11, no. 1–2 (2000): 24. For Papenoe's and Blakenhorn's arguments, see David Blakenhorn, Jean Bethke Elsthian, and Steven Bayme, eds. *Rebuilding the Nest: A New Commitment to the American Family* (Milwaukee: Family Service America, 1991); David Blakenhorn, *Fatherless America: Confronting Our Most Urgent Social Problem* (New York: Basic Books, 1995).

20. In particular, the representation of the family as crippled by violence and miscommunication in *The Field* and *The Butcher Boy* (1997).

21. This presented occasional difficulties. The director's commentary on the DVD

version refers to comments on inconsistencies in Doyle's accent and attributes these to the necessity to occasionally overdub lines, which would be incomprehensible to U.S. audiences in Quinn's original pronunciation.

22. Mim Udovitch, "What Makes Buffy Slay?" *Rolling Stone*, 11 May 2000, 60–65.

23. See Annette Hill and Ian Calcutt, "Vampire Hunters: the Scheduling and Reception of *Buffy the Vampire Slayer* and *Angel* in the UK," *Intensities: The Journal of Cult Media* 1, <http://www.cult-media.com/issue1/Ahill.htm>; and Vivien Burr, "Buffy vs. the BBC: Moral Questions and How to Avoid Them," *Slayage: The Online International Journal of Buffy Studies* 8 (April 2003), for a discussion of this.

24. Nancy San Martin, " 'Must See TV': Programming Identity on NBC Thursdays," in *Quality Popular Television*, edited by Mark Jancovich and James Lyons (London: BFI, 2003), 33.

25. Ibid., 41.

26. Lisa Parks, "Brave New Buffy: Rethinking 'TV Violence,' " in Jancovich and Lyons, *Quality Popular Television*, 125.

27. Dyer, *White*, 210.

28. Ibid.

29. Ibid., 19.

30. See Barbara Creed, *The Monstrous-Feminine: Film, Feminism and Psychoanalysis* (London: Routledge, 1993).

31. See Kathleen Rowe Karlyn, "*Scream*, Popular Culture and Feminism's Third Wave," *Genders* 38 (2003). Karlyn looks at the theme of maternal abandonment in teen culture, rather than the self-sacrificing mother.

32. In *The Conqueror Worm* (1968), UK title, *Witchfinder General*.

33. Dyer, *White*, 210.

34. Ibid.

MAEVE CONNOLLY

"A Bit of a Traveller in Everybody":
Traveller Identities in Irish and
American Culture

TITO RILEY: Are the Travellers cowboys or Indians, Papa?
PAPA RILEY: There's a bit of a Traveller in everybody, Tito.
  Very few of us know where we're going.
—Jim Sheridan, *Into the West*

As a relatively self-conscious fusion of Anglo-Irish literature and revisionist Hollywood Western, *Into the West* (1992) would seem to
constitute an exemplary postmodern text. The central theme of
this highly intertextual narrative, scripted by Jim Sheridan and directed
by Mike Newell, is the loss and recovery of cultural identity and familial
stability through recourse to a rural, preindustrial past. But, significantly,
in *Into the West* this typically postmodern crisis is displaced onto a community of Irish Travellers, an indigenous ethnic minority whose culture
and lifestyle become the subject of a highly romantic representation. Although not related to Gypsies or Roma, Travellers share both their nomadic tradition and their history of persecution and social exclusion.
Of the 25,000 Travellers in Ireland (less than 1 percent of the total Irish
population) one-quarter live in unserviced caravan sites by the side of
the road, without regular refuse collection or running water. They suffer
higher mortality rates than the settled population, as well as restricted
access to education and healthcare.

The opening section of *Into the West*, set in and around the campsites
and tower blocks of north Dublin, foregrounds the marginalization of the

Irish Traveling community, but any attempt at realism is abandoned at an early stage. The narrative centers on a mythic quest undertaken by two Traveller children, Ossie and Tito. Following an encounter with a magical horse named Tir na nÓg, ultimately revealed as the spirit of their dead mother, they leave Dublin for the "wilderness" of the West of Ireland. By the close of the film, they have convinced their father Papa Riley (Gabriel Byrne) to abandon the city in favor of the West and the "old ways" of the Travellers.

Critics have situated *Into the West* within the context of a postmodern turn toward nostalgia in Irish cinema, marking a shift away from the more formally innovative works of the late 1970s and early 1980s. Ruth Barton, for example, includes Sheridan's film in an extensive list of works that can be designated as "heritage cinema" because of their celebration of history as spectacle.[1] Theorists of the European heritage film have tended to focus on the narrative and visual pleasures associated with the re-creation, and occasional reworking, of national histories in costume drama.[2] In keeping with this approach, Barton highlights a series of Irish costume dramas set in the 1950s and 1960s. Her analysis also encompasses a broader range of film narratives, however, which (like *Into the West*) unfold within an ostensibly contemporary setting but nonetheless evoke memories of a past era.

Barton's critique is informed by the social, cultural, and economic changes taking place within the Irish context of production since the early 1990s, and she links the rise of the heritage aesthetic with a shift in the Irish rural economy—from agriculture to tourism. Her analysis also calls attention to the fact that heritage cinema seeks to address a predominantly *metropolitan* audience, by offering an image of the past that is both "pre-industrial" and "uni-racial."[3] *Into the West* clearly operates within the conventions of Irish heritage cinema, with prominent allusions to Anglo-Irish literary myth and highly romantic images of the rural landscape. But because it foregrounds the discrimination experienced by the Traveling community as an indigenous, yet racialized, ethnic minority, the film could also be seen to offer a starting point for a more self-conscious examination of Irish identity.

In her exploration of ethnicity in Irish cinema, Elizabeth Butler Cullingford notes that *Into the West* develops a parallel between the contemporary marginalization of Irish Travellers and the mistreatment of Native American peoples in the United States.[4] She analyzes the recurrent debate within the film between the children and Papa Riley over the true identity of the Travellers. "[Tito] repeats his brother's earlier question, 'Are the Travellers Cowboys or Indians, papa?' Papa's response is evasive, but, since the film's depiction of anti-traveller racism suggests that the travellers are Indians in relation to the settled community, the Southern Irish must be the cowboys . . . [This] identification is familiar but, in a postcolonial context, not necessarily positive. The travellers are white Others who have been 'blackened' by a previous group of white Others, the Irish."[5] Here Cullingford calls attention both to the ambiguous racial status of Irishness at an earlier moment in history and to the subsequent displacement of "blackness" onto Travellers. The apparent continuity between racialized representations of Irishness in the nineteenth century and the contemporary "othering" of Travellers has since begun to emerge as a key issue in Irish antiracist discourse, within the context of a wider campaign for Travellers rights.[6]

During the 1990s and 2000s, a series of Irish and international film narratives—from Irish heritage cinema to postmodern reworkings of more overtly transnational genres—have constructed Travellers as white others. These representations of Travellers in Irish and international cinema are structured by, among other factors, the emergence of Irishness as a globally marketed identity, an identity which holds a particular appeal as a form of ethnicized whiteness.

Representing Travellers in Irish and International Cinema

Prior to the emergence of the heritage cycle of the 1990s, some of the most significant cinematic representations of Travellers were produced by documentary filmmakers, or those with a strong interest in documentary aesthetics. In *No Resting Place* (1950), the acclaimed documentarist Paul Rotha turned to social drama to represent the experiences of a Traveller family. In 1981 Joe Comerford directed *Traveller*, a film based on a script by Neil Jordan, and exemplifying the kind of formal and political innovation that Ruth Barton sees as lacking in the 1990s. It remains one of the few (Irish or international) films to feature a performance by a member of the Traveling community and, as I argue in the latter part of this essay, Comerford's approach to the project was influenced by avant-garde documentary. More recently, film and television documentary has provided a critical forum for the exploration of media images of Travellers.[7]

My analysis is more explicitly concerned, however, with the particular place of Travellers in the cycle of period dramas that have dominated Irish cinema since the early 1990s. In addition to *Into the West*, images of Travellers recur in at least three explorations of Irish history: *The Field* (1990), *This Is My Father* (1998), and *Country* (2000).[8] These films are notably diverse in terms of temporal and narrative structure, yet all engage with familiar themes in heritage cinema, such as emigration, repressive social norms, and traumatic memory. My discussion of these films highlights the fact that Travellers tend to form a key element of the historical mise-en-scène, often providing a figurative or literal link to the past. In her introduction to this volume, Diane Negra notes that global popular culture repeatedly presents Irishness as the "moral antidote" to a range of contemporary ailments, from postmodern alienation to crises over family values. In a set of films produced in Ireland and consumed largely by Irish audiences (*Into the West, This Is My Father, The Field*, and *Country*) this dynamic is slightly modified so that the antidote is provided by Travellers, rather than by the "settled" majority.

In addition to their prominence in Irish heritage cinema, representations of Travellers have also begun to appear in international cinema. Bill Paxton, Mark Wahlberg, Brad Pitt, and Johnny Depp have all played Irish Travellers in narratives that are set outside Ireland. Paxton and Wahlberg take the lead roles in an American independent drama, *Traveller* (1997), focusing on a community of Travellers in the United States. Pitt plays a champion Traveller boxer in the British comedy *Snatch* (2000), and Johnny Depp appears as an elusive Irish "gypsy" in *Chocolat* (2000), a British-American coproduction set in rural France during the 1950s. Both *Traveller* and *Snatch* present an array of ethnic "types" and produce images of male Traveller identity that are highly celebratory, while at the same time deeply problematic. This recasting of the generic hero as an Irish Traveller or gypsy in the cinema of the 1990s and 2000s seems to underscore the international appeal of Irishness as a means of being "white, yet ethnically differentiated."[9] The circulation of these mobile and flexible Traveller identities in international cinema is, however, at odds with a prevailing tendency in Irish cinema to align Travellers with the past.

In order to understand the place of Travellers within Irish and international cinema it is useful to turn to Steven Crofts's critique of national cinema. Crofts highlights a thematic continuity across the commercially and critically successful products of "national cinemas" in the 1990s, a continuity underscored in the discourses of film-festival organizers and distributors. He notes that many of the most prominent exports from this period explore culturally universal themes, such as family madness or artistic ambition, but combine these familiar themes with specific "local inflections."[10] Within this mode of address, Travellers can be seen to function as emblems of both the culturally universal and the local, not least because of the fact that they share the outsider status of artists and the insane. The universal appeal of the Traveller, as a romantic figure, is summed up by Papa Riley in *Into the West* in the epigraph for this essay.

The Irish film *Country* would seem to incorporate many of the key elements of the formula outlined by Crofts, although it conspicuously lacked the uplifting resolution that marked more commercially successful examples of national cinema. An evocation of rural childhood in the 1960s, viewed through the eyes of a young boy, *Country* displays the authentic period detail and picturesque landscape photography typical of the heritage genre. It is set in a small rural community in the early 1960s, decimated by emigration and divided by memories of a traumatic national past. Travellers do not simply "authenticate" this representation of the past. Instead, their (highly romanticized) way of life is constructed in entirely nostalgic terms, as emblematic of childhood itself. The Traveller camp is portrayed as an idealized alternative to the claustrophobia of the nuclear family, and its predictable destruction signifies the (settled) hero's rite of passage into adult responsibility.

An opposition between the extended nomadic clan and the settled nuclear family is also apparent in *The Field*, but the exploration of this dynamic is relatively self-conscious. Noting that the film is characterized by a narrative excess at odds with the heritage aesthetic, Barton describes it a "family melodrama with historical/epic overtones" and a "quasi-Biblical" central character.[11] The action centers on a clash between "Bull" McCabe, a man who has devoted his life to the nurturing of a rented rocky plot, and his rival for the land, an American who wants to build on it. The Bull's investment in the land is both deeply personal and culturally specific, as it concerns a traumatic memory of famine and familial loss. The conflict over the land is paralleled and complicated by an Oedipal narrative concerning the Bull's son Tadgh and a young "Tinker woman" whose unfettered sexuality symbolizes all that is forbidden in settled society. Against his father's wishes, Tadgh rejects his inheritance in favor of romantic love and life on the road. Ultimately, however, his alliance with the Traveller woman proves fatal. Through the death of Tadgh, and the destruction of the male line of inheritance, *The Field* portrays *settled* society (or at least its overtly patriarchal dimension) as doomed. In this sense it offers a useful contrast with *Country*.

It is clear that Travellers occupy a central symbolic role in the negotiation of history and memory in Irish cinema, yet their place within *international* cinema invites further analysis. *Traveller* (the U.S. version), *Snatch*, and *Chocolat* do not share the concern with questions of national or cultural identity that marks *Into the West*, *The Field*, *Country*, and *This Is My Father*. But it is possible to note a number of pronounced points of intersection between these diverse Irish and international films, particularly in terms of the representation of family, ethnicity, and criminality. Joe Cleary's analysis of *Into the West* offers a starting point from which to examine the structural relationship between Irish and American representations of Travellers, not least because it is informed by Fredric Jameson's celebrated discussion of ethnicity and utopia in *The Godfather*.[12] Before proceeding with my exploration of these cinematic images, however, it may be useful to explore some aspects of Traveller identity, within the context of the economic and cultural transformations of the 1990s.

The "Other" Irish: Travellers and Irish Identity

Jim Mac Laughlin has provided one of the most in-depth accounts of the fraught relations between the Traveller and settled communities, from the colonial period to the present day. He emphasizes that in precolonial and early colonial Ireland, Travellers provided seasonal farm labor, various forms of entertainment, and valuable services such as tinsmithing. In fact, he notes that Travellers were "often the only *national* institution, [and they] provided the social cement which bound isolated communities together."[13] Across Europe, however, the appropriation and privatization of property, and the adoption of "petty bourgeois sedentary lifestyles" contributed to a gradual dissociation of nomadic peoples from the stationary majority.[14] This process of separation contributed to the romanticization as well as the vilification of gypsies and nomads, obscuring the interdependency of nomadic and settled economies and cultures. The extended, patrilinear, families of Traveller society came to be seen as echoes of an earlier moment in the history of the settled collective.

In Ireland, anticolonial discourse tended to construct attachment to a nomadic past as an obstacle to modernization. The romantic longing for a primitive past came to be refigured around a shared terrain, rather than tribal or clan structures, and, in the process, Travellers came to be located outside the national body politic. But the disavowal of Travellers occurred later in Ireland than elsewhere in Europe, and their dissociation from the settled population was complicated by the fact that colonial conquest had disrupted the Irish class structure. Mac Laughlin states: "From a purely materialist perspective at least, there was often a very thin divide separating [colonial] 'settlers' from the 'dispossessed' and 'Travellers' in colonial Ireland."[15] By the nineteenth century sections of the settled (and Traveller) population had also begun to emigrate, and an increasing number of seasonal laborers were moving between Ireland and Britain. In the absence of clear distinctions between settled and Traveller societies, attention shifted to the question of origins, often through reference to linguistic or physical markers.

Mac Laughlin, however, is explicitly concerned with highlighting the complex and shifting social and economic relations between the two communities, and to this end he draws on the cross-cultural perspective offered by anthropologist Aparno Rao. According to Rao's model, Irish Travellers can be defined as "peripatetics" or "endogamous nomads who are largely non-primary producers or extractors . . . whose principal resources are constituted by other human populations."[16] Even though peripatetic communities may own land, houses, or even herds, their primary subsistence is derived from commercialism (from the sale of goods or specialized services) and this mode of subsistence obviously requires ongoing interaction with settled communities.

Rao also notes that the marginal social status of Traveling peoples is often paralleled by a "high ritual status," to the extent that nomadic groups are a focus for superstition and myth within settled communities.[17] It has been suggested the distinct social and cultural identity of the Traveling community may have actually developed in response to overt prejudice and racism. For example, Mac Laughlin points out that Travellers may have responded to the spread of clericalism in late-nineteenth-century Ireland by adopting Catholicism as a "protective move," while at the same time preserving "a separate 'hidden' ethnicity and belief system underneath their public image."[18]

A quest to uncover this "hidden" ethnicity can be seen to inform the representation of Irish Travellers since the late 1880s. In his analysis of "pseudo-anthropological" ethnographic representations and Anglo-Irish literary works, Paul Delaney suggests the Travellers were repeatedly rendered "discursively mute" through the trope of the unseen witness. He notes that, in Synge's work, the figure of the Traveller is rarely represented directly, but instead remains a significant offstage presence — the focus for a specifically Anglo-Irish anxiety around the question of national identity. He reads this as a response to the emergence of a dominant (and exclusive) model of Irishness: "The writings of this period, after all, were framed by a series of Land Reform Acts (stretching from 1881 through to 1909) which saw the emergence and consolidation of a rural Catholic peasantry for whom identity was inseparable from a certain kinship with the land . . . One might suggest, therefore, in the final instance, that the problems relating to the representation of Travellers [in Synge's work] prompt the question of whether it is possible to recognise and depict another culture as also Irish."[19] This would suggest that a tendency to employ images of Travellers to represent *other* outsiders, and articulate anxiety around social change, is well established within Irish culture.

Media Representations of Travellers
in Ireland and the United States

The wave of mass emigration from Ireland to the United States during the nineteenth century included small numbers of Travellers and, today, some of their descendants now live in the southern and midwestern states.[20] In contrast with other Irish migrants, Travellers in the United States seem to have gravitated towards rural or small-town communities, establishing a relatively permanent presence in settlements such as Murphy Village, South Carolina. Although a considerable number of American scholars have visited Ireland to document the culture and language of Travellers, sociological and anthropological analysis of Irish Travellers in the United States remains limited.[21] Given the relative absence of scholarly research in this area, my discussion cannot hope to fully engage with the specificity of Traveller culture within the United States.

It *is* possible, however, to propose a number of parallels, and differences, between the Irish and American contexts. For example, Rao notes that each peripatetic community "constitutes a minority wherever it may be."[22] So, in as much as they adhere to nomadic customs, Travellers in the United States are likely to share the marginal social status of their Irish counterparts and to be subject to similar forms of prejudice and discrimination. It is difficult to determine whether Travellers in the United States may form part of a wider Irish American community, but it would appear that as a group Travellers have not developed, or retained, the cultural and political attachments prized by the rest of Irish America.

Recent media coverage of U.S. Travellers, such as the case involving Madelyne Toogood Gorman, would indicate that they are subject to suspicion, curiosity, and, on occasion, overt prejudice. In September 2002, Toogood was filmed beating her four-year-old daughter by parking-lot surveillance cameras outside a store in Mishawaka, Indiana. The footage was played repeatedly on U.S. networks during the buildup to the war against Iraq, prompting one commentator to remark: "First Madelyne. Then Saddam. Then Madelyne. Back to Saddam. Americans are becoming confused: Who's worse?"[23] Predictably, the footage prompted a cultural debate about Toogood's fitness as a mother, echoing a wider media phenomenon—the construction of working-class white women, and women of color, as "delinquent mothers."

Susan J. Douglas and Meredith W. Michaels have explored the idealization and the vilification of motherhood in American popular culture since the late 1980s. They argue that media coverage of maternal violence, abuse, and drug taking has tended to be sensational in tone and to focus primarily on cases involving working-class women or women of color. Although occasionally middle-class, and white, the typical "unfit mother" of such stories was more likely to be "the one who had failed to be upwardly mobile, the one who couldn't control her emotions . . . who probably hadn't played Mozart [to her child] in the womb, the one who insisted that biological ties and gestation were enough."[24]

Douglas and Michaels do not deal directly with the representation of Toogood, but their account does place particular emphasis on surveillance, and the "spectacle" of maternity. They note that media images of maternal delinquency contributed to a process of self-surveillance and authorized a "public inspection" of maternal behavior.[25] In the case of Toogood, however, attention was not exclusively focused on motherhood, as media commentators explicitly attempted to account for her behavior through reference to the "hidden" character of Traveller society, implicitly linked to criminality: "The Travelers are a closed society that has shunned the public eye and avoids public attention. They marry in their own group, they speak their own language, based in part on Gaelic. . . . Authorities say many Travelers are involved in criminal ventures, often conning elderly persons into paying for unneeded residential repairs or for legitimate work that is never completed. Other Travelers, authorities said, specialize in sweetheart scams, telemarketing fraud, sweepstakes and lottery fraud, loan fraud, caregiver cons and shoplifting schemes."[26] Other reports included references to films such as *Into the West* and *Snatch* (both of which feature representations of fraud or crime).[27] Still others focused on the ostentatious lifestyles of Travellers, describing them as "an odd composite of Old World and McWorld" and noting that "Traveler women draw stares when they go into town, dolled up with layers of makeup and halos of hair."[28]

These accounts, with their emphasis on criminality and (implicitly tasteless) ostentation, offer a number of parallels with the construction of white-trash stereotypes in American cinema. Annalee Newitz has examined the theme of "white-on-white class conflict" and the racialization of white poverty in films such as *Kalifornia* (1993) and *Cape Fear* (1991). She suggests that whiteness acquires visibility in these narratives because it is identified as "primitive or inhuman." Citing the work of Marianna Torgovnick, she notes that racial difference is often associated with temporal discrepancy—between a civilized present and a primitive past. She argues that in American cinema "class differences tend to be represented as the difference between civilized folks and primitive ones. Lower class whites get racialized, and demeaned, because they fit into the primitive/civilized binary."[29]

Newitz's account offers an interesting point of contrast with Irish cinema, in that both *Into the West* and *Country* highlight violence directed *against* Travellers as a means of critiquing notions of progress central to the idea of a "civilized present." These films (and those discussed in more detail below) also articulate a more complex relation to the past than is allowed in Newitz's discussion. But her exploration of "inhuman" violence is pertinent to the representation of Irish Travellers, and other nomadic groups in American cinema. In the U.S. feature film *Traveller*, for example, two different modes of Traveller identity are explored and while one is valorized, the other is more clearly associated with a primitive past.

Although Travellers are racialized in the U.S. news media through recourse to the "white trash" stereotype, there is perhaps less evidence of the overt racism that has often marked the Irish context. As Mac Laughlin demonstrates, anti-Traveller prejudice in Ireland became even more pronounced following the formation of the Free State, to the extent that Travellers were "scarcely even considered as citizens and were viewed instead as wards of the state."[30] This situation had worsened by the 1950s, primarily because Travellers' traditional way of life, like that of many craft workers, had been undermined by increased industrialization, and specifically by the displacement of tin goods in favor of plastics. They were increasingly out of step with the dominant modernizing ideology of Ireland under Taoiseach Sean Lemass, a contrast noted by the various British and American anthropologists who "rediscovered" Irish Travellers in the postwar period.[31]

Traveller society did not remain fixed, however, and during the 1960s new forms of employment, such as scrap dealing, began to replace traditional craftwork and differences in class and income within the community became more pronounced. Travellers migrated to cities in larger numbers and several poorly serviced ad hoc encampments developed around the outskirts of Dublin, Limerick, Cork, and Galway, adding to the dissatisfaction of already marginalized working-class residents. Many Travellers continued to participate in traditional gatherings at rural fairs and festivals on special occasions, but again they faced growing hostility from settled communities. Their very presence was regarded as largely incompatible with tourism because, as one local politician pointed out, "they might be photographed by tourists and would show the Irish people in a poor light."[32]

Many urban Travellers gained access to unemployment assistance during this period, and state policy became more focused. Studies such as the *Report of the Commission on Itinerancy* (1963) argued strongly for the assimilation of Travellers into "mainstream" society, through the provision of education and accommodation, a strategy that did little to improve relations between the two communities.[33] Since the late 1960s, the overall population of Travellers in Ireland has increased, partly because many Travellers returned from Britain during the Thatcher years.[34] These returning Travellers, defined by local authorities as "transient," have been greeted with particular suspicion, and their demands for even basic social services are often regarded as an unacceptable burden.

Bryan Fanning has analyzed the social exclusion of Travellers, within the context of a broader study of racism and social change in Ireland. He cites numerous examples of institutional racism in relation to the treatment of Travellers, and provides a detailed case study of policies employed by Ennis Urban District Council (UDC) in county Clare since the 1960s. Fanning points out that the representation of Travellers as a "deviant and dangerous underclass," undeserving of the same rights and entitlements as others, was central to the council's discourse of social exclusion.[35] Elsewhere in his study, he emphasizes various commonalities between the marginalization of Travellers and the more recent experiences of asylum seekers, stating that "forms of racism, spatial exclusion and lesser access to services experienced by dispersed asylum seekers were, in many ways, similar to the forms of apartheid historically experienced by Travellers."[36] For example, in 1972, one member of the Ennis

UDC proposed replacing Travellers' cash benefits with vouchers for essentials. This suggestion was not adopted in relation to Travellers, but in the 1990s it became standard practice to provide vouchers rather than cash to asylum seekers, who are denied the opportunity to work until they achieve refugee status, and are dispersed to reception centers to await processing of their claims.

Fanning emphasizes that the infrastructure of support developed for asylum seekers is as inadequate as that provided for Travellers and notes that "even where right to services exist, in areas such as education and health, asylum seekers along with other members of the new immigrant communities may experience institutional barriers which resemble those encountered by Travellers."[37] Statistics on the nationalities of those seeking asylum in Ireland are difficult to obtain but approximately 50 percent are from two nations: Nigeria and Romania (including large numbers of Roma). The policy of excluding them from employment has contributed to a public perception, fuelled by certain sections of the media, that asylum seekers simply do not wish to work. Similar anxieties have also been articulated with respect to the (predominantly white) citizens of the ten newest EU member states, and their entitlement to work and claim social-welfare benefits in Ireland.[38] It would appear that patterns of suspicion and intolerance, developed in relation to Travellers, are readily extended to encompass other racialized minorities, even when they, too, are classed as "white."

Travellers, Racism, and the Tiger Economy

With the arrival of increased numbers of asylum seekers and migrant workers, academic debate around race and ethnicity in Ireland and the status of Travellers has expanded. Writing in 1997, Michael A. Poole acknowledges "a growing, though not uncontested, opinion that Ireland's Travelers . . . constitute a distinct ethnic group."[39] But he elects to omit both Travellers and "racially defined groups of non-European origin" from his empirical analysis of Irish ethnicity, and instead deals exclusively with the use of the term *ethnicity* to describe Catholic and Protestant traditions. Since 1997, however, academics and activists have focused attention on parallels between the experiences of Travellers and those of other racialized groups in Ireland.[40] Some theorists, most notably Ronit Lentin, have suggested that Irish racism is at least partly rooted in the traumatic collective experience of emigration, an experience painfully reactivated by the increasingly overt presence of migrants.[41]

This collective memory of migration might seem to provide a starting point for an *antiracist* politics, but this memory is fraught with contradiction. This becomes apparent in Elizabeth Butler Cullingford's analysis of intertextuality in *Into the West*. As I have already noted, her discussion highlights the parallels that are established (both directly and through various intertextual allusions) between the contemporary marginalization of Travellers in Irish society and the Native American experience of colonization and forced migration. She emphasizes that the inscription of Irish Travellers as "Indians" is reinforced, and complicated, by the fact that the "racism habitually shown towards [the Travellers] by Southern Irish 'settled people' echoes the racism of *white settlers, including those of Irish descent*, towards the Native Americans."[42] As such, the memory of migration invoked by *Into the West* involves an acknowledgment of the privileged status of whiteness.

Cullingford goes on to imply that *Into the West*'s critical metaphor can be extended to encompass the experiences of other marginalized groups within the Irish context. She states: "The travellers are white Others who have been 'blackened' by a previous group of white Others, the Irish. (Eastern European immigration is currently creating an analogous situation.) While it is Utopian to expect that the experience of racism would, by ideological inoculation, prevent the victims from spreading the contagion themselves, *Into the West* uses the cowboy metaphor to indict the indifference or hostility of the Southern state towards a marginalized sector of its own population."[43] Yet even if the cowboy metaphor acts as a productive reminder of the settled majority's own historical experience (of otherness and othering) *Into the West* can still be seen to perpetuate a tendency to align Travellers with an earlier moment in the settled past.[44] As such its potential as an antiracist critique remains somewhat limited.

Steve Garner has examined the historical development of Irish racial consciousness, with particular attention to the construction of Irishness through various processes of exclusion. Garner notes that nineteenth-century nationalist discourse ignored the presence of indigenous minorities (such as Travellers and Jews) as well as centuries of "métissage" when it located the formation of a "core people" in the twelfth century.[45] He also points towards a parallel process of exclusion in much of the popular discourse surrounding the formation of the Irish diaspora, which fails to address the shifting, and at times contradictory racial status of Irishness.[46] He emphasizes that exclusionary ideologies not based on skin color have a long history within the Irish context, and coexist with newer racisms that may centre on physical appearance or "illegitimate" claims to the nation's resources.

Garner's analysis highlights the fact that racism in Ireland intensified during the boom years of the 1990s. This might seem, at first, to contradict arguments linking racial tension to resource competition. The Celtic Tiger economy (1994–2001) has certainly given rise to greater overall levels of employment and wealth, and a shortage of skilled labor. But levels of social inequality are if anything more pronounced than ever, as the boom period was also marked by an expansion of insecure (contract-based) employment, uneven regional development, declining public services, and increases in personal debt. It is within precisely this context that fears about competition between nationals and foreigners for employment and welfare are likely to become pronounced.[47]

Perhaps most significantly, Garner notes that the boom period has given rise to "increasing tension over defending property, which comprises a growing physical stake in territory."[48] This increasing tension has particular implications for Travellers. Since the 1970s various advocacy organizations have called for the provision of appropriate accommodation for Travellers, in the interests of improving relations between the two communities. Appropriate accommodation (in the form of housing and serviced halting sites) has been repeatedly promised but it has not been provided, partly as a result of ongoing resistance from political representatives.[49]

Citizen Traveller (1999–2002), a communications campaign devised by a number of Traveller groups with the support of the Irish government, highlighted the consequences of this ongoing discrimination. The campaign noted the link between poor accommodation and increased mortality rates within the Traveling community, emphasizing that "Travelers can now expect a life expectancy comparable to that of the settled community in the 1950s."[50] The campaign also explicitly addressed the fears of the settled majority with regard to accommodation: "When Travellers are accommodated in proper serviced halting sites or group housing schemes, opposition to Travellers living in the area greatly diminishes or evaporates. Also, where halting sites are well serviced they have little or no *negative impact on the property market*."[51] This statement is a response to the widespread public perception that property will fall in price if a Traveller halting site is built nearby. If homeowners cannot sell (because of anti-Traveller prejudice or because of a crash in property values) they will of course be rendered immobile, a frightening prospect within an increasingly fluid labor market. It has been suggested that Travellers face particular prejudice because their nomadic way of life is out-of-synch with settled society's valorization of rootedness and property holding. Yet, within the current economic context, Irish settled society has perhaps begun to develop a new relationship with property, as capital. The fear of immobility has (paradoxically) given rise to new forms of territorialism.

In his analysis of social policy in county Clare, Fanning calls attention to the criminalization of nomadism, and to the gradual exclusion of Travellers from unauthorized (yet long established) halting sites around Ennis. In recent years, this policy has acquired even greater legitimacy, following the enactment of the 2002 "Anti-Trespass" Bill.[52] Paul Delaney notes that this legislation is regarded by Travellers' rights groups as assimilationist and in keeping with principles of the 1963 Commission on Itinerancy, which defined nomadism as an outdated custom and sought to obliterate it through the provision of housing. Delaney argues that by identifying nomadism in this way the commission denied its significance and complexity as a living part of Traveller culture, to the extent that the nomadism of Irish Travellers is now often dismissed as "a deterioration of the truly nomadic practices that are carried out by other, more legitimate groups, like the Roma."[53] Citing the Roma scholar Jean-Pierre Liégeois, he emphasizes that nomadism is not dependent on acts of physical movement, but is instead suggestive of a certain approach to life. As Liégeois states, "whereas a sedentary person remains sedentary, even when travelling, the Traveler is a nomad, even when he (or she) does not travel. Immobilised, he (or she) remains a Traveler."[54] This distinction (while perhaps not unproblematic) highlights the fact that Travellers may actually be far *less* mobile than other sectors of the population, by virtue of the fact that their movements are constrained by their lack of security, in terms of accommodation.[55]

One final issue, with respect to the ethnic status of Travellers, needs to be considered before returning to representations of them in Irish and international cinema. One of the key aims of the Citizen Traveller communications campaign was to achieve balanced media coverage of Traveller culture, lifestyles, and achievements. The campaign sought to position Travellers as an ethnic group within Irish society but also to encourage them to embrace their own identity as a community.[56] A billboard and radio campaign was developed, including a number of posters featuring black-and-white portraits of individual men, women, and children. The images largely conformed to the conventions of the professional studio portrait (few details of clothing were visible and the lighting and composition of each shot focused attention on the face of the subject) but each image was overlaid with seven one-word captions, varying in size and color, and featuring the terms *traveller* and *citizen* among a list of different roles.

The rich cultural heritage of Travellers was subtly foregrounded in this poster campaign. So, for example, a middle-aged man was identified not simply as a Traveller and citizen, but also as a "Storyteller," "Carpenter," "Father," "Slagger" (Joker), and "Husband," while the image of a young woman was accompanied by the captions "Flautist," "Mother," "Woman," "Comedienne," and "Midwife." Each poster also included the standard Citizen Traveller slogan: "It's time to value Travellers as people with their own culture, needs and contribution." As already noted, the cultural traditions of Travellers have attracted the attention of professional and amateur enthusiasts since the nineteenth century. Yet the state itself has been relatively slow to support Traveller culture, or even to document its existence.[57] Any recognition of this culture in a state-funded initiative could be seen to represent a step forward. But it is perhaps significant that this appeal for the basic human right of racial tolerance is reinforced by (if not predicated on) claims to a distinct cultural heritage, a commodity that has a particular currency within the Tiger economy.

1–2. The cultural heritage of Travellers is subtly foregrounded in a series of posters produced for the Citizen Traveller Campaign.

Myth, Motherland, and Mobility in *Into the West*

Some of the contemporary anxieties of the settled majority, in relation to issues of home, mobility, and territory, find expression in Irish heritage cinema. In his 1995 analysis of *Into the West*, Joe Cleary examines the various notions of the west mobilized in the film. He notes a profound opposition between the literary, romantic, Celtic west and the political west of the United States, Western Europe, and advanced capitalism, symbolized by the "visually drab, spiritually desiccated world of the city."[58] This binarism is complicated, however, by the construction of a third space — the "Wild West of Hollywood legend: the cinematic west into which Ossie and Tito like to imagine they are fleeing." Through its references to the cinematic west, Cleary suggests that *Into the West* implicitly acknowledges the impossibility of a real escape from the world of advanced capitalism.

Cleary emphasizes that *Into the West* cannot be read as a film that is in any sense "about" the Traveling community in Ireland. Instead, drawing on Jameson's 1979 analysis of *The Godfather*, he suggests that the Travellers function as "the figure of a rather nostalgic desire for a kind of communal collectivity," a collectivity that has been destroyed by advanced capitalism.[59] Jameson's account focuses on the reinvention of the figure of the gangster in the *Godfather* saga and, specifically, on the displacement of the lone hero or anti-hero of classical Hollywood gangster and noir film by an ethnicized family group. This ethnic group is the object of both prejudice and envy: "The dominant white middle class groups — already given over to anomie and social fragmentation and atomization — find in the ethnic and racial groups which are the object of their social repression and status contempt at one and the same time the image of some other collective ghetto or ethnic neighborhood solidarity."[60] Cleary's account also calls attention to a striking *difference* between Irish and American figurations of utopian desire. He notes that, in *Into the West*, the precapitalist Traveller community is presided over by a "Spirit-mother," rather than a "God-father." In this way, the return to the past is coded in terms of a return to maternal origins, perhaps suggesting a culturally specific investment in "myths of motherland."[61]

The consequences of this return to a premodern past, particularly for women, are not fully reconciled within the narrative, and this is evident

3. The implied union between Papa Riley (Gabriel Byrne) and the tracker Kathleen (Ellen Barkin) confirms the restoration of the Traveller family at the close of *Into the West* (1992). (Miramax Films)

in the ambivalent representation of maternity and femininity. Toward the close of the narrative, it emerges that Ossie's and Tito's mother died in childbirth. In the guise of the horse, however, the spirit-mother facilitates a recovery of the family. The only living female within the narrative is the Traveller guide Kathleen (Ellen Barkin). Although she appears to be an independent, strong-willed figure, Cleary suggests that she functions simply as a surrogate for the spirit-mother. When Papa finally comes to terms with the loss of his wife, underscored in the scene in which he burns her caravan and possessions, he is free to enter into a new alliance with Kathleen. This trajectory is, of course, apparent to many viewers from the start because Barkin and Gabriel Byrne were married at the time of the film's production.

In order to fully understand the significance of this imaginary Traveller community, it may be useful to return to Jameson's discussion of *The Godfather*. He reads the Mafia family not simply as a figure of ethnic collectivity, but as a substitution for a very different form of "organized conspiracy"—American business, which (at least in the late 1970s), remained largely immune to popular criticism. Jameson states, "For genuinely political insights into the economic realities of late capitalism, the myth of the Mafia strategically substitutes the vision of what is seen to be a criminal aberration from the norm, rather than the norm itself."[62] From this perspective, the figure of the Traveller in *Into the West* might be read as a representative of social formations that are associated with the *postmodern* (rather than in terms of a more general anxiety around modernity).

In general terms, the Traveller could be regarded as a privileged (mythic) signifier of the peripheral, the marginal, and the mobile. If postmodernity is conceptualized according to the economic, social, and cultural shifts specified by David Harvey, the Traveller economy could be seen to offer certain superficial parallels with highly mobile globalized capitalism, as it has developed within the Irish context. *Into the West* calls attention to similarities between the Traveller and the Tiger economies in various ways. The film opens with a small-scale fraud, in which Ossie and Tito are temporarily renamed (by Papa Riley) so that another family can claim larger social-welfare benefits. The Travellers are not the only Irish community to evade regulation, however, and much of the film's plot centers on another fraud, in which an unscrupulous horse breeder, with the assistance of a corrupt Garda sergeant, steals Tir na nÓg and turns him into a show horse. Given that the horse-breeding industry continues (like multinational capital in general) to benefit from Irish tax concessions, the personification of state and corporate corruption in this way seems highly suggestive. But although the Traveller and big-business economies are portrayed as equally fraudulent, *Into the West* ultimately positions the Travellers (and particularly Ossie and Tito) in an opposing relation to capitalist interests. The children rescue Tir na nÓg from the film's only true gangster, the horse breeder, and their action forces Papa Riley to abandon his fraudulent lifestyle.

Memory, Trauma, Migration

As Cleary demonstrates, *Into the West* fails to offer any alternative to dependency, other than the mythic land of Tir na nÓg. A small number of films have, however, attempted to disrupt the dominant pattern of representation, whereby Travellers are constituted as others through an alignment with the past. At least one challenge to the dominant mode has emerged from the margins of Irish heritage cinema, a genre that in recent years has been marked by a particular concern with traumatic memory.[63]

In *This Is My Father*, James Caan (who first came to prominence in *The Godfather*) plays Irish American Kieran Johnson, a middle-aged man in crisis. His career as a Chicago high-school teacher is unsatisfying, and his failure to achieve career (or personal) ambition is portrayed as a function of his troubled family history. Kieran never knew his father, and although his mother is still living, she is in many ways absent from his life, as she refuses (and perhaps cannot) speak about the past. A breakdown in communication has also occurred between Kieran's sister and her son, and a trip to the "homeland" is proposed as a form of therapy.

In many ways the character of Kieran is reminiscent of Sean Thornton, the quiet man from the film of the same title who sought to recover a past coded in maternal terms. In Ireland, Kieran acquires a maternal figure in the guise of an elderly Traveller woman, and professional storyteller, Mrs. Kearny. She was a witness to many of the key events in Kieran's mother's life and her willingness to verbalize the past stands in pointed contrast to the other woman's silence. By framing the past as the story of a Traveling woman, *This Is My Father* might be seen to conform to dominant patterns of representation, whereby Travellers are constituted as the literal and metaphorical representatives of an earlier moment in the history of the settled community. Yet this familiar temporal relation is disrupted in various ways. Mrs. Kearny is herself a mother, and her son Seamus owns the bed and breakfast in which Kieran and his nephew are staying. As played by Colm Meaney, Seamus is a camp, kitsch " 'Mammy's boy," and something of a caricature. Yet *This Is My Father* remains one of the few Irish film narratives to feature a Traveller engaged in gainful employment within a contemporary setting. Seamus's position as the bourgeois owner of a bed and breakfast also tends to work against romantic, essentialized notions of nomadism in Traveller culture.

A certain disjunction between the landscapes of past and present also becomes apparent as the narrative unfolds in a series of flashbacks linked to Mrs. Kearny's stories. The landscape of the present seems largely devoid of aesthetic appeal, framed as a blighted byproduct of mismanaged industrialization (and likened by Kieran's nephew to Chernobyl). By contrast, the predominantly agricultural past retains a desolate beauty, in accordance with the realist conventions of "hard primitivism."[64] Yet the veracity of this remembered landscape remains uncertain. Many of the storytelling sessions take place in the dining room of the bed and breakfast, which is decorated by a kitsch oversized poster of a tropical beach. Recalling the scenic backdrops employed in *The Quiet Man*, this setting serves as a reminder of the charged relationship between memory, landscape, and desire. Ultimately the distinction between the remembered past and the present is rendered ambiguous, particularly at the point when Mrs. Kearney finally reveals the fate of Kieran's father. He was found hanging from a tree on a hill — in a landscape that is uncannily similar to one encountered by Kieran in a book about Ireland, *before* undertaking his journey.

Through its exploration of the interplay between past and present, and between Kieran and Mrs. Kearney, *This Is My Father* seems to suggest a parallel between the figure of the Traveller and the condition of the migrant. This exploration of Traveller subjectivity remains somewhat underdeveloped, however, and in order to find a film drama that is explicitly concerned with this issue it is perhaps necessary to return to a much earlier moment in Irish film culture. Joe Comerford's *Traveller* (1981) forms part of the new wave of Irish filmmaking, which emerged in the late 1970s with the support of Irish and international state funding.[65] It is loosely based on a script by Neil Jordan, which in turn reworks elements of Synge's *Playboy of the Western World*, and the production team featured a number of other Irish filmmakers, such as Thaddeus O'Sullivan and Cathal Black.

The narrative of Comerford's film centers on the relationship between two young Travellers (Angela and Michael) who are unwillingly matched and forced to marry. On a trip to the north of Ireland, smuggling goods at the behest of Angela's father, they meet Clicky, a hitchhiker with a mysterious Republican past. Angela develops a bond with Clicky, telling him of abuse suffered at the hands of her father, which resulted in her institutionalization. They part company and, after Michael robs a post office, the couple hide out in a series of desolate locations (a decaying rural mansion, an off-season seaside town) and begin to resolve their differences.

On their return to Limerick they are reunited with Clicky, and Michael uses Clicky's gun to kill Angela's father.

Traveller could perhaps be seen to rehearse a familiar opposition between familial belonging and individual freedom. But while comparable narratives such as *Into the West* can be seen to borrow from the classical Hollywood western, Traveller's mode of address is far more indebted to European and British avant-garde cinema. Various formal strategies are employed to disrupt identification; visual barriers such as reflective or distorted glass are repeatedly employed, and short animation sequences map the movements of the three central characters. There is little synchronized speech, and the disjunctive use of voice-over undercuts the development of the plot.

Comerford also chose to work primarily with nonprofessional actors and the lead roles of Michael and Angela are played by Davy Spillane, a well-known Irish traditional musician, and Judy Donovan, a member of the Traveling community. Donovan's participation might be thought to lend an air of authenticity to the production, but expectations of authenticity are countered by the use of sound, and the thematic exploration of performativity. Donovan's character is in fact voiced by, and openly credited to, another actress (Marian Richardson). This use of dubbing was not intended to make the film more accessible to international audiences, because Richardson delivers the lines with a strong accent, and the finished film was actually subtitled in English for distribution in Britain.

Instead, the use of dubbing seems to recall strategies from avant-garde film. In Godard's *Tout Va Bien* (1972), for example, the voice of Jane Fonda is frequently misdubbed, precisely in order to "sabotage the fictive unity of voice and image."[66] Similarly, Amy Lawrence points out that avant-garde documentary filmmaker and theorist Trinh T. Minh-ha employs English-speaking actresses to re-voice the words of Vietnamese women in her film *Surname Viet, Given Name Nam* (1989). Lawrence suggests that "the use of actresses—literally putting one person's words into another body—seemingly undermines the traditional documentary's construction of speech-as-subjectivity where sync 'proves' an essential link between image/sound track/being."[67]

In addition to its exploration of form, *Traveller* is characterized by a thematic concern with gender and performativity. For example, at Angela's and Michael's wedding reception, the singer Agnes O'Donnell (positioned off-screen) launches into the song "One Day at a Time." As she sings the words "I'm only a woman," we see O'Donnell for the first time and she is revealed as a strikingly androgynous older woman, dressed in a tuxedo. In a later scene, set in a Republican social club, Angela and Michael both take to the stage as performers, exposing the inauthenticity of Angela's singing voice. Finally, in a scene that marks her growing dissatisfaction with her lot as wife and daughter, Angela decides to change her own identity and she swaps her wedding ring for fashionable new clothes.

In a contemporary review, Kevin Barry highlights Comerford's pronounced and deliberate use of "impaired speech, silence and music," reading it in terms of an exploration of disjunctive cultural identity.[68] More recently, Comerford has stated that the various alienating strategies employed in *Traveller* constituted a *response* to the experience of working with performers like Donovan. He notes that, during the course of the production, the actress's own persona altered: "She started changing, she started using lipstick for the first time, she started dressing in a nontraditional way. But this was happening in her life. It wasn't a film. It was happening in her life."[69] The temporal and narrative inconsistencies of *Traveller* can, then, be read as the product of Comerford's self-reflexive engagement with the conventions of film documentary, and his experience of working with a member of the Traveling community.

Keith Hopper, however, is highly critical of Comerford's approach, and he suggests that Comerford's film invites an "allegorical reading," whereby Travellers stand for "the dispossessed people of the North."[70] Hopper argues that the film fails to address the "real" marginalization of the Traveling community. But Comerford's film is, arguably, one of the few Irish film dramas to *reject* the reduction of Travellers to the status of symbol.[71] Instead, anticipating projects such as Citizen Traveller, it refuses to essentialize Traveller culture and foregrounds a mobile identity that is structured by many of the same historical and social forces that shape settled society.

Finally, instead of relegating Travellers to the periphery of settled history, or to a rural West that is coded as premodern, Comerford's film concludes with an exploration of the various possible futures open to Michael, Angela, and Clicky. The final (animated) sequence suggests that all three will follow in the footsteps of earlier migrants — tracing familiar routes to the United States, England, and even Australia. By recasting its central characters as migrants in this final sequence *Traveller* invokes a wider cultural memory of migration. In this respect it anticipates (and offers parallels with) the exploration of memory in *This Is My Father*.

Beyond the National Context:
Travellers outside Ireland

In many of the Irish films that I have discussed, images of Travellers provide a means of negotiating the dynamics of migration, memory, and identity, and some of these themes can be seen to recur in the non-Irish films *Chocolat* (U.K./U.S.), *Snatch* (U.K.), and *Traveller* (U.S.). In each of these narratives, Traveller characters are positioned in relation to an array of other types and clearly marked as heroic, perhaps confirming the appeal of Irishness as an ethnic identity in late-twentieth-century U.S. culture. *Snatch* and *Traveller* both explore an ethnicized criminal underworld, but *Chocolat* is more easily located in relation to the heritage genre.

Chocolat is a comic romance, set in rural France in the 1950s. The central character, Vianne (Juliette Binoche), is a habitual wanderer torn between her daughter's need for the security of small-town life, and her own need for independence. Her nomadic lifestyle and skill with chocolate are both explained in racial terms, as a consequence of her maternal ancestry — she is a descendant of a mythic Aztec tribe. Vianne decides to settle temporarily in a conservative small town, and begins to dispense chocolate in an effort to undermine the repressive social order represented by the devoutly Catholic mayor. When the unexpected arrival of a band of gypsies exposes the prejudices of the townsfolk, Vianne provocatively establishes an alliance with their leader Roux (played, with a touch of an Irish lilt, by Johnny Depp). Roux and Vianne flirt but she is reluctant to enter into the traditional role of wife and mother, a reluctance that seems justified, not least because her independence allows her to rescue other women from domestic abuse. In the course of the narrative, however, Vianne is forced to confront her own past, and she eventually decides to settle for her daughter's sake, breaking the pattern of wandering inherited from her own mother. This compromise is softened, however, by the likelihood that she could develop an open and equal relationship with the open-minded and free-spirited Roux.

Like *Chocolat*, *Snatch* is a highly stylized work. It operates within the conventions of the heist movie, and features a crew of assorted colorful criminals and a complex score. Moving between American and British settings, it recycles an array of familiar stereotypes, from dapper mafiosos and cheeky cockneys to Jewish hustlers and somber Eastern Europeans. The "Pikeys," led by Mickey O'Neill (an unbeatable boxer, played by Brad Pitt) are the newest addition to this ethnic assortment, and their incomprehensible dialect provides the focus of the film's humor. In his review of *Snatch*, Roger Ebert reads the presence of the Pikeys as a comment on the reception of Ritchie's earlier film, *Lock, Stock and Two Smoking Barrels* (1998). He states, "In the previous film, some of the accents were impenetrable to non-British audiences, so this time, in the spirit of fair play, Ritchie has added a character played by Brad Pitt, who speaks a gypsy dialect even the other characters in the movie can't understand."[72]

Snatch would seem to have evaded criticism within the British and U.S. press because of its evenhanded stereotyping, its novelty, and its nonnaturalistic form. Irish critics have, however, noted that *Snatch* perpetuates some very well-established conventions in its representation of Irishness as otherness, most notably the (acknowledged) "simianization" of Pitt through makeup and prosthetics.[73] *Snatch* also shares a number of thematic similarities with Irish film narratives, in terms of its emphasis on the maternality of Traveller society. Mickey O'Neill's family is dominated by a beloved matriarch, and her sudden death motivates much of the action. Pitt's character is in fact a highly exaggerated version of a very familiar cinematic figure—the tough working-class boxer with a soft heart—motivated by commitment to family and community. It is perhaps significant that Pitt's performance as Mickey O'Neill was read by some critics as a "satiric" commentary on an earlier work, *Fight Club* (1999).[74] In *Fight Club*, Pitt played a hypermasculine character, ultimately revealed as the fantasy product of an office worker's nervous breakdown. Ritchie's film, however, seems to recover an image of heroic masculinity from an earlier cinematic moment, through reference to contemporary stereotypes surrounding Traveller society.

The U.S. independent film *Traveller* seems to be informed by a more personal concern with the experiences of Irish Travellers. Yet it many respects it, too, perpetuates familiar myths and stereotypes, offering parallels with both Irish cinema and ethnic sagas such as *The Godfather*, but also working within the conventions of the heist movie. Coproducer and leading actor Bill Paxton plays Bokky Sherlock, a Traveller and a successful con artist who pays his dues to the family boss but works independently. His routine is disrupted by the arrival of Pat O'Hara (Mark Wahlberg), the son of a deceased Traveller and a settled woman. Pat demands to be inducted into the Traveller clan, and this provides a narrative device whereby the "hidden" ways of the community are revealed. In the course of his induction into the community, Pat learns that Travellers have a tradition of early "fixed" marriage and a private language called Cant (because, according to Bokky, "we can speak it and they can't"). He is taught to distinguish between Irish, Scottish, and "Turkish" Travellers and to perform a number of reliable scams. All of those outside the clan are fair game, as evidenced in one scene where Bokky attempts to distract a possible "mark" with comments about her "Irish" red hair.[75]

Bokky and his cohorts ply their trade in the suburbs, while staying in motels, and by comparison with the Turks (or indeed the Pikeys) they retain a degree of anonymity. They return to the clan only for family gatherings, and it is at a communal funeral that the structure of the community is first revealed to Pat. This scene is set in a forest clearing and marked by a certain southern-gothic ambiance, not least because of the unlikely proximity between the family graves and trailers. The otherworldly character of the community is also underscored by the figure of Ganny, Bokky's elderly blind grandmother. As guardian of Traveller lore, she upholds Pat's claim to Traveller ancestry with these words: "Though a man lose his way on the dark roads of life, if he come from the belly of a *real Traveler woman*, isn't that man yet a Traveler on the day he dies? The boy's got the blood and blood don't lie." This statement is perhaps significant, although highly contradictory, in that it defines Traveller identity in terms of the *maternal* line (a definition that would actually exclude Pat, since his mother was a settled woman). The emphasis on the maternal, as source of authentic identity, becomes more pronounced as the narrative unfolds. Following Ganny's death we learn that Bokky's own wife died in childbirth, and it is only through coming to terms with this event that he is able to begin a new life, with a settled single mother and her daughter.

Traveller offers striking parallels with *This Is My Father* and *Into the West*, in terms of its privileging of the maternal supernatural, its failure to engage with experiences of living women, and its focus on male trauma. *Traveller* is also clearly marked by an opposition between the realm of family and domesticity and the sphere of business. The Traveller economy is governed by the boss, and much of the plot centers on Bokky's and Pat's rivalry for his approval and power, a dynamic explored through Pat's affair with the boss's daughter. Bokky and Pat clearly represent two quite different notions of Traveller identity—Bokky's allegiance is to the free-wheeling independent life (and to the memory of his wife) while Pat seeks the reassurance of blood ties. It is through the character of Bokky that the Travellers are Americanized, and rendered "sympathetic." At one point Bokky is pictured with a beer in his hand, enjoying the World Series and relaxing with his friends and family at a barbeque—just like any other American. In contrast, Pat's desire for acceptance and status in this close-knit community appears somewhat obsessive.

The representation of Travellers as conmen also invites analysis. In many ways the film anticipates, and perhaps exploits, the desire for inside knowledge articulated in the media coverage of the Toogood case. But while U.S. media accounts have tended to censure Travellers as untrustworthy or duplicitous, *Traveller* seems to celebrate the artistry and independence of the con artist. The scenes in which Bokky teaches Pat the tricks of the trade evoke a cinematic tradition extending from *Paper Moon* (1973) to *The Grifters* (1990). Many of the scams are perpetrated against unsuspecting suburbanites, portrayed as naive and greedy, and they are structured by a moral code. So when Bokky unwittingly defrauds an impoverished single mother, Jean, he feels he must make amends—against the wishes of Pat. This honest act initiates a relationship that will ultimately lead Bokky away from the clan.

As is typical of the heist or con genre, the drama culminates in one final, large-scale, scam—involving in this case the sale of currency plates to a rival gang of Turkish gypsies. The sting lies in the fact that the currency plates do not exist and the high-quality "forgeries" shown to the "Turks" are actually real banknotes. When the con is discovered, the gang members kill one of the Travellers and pursue Bokky and Pat to Jean's home. In a scene of extreme violence, typical of the kind foregrounded by Annalee Newitz in her discussion of racialized primitivism, the gypsy gang attack Jean and her daughter. Bokky and Pat are rendered helpless and are saved only by the arrival of the Traveller boss and an armed posse, who meet violence with violence.

The resolution of the narrative confirms the opposition, established throughout the narrative, between the two modes of identity represented by Bokky and Pat. Two new unions are formed; Pat returns with the boss to the clan and Bokky leaves town with Jean and her daughter. Given his earlier involvement with the boss's daughter, it seems likely that Pat will finally acquire the status of a "real" Traveller. Yet his claim to Traveller identity is undercut by the fact that the structure of the clan is patriarchal and so not fully authentic according to the maternal terms specified by Ganny. By establishing a union with the independent single mother Jean, Bokky seems to abandon his identity as a Traveller. But it is only through his knowledge, and acceptance, of traumatic memory (facing the loss of his wife) that Bokky can enter into a new, and different, relationship.

Conclusion

This analysis of Traveller identities, as they are constituted in Irish and international cinema, would seem to suggest that the figure of the Traveller provides a conduit to the recovery of the past, a recovery coded as therapeutic. My analysis highlights a recurrent romantic investment in the spiritual, familial, and communal values that these white others are thought to possess—values that are no longer securely located in post–Celtic Tiger Ireland. This recovery of the past sometimes enables the establishment of new relationships, or more progressive forms of social and familial organization. This dynamic is perhaps most pronounced in the international films discussed, such as *Chocolat*, *Traveller*, and *This Is My Father*. Yet it is also suggested by the conclusion of Joe Comerford's film, one of the few narratives to deal explicitly with the experiences of a Traveller woman. In some of the Irish examples discussed, however, such as *The Field* and *Into the West*, the recovery of lost histories fails to disrupt the dominant order.

The prominent position of Travellers in Irish heritage cinema is clearly structured by cultural, social, and economic factors extending beyond the Irish context. Mac Laughlin, Garner, and Lentin suggest that representations of Travellers have been shaped by a variety of historical factors associated with the experience of colonization and migration, and the formation of Irish nationalism. In its current form, however, Irish racial discourse is also underpinned by the Celtic Tiger economy, which has contributed to an increased investment in property as capital, and growing tensions around ethnic and cultural difference. As Irish society has become more overtly ethnically diverse, patterns of intolerance established in relation to Travellers have continued to inform attitudes toward other, newer, minorities.

One of the key issues to emerge from this analysis of Irish and international cinema is the recurrent emphasis on Traveller society as inherently, and ideally, maternal. The coding of the settled past (and by extension Traveller culture) in this way would seem to have particular implications for women, and this invites further analysis. Another key issue is the extent to which Irish cinema can hope to engage with the lived experiences of Travellers, given the place that they have been assigned within the Irish, and international, cultural imaginary. A possible point of departure is suggested by Comerford's *Traveller*. Through its exploration of performativity, and female subjectivity, it articulates a critique of the traditions of representation that continue to shape relations between Travellers and the settled majority in contemporary Ireland.

Notes

This essay forms part of a larger research project, funded by the Irish Research Council for the Humanities and Social Sciences. I am grateful to Stephanie McBride and Luke Gibbons for their guidance throughout this project, to Diane Negra for her assistance in researching representations of Irish Travellers in the U.S. media, and to Dennis McNulty for assisting me with the illustrations.

1. Ruth Barton, "From History to Heritage: Some Recent Developments in Irish Cinema," *Irish Review* 21 (1997): 41–56.

2. See Andrew Higson, "Re-presenting the National Past: Nostalgia and Pastiche in the Heritage Film," in *Fires Were Started: British Cinema and Thatcherism*, edited by Lester Friedman (Minneapolis: University of Minnesota Press, 1993), 109–29.

3. Barton, "From History to Heritage," 51.

4. Elizabeth Butler Cullingford, *Ireland's Others; Gender and Ethnicity in Irish Literature and Popular Culture* (Cork: Cork University Press, 2001), 183. She emphasizes that the film is marked by a thematic exploration of memory and nostalgia and highlights various intertextual references to nostalgic screen fictions, such as *Butch Cassidy and the Sundance Kid* (1969) and *Back to the Future Part III* (1990).

5. Cullingford, *Ireland's Others*, 183.

6. See Sinéad Ni Shuinéar, "Othering the Irish (Travellers)" in *Racism and Anti-Racism in Ireland*, edited by R. Lentin and R. McVeigh (Belfast: Beyond the Pale, 2002), 177–92.

7. An exploration of contemporary Traveller identity can be found in the feature-length documentary *Southpaw: The Francis Barrett Story* (1999) about Francis Barrett, an Irish Traveller and Olympic boxer. The documentary *Traveller* (2001) also develops a complex examination of the relationship between a photographer and his former subjects, a group of Travellers.

8. See the analysis of *Trojan Eddie* (1996), *Southpaw*, and MacWhiney's *Traveller* in Ruth Barton, *Irish National Cinema* (London: Routledge, 2004), 185–86.

9. Diane Negra, in the introduction to this volume, 13.

10. Stephen Crofts, "Reconceptualising National Cinemas," *Quarterly Review of Film and Video* 14, no. 3 (1993): 58.

11. Barton, "From History to Heritage," 50.

12. Joe Cleary, "Into Which West? Irish Modernity and the Maternal Supernatural," in *Literature and the Supernatural*, edited by Brian Cosgrave (Dublin: Columba Press, 1995), 147–73; Fredric Jameson, "Reification and Utopia in Mass Culture" (1979), in *Signatures of the Visible* (New York: Routledge, 1992), 9–34.

13. Jim Mac Laughlin, *Travellers and Ireland: Whose Country, Whose History?* (Cork: Cork University Press, 1995), 19.

14. Mac Laughlin, *Travellers and Ireland*, 9, emphasis added.

15. Ibid., 11.

16. Aparna Rao, "The Concept of the Peripatetics: An Introduction," in *The Other Nomads* (Cologne: Bohlau Verlag, 1987), 12.

17. Ibid., 9.

18. Mac Laughlin, *Travellers and Ireland*, 16.

19. Paul Delaney, "Representations of the Travellers in the 1880s and 1900s," *Irish Studies Review* 9, no. 1 (2001): 65.

20. Irish Traveller groups, such as the Pavee Point Travellers' Centre, estimate the

numbers of Travellers in Britain and the United States at 15,000 and 10,000. In the United States, Traveller communities can be found in Texas, Indiana, South Carolina, and Tennessee.

21. See especially the work of George and Sharon Gmelch, "The Emergence of an Ethnic Group: The Irish Tinkers," *Anthropological Quarterly* 49, no. 4 (1976): 225–38; *The Irish Tinkers: The Urbanization of an Itinerant People* (Menlo Park, Cal.: Cummings, 1977). I have found little evidence of in-depth research by American scholars into Irish Travellers in the United States, with the exception of linguistic analyses such as Ian Hancock, "The Cryptolectal Speech of the American Roads: Traveler Cant and American Angloromani," *American-Speech* 61, no. 3 (1986): 206–20. In contrast, the history and culture of Irish Travellers in the United States has proved to be of some interest to Irish scholars and filmmakers. See Sinéad Ni Shuinéar, "Travellers Outside Ireland," in *Encyclopaedia of Ireland*, edited by Brian Lalor (Dublin: Gill and Macmillan, 2003), 1073–74; and also the profile of the Irish Traveller community in Murphy Village, North Augusta in the documentary *Stories from Irish America: The Travellers of Murphy Village* (1995). I am indebted to Kevin Whelan for calling my attention to both the encyclopedia entry and the film.

22. Rao, "Concept of the Peripatetics," 11.

23. Margery Eagan, "Options Available for Girl in Taped Beating Not Toogood," *Boston Herald*, 24 September 2002. Toogood was eventually released, after serving a custodial sentence.

24. Susan J. Douglas and Meredith W. Michaels, *The Mommy Myth: The Idealization of Motherhood and How it has Undermined Women* (New York: Free Press, 2004), 151.

25. Ibid., 170–71.

26. "Arrest Aims Light on Nomad Travellers," *Washington Times*, 7 October 2002. See also Melody McDonald, "Woman Videotaped Hitting Child Believed Linked to Irish Travellers," *Fort Worth Star-Telegram*, 20 September 2002.

27. Jennifer Mathieu, "Ties of Texas," *Dallas Observer*, 10 October 2002.

28. Amanda Ripley, Mairead Carey, and Daren Fonda, "Unwelcome Exposure," *Time*, 7 October 2002, 10

29. Annalee Newitz, "White Savagery and Humiliation, or A New Racial Consciousness in the Media," in *White Trash: Race and Class in America*, edited by Matt Wray and Annalee Newitz (New York: Routledge, 1997), 135.

30. Mac Laughlin, *Travellers and Ireland*, 34.

31. Ibid., 36.

32. Brian Fanning, *Racism and Social Change in the Republic of Ireland* (Manchester: Manchester University Press, 2002), 136.

33. The *1963 Report of the Commission on Itinerancy* (Dublin: Government Publications) remains an influential work, and its publication confirmed the rise of the term *itinerant*, in place of the pejorative *Tinker*. *Itinerancy* clearly carries negative associa-

tions, however, and the term *Traveller* is prominently foregrounded in contemporary antidiscrimination campaigns.

34. Mac Laughlin, *Travellers and Ireland*, 45.

35. Fanning, *Racism and Social Change*, 136.

36. Ibid., 172.

37. Ibid., 173.

38. The ten new countries are Cyprus, Czech Republic, Estonia, Hungary, Latvia, Lithuania, Malta, Poland, Slovakia, and Slovenia. See Damien Kiberd, "Keep the Door Open to a Labour Opportunity," *Sunday Times*, Business and Money, Irish edition, 15 February 2004, 6

39. Michael A. Poole, "In Search of Ethnicity in Ireland," in *In Search of Ireland: A Cultural Geography*, edited by Brian Graham (London: Routledge, 1997), 129.

40. Two recent publications dealing with both racism and antiracism in Ireland incorporate analyses of the experiences of Travellers. See Ronit Lentin and Robbie McVeigh, eds., *Racism and Anti-Racism in Ireland* (Belfast: Beyond the Pale, 2002); and Fintan Farrell and Philip Watt, eds., *Responding to Racism in Ireland* (Dublin: Veritas, 2001).

41. Ronit Lentin, cited by Steve Garner in *Racism in the Irish Experience* (London: Pluto Press, 2004), 24.

42. Cullingford, *Ireland's Others*, 181, emphasis added.

43. Ibid., 183.

44. This strategy is very much in keeping with the processes critiqued by Johannes Fabian in *Time and the Other: How Anthropology Makes Its Object* (New York: Columbia University Press, 2002).

45. Garner, *Racism in the Irish Experience*, 89.

46. Ibid., 112–13.

47. Ibid., 196.

48. Ibid., 48.

49. Ibid., 131.

50. Citizen Traveller, "Fact Sheet Traveller Health Issues," Dublin, 1999.

51. Ibid., emphasis added.

52. Nomadism has effectively become a criminal offense following the enactment of section 24 of the Housing (Miscellaneous Provisions) Act of 2002, commonly known as the Anti-Trespass Act. The legislation has already resulted in the conviction of members of Traveller families.

53. Paul Delaney, "A Sense of Place: Travellers, Representation, and Irish Culture," *The Republic: A Journal of Contemporary and Historical Debate* 3 (2003): 85.

54. Jean-Pierre Liégeois, cited by Delaney, "A Sense of Place," 86.

55. Delaney cites Jane Helleiner's research into this area, which notes that "housed" or so-called "settled" Travellers are often more mobile than other members of their community, who fear loss of access to facilities (86).

56. Citizen Traveller Charter, Dublin, 1999. Documentation of some of the campaign images can be found on the website of the Irish Traveller Movement at <http://www.itmtrav.com/frame2.html>.

57. Mac Laughlin points out that the Irish Folklore Commission established to document Irish traditions and customs largely ignored Travellers (*Travellers and Ireland*, 37).

58. Cleary, *Into Which West?* 155.

59. Ibid., 159.

60. Jameson, *Signatures of the Visible*, 32–33.

61. See Richard Kearney's analysis "Myths of Motherland," in *Postnationalist Ireland: Politics, Culture, Philosophy* (London: Routledge, 1997), 108–21.

62. Jameson, *Signatures of the Visible*, 32.

63. *The Butcher Boy* (1998), *The Magdalene Sisters* (2002), and the television film *Sinners* (2002) all deal with institutional abuse and its denial. Traumatic memories associated with migration and social deprivation also find expression in *Korea* (1995), *Angela's Ashes* (1999), *I Could Read the Sky* (1999), and *This Is My Father*. The latter film is the only one of this series to incorporate a representation of Irish Travellers.

64. Luke Gibbons, "Romanticism and Realism in Irish Cinema," in *Cinema and Ireland*, edited by Kevin Rockett, Luke Gibbons, and John Hill (London: Routledge, 1988), 200.

65. Comerford's film was cofinanced by the Irish Arts Council and by the Production Board of the British Film Institute, an agency responsible for the funding of a diverse range of avant-garde works. For an analysis of the role of the Production Board in Irish avant-garde film culture see Maeve Connolly, "Visibility Moderate? Sighting an Irish Avant-Garde in the Intersection of Local and International Film Cultures," *boundary 2: International Journal of Literature and Culture* 31, no. 1 (2004): 244–65. For details on Travellers within the context of Irish cinema see Richard Haslam, "Irish Film: Screening the Republic," in *Writing in the Irish Republic: Literature, Culture, Politics 1949–99*, edited by Ray Ryan (Basingstoke, England: Macmillan Press, 2000), 130–46.

66. Ella Shohat and Robert Stam, "The Cinema and Babel: Language Difference and Power," *Screen* 26, no. 3–4 (1985): 51.

67. Amy Lawrence, "Women's Voices in Third World Cinema," in *Sound Theory, Sound Practice*, edited by Rick Altman (London: Routledge, 1992), 189.

68. Kevin Barry, "Discarded Images: Narrative and the Cinema," *Crane Bag* 6 (1982): 45–51.

69. Joe Comerford, interview by the author, 8 May 2001.

70. Keith Hopper, " 'A Gallous Story and a Dirty Deed': Word and Image in Neil Jordan and Joe Comerford's *Traveller* (1981)," *Irish Studies Review* 9, no. 2 (2001): 186.

71. Alaina Lemon calls attention to a parallel current within contemporary Russian cinema, an exploration of identity (as both hidden and mobile) articulated in

farces such as *Shirly-Myrly* (1995). *Between Two Fires: Gypsy Performance and Romani Memory from Pushkin to Postsocialism* (Durham, N.C.: Duke University Press, 2000), 68–69.

72. Roger Ebert, "*Snatch* (Review)," *Chicago Sun-Times*, 12 January 2001.

73. Sinéad Ni Shuinéar, "Othering the Irish (Travellers)," 189.

74. See Mick LaSalle, "Pitt finds his Groove," *San Francisco Chronicle*, 19 January 2001.

75. See Amanda Third's essay on the semiotics of redheadedness in this volume.

MICHAEL MALOUF

Feeling Éire(y): On Irish-Caribbean
Popular Culture

Book your trip by plane or ferry
Once you get here you'll be glad,
Further west than Londonderry
Somewhere east of Trinidad
Begorrah and olé
Credit cards okay
— Stewart Parker, *Kingdom Come*

The commercial phenomenon that was Irish culture in the 1990s
can be traced to two controversial popular events in 1992, which
notably did not take place in Ireland, but across the Atlantic in
the United States. In May of that year, Sinéad O'Connor appeared on the
American television show *Saturday Night Live*, and, in a notorious gesture
of rebellion, ripped up a picture of the pope.[1] Her literally iconoclastic
performance was followed that fall by Neil Jordan's film about an interracial love story between an IRA soldier and a transvestite, *The Crying
Game*, which was received with popular and critical acclaim in the United
States after a tepid reception in England.[2] Significantly, the two events depend on opposite tactics: while O'Connor's performance was concerned
with acts of full disclosure — outing herself, the pope, the plight of Irish
women — *The Crying Game*'s success depended on audiences and critics not revealing the film's "real" disclosure — the biological sex of Dil,
the love interest of both the British soldier Jody and the IRA soldier Fergus. While it might be said that the "shock" of these two cultural events
was heightened by the sensationalizing habits of the media-saturated U.S.

market, it is worth noting the impact at home insofar as they each played on a paramount ideological fault line in Irish culture: Roman Catholicism and Irish Republican Nationalism, respectively. As a result, they participated in an ongoing generational rebellion against the Catholic-Nationalist pieties associated with the reign of Eamonn De Valera from the 1930s into the 1960s that dominated the ethos of postcolonial Ireland. As representatives of a commercially viable avant-garde aesthetic, Jordan and O'Connor suggested some alternative directions that Irish popular culture might take in the following decade.

In creating these controversial games of hide and seek, Jordan and O'Connor cloaked their transgressive acts in the guise of Afro-Caribbean culture. O'Connor appeared on snl wearing a Star of David around her neck to show her sympathy with Rastafarianism and sang reggae star Bob Marley's "War" a cappella while tearing up the pope's picture. Jordan's film features two black British characters, one of whom, the soldier Jody, grew up in Antigua before emigrating to Tottenham, while the transvestite Dil's indeterminate national and racial backgrounds help to reinforce her biological sexual ambiguity. The subtext of race, then, follows the same logic of repression and disclosure that marks the shock value of these controversial appearances. In O'Connor's case, it is "seen" in the Rastafarian symbols, but not mentioned, since the main object of attack is the church; while in Jordan's film, race is also "seen" but not mentioned, as the film's main concern is with rigid conceptions of Irish nationalism and masculinity. In a sense, then, these two performances engage with Afro-Caribbean culture as part of a process of engaging with a recalcitrant official Irish culture. Yet their Caribbean detours are distinctive in how these representations implicitly constitute the relationship between Irish and Caribbean communities in England and elsewhere.

The absent presence of race evident (or not so) in these two popular cultural events is indicative of the ambivalent shape that discourses of race were to take over the next decade in Irish society. No longer an "export" culture in which its agricultural products and its people were sent abroad, Ireland became in the 1990s an "import" culture as many middle-class Irish migrants returned, U.S. multinational corporations in technology and health sciences entered, and large-scale immigration from Africa and Eastern Europe began to take place. Despite its history of

colonialism and the existence of anti-Irish racism in England and elsewhere, Ireland reacted to the arrival of asylum seekers in much the same
way as other countries like France and England. On the one hand, the
government promoted advertisements calling for inclusiveness while at
the same time sanctioning policies such as welfare restrictions and restrictions from employment that excluded the asylum seekers from Irish
society.

However small the actual number of asylum seekers that have arrived in Ireland (though a relatively large group considered per capita),
the dominant impression fostered by the government and media is of
the threat of the country being swamped and exploited by the recent
arrivals in north Dublin's "Little Africa."[3] As a result, there have been
vocal and violent reactions against the asylum seekers, including acts of
vandalism, verbal abuse, and even arson directed at asylum hostels. For
these "Irish-Irelanders," as Bryan Fanning refers to the extreme nationalist position underwriting such behavior, Irish nationalism and its anticolonial struggle against the British justify entitlement to an exclusive,
Catholic, monocultural Ireland.[4]

Notably, there has been much useful work by Irish historians, activists, and sociologists over the past few years to counter this misconc-
eption of Ireland as a homogenous, monocultural society. From the
"Cross-Currents" pamphlets sponsored by President Mary McAleese to
the academic sociological and critical studies published by Pluto and the
Manchester Press, a strong, and relatively coherent, antiracist position
has been expressed.[5] For the antiracists, Ireland has an internationalist
history of migration and anticolonial struggle that can justify an inclusive
Irish nationalism.[6] Thus far, this position has tried to create an argument
out of a recovered history of Irish experiences of race either in Ireland,
through Belfast's engagement with the slave trade, and abolitionist visits
to Ireland by Olaudah Equiano and Frederick Douglass, or in Irish experiences of race abroad, whether in the United States or while serving
as part of the British Empire. The antiracist position uses this mixed history of solidarity to build a politics of tolerance, sympathy, and support
for the concept of a multicultural Ireland expressed by figures who have
traditionally escaped nationalist histories such as the midcentury Irish
Protestant cultural critic, Hubert Butler.[7]

A crucial element in the antiracist argument, therefore, has been this search in the archives for an "alternative history," as Rolston and Shannon put it, "one of mutual respect between Irish and black people—which produced such key figures as Daniel O'Connell and Frederick Douglass" where the goal is to "confront the history of the past, to know the roots of racism and also the ferment of anti-racism, and thereby to reject the former and nurture the latter."[8] Such mixed strategies of self-criticism and historical retrieval exemplify the paradoxes of race within the tradition of Irish nationalism. Inevitably, these critical acts of retrieval have to face the lack of many positive, selfless acts of solidarity by Irish nationalists with black activists from America or anywhere else (in fact, *race* appears to stand in for a diverse range of black identities, including African American, black British, Afro-Caribbean, or the many African cultures that have been the main source of recent immigration in Ireland). The often-cited examples of the San Patricio Corps as one of these moments of solidarity between the Irish in America and nonwhites, or of Irish nationalists and the Boers, illustrate the desire—and the necessity—for such a history. Yet, at the same time, the ensuing controversies that follow such examples suggest the difficulty in making this alternative canon accepted according to historicist terms.[9]

The Irish sociologist Steve Garner describes the black-Irish history of exchange and solidarity as a "one-way traffic" which, in its dependence on moments of black activists reaching out to Irish nationalists, has inhibited the potential of the antiracist argument. So far, much of the antiracist position has been defined by social-science rhetoric that assumes a form of rights-based and emancipatory politics within the nation state. As necessary and valuable as these approaches have been, any effort to create an alternative tradition of Irish culture needs to reconcile its objectives with the forms of racialization in Irish popular culture if it is to make any kind of lasting intervention.

This essay is part of a series of attempts to rethink this traffic flow of exchange and solidarity by reconsidering the Irish side of the street, as it were.[10] My title alludes to the Rastafarian adjective *Irie* which is defined as "nice," but is often used as a signal of approval or brotherhood in greetings. It is this latter meaning that this title emphasizes: how have Irish artists and intellectuals used Afro-Caribbean culture as a way of fashioning Ireland as part of a cosmopolitan brotherhood? What happens to the more "authentic" conceptions of monocultural Ireland in this hybrid construction? Invocations of the Caribbean in Irish culture and Irish-inflected popular culture from the 1970s to the present reveal the ways in which diverse Irish intellectuals and artists have represented changing conceptions of Irishness and race. I want to explore these cultural appropriations in order to try and clear a space between the essentialist narrative of Irish authenticity and an antiessentialist postmodernism in which Irish identity becomes only a "fiction" within a dominating European identity. The underlying question is, what can popular culture tell us about the boundaries of nation and identity through which the politics of antiracist intervention have so far been imagined?

Northern Tropics: Neil Jordan and Stewart Parker

The transatlantic history of Neil Jordan's *The Crying Game* has become part of its own personal folklore as the controversial indie film that made good overseas.[11] Its tepid reception in the UK has been attributed to the renewed IRA bombing campaign in London, while its popularity in the United States is often seen as the result of a cleverly teasing publicity campaign. Certainly, the traditionally romanticized perception of the IRA in the United States also made the image of Stephen Rea's "IRA soldier with a conscience" more palatable for audiences. But, in terms of the Irish films of the 1990s, it appears that Jordan's film may have been more influential for its shrewd marketing strategies in the United States than for its challenging subject matter.

As Debbie Ging has noted, the majority of Irish films made during the heyday of the Celtic Tiger faithfully reproduced commercial expectations of Irishness for the U.S. marketplace.[12] But those films occupy a different stratum of popular culture from Jordan's film, which revealed its aspirations to an art-house audience by not playing into such received conceptions of Irishness. Indeed, the film critic Frann Michel argues that *The Crying Game*'s scrutiny of borders, both individual and national, is conveyed through Ian Wilson's camera, which "looks through windows and doorways; shots are framed by carnival booths, by furniture, by the architecture of a construction site, a bar, a stage" so that "what we see is constructed by the frameworks available to us, foregrounding the film's interrogation of conventional boundaries and leading us to recognize and to challenge oppressive conventions of representation."[13] Bell hooks summarizes this viewpoint: "In the best sense, much of this film invites us to interrogate the limits of identity politics, showing us the way desire and feelings can disrupt fixed notions of who we are and what we stand for."[14]

The film's interrogation of these boundaries, however, is limited. As hooks further argues in "Seduction and Betrayal": *The Crying Game* "seduces" by suggesting the pleasure of crossing boundaries, escaping our identities, but it "betrays" that promise by reinscribing conventional racial and gender roles. Ultimately, Jordan's black characters, Jody and Dil, embody stereotypical neoprimitive figures who exist to consolidate the subjectivity of a white male. Jordan's "interrogation" of these interpellated social identities is only formal, questioning essentialist identities while remaining "indifferent," in the words of Joe Cleary, "to the structures of power that constitute the various minorities [the film] features."[15] What has not been fully considered by the film's critics is the significance of the Caribbean origins that Jordan lends Jody and Dil. This might be due in part to the fact that Jody's background arises only briefly during Jody and Fergus's conversation when Jody remarks on the difference between playing cricket in Antigua and in England where it is less popular and more of a "toff's game." While his reference to cricket gains in significance over the course of the film, not only with Fergus's later visions of Jody in his cricket whites, but also when he dresses Dil up in Jody's old sweater at the end of the film, the relation between cricket and Antigua is left behind as its meaning shifts from signifying Jody's national-racial passing to Dil's passing as a male.

As Cleary has argued, the sympathy between these two characters with similar working-class, colonial backgrounds is dismissed when Jody is repeatedly seen to represent official forms of British identity: first, with the British army, and later, with cricket; as a result, "the film effectively identifies British Blacks with the British State . . . and thereby establishes the relationship between Black Englishmen and Northern Irish nationalists as strictly one of murderous antagonism" (135). While this "antagonism" does not necessarily characterize Jody and Fergus (notably, it is Fergus's inability to murder Jody that precipitates much of the action), the perception of Irish–black British relations as hazardous is apparent in Jody's death and later in Fergus's imprisonment.

Jody is also something of an outsider as a black British soldier serving as part of an occupying force in Northern Ireland: "Just my luck to be sent to the only place in the world they call you nigger to your face. Go back to your banana tree, nigger! No use telling them I came from Tottenham."[16] As Cleary aptly notes about this speech, it is as if there were no such racism in England, much less in the British army. By sharing this anecdote, Jody portrays Irish views of race as primitive in comparison to a modern, multicultural Britain. Not only is this view mistaken with regards to the experience of black British soldiers, but it also ignores the complex history of race in the North.[17] According to Rolston and Shannon, rather than regarding northern antiblack racism as atavistic, it should be understood in terms of the contact experience with American troops stationed in the North during World War II which brought black American soldiers to the area as well as the racial attitudes of the white American troops. This historical context to race attitudes in the North suggests the ways race in Jordan's film is separated from other contingencies of power and history. The aestheticization of race in *The Crying Game* makes it difficult to engage with this and other complexities attached to the fact that Jody as a soldier represents a culture that has long perceived the Irish by the same racist terms that are being turned back on him.

Throughout the film, Jody and Dil function as model minorities who are unlike the recalcitrant Irish Catholics in that they find ways of working within the system; indeed, they become the system. Whether it is Jody as the black man in the white English cricket sweater, or Dil identifying with the role of a nurturing female, they are both "passing" as a way of accommodating themselves to colonial power. Their differences extend to how they see the world: when Fergus goes to London and follows Dil to the Metro he is notably out of place, confused about what drink to order, and unable to recognize his surroundings as a drag bar. It is only later, after the famous recognition scene, that he returns to the bar and sees it, demystified, for the first time. The implication is that the Catholic Irish nationalist, who is defined by national boundaries, is unable to recognize the polysemous, postmodern world of the cosmopolitan, while it is second nature for the black British subject.

According to Jane Giles, Jordan claimed that one of the goals of *The Crying Game* was to "contrast black and Irish experiences in Britain."[18] Jordan's use of black Britishness as exotic, aestheticized counterpart to the problematic Irish subject is not exclusive to *The Crying Game*, however. His 1985 film *Mona Lisa*, where he also paired a tragic mulatto figure with a white working-class male works similarly. The roots of these cinematic examples can be traced to a Jordan short story, "Last Rites" (1976) where he depicts the despair of an Irish working-class male in London.[19] Jordan has remarked that "the London of *The Crying Game* is entirely based on my memories of it as a working Paddy's city when I first came here."[20] It is this Irish working-class view of London that is the subject of "Last Rites."

The story has two overlaying narratives: a conventional first-person narrative, which describes the thoughts of an Irish construction worker while he goes to a public bath at the end of the week, and an omniscient narration, rendered in italics, which interrupts occasionally to describe the perspectives of other characters in the world around this Irish laborer. In short, the somber story describes the anonymous worker's thoughts as he enters the shower, masturbates, and then slashes his wrists. Arising from the elegiac tradition of poetry and songs about the Irish exile in England, "Last Rites" strives to render this convention in contemporary terms by showing the changing community of migrant labor in which the typical Irish worker finds him or herself. No longer an all-Irish clan of workers, the migrant labor community Jordan describes has become a hybrid mixture of Irish and West Indian laborers. But, for Jordan, this is an occasion for regret and nostalgia; the changing content of the community resembles for him a kind of descent into postmodern difference that only furthers the laborer's sense of isolation and anomie.

We first encounter the "pastiche" of the postmodern, materialist culture in the image of white paint that the Irishman tries to wash off in the shower, which had been put there by his fellow worker, "the negro painter," who had "slapped him playfully with his brush." Washing away this dash of paint is like washing away "the world, that world he inhabited, the world that left grit under the nails, dust under the eyelids. He scrubbed at the dirt of that world, at the coat of that world, the self that lived in that world, in the silence of the falling water."[21] The humiliation

1. Fergus (Stephen Rea), the IRA soldier turned laborer in London, is covered in white dust in *The Crying Game* (1992). (British Film Institute)

of this white dash of paint has a correlative in *The Crying Game* where we first see Fergus covered in white dust at the building site in London where he is disdainfully referred to as "Paddy" (figure 1). In both cases, the white paint and dust represent the actual distance between the characters' status as migrant laborers and any kind of symbolic "whiteness" in British society. Their humiliation comes from the fact that this pastiche of whiteness points to their lack of any real white identity (in terms of social capital). In "Last Rites," however, the fact that this dash of paint on the Irishman's cheek comes from a black worker suggests that working among black laborers puts his whiteness in crisis. As a result, he not only wants to make himself "totally, bleakly clean" but to recover his whiteness: "White, now. Not the sheer white of the tiles, but a human, flaccid, pink skin-white." In contrast to the perception of whiteness as marking a social advantage, it rather becomes something like a "castle of skin," to use George Lamming's phrase, as he thinks of his anonymous existence in terms of the shower room: "He thought it somehow appropriate that there should be men naked, washing themselves in adjacent cubicles, each a foreign country to the other."[22]

Jordan reinforces this difference when, after the Irish laborer masturbates in the shower, the story abruptly shifts to the other voice of omniscient narration where we learn the thoughts of the young man showering in the cubicle next to him. "The young Trinidadian in the next cubicle squeezed out a sachet of lemon soft shampoo and rubbed it to a lather between two brown palms. Flecks of sawdust — he was an apprentice carpenter — mingled with the snow-white foam. He pressed two handfuls of it under each bicep, ladled it across his chest and belly and rubbed it till the foam seethed and melted to the colour of dull whey, and the water swept him clean again, splashed his body back to its miraculous brown and he slapped each nipple laughingly in turn and thought of a clean body under a crisp shirt, of a night of love under a low red-lit roof, of the thumping symmetry of a reggae band."[23] Significantly, the man in the next cubicle is neither white nor Irish, literally rendering him the "foreign country" that the laborer imagined. In contrast to the Irish laborer who desperately washed the dash of paint off of his white skin, this Trinidadian cheerfully washes off the sawdust with the white foam of the soap to recover his "miraculous brown" skin. Where the Irishman's masturbation suggests a sexual life based on guilt and repression, the Trinidadian embodies its opposite, not only a confident, fulfilled sense of his sexuality, but also a sexuality that might safely display itself for public consumption.

Notably, the Trinidadian's thoughts are rendered in the italics of the omniscient narrator, signaling the degree to which they are beyond the comprehension of the Irish laborer. The Trinidadian appears in his thoughts only indirectly, when the Irishman overhears him being called out to by his friends who tell him to "move that corpse, rassman. Move!"[24] The word *corpse* ironically refers to the Irishman who, at that moment, is proceeding full of "passion and shame" to cut his wrists with his razor. He is discovered by the other workers, one of whom, a "middle-aged, fat and possibly simple negro," concludes the story by remarking: "*Every day the Lord send me I think I do that. And every day the Lord send me I drink a bottle of wine and forget 'bout doin' that.*"[25] Again, these thoughts are conveyed in the italicized voice of the omniscient narrator, which imposes the sense of absolute difference on black expressions.

Because it was originally published in 1976, "Last Rites" might be passed off as an anachronism were it not for the fact that Jordan repeats the same binary of expressive black bodies and repressed, overly interiorized Irish bodies in *The Crying Game* fifteen years later. While he does recognize that the Irish laboring community in England is no longer isolated (though it is debatable if it ever was), but inextricably bound up with working-class black British subjects, he cannot depict race in any other terms than those of absolute difference. At the same time, the black British are not seen in terms of their shared class position but as the beneficiaries of the British state: not only usurping traditional Irish jobs but also making matters worse by accommodating themselves to power and actually enjoying it.

An early and little-known progenitor of Jordan's attempt to displace Northern Irish politics onto Afro-Caribbean bodies can be found in *Kingdom Come*, a play by his contemporary, Stewart Parker. Billed as "a colourful and humorous Irish-Caribbean musical," Parker's play had a limited run in 1978 at the King's Head Theatre in London and again at the Lyric Theatre in Belfast in 1983 (figure 2). Best known for his trilogy of Belfast history plays *Northern Star*, *Heavenly Bodies*, and *Pentecost*, the latter of which was produced by Field Day in 1987 (shortly before his premature death from cancer in 1988), Parker wrote *Kingdom Come* on a commission for the King's Head.

Starring both black and white characters who are themselves a mix of Protestants and Catholics, the screwball plot describes an island community divided along both racial and religious lines that is anticipating the arrival of the queen of England. There are at least four groups contending for power in the play: a parodic British colonial governor, a group of Republican agitators, an opposing group of Loyalist sympathizers, and a final character representing the "modernizing solution" of tourism. The island's divisions arise around the problem of how to best represent the island in a jubilee to welcome the queen. The final judgment is a populist "curse on both your houses" as the attempts by the two main camps—ostensibly Catholic and Protestant—mutually destruct and the lone character, Teresa (representing "the people"—yet another group), ends by singing a closing song of liberation, "Jubilo": "There's no way to eliminate me/I've had all that I plan to take/Don't you try to intimidate me/This little child is wide awake."[26]

In contrast to the commercial success of *The Crying Game*, however,

2. Program for *Kingdom Come* at Belfast's Lyric Theatre, 1983. (Courtesy KP Graphics, Belfast)

the play's career was disposed of in a single-paragraph review in the *Observer* by the influential theater critic Robert Cushman who called it confusing, as "much vital information is lost in transit and never recovered."[27] Yet, Cushman does commend the "infectious performances" and the music by Shaun Davey, which, he notes is more Caribbean than Irish (unfortunately, there is no soundtrack). But the play was significant enough to provoke a passionate response by Conor Cruise O'Brien. Describing its message as "strong, valid, and urgent," O'Brien regards the play as dramatically recasting recent northern events, particularly the failed Loyalist strike in May 1977 and the Catholic Women's Peace March.[28] In this way, Parker's purpose is similar to the "contemporary melodramas," such as *The Colleen Bawn* and *The Shaughran*, created by the Irish playwright Dion Boucicault in the nineteenth century. For O'Brien, the recent acts of defiance by the Protestant and Catholic groups of both Ian Paisley and the IRA are replicated in the populist message of

"Jubilo," as the "people" shake off the influence of their so-called political representatives.

Still, however timely the play's theme, it is equally significant that this message was not only lost on Cushman but on the audiences as well. O'Brien argues that he and his company (his son and daughter-in-law) were "more moved and impressed by the comedy" than the rest of the English audience. In this way, his supplementary review resembles crib notes passed by a native informant qualifying the authenticity and value of this production from an Irish perspective. It is striking, then, that when *Kingdom Come* was produced in Belfast in 1983 these events were already lost on the local reviewers.[29] Of course, the Protestant strike of 1977 seemed dated and even benign after the IRA hunger strikes drastically altered the political landscape in 1981.

While O'Brien's interpretation may be accurate for 1978, however, he recognizes only the play's northern references (which might explain the play's "dated" quality today). Just as in Jordan's film, the role of the Caribbean is, in the words of the *Sunday Irish Times*, as a touch of "exotic flavour," relegating the Caribbean to a mere backdrop, playing Thebes to Belfast's Athens and limiting the satire to only its local emotions. Parker reinforces the mainly Irish-centric purpose of the play in a 1983 interview where he responds evasively to an interviewer's supposition that the "message" of the play is "Brits go home": "It's not really a statement, it's an exhortation to get politicians off their backsides and make some assertion, and I wanted to write something with a bit of joy in it too. The people of the North have asserted themselves many times, but that self-assertion seems to have gone underground again. I'm basically a socialist. I'd like the two communities here to see that as they have bad housing, unemployment, appalling living conditions, they have everything in common to fight for. If we could persuade them to recognise that, with an exhortation, it would be worthwhile."[30] Parker's description of the play as merely an "exhortation" appears again in a review by the *Belfast Telegraph*, which remarks favorably that the play shows "no deep insight" into the troubles and is "sheer entertainment." In both positive and negative reviews in Belfast, the Caribbean connection is only seen as a conceit, merely revealing how "our problems become ludicrous in the sky blues of a Caribbean isle."[31]

While Parker seems to share with Jordan a desire to use the juxtaposition of northern troubles with Caribbean tropics as a means of defamiliarizing an Irish problem, *Kingdom Come* can be seen as doing more with this conflation of Atlantic cultures than is evident from either Parker's comments or its reception. I have to admit at the outset that it is difficult to discuss critically a play which depends so much on music and burlesque staging without seeing it performed, but, judging by the script, it can be argued that the play combines the problems of Ireland with those of the Caribbean during the 1970s in a way that might not have been so evident to its English and Belfast audiences. We can see this first in the overture, "Macalla" (which is the given name for the mythical island, based loosely on the history of Montserrat), where, in the British musical tradition of Gilbert and Sullivan, Parker introduces the play's main themes. Since the play is unpublished and mostly unknown, I will quote this song in its entirety.

Hello and welcome to this sceptred isle
This earth of majesty, this seat of Mars
This other Eden, demi-Paradise
This emerald gem set in the silver sea!
Book your trip by plane or ferry
Once you get here you'll be glad,
Further west than Londonderry
Somewhere east of Trinidad
Begorrah and olé
Credit cards okay
Macalla Macalla
Come and sip a sup of marsala
Macalla Macalla
While you pass your pal a marshmallow
Macalla Macalla
You'll enjoy the picturesque squalour
In the heart of downtown Macalla
So unpack your maraccas and play,
Follow me down to Valhalla
Thomas Cook will book you today.

By the statue of St. Patrick
Cricket games are never done
Once a bowler bowled a hat-trick
Back in 1921
Sláinte and pip-pip
Don't forget to tip
Macalla Macalla
Bring your mem-sahib or your wallah
Macalla Macalla
You can buy a synthetic mandala
Macalla Macalla
We can rent you a nice Ford Impala
Don't go home till you've spent your last dollar
We can lease you a small Galway Bay,
Follow me down to Valhalla
And buy all your troubles away.
Life here has such varied facets
From the mansion to the slum
You can share our liquid assets
Drown the Shamrock in your rum
Though the natives have grown restless
In this well-known trouble spot
Don't let our hotels stay guestless
Visitors are seldom shot
Come and join the fray
Happy holiday
Macalla Macalla
You can take your girl to a gala
Macalla Macalla
You can hear a steel band playing Mahler
Macalla Macalla
Though it may not be up to La Scala
It possesses a je ne sais quali-
ty ever so quaintly outré,
Follow me down to Valhalla
It's like living a part in a play.[32]

The phrase, an "emerald gem in the silver sea," places the scene on the Leeward island of Montserrat, which refers to itself as the "other emerald isle" due to its history of Irish settlement. And this invocation — reinforced by the description of the island as "west of Londonderry and east of Trinidad" — signals at the beginning of the play that the interest here is not limited to the north of Ireland. The song depicts a society torn by the "three beasts" of third-world development: poverty, violence, and tourism. While the relation of tourism and violence was lost on reviewers, it appears repeatedly in the play as part of the debate between the two sides of the civil war. One side, socialist in impulse, wants to reveal the island's economic dependency and underdevelopment in the jubilee, while the opposing side, the "Protestant" ruling class, wants to portray the island as "modernizing" through the development of tourism as an industry. While certainly troublesome as a rhyme, "our steelbands play Mahler," points to the colonial mimicry sought after by the tourist industry which paradoxically desires the other to be so nearly like ourselves, if only to reassure us that we are not like "them." This "mimicry" has another resonance in the name of the island, Macalla, which is the Irish word for "echo." The figure of the Caribbean island as an "echo" problematizes any critical desire to read the play as solely about Northern Ireland.

The provocative connection that Parker's play raises between tourism and violence resonates with politics and culture in Ireland and Jamaica in the 1970s.[33] In a 1979 *Crane Bag* editorial, Seamus Deane noted that it was a sign of the times when the Irish Dáil responded to the 1972 Bloody Sunday massacre not by condemning British aggression but by debating the possible repercussions for tourism in the Republic.[34] In a contrasting example from the Caribbean, Jamaica underwent a political revolution from the mid-1960s to the 1980s that also took a violent form when the two main political parties mobilized elements of class warfare and intimidation tactics as political strategies. While they had their roots in the anticolonial struggles of the 1940s, such tactics peaked in the 1960s when, the sociologist Anita Waters notes, "a number of members of the lower class were armed with guns and were paid retainers by the parties to 'protect' other party supporters. In some cases, entire gangs were co-opted by the parties . . . By 1976 and 1980, there were many incidents of violence outside [Western Kingston], in rural areas and in other sections of the

Corporate Area. In the everyday speech of Jamaica, the phenomenon is known as 'tribal war.' "[35]

Both the rival parties, Edward Seaga's People's National Party (PNP) and Michael Manley's Jamaican Labor Party (JLP) enlisted the help of local "rough boys" during this period, decisions that led to the state of perpetual civil war still affecting the island. With this expanded sense of terrorism, it could be said that both island regions find their own autonomy and sovereignty contradicted by the influence of violence—in terms of both drugs and arms—and by their economic dependence on multinational corporations, particularly through the tourist industry. As a result, they suffer from two dominating, yet contradictory, reputations: as hopelessly violent and as perpetual paradises untouched by modernity in which "natives" are alternately mindlessly violent and wonderfully cheerful and at peace. Parker's song highlights the inherent contradiction of these reputations: "Though the natives have grown restless/In this well-known trouble spot/Don't let our hotels stay guestless/Visitors are seldom shot."

The problem of tourism on a cultural level is similar to that of terrorist violence at a political level insofar as both represent struggles over the right to representation. Who gets to speak for the people—which O'Brien aptly notes as the play's theme—is only one form the problem can take. It also asks through its own formal experimentation how one can justify a right to representation—political or cultural—when the real power exists outside of the island itself? Here that power is embodied in the imminent arrival of the queen, the metropolitan or tourist "eye" which instigates the turbulent plot. Parker uses the musical's carnivalesque tradition to create an ambivalence around the normative identities of these two regions by bringing out the contradictions inherent in these representations. The play's complex interaction of identities and roles that switch with almost every song not only complicates the easy "transmission of information" (to cite Cushman's complaint) but also emphasizes the processes of recognition between metropole and periphery involved in the construction of these identities.

It is suggestive, then, that these complex issues of recognition appear in a play with its own problems of representation in the contradictions and unevenness of its hybrid dramatic structure. Nonetheless, this is a reading based on a silent typescript from the archives of Belfast's Linen Hall library. How it was received in its 1978 and 1983 performances also has to be part of this account. The indecipherability of Parker's text to its metropolitan audience reminds us of the impossibility of representing Irishness or Caribbeanness without their local signifiers (the tribal rituals of cricket and hurling that define Jody and Fergus in Jordan's film, for example) while the Caribbean's own touristic veneer is briefly disturbed so as to reveal the racial divisions, poverty, and endemic violence constructed around transnational contraband trade (drugs and guns), which are similar in form (if different in intention) to those in the North during the turbulent period of the late 1970s. While covering similar terrain as Jordan, Parker's play does not limit the Irish-Caribbean comparison in the same way. For Parker, Ireland and the Caribbean "echo" as the same in this play through their relatively similar positions on a map of transatlantic power. At the same time, Parker's hybrid form of representation also defamiliarizes both groups—not just Ireland—at least momentarily to the audience. If we no longer know where we are, Ireland or the Caribbean, if we no longer recognize these cultures by the transparent identities we have invented, then it might be Valhalla indeed.

Outside History: Sinéad O'Connor's Celtic Rastafarianism

In both its "dated" themes of the mid-1970s troubles and Jamaican civil strife and in its medium as a rarely performed musical comedy, Parker's play reminds us of the ephemeral experience of popular culture and the problems in reading popular cultural texts as models for understanding social practices. While the inaccessibility of *Kingdom Come* is extreme, it is also relevant for understanding Jordan's films and stories and O'Connor's music, which are similarly tied to their performances in particular moments.

Where Jordan's attempt to represent the reality of Irish-Caribbean relations in England has resulted in depicting them in terms of absolute difference, pop singer O'Connor has developed in her own work a cross-cultural synthesis of ancient Celtic and contemporary Rastafarian religion and music. O'Connor dedicates her 2001 album *Faith and Courage* to "the Rastafarian people for their great faith, courage, and above all, inspiration" while adorning it with images of the Rastafarian Lion of Judah, the fire of the Pentecost, and Celtic Crosses (figure 3). She concludes the liner notes to her recent album of traditional Irish songs, *Sean-Nós Nua* (which translates as "New Old Style"), by describing the sean-nós as "true soul music" and proclaiming "All Glory to Jah the highest."[36] In interviews, O'Connor has said that while living in London for thirteen years she met Rastafarians and "fell in love with their culture, their sense of spirituality."[37]

According to the Reggae cultural historian Lloyd Bradley, this empathy between Irish and Afro-Caribbean cultures in London has a long precedent. In the 1950s, the house parties held by Jamaican emigrants were called "shebeens" after the Gaelic word for weak beer, and Bradley remarks that "it wasn't unusual to find Irish women in West Indian shebeens, as by the end of the 1950s a considerable esprit de corps existed between these two sets of often-despised arrivals."[38] By validating this cross-cultural empathy, even in these spiritual terms, O'Connor represents an important contrast to Jordan's negative view of Irish-Caribbean relations in England.

As I noted earlier, O'Connor first made her Rastafarian sympathies clear in her controversial appearance on *Saturday Night Live*. In aligning herself with the global celebrity of Bob Marley and recording the song "Empire" with Benjamin Zephaniah, while symbolically attacking Irish institutions, O'Connor has been trying to situate Irish music in cosmopolitan terms as part of a radicalized Third World sound. She further confused and frustrated music journalists when she admitted in interviews to being a Rastafarian, which is surely a paradox since not only had she already been ordained as a Catholic priest within the Tridentine sect, but both religions are notoriously insular and misogynist. The cultural critic Elizabeth Cullingford sees O'Connor's use of religion, including Rastafarianism, as a form of "critical Catholicism" which recognizes Catholicism's negative effects while retaining "a connection to a religious tradition that, for better or for worse, has helped to define the Irish experience."[39] O'Connor defends her choices by portraying herself as a "bridge" between these traditional spiritual cultures and the contemporary world: "I believe in not throwing the baby out with the bath water . . .

3-4. The front and back cover for Sinéad O'Connor's *Faith and Courage*
(2000) with the dedication and the Rastafarian Lion of Judah.

To me it's a most Rastafarian act to become a Catholic priest, and try and lay yourself down as a bridge between what's good about the old and traditional and what's good about the future."[40] In the notes to the traditional Irish song "The Singing Bird" on *Sean-Nós Nua*, she remarks that "the song acknowledges the greatness of Jah above all powers," as if finding a Rastafarian spirit in music celebrating Irish nature. To her credit, she enters these religions with a reformist agenda; she wants to open the Catholic Church to women, "beat up the hate that Rastafarians feel to any other church," and counter the fundamentalist forms of Rastafarianism currently popular in Jamaican dancehall culture.[41]

In addition to recognizing their connection in England, O'Connor also acknowledges a historical, spiritual, and musical connection between Ireland and the West Indies:

> I guess the thing is that there are similarities in the culture in that we're both colonialist countries; we've both been colonized by the same people and both cultures have had the same experience of the church, having been colonized by the English and the church. You know what I mean? There's a certain rebelliousness to the music. And there are huge Irish influences in the West Indies. The island of Montserrat still has street names that are Irish, you know. And at the height of the sugar trade in the West Indies there were tons of Irish convicts sent there to work. And then after awhile there was a request sent to the British not to send any more Irish people because they were inciting everyone to rebellion, you know. Even in some of Bob Marley's work—most obviously in tracks like "So Much Trouble in the World"—you can hear the Irish whistle.[42]

In this account, O'Connor advances an analogous argument by describing Ireland and Jamaica as "both colonialist countries," and a syncretic one in her description of Montserrat and the whistle in Marley's music. Notably, she feels the need to provide a historical basis for her turn to Afro-Caribbean culture, and, unlike Jordan, she at least draws attention to the British colonial structures of power that put these two cultures into a similar context. Yet a question arises about how we should approach the fact that O'Connor gets some of the particulars of her history wrong. For instance, Ireland and the Anglophone Caribbean did not have the same experience of the church; the Irish mostly worked as indentured servants, not slaves, and their labor in fact decreased, and African slave labor increased, during the conversion from tobacco to sugar. However, it is not my interest here to enter into a full-length historical exegesis of the "real" history of the Irish in the Caribbean, but rather to draw attention to the milieu of a popular historical understanding of that experience in which O'Connor is faithfully participating. The fact is, O'Connor is not alone in making these connections between Irish and Caribbean histories. Her characterization represents a radical populist understanding of the Irish Atlantic that has recently been the subject of a number of recent histories and historical novels from different ends of the political spectrum by writers such as Kate McCafferty, Donald Akenson, and Sean O'Callaghan.

O'Callaghan's provocative moral history of Irish indentured labor, *To Hell or Barbados* (2000), and the historical novel by the Irish American McCafferty, *Testimony of an Irish Slave Girl* (2002), each tell a searing tale of how Irish Catholics were kidnapped, or "barbados'd" to the Caribbean as a form of ethnic cleansing by Cromwell and his policy of colonial settlement in Ireland. While *To Hell or Barbados* is written as a history, it is presented as part of O'Callaghan's larger project on the contemporary slave trade in the late twentieth century, in particular, the problem of "white and yellow slavery" in the Sudan, Europe, and the Far East. For O'Callaghan, the Irish experience in the seventeenth century is a historical precedent for this contemporary problem, and just as the Irish case has been ignored by historians, so we are also blind to these existing humanitarian abuses.

His investment, however, in a theoretical conception of slavery blinds O'Callaghan's analysis to the significant differences between indentured servitude and chattel slavery. Written in a polemical style, *To Hell or Barbados* never engages with historians of slavery such as David Brion Davis, Robin Blackburn, or Eric Williams, just to cite the most prominent, who clearly distinguish between the two forms of servitude.[43] His method is to confuse form with content; for instant, just because the same ships used to bring African slaves were also used to bring Irish indentured servants does not make the content of the shipment the same. Just because the nature of work and the form of penal punishment endured by the Irish was similar to that of African slaves, it does not make their formal status the same. While O'Callaghan's cause is just, his dependence on the term *slavery* tends to exclude other relevant lessons that might be learned from the Irish experience and to depoliticize the calamity by drawing it too broadly.[44]

As a work that also tries to find a contemporary relevance in the Irish experience, *Testimony of an Irish Slave Girl* emphasizes a narrative of resistance rather than one of exploitation. "The Irish perspective is important," McCafferty writes in the preface, "to the history of resistance to colonialism. It is also important because involuntary indentured servants 'laid the foundation for African chattel slavery in Barbados.' But perhaps it is most important, at the beginning of the twenty-first century, as part of a little-known history of affiliation, across race and ethnicity, between groups conventionally defined as incompatible."[45] Defining her project in terms of contemporary multiculturalist politics, McCafferty is under an obligation to portray black and Irish characters as different yet the same, a paradox that can be as binding and reductive as the racist categories which maintain them as essentially "incompatible." As a result, all the slaves (and the Irish are categorized uncritically as such) are noble and idealist and all the slaveholders are evil and corrupt as the novel fails to develop into more than a conventional morality play.

Like O'Callaghan, McCafferty has no qualms about using slavery to describe the Irish experience.[46] She briefly reviews the history of Irish exploitation, relying mainly on research by the Caribbean historian Hilary Beckles, but without the subtle distinctions he makes between indentured servitude and slavery.[47] By using *slave* in her title to describe the Irish experience on Barbados in the sixteenth century, she conflates two different modes of production and forms of ownership, while also obscuring the role of racial classification by skin color (as opposed to religion and nationality) that was crucial to the ideological construction of slavery during the early modern period.[48]

It is this type of idealist perspective of the West Indies in the seventeenth century that compels Donald Akenson to write his own counter-Hibernicist history of the Irish in the region, *If the Irish Ran the World, Montserrat, 1630–1730*.[49] In stark contrast to O'Callaghan's and McCafferty's narratives of exploited Irish men and women shipped involuntarily across the Atlantic, Akenson's narrative depicts the Irish as self-interested agents for whom the West Indies was an opportunity for gaining success and wealth otherwise inconceivable at home. Despite Akenson's ideological differences from O'Callaghan and McCafferty, the premise for his study is also presentist in its concern. "So, what if the Irish had controlled more of the world in the modern era, say from the Protestant Reformation onwards? How would they have acted?"[50] Akenson's answer to this "counterfactual" historical question, not surprisingly, is that they would have been just about the same as everyone else. His dispute is with the assertion that the propertied Catholic Irish who were the dominant landowners on the island of Montserrat for almost a hundred years were more benevolent than their Anglo-Protestant counterparts on other islands, and that they left a discernable Irish heritage as part of Montserratian culture. In countering this Hibernicist perspective he relies on work by the Montserrat poet and historian Howard Fergus who has sought to recuperate an Africanist perspective on Montserrat's history.[51] But while Fergus's work aspires to a form of cultural nationalism that has as its object the island's independence from Britain (Montserrat is an overseas dependency), Akenson disparages any claims for independence and considers the Africanist tradition to be as "invented" as the Hibernicist history. In the end, Akenson's view of the Caribbean is as a site of inauthenticity, invented traditions, and Naipaulian "mimic men."[52] The result of his own "historical clarity" is to argue for the inherently dependent relation of a small island that should persist as one of the last remaining British colonies.

While each of these works positions itself as relevant to the contemporary Caribbean, their real interest lies with contemporary Ireland. As his title reveals, Akenson's real argument is with "politically correct" Irish historians, and O'Callaghan's and McCafferty's concerns with the poor whites of Barbados are only salutary; the actual Caribbean appears in their works only as part of a traditional narrative of decline and loss—the sultry tropics once again overtaking history. As a result, while they study the Irish in the Caribbean, these histories and historical fictions each reassert a hierarchical difference between the two sites as inherently incompatible. By appropriating the position of "slave" from Afro-Caribbean history, O'Callaghan and McCafferty contribute to an increasing sense of global Irishness in which Irish history provides a correlative — or analogous form — for any historical experience of suffering by others, whether it is in describing the famine as a holocaust or indentured servitude as slavery. Much like the famine, this period of Irish diasporic history can be usefully explored for what it reveals about the social effects of cruel economic policies; in this, O'Callaghan's comparison of the Irish experience in Barbados to that of migrant labor in Europe (and Ireland) is apt, though unfortunately it is never explored beyond a casual reference in his preface.

These three histories reveal the divergent interests in writing about the Irish-Caribbean connection from the perspective of contemporary Irish culture. What appears to be consistent for all of these writers is the relevance of the comparison for Ireland, which always occupies the position of the dominant identity seeking either confirmation or explanation through its meeting with an "other" whose own identity — whether authentic in the case of McCafferty or unredeemably inauthentic in the case of Akenson — is easily "known" from the Irish perspective.

In contrast to these projections of Ireland onto the Caribbean, O'Connor incorporates Rastafarianism as a framework through which she engages with Irish culture, redressing her past and revising herself and her culture in cosmopolitan terms. One can see this as part of a process, since the first title for *Faith and Courage* was "Green on Black."[53] Now, this final version might be considered "Black on Green" as she uses this album to revisit the controversy that ensued after her appearance on snl, which engulfed and overwhelmed her career for the rest of the decade. She discusses this incident and her embattled relations with Irish Catholics in a song, "The Lamb's Book of Life," which mixes low Irish whistles with a background of syncopated reggae bass line and drums. In the song she apologizes for the pain that her exploit may have caused (even though in her interviews she does not regret the incident), "I know that I have done many things/To give you reason not to listen to me/But if you knew me maybe you would understand me/Words can't express how sorry I am/If ever I caused pain to anybody/I just hope that you can show compassion/And love me enough to just please listen." Unlike most pop songs, which merely preach to the converted, her song is a direct call to those in Ireland, the United States, and England who may have stopped listening to her as a result of her actions on *Saturday Night Live*. The song's opening lines — "Out of Ireland I have come/Great hatred and little room/Maimed us at the start" — describe Ireland in terms of a cultural trauma. O'Connor justifies her actions by arguing that they arose from the same "great hatred" as the violent reaction it created.

The "little room" in Ireland cultivates these extreme forces as each action engenders its opposite reaction. In the final stanza, the opening line has changed from the first-person to the collective *we*: "Out of history we have come/With great hatred and little room/It aims to break our hearts/Wreck us up and tear us all apart/But if we listen to the Rasta man/He can show us how it can be done/To live in peace and live as one/Get our names back in the book of life of the lamb." In what sense have the Irish come "out of history"? On the one hand, the line suggests history as the past which has created such hatred, while on the other it could refer to an image of contemporary Ireland as having come out of history in the sense of having left it behind. O'Connor describes a country that has been traumatized by its colonial past but which might find reconciliation through "the Rasta man" who is to show the Irish the way back to a spiritual life.[54]

"The Lamb's Book of Life" is produced by the American R&B producer, Kevin "She'kspere" Briggs, who has become well-known for his work with U.S. performers like Destiny's Child, Mariah Carey, and Boyz II Men, though his work here suggests the recent influence of Jamaican dancehall and reggae on contemporary American R&B. Notably, the song was mixed by the British reggae and dub impresario Adrian Sherwood, who produces, along with the guitarist Skip McDonald, four other songs on the album, "The Healing Room," "If U Ever," "What Doesn't Belong to Me," and "Kyrié Eléison," as well as coproducing *Sean-Nós Nua*. O'Connor's relationship with Sherwood is indicative of her relation to Rastafarianism and reggae since Sherwood, as the innovative founder of On-U Sound records in the 1980s, established a British style of reggae music called "Nu Roots" that was seen by many as opposed to the form's "purist" roots in Jamaica. In interviews, Sherwood has described the UK scene as more open to avant-garde and alternative cultural influences including a belief in the use of voice rather than electronic "steppers rhythms."[55] By thinking of O'Connor's recent turn to reggae sounds in terms of a collaboration with a producer like Sherwood, it is possible to understand the ways in which she is situated in relation to contemporary reggae music. This also suggests the ways in which the music production mirrors the song's themes. Just as "Lamb's Book of Life" and "Kyrie Eléison" provocatively dislodge Rastafarianism from its local references to Afro-Caribbean belief, so O'Connor is working with a producer who has been trying to create a "less pure" form of roots reggae.

The hybrid form they create can be found in the low Irish whistle of "Lamb's Book of Life," which is played by Kieran Kiely within the strictures of the syncopated bass line rather than floating above the music. In the same way, O'Connor's voice, which is famous for its clear intensity that rises above a rock sound, here obeys the clipped rhythms of the bass line. An instructive contrast might be found by comparing "Lamb's Book of Life" to Kiely's whistle and O'Connor's voice in the following song, "If U Ever," where both assume their conventional ethereal and inspirational sounds. The disruption of expectation that occurs with the subservience of the Irish whistle and O'Connor's "Irish" voice in "Lamb's Book of Life" suggests O'Connor's desire for Irish culture to redeem itself by recovering a spiritual relationship to a greater power.

As the music sociologist Simon Frith has argued, the singing voice in popular music must be seen as a form of identity, as representing a personality as much as a sound.[56] In this sense, then, I do not want to argue that the "star quality" of O'Connor's voice is changed by being incorporated into the music, but rather that, in "Lamb's Book of Life" this overdetermined personality — "Sinéad O'Connor" — is put into dialogue with the song's reggae sounds. The relation the song creates formally in the music is similar to the relation O'Connor is asking the Irish people to have with Rastafarian-style spirituality. Significantly, O'Connor is not asking the Irish people to "become" something else, she's not asking them to become Rastafarians, but to reconsider the ways in which Irish identity defines itself against forms of alterity.[57]

Aside from its significance within Rastafarianism, "Lamb's Book of Life" is interesting in comparison to the forms of historical and personal revision we have seen so far by Irish artists and historians. Here, O'Connor chooses a reggae-influenced song as the form in which she redresses the earlier traumatic events in her life. As Parker describes the two island cultures as an "echo," O'Connor does not use the voice of the trans-atlantic other as an analogy for her experience, but as a means of rewriting her relationship to the past, in order to reinvent herself and Ireland in cosmopolitan terms. The song is not only about her "coming out" of Ireland but of Ireland's coming out of its past — "out of history" — through a cross-cultural relationship with the other. Ultimately, her adoption of Rastafarian beliefs is tied in with her view of Ireland as an oppressed country and of Catholicism as a radically universalist belief. In order to leave its past history of "great hatred," Ireland must at the same time leave its so-called "insular sensibility" and, according to this logic, adopt a cosmopolitan vision of the world.

As a result, O'Connor's performance of Rastafarianism recalls many of the declarations of a cosmopolitan, multicultural Ireland that have been expressed by critics over the past ten years. Rastafarianism allows her to address critically an Irish culture that is in a state of cultural conflict, and, when seen within her own political agenda of reforming Irish society, O'Connor's cross-cultural beliefs represent a suggestive model for how Irish culture might imagine change while maintaining continuity — in O'Connor's phrase, of "not throwing the baby out with the bathwater." While the Babylon of Rasta belief arose from the social inequities of Jamaican society, its reference is also to the institutionalization of those inequities, and in that sense it always contained within it a sense of Jamaica as part of an international imperialist complex. At the same time, the Rastafarian criticism of the church resonates with O'Connor's purpose since, as Enna Edmonds notes, for the Rasta, "the church is implicated for participating in mentally enslaving the people."[58] So by invoking the "Rasta man" as her model and by expressing herself in a song like "Lamb's Book of Life," O'Connor mobilizes a Rastafarian critique of colonial history and its persistence in forms like established religion that she feels is unavailable in Irish Republican nationalism.

It might be argued that, in the end, O'Connor's Rastafarianism is not so different from Jordan's portrayal of Afro-Caribbean figures in *The Crying Game* insofar as she finds in the Caribbean other a means of recuperating a problematic Irish subjectivity — in this case, her own. Seen in the perspective of the 1990s Irish culture which they straddle, Jordan and O'Connor travel between cultures as a means of traveling "out of history" in order to create their own forms of cosmopolitan Irish culture. How they differ is in their visions of this cosmopolitanism: where it is Jordan's desire to assimilate the Irish within a cosmopolitan majority culture, O'Connor's objective in part is to take on the mantle of Bob Marley and situate Irish culture as part of a radical cosmopolitanism from below. In contrasting Irish and Caribbean figures in *The Crying Game* and "Last Rites," Jordan follows the analogous reasoning that has been integral to antiracist politics. The problem his work encounters is not so different from the paradoxes of the emerging antiracist position in Ireland: where the focus of Jordan's narrative is ultimately on the recovery of a consolidated white subject, so the search for a revisionist Irish antiracist history has been similarly one-sided in its use of recuperative black subjects as well as its affiliation and disaffiliation with blackness as it becomes useful.

By contrast, the cross-cultural forms presented in plays like Parker's *Kingdom Come* and expressed by O'Connor's own enigmatic Rastafarianism frustrate any search for analogy between Irish and Caribbean cultures. Instead, they incorporate the Caribbean into their own expressions of Irishness in such a way as to disrupt the search for a continuous identity. It might be that these examples are moments of popular self-fashioning, as David Scott puts it in his discussion of Jamaican dancehall, which also suggests new forms of political subjectivity outside the "nationalist-liberationist" model.[59] The problem facing contemporary Irish multiculturalism is the mixed history of Irish nationalism with regards to its racist, imperialist, and anti-imperialist lineage. To follow the advice of Rolston and Shannon and "reject one and nurture the other" would be to risk "being sucked into nationalist quicksand," as Garner puts it. In other words, it is necessary to consider the ways in which antiracist politics can be defined in terms other than those of Irish Republicanism or other political narratives of Irish identity. This involves moving away from reading forms of colonial representation and trying to retheorize the space of antiracist politics.

O'Connor's persistent self-fashioning completes what is attempted and ultimately fails in Jordan's film and story. Also, instead of having to go outside of Ireland for these transformative experiences, as in Jordan's London, for O'Connor difference resides just as easily at home. An example of this is in the liner notes to *Sean-Nós Nua* where she introduces the traditional Irish song "Her Mantle So Green" by situating the story of a young soldier returning home to his lover in disguise in terms of the "new culture of Ireland": "For me, the song is really about the love of the people of Ireland for their culture and their experiences of having to let the culture die in order to be born again as something more joyous. That is what I believe is taking place right now in Ireland—a God-sent miracle. The new culture of Ireland, as represented by the narrator in disguise, shows that the Ireland we romanticised for so long about is going to be something much better than we were taught to long for, which was an Ireland united by bullshit, instead of united by love. From war or bad circumstance, Jah comes in disguise as people in need of our aid, with all the golden gifts they bring."

The desire expressed by the antiracist position to integrate itself with the nationalist-modern project reveals its dependence on a narrative of liberation in order to be viable in a liberal electoral politics. What O'Connor expresses here is a sense of how that modernizing project is no longer the only available language for developing expressions of social community. The image of the "new Ireland" as a figure in disguise suggests the possibility of taking on and adopting multiple identities in a way that opens up the potential for developing communities that might also describe multiple ways of being citizens.

It should be possible for critical discussions of Irish culture to expand beyond the traditional narratives of island politics to try and understand how alternative narratives of Irishness from home are played out abroad. One way, only suggested here, is to consider how Ireland is read differently within that "one-way traffic" by figures like Marcus Garvey and Claude McKay, and how so doing can reveal something more about what Ireland is today than we can learn from revising yet again a fraught internal history. Another way is by considering how the cross-cultural vision of Irish popular culture offers new perceptions of political subjectivity. Rather than trying to explain away these instances of cross-cultural expression as aberrations from the cultural norm, as instances of artists and intellectuals invoking other cultures but only "getting it wrong," we should strive to understand what these complex dialogues and circulations of influence and knowledge tell us about the role of transnational imagining in our conceptions of nationalism.

Notes

I would like to thank Kristina Olson, Cóilin Parsons, and Diane Negra for their many helpful comments and suggestions.

1. For an insightful analysis of this event and its repercussions see Elizabeth Butler Cullingford's two essays on O'Connor: "Seamus and Sinéad: From 'Limbo' to Saturday Night Live by Way of Hush-a-Bye Baby," in *Ireland's Others: Ethnicity and Gender in Irish Literature and Popular Culture* (Cork: Cork University Press), 234–57; and "Virgins and Mothers: Sinéad O'Connor, Neil Jordan, and *The Butcher Boy*," *Yale Journal of Criticism* 15, no. 1 (2002): 185–210.

2. On the history of the film's circulation and reception in the United Kingdom and the United States, see Jane Giles, *The Crying Game* (London: British Film Institute, 1997), 39–52.

3. Steve Loyal, "Welcome to the Celtic Tiger: Racism, Immigration and the State," in *The End of Irish History?: Critical Reflections on the Celtic Tiger*, edited by Colin Coulter and Steve Coleman (Manchester: Manchester University Press, 2003), 74–94.

4. Bryan Fanning, *Racism and Social Change in the Republic of Ireland* (Manchester: Manchester University Press, 2002).

5. For just a sampling of this increasing literature see Declan Kiberd and Edna Longley, *Multi-Culturalism: The View from the Two Irelands* (Cork: Cork University Press, 2001); Ethel Crowley and Jim Mac Laughlin, *Under the Belly of the Tiger: Class, Race, Identity and Culture in the Global Ireland* (Dublin: Irish Reporter Publications, 1997); Bill Rolston and Michael Shannon, *Encounters: How Racism Came to Ireland* (Dublin: BTP Publications, 2002); Steve Garner, *Racism in the Irish Experience* (London: Pluto Press, 1994); Fanning, *Racism and Social Change*; and Coulter and Coleman, *The End of Irish History*.

6. On the term *antiracism*, see Paul Gilroy, "Two Sides of Anti-Racism," in *There Ain't No Black in the Union Jack: The Cultural Politics of Race and Nation* (Chicago: University of Chicago Press, 1987), 114–52.

7. Described by Edna Longley as a "multi-culturalist martyr," Butler was an Irish nationalist and Irish Protestant who was an expert on Russia and Eastern Europe, particularly Yugoslavia, as well as a cultural critic who emphasized Ireland's European identity and was a gadfly to the Catholic State in the 1950s. See Longley, *Multi-Culturalism*, 1.

8. Rolston and Shannon, *Encounters*, 88.

9. On this specific example of the San Patricio Corps, see Garner, *Racism in the Irish Experience*, 104, 219; and David Lloyd, *Ireland After History* (South Bend, Ind.: Notre Dame University Press, 1999), 105. For a historicist counterargument, see Stephen Howe, *Ireland and Empire: Colonial Legacies in Irish History and Culture* (Oxford: Oxford University Press, 2000), 56–58; and "Afterword: Transnationalisms Good, Bad, Imagined, Thick and Thin," *Interventions* 4, no. 2 (2002): 87.

10. I explore the paradoxes involved in this kind of revisionist historiography in my essay on Sinn Féin, "With Dev in America: Sinn Féin, Marcus Garvey, and Recognition Politics," *Interventions* 4, no. 2 (2002): 22–34. Also, it is necessary to recognize that the "one-way traffic" from black activists is also defined by its own political and historical contingencies and requires its own particular scrutiny, which I attempt to provide in "Other Emerald Isles: Caribbean Revisions of Irish Cultural Nationalism" (Ph.D. diss., Columbia University, 2004), which studies the "readings" of Irish nationalism by Marcus Garvey, Claude McKay, and Derek Walcott.

11. Emer Rockett and Kevin Rockett, *Neil Jordan: Exploring Boundaries* (Dublin: Liffey Press, 2003), 267.

12. Debbie Ging, "Screening the Green: Cinema under the Celtic Tiger," in *Reinventing Ireland: Culture, Society and the Global Economy*, edited by Peadar Kirby, Luke Gibbons, and Michael Cronin (London: Pluto Press, 2002), 177–95.

13. Frann Michel, "Racial and Sexual Politics in *The Crying Game*," *Cineaste* 20, no. 1 (1993): 30.

14. bell hooks, "Seduction and Betrayal—*The Crying Game* Meets *The Bodyguard*," in *Outlaw Culture: Resisting Representation* (New York, Routledge, 1994), 60.

15. Joe Cleary, *Literature, Partition and the Nation-State: Culture and Conflict in Ireland, Israel and Palestine* (Cambridge: Cambridge University Press, 2002), 136.

16. Neil Jordan, "The Crying Game," in *A Neil Jordan Reader* (New York: Vintage, 1993), 191.

17. For a provocative account of the racial and class differences in the British army from a black British perspective, see Odimumba Kwamdela, *Black British Soldier* (1969; reprint, New York: Kibo Books, 1999).

18. Giles, *The Crying Game*, 9.

19. Jordan, "Last Rites," in *A Neil Jordan Reader*, 5–14. Originally published in *Night in Tunisia and Other Stories* (Dublin: Irish Writers' Cooperative, 1976).

20. "Production Notes," *The Crying Game*, dir. Neil Jordan, Artisan Entertainment, 1998, DVD.

21. Jordan, "Last Rites," 11–12.

22. Ibid.

23. Jordan, "Last Rites," 13.

24. Ibid.

25. Ibid., 14.

26. Stewart Parker, *Kingdom Come*, unpublished. All citations from *Kingdom Come* appear courtesy of the Parker estate and The Linen Hall Library's Theatre and Performing Arts Archive.

27. Robert Cushman, "Theatre," *The Observer*, 22 January 1978, 30.

28. Conor Cruise O'Brien, "A Song of Disembafflement," *The Observer*, 29 January 1978, 28.

29. The headlines for the reviews describe something of its reception in Belfast:

"A Dramatic Disappointment," "Not So Hot in the Tropics," and "Calypso Chaos." See Brian Sexton, "Not So Hot in the Tropics," *Irish News*, 20 November 1983; and "A Dramatic Disappointment," *Sunday Irish Times*, 14 November 1983.

30. Kate Hingerty, "Belfast Festival — Peaceful Enjoyment," *Irish Press*, 25 November 1983.

31. The first quote is from the *Sunday Irish Times*, 14 November 1983; and the second from "Ireland in the Sun!" a review in *New Letter* (1983).

32. Parker, *Kingdom Come*.

33. This has not escaped the attention of advertisers, however. Diane Negra and Mark Crispin Miller have both astutely observed the ways in which the threat of terrorist violence is addressed and deflated in tourist advertisements to Ireland and Jamaica. See Mark Crispin Miller, "Massa, Come Home" in *Boxed In: The Culture of TV* (Evanston, Ill.: Northwestern University Press, 1988), 31–41; and Diane Negra, "Consuming Ireland: Lucky Charms Cereal, Irish Spring Soap and 1–800-SHAMROCK," *Cultural Studies* 15 (2001): 76–97.

34. Seamus Deane, "Postscript," *Crane Bag* 3, no. 2 (1979): n.p.

35. Anita Waters, *Race, Class, and Political Symbols: Rastafari and Reggae in Jamaican Politics* (Oxford: Transaction Books, 1985), 58; and Anthony J. Payne, *Politics in Jamaica*, rev. ed. (New York: St. Martin's, 1995).

36. Sinéad O'Connor, *Faith and Courage* (Atlantic, 2000); and *Sean-Nós Nua* (Hummingbird, 2002).

37. Grzegorz Brzozowicz, "Building Bridges: Sinéad O'Connor," *Machina Magazine* (Poland), 15 September 2000, <http://dcebe.tripod.com/fac_int0915.htm>; and Jeffrey Overstreet, review of *Faith and Courage*, "O'Connor's Pop Therapy Session," <http://www.promontoryartists.org/lookingcloser/music/july2000>.

38. Lloyd Bradley, *This is Reggae Music: The Story of Jamaica's Music* (New York: Grove Press, 2000), 117.

39. Cullingford, "Seamus and Sinéad," 257.

40. Aaron Hicklin, "Angelic Upstart," *Sunday Herald* (Glasgow), 25 June 2000, 6.

41. Brzozowicz, "Building Bridges."

42. Richard Fahle, "'Mommy's a Brilliant Singer': An Interview with Sinéad O'Connor," *Borders Chain Magazine*, 17 October 2002, <http://www.sinead-oconnor.com/news>.

43. See, in particular, Blackburn, "Plantation Labour: From Indenture to Slavery," in *The Making of New World Slavery: From the Baroque to the Modern, 1492–1800* (New York: Verso, 1997), 315–31.

44. O'Callaghan and McCafferty are also part of a larger trend in Irish and Irish American cultural representation of Irish history in terms of victimization that Catherine Eagan discusses more comprehensively in her essay in this collection, "Still 'Black' and 'Proud': Irish America and the Racial Politics of Hibernophilia."

45. Kate McCafferty, *Testimony of an Irish Slave Girl* (New York: Viking, 2002), ix.

46. This is too bad, because there is much in the book that does contribute to a more complex understanding of the early Caribbean plantation society. This is achieved in part by balancing Cot Daley's "testimony" with the story of her English interviewer, Peter Coote, who as a propertyless gentleman falls outside the parameters of the slaveholders. Caught between his obligations to the colonial governor and his own self-interest in acquiring property, Coote painfully becomes aware of his own unfortunate place within a hierarchical society. The form of the novel allows McCafferty to examine these different subjective experiences of living in a society based solely on a system of exploitative capitalism. Despite her interest in "Irish resistance," McCafferty also draws attention to the lack of modern notions of nationality, particularly among the settlers; for instance, when Coote replies to the governor that he is protecting the interests of "all Englishmen, whose colony this is" the governor's response is a challenge to nationalist colonial histories: "That it is not! . . . Many an English rogue shipped here in chains has been freed from servitude to foul our shores . . . Problems. Problems, to be sure" (26). Rather than describing the Irish as slaves within an English colony, McCafferty conveys the more complicated idea of exploitation based not on race but mainly as a result of power and profit.

47. She also cites a "noted authority on global slavery," Orlando Patterson, but miscites him in her endnotes, leaving his reference somewhat obscure. She also similarly simplifies and levels the subtle historical arguments advanced by Beckles which can be found in his article, "A 'Riotous and Unruly Lot': Irish Indentured Servants and Freemen in the English West Indies, 1644–1713," *William and Mary Quarterly* 47 (1990): 503–22. For other sources on the Irish experience which McCafferty does not cite, see Jill Sheppard, *The "Redlegs" of Barbados: Their Origin and History* (Millwood, N.Y.: KTO, 1977); and Richard Dunn, *Sugar and Slave: The Rise of the Planter Class in the English West Indies 1624–1713* (New York: Norton, 1973), 57, 69, 72–73. The most noted authority on the Irish in the sixteenth-century Caribbean is Aubrey S. J. Gwynn, "Early Irish Emigration to the West Indies (1612–1643)," *Studies* 18 (1929): 377–93; "Indentured Servants and Negro Slaves in Barbadoes," *Studies* 18 (1929): 648–63; "Cromwell's Policy of Transportation — Part I and Part II," *Studies* 19 (1930): 607–23, and *Studies* 20 (1931): 291–305; "The First Irish Priests in the New World," *Studies* 21 (1932): 213–28; and "Documents Relating to the Irish in the West Indies" and "An Irish Settlement on the Amazon, 1612–29," *Analecta Hibernica* Irish Manuscripts Commission 4 (1932): 139–286.

48. See Blackburn, *Making of New World Slavery*, 14–15, 315–31.

49. Donald Akenson, *If the Irish Ran the World, Montserrat 1630–1730* (Montreal: McGill-Queens University Press, 1997).

50. Ibid., 4.

51. Howard Fergus, *History of Alliouagana: A Short History of Montserrat* (Plymouth, Monserrat: University Centre, 1975); "Montserrat, the Last English Colony? Prospects for Independence," *Bulletin of Eastern Caribbean Affairs* 4, no. 1 (1978): 15–

24; "Montserrat, 'Colony of Ireland': The Myth and the Reality," *Studies* 70 (1981): 325–40; *Montserrat: Emerald Isle of the Caribbean* (London: MacMillan, 1983); *Rule Britannia: Politics in British Montserrat* (Montserrat: University Centre, University of the West Indies, 1985). Also, see Fergus's book of poetry *Lara Rains and Colonial Rites* (Leeds: Peepal Tree Press, 1998). For other perspectives on Montserrat, particularly the dispersal of the population due to the volcanic eruption, see Polly Patullo, *Fire From the Mountain: The Tragedy of Montserrat and the Betrayal of Its People* (Kingston, Jamaica: Ian Randle Publishers, 2000). Another, very controversial, account of the legacy of the Irish slaveholders on the culture of Montserrat was compiled by the American anthropologist John C. Messenger in the 1960s and 1990s, "The 'Black Irish' of Montserrat," *Eire/Ireland: A Journal of Irish Studies* 2, no. 1 (1967): 27–40; and "St. Patrick's Day in 'The Other Emerald Isle,'" *Eire/Ireland: A Journal of Irish Studies* 29, no. 1 (1994): 12–23. Based on his ethnographic observations, including the use of photographs, Messenger claimed that the Montserratians he studied had an Irish appearance, that their speech resembled that of Irish peasants, and pictures of Montserratians driving their cars revealed "distinctively Irish motor habits."

52. See, for instance, his concluding chapter, "Usable Traditions," and his sympathy with V. S. Naipaul's dismal assessment of Caribbean history in Akenson, *If the Irish Ran the World*, 171–87; 250 n. 17.

53. See the O'Connor fan club website, <http://www.members.tripod.com/dcebe/newalbum.htm>.

54. She does not limit her spiritual advice to Ireland, either. She has a similar song, "A Prayer for England," which she cowrote and sang with the British trip-hop band, Massive Attack, from their album *100th Window* (Virgin Records, 2003). With a dark, urban-sounding bass line behind her recognizable voice, O'Connor sings in the name of, "and by the power of/the Holy Spirit," to intercede for "the children of England." As with Ireland, the people of England have been led astray from the spiritual life and need to be reconciliated with the spirituality associated with "Jah." By extending her vision beyond Ireland, O'Connor removes the sense of Irish exceptionalism that might be seen from only hearing the call for Ireland to "get back in the book of the Lamb."

55. Greg Whitfield, "The Adrian Sherwood Interview: The On-U Sound Experience, the On-U Sound Family," <http://www.uncarved.org/dub/onu/onu.html>. For more on the different styles of UK and Jamaican roots reggae see Bradley, *This is Reggae Music*, 382–83.

56. Simon Frith, *Performing Rites: On the Value of Popular Music* (Cambridge: Harvard University Press, 1996), 196.

57. In an online essay, O'Connor has expressed this concept of cross-cultural relations in spiritual and national terms: "I had a great dream a while ago which I loved, which was that An Post were using posters of pregnant African ladies to advertise themselves—and this became the symbol of Ireland: pregnant African women. I just loved that. And I think this whole thing has been a miracle that we should be very

grateful for. It's fucking disgusting to see how against it a lot of people are, and how racist we are. I think we should be so grateful to these immigrants, for deigning to grace us with their presence. We should be on our knees thanking them." See O'Connor, "'90s: Lion's Daughter."

58. Ennis B. Edmonds, "Dread 'I' In-A-Babylon: Ideological Resistance and Cultural Revitalization," in *Chanting Down Babylon: The Rastafari Reader*, edited by Nathaniel Samuel Murrell, William David Spencer, and Adrian Anthony McFarlane (Philadelphia: Temple University Press, 1998), 27.

59. David Scott, *Refashioning Futures: Criticism After Postcoloniality* (Princeton: Princeton University Press, 1999), 224.

DIANE NEGRA

Irishness, Innocence, and American Identity Politics before and after September 11

A large and growing body of work has come into existence analyzing the rapid transnationalization of Irishness spurred by Celtic Tigerism. At one extreme in the spectrum of this scholarship we find the suggestion that Irishness is now essentially an impossible category. To borrow a phrase from Colin Graham's *Deconstructing Ireland*, the contemporary global environment is one in which "an idea of 'Ireland' [is] produced more often as a citation than an actuality."[1] In this article I want to emphasize the politicized nature of the fantasies of nostalgia and innocence in which Irishness is so often embedded in the United States. How does Irishness work for a culture that is at once highly sentimental with respect to its own interests and most often coldly unsympathetic to the interests of others? I will explore certain aspects of an American national expressive culture that strategically mobilizes Irishness in its self-narrativization.

Of course, as I have argued elsewhere, the lifestyling of Irishness has been a bona fide cultural phenomenon in the United States for nearly a decade.[2] Conferring ethnic legitimacy on white Americans newly beset in the 1990s multiculture, claims of Irishness catalyzed a heritage fantasy that has both domestic and touristic functionality. In the late 1990s, the uses of such claims expanded further, with a wave of Irish American– and Irish-themed television sitcoms and dramas giving evidence of the new ways that Irishness figured in a representational lexicon compatible with family values. The commercial exploitation of Irishness in everything from popular music and print fiction to coffee and cholesterol-medication advertisements and chain restaurants marked its emergence as the most marketable white ethnicity in late-twentieth-century American culture. The strikingly anodyne nature of the Irishness conceptualized in such formats indicated its use value as a consoling ethnic category. The tendency, above all, to use Irishness as a way of speaking a whiteness that would otherwise be taboo was well underway before the events of September 11.

As Irishness has acquired the status of an ethnicity at large in American culture, its uses as an imagined state of innocence have become evident in a growing number of commodity categories. For instance, fantasies of innocence are central to the work of Thomas Kinkade, a painter whose specialization in scenes of cozy homes and picturesque hometowns has struck a resonant chord with the contemporary American middle class. Kinkade, whose phenomenal popularity provides a uniquely literal spin to the phrase *cottage industry*, uses light to thematically convey the warmth of home, the virtues of small town life, and the fantasy integration of development with unspoiled nature. His success in recent years has been vast, with his landscape paintings, merchandizing, and most recently serenity-themed self-help books feeding a franchise that in 2000 amounted to more than $2 billion a year in revenue. (Kinkade is the kind of fully mainstreamed artist who has his own shops in malls—a largely unprecedented phenomenon). The *Irish Times* reported in 2002 that Kinkade's work hangs in one out of every twenty American homes.[3]

Art historian Karal Ann Marling characterizes Kinkade's art as "suffused with nostalgia," arguing that the appeal of the paintings lies in the fact that they "create a sense of safety and light in a darkened world."[4] Several of Kinkade's works are set in Ireland, notably "Emerald Isle Cottage" and "A Peaceful Time." Reliant on hackneyed images of the warmly lit, thatch-roofed cottage, Kinkade's Irish-themed work feeds a retreatist American sensibility. In the blurb that accompanies "Emerald Isle Cottage" in the 2002 Kinkade catalogue, for example, the painter says, "To me, Ireland means tradition and stability . . . charming customs, love of family, a faith as enduring as the austere, ruggedly beautiful countryside itself." While Irishness, as I shall discuss further, seems increasingly well

1. Thomas Kinkade's *Emerald Isle Cottage* links nostalgic Irishness to themes of security and safety. (Thomas Kinkade Company)

suited to re-mythologize the white working class and to stage political innocence, it is used here to fantasize removal from present-day exigencies and the re-embrace of traditionalism. Kinkade's reliance on expressive, often unpopulated landscapes, generates a pictorial/geographical innocence in which Ireland, as frequently has been the case in tourist advertising, figures as the site for rejuvenating reconnection with the past.

This impulse is elaborated in certain forms of television drama which feature protagonists who long to be excused from present-day dilemmas of citizenship and family life and to retreat back into history. One example is the CBS made-for-television movie *Yesterday's Children* which centralizes the production of an "instant past" through an ingenious yet perhaps inevitable permutation of the heritage narrative—the reincarnation drama.[5] In *Yesterday's Children* the psychic route toward Ireland is linked with American family formation and rejuvenation. Jane Seymour plays Jenny Cole, a forty-two-year-old Allentown, Pennsylvania, mother whose surprise late pregnancy materializes at the same time as

2. Dilemmas of citizenship
and family life are resolved
by a trip to Ireland in the
made-for-television movie
Yesterday's Children (2000).
(CBS Television)

a series of dreams of a prior life in 1930s Ireland. Scenes of family life
in the Cole household depict patronizing and distant relations between
husband and wife (who argue about Jenny's pregnancy) and a classically
alienated teenage son. Jenny and her husband Doug had been on the cusp
of the empty-nest phase, but Jenny's pregnancy occurs just as her only
child, Kevin, is making plans to leave home to attend college as far away
as possible on the West Coast.

Jenny's dreams become increasingly intense flashes of the life of an
abused wife, Mary (Seymour as well), her husband John, and their children. Mary loses a stillborn child, and though her doctor warns that she
cannot survive another pregnancy, John rapes her and Mary dies giving
birth, after entreating her oldest son, Sonny, to keep the children together
at all costs. Jenny's mother Maggie is the only one around her who takes
her dreams seriously and refers her to a psychiatrist who hypnotizes Jenny
into further recollections. The psychiatrist soberly informs her, "These
aren't dreams, Jenny. These are your memories," and urges her to discover "how [her] life now is connected to [Mary's] life then." With this
establishment of her proprietary relationship to Irishness, Jenny's heri-

tage journey enables her to recover and legitimize her childhood dreams of Ireland (she begins her quest with sketches of Ireland she had drawn as a child, that reveal the Swords Road in Malahide and a local church).

When Maggie gives the family tickets to Ireland, Jenny tracks back to Malahide, where she and Kevin quiz local residents about whether they remember the family of her visions. In her new role and on Irish soil, Jenny acquires a dignity and an agency that she never possessed back home. Notably, her husband and son experience distinct personality changes on arriving in Ireland. The surly Kevin transforms into a kind and concerned son, an accessory figure to his mother's identity quest. Doug, who had brusquely dismissed his wife's visions as reveries unrelated to their present life, inexplicably shifts to a position of warm support once he arrives. Jenny's agency is recognized by the local parish priest whose help she enlists — Father Kelly tells her, "The spirit of this woman could be speaking through you to find her children." When Jenny locates Sonny (a dubiously accented Hume Cronyn) and is able to gather together Mary's other surviving children (who have been separated since being placed in an orphanage) Father Kelly tells her, "You've done a glorious thing."

In its emphasis on the positive transformations of the Cole family in Ireland, *Yesterday's Children* well illustrates tendencies I have already discussed for Ireland to be figured as a therapeutic heritage zone for middle-class, white Americans. Yet it makes a somewhat original intervention as well, drawing from the generic power of the made-for-television movie and its ability to figure quasi-autobiographical stories of women's experience that act to validate female subjectivity.[6] *Yesterday's Children* operates as a narrative of maternal reconsolidation as Jenny reunites and repairs the family of the past as well as the family of the present. Fortified by having intervened on historical injustices, the Cole family learns to practice better family values through its encounter with a negative historical example. While it means to draw attention to the therapeutic intervention made by Jenny Cole on an Irish family, *Yesterday's Children* highlights just as decisively the beneficial therapeutic effect that she and her family receive. Her pregnancy no longer a subject of contention and her son transformed, by the conclusion Jenny has symbolically ascended to the role of the revered Irish mother whose innocence and altruism make her unassailable.

Another instance in which pre–September 11 popular culture equated Irishness with a re-essentialized, simplified epistemology can be found in a television- and radio-advertising spot used by Bennigan's Irish-American Bar and Grill, one of the most successful ethnic-themed chain restaurants in the United States. Heavily broadcast around St. Patrick's Day, the ad called "Pocket Money" features a nondescript guy who celebrates the discovery of ten dollars in his jeans pocket, and chooses to express his delight by taking himself (and his money) to Bennigan's. In part through its use of stylized intertitles fashioned to resemble those of silent film, the ad tacitly promises to turn back the clock to an era in which ten dollars was a meaningful amount of money. By linking this to themes of Irishness, Bennigan's perpetuates a long line of popular cultural constructions of Irishness as pleasingly anachronistic. More than this, however, it also cultivates a fantasy of financial innocence. This fantasy has a slightly ugly undertone to it as we witness a ridiculous figure who deems himself "a wealthy man of means" on finding $10; yet the prevailing tone of the piece is cheery and upbeat and utterly in keeping with the cultivation of innocence that links the majority of recent presentations of Irishness.

For all these similarities, the experience of national trauma after September 11 clearly necessitated and triggered new ways of speaking regionalism and whiteness through Irishness. At the 25 October 2001 benefit concert held at Madison Square Garden to celebrate the efforts of New York's police and fire departments after September 11, Mike Moran, a New York City fireman, took the microphone to deliver a feisty challenge to Osama Bin Laden. The rhetorical terms of this mode of address are what interest me and inspire a starting point for this section of my analysis. For at a moment when intense professions of American national identity were the norm, Moran invited the radical Arabic leader to "kiss [his] royal Irish ass!"[7]

This episode, which went into heavy rotation as a video clip to promote rebroadcasts of the concert and as an audio clip on New York–area radio stations, speaks forcefully to the emergence of the trope of Irishness

3. Ads for Bennigan's Irish-American Bar and Grill encode Irishness as good fortune.

4. Post–September 11 tributes such as "The Ballad of Mike Moran" emphasized Irish themes. (From the now-defunct Fireman Song website)

as white ethnic legitimacy and empowerment in contemporary American culture.[8] While it is hardly surprising that a reference to Irish identity would emerge at a benefit for police and fire officers (this reference, after all, continues a long-established association between the Irish and policing in America) the circulation of this clip suggests how Irishness has become a crucial discursive platform for articulating white working-class legitimacy and innocence. Amidst the exigencies of politics and the marketplace, invocations of Irishness give shape and substance to nebulous, unstable, and/or discredited notions of national and ethnic identity. Moran's remark, in fact, catapulted him to a revered cultural status, with Steve Hochman writing admiringly, for example, in the *Los Angeles Times* that "there was simply no bigger, better rock star in 2001 than New York City firefighter Michael Moran."[9] Indeed, it seems that Moran was able to inscribe an Irish connection to September 11 that even Bono envied, as he quoted Moran repeatedly during U2's fall concerts and subsequently invoked him again in an appearance on *The Tonight Show with Jay Leno*.

The resonance of Moran's assertion of white Irishness to others is suggested not only by the fact that it was this moment of the concert that was picked up and replayed incessantly by media in New York, New Jersey, and Connecticut. Moran's remark inspired Doug Cogan and Christopher Storc to adapt John Kegan Casey's "The Rising of the Moon" into

"The Ballad of Mike Moran," a song that celebrates Moran and other fire-fighters.[10] In their promotional website for "The Ballad of Mike Moran" Cogan and Storc state that the song is meant to "pay tribute to all of the brave men who lost their lives on September 11, 2001. As songwriters, we hope that it also offers a sense of empowerment to those who hear it."[11]

This rhetoric of empowerment is striking when we consider that prior to September 11, the majority of representations of white male firefighters and police officers stressed a sense of anxiety about a perceived loss of status in a society that no longer valued their brand of masculinity. As sociologist Neal King demonstrates, 1980s and 1990s "cop action films" endlessly rehearsed plots in which guilty white masculinity both recognizes itself and strives to reassert its relevance. In such films "cops see their world hurtling into monopoly capitalism and multicultural strife, too busy to defer to working-class joes. The largely white and male ranks of police workers feel that they have lost an esteem they once enjoyed as otherwise unmarked everyman Americans, not simply to declines in discrimination and shifts in industry, but also to the corruption over-running their world."[12] In this light, the events of September 11 may be seen as something of a boon for a class of white male workers driven by a sense of "lost ground" and awkwardly positioned in the space between the service and professional classes.[13]

Mike Moran's characterization of himself as "royal/white" and "Irish" and the subsequent elaboration and celebration of these traits indicate something of the use-value of Irishness to the broader American cultural conversation about the heroism of working-class white males that emerged post–September 11.[14] It is important to note here that in the wake of the World Trade Center attack, the New York Fire Department (FDNY) remained 93 percent white, an astonishingly skewed racial percentage given the multiracial character of urban New York.[15] While Moran or any other member of the New York police or fire departments would have been unlikely to trumpet a proud assertion of whiteness at the concert (the NYPD, after all, drew national attention several times in the 1990s for abuse cases involving racial minorities) Moran crucially identifies himself not just as white, but as Irish. By making these proximate terms, Moran insulates himself from any perception of racism, while Cogan's and Storc's song elaborates Moran's bid for identity capital by situating it in a historical continuum of Irish national resistance to British oppression.

Ultimately this sort of conservative appropriation of Irishness is highly complementary to American hypernationalism. In fact, it may be seen that aggressive American machismo and sentimentalized Irishness are utterly uncontradictory when framed in these terms. In American culture at present, Irishness may be more and more a pose that enables a hard, masculine Americanness a foray into sentiment and recollection without engendering any deviation from identity as stipulated. On the other hand, and this is where I believe the meanings of Moran's comment exceed anything he may have consciously intended, in naming himself (or at least his representative body part) Irish, Moran was expressing national outrage without the responsibility of citizenship. The attractions of this gambit are evident in the wide circulation and celebration of Moran's remark in both attributed and unattributed forms. One example of the latter can be found in an episode of the Denis Leary sitcom *The Job* titled "Anger Management" in which Leary's New York police officer, Mike McNeil, suffering from nicotine withdrawal and a more generalized sense of misanthropy, assaults a Russian taxi driver and is obligated to undergo two weeks of anger-management therapy. Leary's abrasive, caustic demeanor proves decidedly at odds with the therapeutic environment, and he finally walks out of the session asserting his Irish whiteness as an identity credential. The concluding invitation of his speech employs the Moran catchphrase as Leary tells the group, "You can all kiss my white Irish ass."

The celebration of Mike Moran and his Irish-inflected response to the events of September 11 is best understood in my view not as an anomaly but as, in some sense, a highly predictable reaction that draws from a cultural reservoir of associations between Irishness and innocence. It's important to recall that despite the massive sense of shock and sadness experienced by many Americans in the wake of the World Trade Center attacks, one element of the response was also a kind of calm and unsurprisedness that suggests that for some, this event represented not so much an aberration as a culmination.[16] Given the broader themes of survivalism and apocalyptic expectancy that have played through American popular culture over the last decade, and the fact that the 1993 attack on the World Trade Center was a literal rehearsal for the tragically full-fledged destruction of September 11, it is, to me, at least credible that many Americans perceived the attacks as a millennial reckoning, slightly delayed perhaps but nevertheless anticipated.[17]

Since the vast majority of millennial-themed destruction scenarios position America (sometimes humanity at large) as guilty of a multitude of sins (hubris, hypercommercialism, grandiosity, environmental neglect, and abuse) this cast over the events of September 11 suggests the necessity of exactly the kind of response that was widespread after the attack — the generation of counternarratives of innocence and virtuous heroism. I want to point out here that Irishness is one ingredient in the broader gendering of the September 11 narrative which cast men as heroes or villains and largely reduced women to the role of mourners, singling out in particular the upper-middle-class suburban white widow in anchoring public grief and designating whose losses we should be concerned with.[18] In these ways, the figure of the affluent suburban widow or the body of the white working-class male rises to exclude others. While I have concentrated on the more sanguine formulations of Irishness post–September 11, there were mournful ones as well, notably the draping of Irish flags at Ground Zero and the massive success of Enya's New Age ballad "Only Time" in the weeks following the attack, with the single becoming essentially the soundtrack for national grief (with the mourning voice kept both Irish and female).[19]

It should be noted that a number of accounts have highlighted the heavily Irish American character of the September 11 victims, both among the police and firefighting squads and the financial-services employees who made up a high percentage of the casualties. Some have stressed the ubiquity of Claddagh jewelry on the victims and the FDNY itself makes available for purchase a Claddagh pin that features the U.S. and Irish flags.[20] A website, IrishTribute.com, was established celebrating the Irish victims of September 11. Meanwhile newspaper profiles relentlessly figured the events of September 11 in terms of Irishness.

Because Irishness was already in place as a stock element in fantasies of nostalgia and cultural innocence, the Michael Moran phenomenon is actually a predictable response to the traumatic perception of discredited/dysfunctional national identity implicit in coverage of September 11. In fact, Kirby Farrell's argument would be that in many respects U.S.

culture operated in a "post-traumatic mode" all through the 1990s, and this provides a particularly helpful way of understanding the therapeutic functions of commodified Irishness. Deployed across a multitude of representational and cultural sites in the 1990s, the experience and endurance of trauma became an ongoing operative metaphor through which many Americans negotiated the vivid prospect of social death under governmental and economic terms that compromised individual and communal health. According to Farrell: "People may use [the trope of trauma] to account for a world in which power and authority seem staggeringly out of balance, in which personal responsibility and helplessness seem crushing, and in which cultural meanings no longer seem to transcend death. In this sense the trope may be a veiled or explicit criticism of society's defects, a cry of distress and a tool grasped in hopes of some redress, but also a justification for aggression."[21]

In such a climate, the embrace of Irishness as a psychic defense capitalized on popular cultural associations between Irishness and an anachronistic experience of peace, serenity, and innocence. The theme of removal to an experience of past serenity coded as Irish illustrates in part the depth of the craving for innocence in contemporary American culture and the further fact that when it cannot generate innocence internally, that culture will appropriate other national/ethnic categories to do so. Indeed, it vividly illustrates Henry Giroux's observation that "innocence has a politics."[22]

If before September 11 Irishness was most often invoked to negotiate the traumas of deficient family values or to assuage a sense of capitalism run amok, its flexibility is such that after this seminal event, it could be differently mobilized to stave off an anxious, traumatized perception of American identity. Irish inflections in the post–September 11 national discursive environment were hardly confined to Michael Moran, and there is currently no better example of the invocation of Irish innocence than the reassembled remains of the county Mayo cottage that sit one block from Ground Zero. Ostensibly a famine memorial, the cottage is a key feature of the compensatory landscape emerging in place of the post-disaster geography of dislocation and trauma. Out-of-town visitors are likely to tour the area by walking up from Battery Park whose southern end is now home to "The Sphere," a public-art work by Fritz Koenig that stood for thirty years at the World Trade Center and was resituated on 11 March 2002, in its now half-demolished state. Vendors sell memorial plaques, photo books of the disaster, and patriotic paraphernalia in this area of the park, but as one walks north these give way to residual non-commercial displays of photos, tokens, and tributes related to the attack victims and the rescuers, and finally to the memorial cottage.[23]

Even though functionality and memorialization coincide here to produce strange juxtapositions (well-dressed corporate workers now neatly zigzag around the still blocked-off areas), the deliberately unstylized, unprettified entrance to the Mayo cottage is nevertheless startling. One simply steps from the sidewalk into a steep, rocky field (sparsely dotted with plant species imported from Connemara) toward the reassembled remains of the site. With corporate towers looming overhead, this is surely the most anomalous Irish cottage one could ever expect to see. Yet with the former World Trade Center site literally in view, it is as if one anomaly in the local landscape motivated another.

What is crucial about the county Mayo famine cottage is that it is essentially a ruin, one which was designed to inspire somber reflection on a historical experience of loss and displacement, yet it is placed in such a way that its meanings inevitably turn toward the contemporary. Like Ground Zero, it is largely a void space whose elements endow absence with meaning.[24] The cottage "explains" loss on innocent discursive terms that carry over to the present. Calling on an understanding of the famine that has been heightened in America in recent years, the memorial obliquely celebrates the tenacity, endurance, and moral unassailability of Irishness. In effect, the placing of one ruin next to another invites us to perceive the sense of injustice many Americans associate with the famine as equally applicable to Ground Zero. In this respect, the famine cottage functions as U.S. constructions of Irishness so often do, as a flattering prism for American national identity.

Even if its physical site did not already inspire connections to September 11, the cottage is also framed within a suggestive rhetoric that makes these connections more manifest. In an exit passageway from the site inscribed with various facts and commentary relating to the famine, one citation is particularly illustrative of the connections that underwrite this staging of Irish innocence beside Ground Zero: "The French writer Louis Paul Dubois warned that "Emigration will soon cause it to be said that Ireland is no longer where flows the Shannon, but rather besides the banks of the Hudson River and in that greater Ireland whose home is the American Republic." As vigorous debates continue to play out over the most appropriate way to memorialize the victims of September 11, the "borrowed innocence" that accrues to Ground Zero from the famine cottage has met with a warmly appreciative and politically unproblematic reception. There would appear to be widespread agreement that it is both a poignant and appropriate memorial, though the question of where its memorializing capacities are directed is a complex one, as I hope to have shown.

What these far-flung examples from disparate forms of popular culture illustrate is the functionality of Irishness in American fantasies of political, familial, financial, and geographic innocence. They could certainly be further compared to other recent phenomena that work on similar terms, for instance at this writing, historically based Irish-themed gangster narratives seem to be enjoying a run in the "prestige picture" category (*Road to Perdition*, *Gangs of New York*). It is tempting to say that such old-fashioned crime feels almost "innocent" beside contemporary global terrorism. Indeed the process of activating Irish-inflected discourses of innocence around September 11 might be seen to culminate in *Gangs of New York* which in its conclusion audaciously emulsifies the depiction of brawling turbulent nineteenth-century Five Points New York with an invocation of achievement symbolized by the Twin Towers. The image of the towers is paired with U2's (now Grammy-winning) song "These Are the Hands That Built America," that also plays over the closing credits and which invokes lyrically the sense of innocence that the towers are meant to connote visually. The song opens, "Oh my love, it's a long way we've come. From the freckled hills, to the steel and glass canyons," and closes, "It's early fall, there's a cloud on the New York sky line. Innocence, dragged across a yellow line. These are the hands that built America. Ahhh America." By linking a closed chapter of American urban ethnic history with the sense of loss attached to September 11, the film's conclusion tries for a sense of political decontamination, that is to say it participates in a broader process of rendering both distant and recent history sentimental and safe.

If I have given the impression thus far that Irishness operates inevitably as a form of political protection in a deeply conservative American popular culture, I would be remiss in not pointing to one recent fiction which strikingly desentimentalizes Irishness. In impressive contrast to reflexive invocations of "innocent" Irishness (in forms as disparate, as I have illustrated, as reincarnation fantasies and scenarios of dumbed-down consumerism), Spike Lee's 2002 *The 25th Hour* rigorously interrogates the uses of Irishness as bulwark against the responsibilities of citizenship. From its earliest moments, the film strongly signals that it will reject the contrivances of recent cinema to imaginatively recover pre–September 11 New York. Instead, a devastating early sequence insists on both the towers' absence and the impulse to fill their vacant space in an extended aerial tour of the "Tribute in Light," the somber blue beams that temporarily stood in for the towers in early 2002.

On his last day in the city before he must report to prison, convicted Irish American drug dealer Montgomery Brogan (Edward Norton) takes the measure of the place he both loves and hates, his feelings encapsulated in an extended rant delivered to his own mirror reflection in the bathroom of his father's Irish bar. Monty's "fuck this city" rant, an astonishing, sweeping condemnation of nearly every ethnic, racial, and sexual constituency in multicultural New York concludes with a now-familiar rhetorical flourish. After bitterly repudiating the interest politics of a wide variety of social groups (including Irish Americans), Monty invites them all to "kiss [his] royal Irish ass!" Yet in this context the phrase operates very differently from what we have previously seen, its status as a defense mechanism laid bare in a film that elaborates and meditates on concepts of national and regional identity and instead of romanticizing innocence is unafraid to explore the dynamics of guilt. *The 25th Hour* thus culminates a flurry of post–September 11 references to the Irish body that cumulatively displace an earlier generation's ethnic catchphrase, the blithe (and now very quaint-seeming) "Kiss me, I'm Irish."

Many of the essays in this collection have shed additional light on the ideological components of the Celtic Tiger and the recruitment of Irishness for global capitalism and political insulation. My goal has been to sketch particular conditions of national sentimentality in which Irishness plays quite a large part. These apparently ephemeral phenomena play a strong role in cultivating the attractions of Irishness in contemporary American culture. They interrelate with more pragmatic signs of the embrace of Irish identity in America, signs such as the doubling of applications for Irish citizenship from the United States over the last decade, and the quintupling of the Ireland Fund's donor base between 1995–2000.[25] More than this, however, they give evidence of a largely undetected, but I believe rather widespread, historical/cultural dilemma at work in the national psyche—this dilemma finds expression in the longing for an innocent, anachronistic citizenship.

Notes

Stephanie Rains, Maeve Connolly, and Breandan Mac Suibhne all generously shared with me material related to this discussion, while audiences at the 2002 Keeping It Real conference at University College, Dublin and the 2003 Notre Dame Irish Seminar offered feedback and encouragement. Przemek Budziszewski helped both in researching and reformatting several versions of this piece.

1. Colin Graham, *Deconstructing Ireland: Identity, Theory Culture* (Edinburgh: Edinburgh University Press, 2001), flyleaf.

2. See "The New Primitives," *Irish Studies Review* 9, no. 2 (2001): 229–39.

3. D. Campbell, "Land of the Twee," *Guardian*, 8 July 2002, 12. The same article also reported on the development of a themed housing community based on the Kinkade aesthetic.

4. "Despite Elitist Gripes, He's America's Most Popular Artist," *Chronicle of Higher Education*, 22 February 2002, B4.

5. *Yesterday's Children* aired 16 October 2000.

6. The made-for-television movie has historically been a slot in the network schedule that gives a particular shape and substance to women's experience, as Elayne Rapping so successfully argues in *The Movie of the Week: Private Stories/Public Events* (Minneapolis: University of Minnesota Press, 1992). For a cogent discussion of the symbolic and expressive landscapes of post–September 11, see Susan Willis, "Old Glory," *South Atlantic Quarterly* 101, no. 2 (2002): 375–83.

7. It is important to point out that as often as not, Moran was cited as having invited Bin Laden to kiss his "*white* Irish ass." Regardless of the specific construction (whether "white Irish" or "royal Irish") the phrase carries similar connotations of a sense of privilege (racial, aristocratic) that is then rationalized/offset by the invocation of Irishness.

8. Although I do not have space to discuss them here, it is worth pointing out that the persistence of these themes is abundantly demonstrated in the Irish American-

themed firefighter drama *Ladder 49* (2004) and in the FX television series *Rescue Me*. The latter is in many ways continuous with star Denis Leary's earlier television sitcom, *The Job*, which I briefly discuss later in the chapter.

9. Steve Hochman, "Pop Music; Pop Eye—Start Spreading the News: A New York Firefighter Upstages the Superstars," *Los Angeles Times*, 23 December 2001.

10. I am indebted to ethnomusicologist Mick Moloney, who made me aware of some of the historical and thematic connotations of Casey's Fenian anthem.

11. The website address <http://www.firemansong.com> takes its name from the way that Cogan's and Storc's song came to be popularly known by radio listeners.

12. Neal King, *Heroes in Hard Times: Cop Action Movies in the U.S.* (Philadelphia: Temple University Press, 1999), 12–13.

13. William Langewiesche discusses the proprietary and preferential status of the "uniformed personnel" at Ground Zero, briefly linking the tribalism that dominated recovery and removal work to the white ethnic cultures of workers' outerborough neighborhoods and families. *American Ground: Unbuilding the World Trade Center* (New York: North Point Press, 2002), 154–55.

14. "The Ballad of Mike Moran" constitutes an example of the way that Irishness is used to convey the pride and defiance of white working-class masculinity, while *9/11*, a CBS television "special event" broadcast in early March 2002 used Irishness in a more elegiac mode. The highly publicized and well-watched documentary account of the World Trade Center collapse through the perspective of a probationary firefighter and two French filmmakers closes with Ronan Tynan's "Danny Boy" as the soundtrack accompaniment to a montage of firefighter photos.

15. Niall O'Dowd asserts that it also remains 92 percent Catholic, "with those of Irish and Italian roots forming the overwhelming majority of the firefighters." *Fire in the Morning: The Story of the Irish and the Twin Towers on September 11* (Dingle: Brandon, 2002), 52. He does not provide a source for this information.

16. The most common expression of this was the widely reported observation of those at the scene of the attack and those who watched it on television that they had somehow "seen this before."

17. Bill Luhr made exactly this point during a roundtable discussion called "The World Trade Center Disaster and the Media," held during the University Seminar in Cinema and Interdisciplinary Interpretation at Columbia University on 21 February 2002.

18. In their book on female firefighters, police officers, and emergency medical workers, Susan Hagen and Mary Carouba cite the "invisibility of women at Ground Zero" and note that "the media presented story after story about 'the return of the manly man' and made daily unapologetic references to 'the brothers' and 'our brave guys.'" *Women at Ground Zero: Stories of Courage and Compassion* (Indianapolis: Alpha, 2002), xi–xii.

19. I am grateful to Kevin Rockett for reminding me of the ubiquity of Enya's music

in September and October of 2001, and its relevance to the dynamics of ethnicity and gender I attempt to sketch here.

20. See Jim Dwyer, "Sonuvagun, If It Isn't Dominion," for an example of journalism that stresses the Irish dimensions of September 11. *New York Times Magazine*, 11 November 2001. An example of the Claddagh pin can be found at <http://www.fdnypins.com/pins.htm>.

21. Kirby Farrell, *Post-Traumatic Culture: Injury and Interpretation in the Nineties* (Baltimore: Johns Hopkins University Press, 1998), 14.

22. Henry Giroux, *Stealing Innocence: Youth, Corporate Power and the Politics of Culture* (New York: St. Martin's, 2000), 21.

23. It should be noted that these displays, although officially noncommercial, often welcome donations to firefighter, police, and other emergency personnel organizations and have prominently placed collection baskets.

24. The very muteness and simplicity of the cottage were, it might be argued, all the more necessary in the face of events so staggering they prompted a kind of crisis of public eloquence. When articulate, sensitive assessment on the order of Rudolph Giuliani's pronouncement that the losses at the World Trade Center would surely be "more than any of us can bear" were made they were repeated again and again as a kind of public consolation. More often, the response to September 11 was a babble of ineloquence (of the kind available twenty-four hours a day on cable television) and otherwise, a kind of speechlessness. An article detailing the lack of forceful original rhetoric in the upcoming annual commemoration ceremony, noted "speechlessness may also suit the times. Politicians are not trained in oratory, and their audience is skeptical and impatient. In a society fragmented by race, ethnicity and class, it is harder to find language and allusions that resonate widely and to find meanings that can be broadly embraced." "The Silence of the Historic Present," *New York Times*, 11 August 2002, 31. An account of the cottage is provided by Patrick Smyth in "A Field in New York that is Forever Ireland," *Irish Times*, 20 July 2002, 12.

25. Maureen Dezell, *Irish America Coming into Clover: The Evolution of a People and a Culture* (New York: Doubleday, 2000), 202–3.

CATHERINE EAGAN received her Ph.D in English at Boston College, completing a dissertation entitled " 'I Did Imagine . . . We Had Ceased To Be Whitewashed Negroes': The Racial Formation of Irish Identity in Nineteenth Century Ireland and America." She has published in *Eire-Ireland*, *American Quarterly* and *Working Papers in Irish Studies* and is an Instructor of English at Las Positas College.

SEAN GRIFFIN is an associate professor in the division of cinema-television at Southern Methodist University. He is the author of *Tinker Belles and Evil Queens: The Walt Disney Company from the Inside Out*, coauthor of *America on Film: Representing Race, Class, Gender and Sexuality at the Movies*, and coeditor of *In-Focus: Queer Theory, The Film Reader*.

NATASHA CASEY is currently researching a Ph.D at McGill University on contemporary Irish-American identity and popular culture. As a freelance writer, her articles on Irish politics and culture have been published in a variety of newspapers including the *Fort Worth Star Telegram*, *St. Louis Post-Dispatch*, and the *Chicago Tribune*. She currently teaches at Webster University in St. Louis.

MARIA PRAMAGGIORE is an associate professor of English and director of film studies at North Carolina State University. She is the coauthor, with Tom Wallis, of *Film: A Critical Introduction* and coeditor, with Donald E. Hall, of *Re-presenting Bisexualities: Subjects and Cultures of Fluid Desire*. She has also written essays on feminist performance, women and film, and Irish film that appear in *Theatre Journal*, *Cinema Journal*, and *Screen*.

STEPHANIE RAINS lectures in cultural theory at Dun Laoghaire Institute of Art Design and Technology in Dublin. She has also held an assistant lectureship in communication at Dundalk Institute of Technology and has published articles on Irish cultural policy and cultural tourism. Her Ph.D thesis at Dublin City University focused upon Irish-American diasporic representations of Ireland and Irishness in popular culture.

LAUREN ONKEY is an associate professor of English at Ball State University where she teaches Irish and other postcolonial literatures. She has recently published essays on Irish-American playwright Ned Harrigan, James Joyce, the Irish theatre group Passion Machine, and a study of Jimi Hendrix and the politics of race.

MARY MCGLYNN is an associate professor of English at Baruch College, City University of New York. Her publications include articles in *Contemporary Literature*, *Scottish Studies Review*, *Studies in the Novel*, and *New Hibernia Review*. She is currently at work on a study of recent Scottish and Irish fiction of the working class entitled *Urban Peripheries: Contemporary Vernaculars of the British Isles*.

AMANDA THIRD is a lecturer in media and communication studies at Monash University in Melbourne, Australia. She has previously taught in media and cultural studies, critical theory, mass communication, screen studies and professional writing at Curtin University and Murdoch University in Western Australia. She has recently completed her doctoral thesis at Curtin University on popular representations of female terrorists active in the United States in the 1960s and 1970s.

GERARDINE MEANEY is the director of Irish studies at University College Dublin. She is the author of *(Un)Like Subjects: Women, Theory, Fiction* and of a short study of Pat Murphy's film *Nora*, for the *Ireland into Film* series. Her articles on gender and Irish culture have appeared in *Colby Quarterly*, *Textual Practice*, and *Women: A Cultural Review*. She is a co-editor of the *Field Day Anthology of Irish Writing: Women's Writing and Traditions*, volumes 4 and 5.

MAEVE CONNOLLY lectures in film, animation, and visual culture at Dun Laoghaire Institute of Art, Design and Technology, Dublin. She recently completed her doctoral thesis on Irish film culture and the avant-garde and she is the coeditor of *The Glass Eye: Artists and Television*. Her articles on film and art have appeared in *boundary 2*, *Moving Worlds*, *Irish Com-*

munications Review, *Contemporary Visual Culture in Ireland*, *Variant*, and *Filmwaves*.

MICHAEL MALOUF is an assistant professor of English at George Mason University. He received his Ph.D from the department of English and comparative literature at Columbia University where he completed a dissertation on Caribbean revisions of Irish Cultural nationalism. He has published articles and reviews on Irish and postcolonial topics in *Interventions*, *Jouvert*, *Workplace*, and *James Joyce Quarterly*.

DIANE NEGRA is a senior lecturer in the School of Film and Television Studies at the University of East Anglia. She is the author of *Off-White Hollywood: American Culture and Ethnic Female Stardom*, and coeditor of *A Feminist Reader in Early Cinema* and the forthcoming *Interrogating Postfeminism: Gender and the Politics of Popular Culture*. Her articles and reviews have appeared in a number of anthologies and journals including *Cultural Studies*, *Irish Studies Review*, *Genders*, and *The Velvet Light Trap*.

INDEX

Library of Congress Cataloging-in-Publication Data

The Irish in us : Irishness, performativity, and popular culture /

Diane Negra, editor.

p. cm.

Includes bibliographical references and index.

ISBN 0-8223-3728-2 (cloth : alk. paper)

ISBN 0-8223-3740-1 (pbk. : alk. paper)

1. Irish Americans in popular culture. 2. Art, Irish — Influence.

3. Art, Irish — Cross-cultural studies. 4. Irish Americans — Ethnic identity.

5. Whites — Race identity — United States. 6. Ethnicity — United States.

I. Negra, Diane, 1966-

E184.I61685 2006

700.'4529916200973 — dc22   2005026006